Uncertain Europe

Over a decade has now passed since the Cold War ended. During that time, Europe has seen major conflicts in the Balkans, a variety of tensions in both its eastern and western halves, and uncertainty about the future development of the European Union and NATO. As a result, many Europeans today feel a sense of uncertainty about the future security of their continent.

This book offers a broad and up-to-date overview of the state of European security at the beginning of the twenty-first century, and is written by a specially commissioned team of experts, spanning the spectrum of related disciplines: international relations, security studies and European studies. The chapters explore: core concepts of 'order', 'security' and 'identity' in post-Cold War Europe; the contemporary relevance of these concepts in relation to primary European institutions; and regional/national perspectives from the USA, Western Europe, Central and Eastern Europe, Russia and the Balkans.

Uncertain Europe gives a comprehensive overview of the pan-European security debate. Throughout, the chapters consider, critically assess and develop the idea that enlargement of EU and NATO membership will be pivotal in deciding the success or failure of the attempt to extend the boundaries of the 'security community' that currently exists in the western part of Europe. This topical and accessible book will be an essential resource for students and academics interested in politics, international relations, security and European studies.

Martin A. Smith is Senior Lecturer in Defence and International Affairs at the Royal Military Academy, Sandhurst. He is the author of *NATO in the First Decade after the Cold War*. **Graham Timmins** is Senior Lecturer in Politics at the University of Stirling. He is the author of *Organised Labour and German Unification*. In addition, the editors recently co-authored *Building a Bigger Europe: EU and NATO Enlargement in Comparative Perspective*.

Routledge Advances in International Relations and Global Politics

Uncertain Europe

Building a new European
security order?

**Edited by Martin A. Smith and
Graham Timmins**

London and New York

First published 2001 by Routledge
11 New Fetter Lane, London EC4P 4EE

Simultaneously published in the USA and Canada
by Routledge
29 West 35th Street, New York, NY 10001

Routledge is an imprint of the Taylor & Francis Group

Typeset in 10/12pt Baskerville by Graphicraft Limited, Hong Kong
Printed and bound in Great Britain by Biddles Ltd, Guildford and King's Lynn

British Library Cataloguing in Publication Data
A catalogue record for this book is available
from the British Library

Library of Congress Cataloging-in-Publication Data
Uncertain Europe: building a new European security order? /
edited by Martin A. Smith and Graham Timmins.
    p. cm. – (Routledge advances in international relations and
politics; 15)
    Includes bibliographical references and index.
    1. National security–Europe. 2. Europe–Defenses.
3. Europe–Military policy. I. Smith, Martin A. II. Timmins,
Graham. III. Series.

UA646.U475 2001
327'.094–dc21   2001019464

ISBN 0-415-23735-1

Contents

Contributors

Clive Archer is Research Professor in the Department of Politics and Philosophy, Manchester Metropolitan University. He was, until 1996, Jean Monnet Professor at the University of Aberdeen. His main research interests are in the international relations of the Nordic, Arctic and Baltic regions. He is chairman of the University Association for Contemporary European Studies and was, until September 2000, editor of the *Contemporary European Studies* series. Books by Professor Archer include *International Organizations* (3rd edn 2001), *Organizing Europe* (1994), *The European Union: Structure and Process* (3rd edn 2000) and, with Ingrid Sogner, *Norway, European Integration and Atlantic Security* (1998). He has also co-edited, with Lena Jonson, *Peacekeeping and the Role of Russia in Eurasia* (1996). He has written a number of articles for *European Security, Journal of Common Market Studies, Journal of Peace Research* and *Journal of European Integration.*

Robert Bideleux is Reader in Politics and Director of the Masters programme in European Politics at the University of Wales Swansea. His publications include *Communism and Development* (1985, revised 1987), *A History of Eastern Europe* (1998) with Ian Jeffries and large parts of *European Integration and Disintegration: East and West* (1996). He is currently writing *The Balkans and East-Central Europe: A Contemporary History* with Ian Jeffries and books on civil society, democracy and the state.

Laura Richards Cleary is a Lecturer in International Politics at the University of Stirling. She received her BA in Politics and History from Indiana University and a Ph.D. from the University of Glasgow. The focus of her research is defence transformations in the former Soviet Union and Central and Eastern Europe. She is the author of *Security Systems in Transition* (1998), a comparative analysis of defence conversion in the United States and Russia. More recently her work has focused on the establishment of democratic civil–military relations in Bulgaria. As a result of that work she has edited the volume *Civil–Military Relations: A Guide* (1999) and published a number of articles.

Andrew Cottey is a Lecturer in the Department of History, University College Cork, and the Department of Peace Studies, University of Bradford. He has previously worked for the EastWest Institute, Saferworld and the British American Security Information Council and been a NATO Research Fellow. He is the author of *East-Central Europe after the Cold War: Poland, the Czech Republic, Slovakia and Hungary in Search of Security* (1995) and editor of *Subregional Cooperation in the New Europe: Building Security, Prosperity and Solidarity from the Barents to the Black Sea* (1999).

Stuart Gordon is a Senior Lecturer in Defence and International Affairs at the Royal Military Academy, Sandhurst. In addition to British foreign and security policy, his research interests include civil–military relations in complex emergencies. His most recent publication is *The Ethical Foreign Policy: The Road to Sierra Leone* (2000).

Jackie Gower is Honorary Senior Lecturer in the Department of Politics and International Relations at the University of Kent at Canterbury. She served as the specialist adviser to the House of Lords Select Committee on the European Communities' recent inquiry on EU enlargement. Her publications include an edited book, *Enlarging the European Union: The Way Forward* (2000) with John Redmond, 'Russia and the European Union' in M. Webber (ed.), *Russia and Europe: Confrontation or Cooperation?* (2000) and 'EU Policy to Central and Eastern Europe' in K. Henderson (ed.), *Back to Europe: Central and Eastern Europe and the European Union* (1999).

Paul Latawski is a Senior Lecturer in Defence and International Affairs at the Royal Military Academy, Sandhurst. He is also an Associate Fellow at the Royal United Services Institute for Defence Studies in London and an Honorary Visiting Fellow at the School of Slavonic and East European Studies, University of London. His principal research interests include contemporary Poland and security in Central and South-eastern Europe. He has published widely on these topics.

Wyn Rees is a Senior Lecturer in International Relations at the University of Leicester, where he is also Deputy Director of the Centre for European Politics and Institutions. Among his publications are *The Western European Union at the Crossroads: Between Trans-Atlantic Solidarity and European Integration* (1998) and the co-authored *The Enlargement of Europe* (1999).

Martin A. Smith is a Senior Lecturer in Defence and International Affairs at the Royal Military Academy, Sandhurst. He was previously at the Department of Peace Studies, University of Bradford, from where he received his Ph.D. in 1994. His publications include *Superpowers in the Post-Cold War Era* (1999) with Ken Aldred and *Building a Bigger Europe: EU and NATO Enlargement in Comparative Perspective* (2000) with Graham

Timmins. He is presently working with Paul Latawski on *Kosovo and the Paradoxes of a Humanitarian War.*

James Sperling is Professor of Political Science at the University of Akron. He is editor of *Two Tiers or Two Speeds? The European Security Order and the Enlargement of the European Union and NATO* (1999) and co-author of *Recasting the European Order: Security Architectures and Economic Cooperation* (1997).

Graham Timmins is Senior Lecturer in European Politics in the Department of Politics at the University of Stirling. He previously worked at the University of Huddersfield. His publications include *Building a Bigger Europe: EU and NATO Enlargement in Comparative Perspective* (2000) with Martin A. Smith and *German Unification and Organised Labour: Social Partnership under Pressure.* He is presently working on a study of the EU as a 'soft security' actor.

R. E. Utley holds a Leverhulme Research Fellowship in the Department of Politics, University of York, having previously held a research position in the School of History, University of Leeds. Her interests relate to French defence and security policies during the Fifth Republic, French relations with NATO and France's role in European security issues. Her current research project concerns France and European security since 1958. She is the author of *The French Defence Debate: Consensus and Continuity in the Mitterrand Era* (2000), as well as several articles on French external military interventions.

Preface and acknowledgements

This edited volume developed out of our co-authored book, *Building a Bigger Europe: EU and NATO Enlargement in Comparative Perspective*. As this earlier work was being completed, it became clear to us that studying institutional enlargement in Europe had offered a useful stimulus for considering a more general assessment of key underlying concepts, as well as wider debates and issues. We had deliberately avoided being drawn into more profound debates in *Bigger Europe* as that book is specifically about the EU and NATO enlargement processes and the ways and extent to which these impacted upon each other during the 1990s. We were aware of the many important uncertainties in the larger picture, however, and had concluded by stating that 'a bigger Europe there will most certainly be, but whether this becomes a better Europe is less clear'.

At the outset of this project this seemed true, in our view, for three main reasons. First, not all countries that desire to become members of either or both the EU and NATO will gain entry. These two institutions and their members are, therefore, challenged with the task of coping with the demands, expectations and concerns of 'outsiders'. Second, the impact of enlargement, together with changing institutional agendas and changes in the overall strategic and political environment within which the institutions operate, is having extensive implications for the institutions themselves – with which the member states are struggling to come to terms. Third, and most fundamentally, our understanding of the nature of 'order' and 'security' is by no means settled or agreed and is indeed the subject of much ongoing discussion.

Relevant academic research can, broadly speaking, be split into three categories. There is, first, a large and growing body of published work on the process and mechanics of institutional enlargement. Second, significant attention has also been given by scholars and other writers to more general debates and perspectives that surround the main international institutions in Europe. Finally, interesting and useful theoretical work is being done on the changing nature of order and security. Our intention in this volume has been to assemble a team of specialist contributors spanning the academic disciplines of International Relations, Strategic Studies and European Area Studies. As such the coverage and approaches of the chapters which follow should be of use and relevance to students, researchers and practitioners with an interest in any one or more of the issue-areas outlined above.

The book is divided into four parts. In the first, the emphasis is on exploring three key concepts as they relate to contemporary Europe. These are 'order', 'security' and 'identity'. Unless the last is taken into account, order and security are unlikely to acquire much real meaning. Our second part considers perspectives and debates within and about the leading European institutions: the OSCE, NATO and the European Union. A fourth institution – the WEU – seems at the time of writing to be poised to disappear, or at least be effectively cannibalised by the EU. An understanding of how and why this situation came about sheds much useful light on the wider institutional debates, and in particular the potential for the EU to develop as a 'hard' security actor. The third part of this volume brings together a series of national and regional perspectives on order, security and identity. In addition to assessing the nature, relevance and importance of these debates and issues in their particular countries or regions, our contributors here also consider attitudes to, and debates about, the institutions; most particularly the EU and NATO. Our fourth and concluding part offers us, as editors, the chance to draw together the main arguments and debates that have been uncovered and developed by our contributors. This chapter is not intended to be a mere summation, however. In it we tackle two core questions. On the basis of the contributions to this volume, we ask, first, what should be the main elements to a 'genuine' European security order? We then assess the extent to which such an order is, in fact, in the process of being constructed in the post-Cold War context in Europe.

'Europe' is an endlessly topical source of controversy and debate. It is also seemingly in a state of permanent flux. We are particularly grateful, therefore, to all our contributors for responding both positively and with good grace to the tight deadlines which we suggested for the submission of their chapters. In addition, our appreciation goes to Clive Archer for hosting the workshop at Manchester Metropolitan University in January 2000 at which this project began to assume tangible shape. Our thanks, too, go to Craig Fowlie and Milon Nagi at Routledge for their consistent support and encouragement, and to the two anonymous referees who offered valuable suggestions and, most especially, reminded us of the importance of coherence in any edited work. Finally, our usual gratitude goes to our long-suffering families and friends for their patience and indulgence as the editing and preparation of this book imposed ever-increasing demands on our time.

Martin A. Smith and Graham Timmins
Camberley and Stirling
November 2000

List of abbreviations

ASEAN	Association of South-East Asian Nations
CEE	Central and Eastern Europe[an]
CEFTA	Central European Free Trade Area
CEI	Central European Initiative
CESDP	Common European Security and Defence Policy (EU)
CFSP	Common Foreign and Security Policy (EU)
CIS	Commonwealth of Independent States
CJTF	Combined Joint Task Forces (NATO)
COREPER	Committee of Permanent Representatives (EU)
CSBMs	Confidence and Security-Building Measures
CSCE	Conference on Security and Co-operation in Europe (1975–94)
CSCM	Conference on Security and Co-operation in the Mediterranean
DCI	Defence Capabilities Initiative (NATO)
EC	European Community (1987–93)
ECSC	European Coal and Steel Community
EDC	European Defence Community
EEC	European Economic Community (1957–87)
EFA	European Fighter Aircraft
EMU	Economic and Monetary Union (EU)
EPC	European Political Co-operation
ESDI	European Security and Defence Identity (NATO)
EU	European Union (1993–)
FRY	Federal Republic of Yugoslavia
FSU	Former Soviet Union
KFOR	Kosovo Force
HCNM	High Commissioner on National Minorities (OSCE)
ICG	International Crisis Group
JACS	Joint Armaments Co-operation Structure
KVM	Kosovo Verification Mission (OSCE)
MAP	Membership Action Plan (NATO)
MAPE	Multinational Police Advisory Element (WEU)

MCG	Mediterranean Co-operation Group (NATO)
NAA	North Atlantic Assembly (NATO)
NACC	North Atlantic Co-operation Council (NATO)
NATO	North Atlantic Treaty Organisation
NPA	NATO Parliamentary Assembly
ODIHR	Office for Democratic Institutions and Human Rights (OSCE)
OSCE	Organisation for Security and Co-operation in Europe (1994–)
PARP	Planning and Review Process (NATO)
PCA	Partnership and Co-operation Agreement (EU)
PfP	Partnership for Peace (NATO)
PHARE	Pologne et Hongrie assistance à la reconstruction économique (EU)
PSC	Political and Security Committee (EU)
SACEUR	Supreme Allied Commander Europe (NATO)
SDR	Strategic Defence Review (UK)
SFOR	Stabilisation Force
SHAPE	Supreme Headquarters Allied Powers Europe (NATO)
TACIS	Technical Assistance for the Commonwealth of Independent States (EU)
TEP	Transatlantic Economic Partnership
UN	United Nations
UNMIK	United Nations Interim Administration Mission in Kosovo
WEAG	West European Armaments Group
WEU	Western European Union

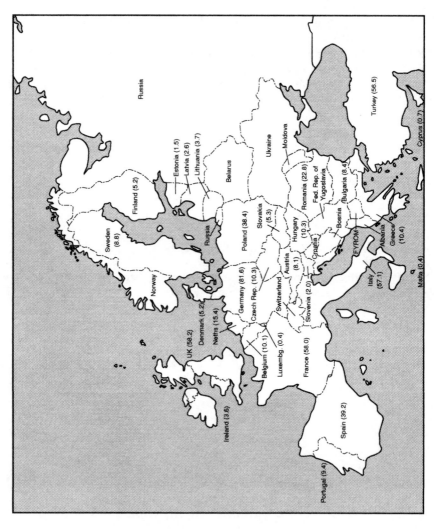

Map showing the European Union and applicant states with populations (in millions)

Part I

Key concepts

Order, security and identity

1 What security? What order?

Clive Archer

Introduction

This chapter aims at examining two concepts in the context of Europe at the start of the twenty-first century: order and security. As will be seen, the ideas are linked, though there is some disagreement over the nature of this link. The chapter will investigate their meanings and will suggest how an understanding of the terms might affect one's view of the identity, institutions and policies of Europe at the turn of the twenty-first century.

These two notions, order and security, are to be discussed in this book in the context of a Europe that has emerged from the Cold War period into a period of uncertainty. After all, the Cold War appeared to be a time of certainty. Europe was divided into two main alliances – NATO and the Warsaw Treaty Organisation – that were dominated by the United States and the Soviet Union. These two countries were to some extent European powers – the latter more than the former – but were also superpowers with wide interests outside Europe. Talk of 'order' and 'security' in Europe thus seemed to be tied to ideas dominated by those two superpowers, with Europe being an object. It may appear in retrospect that the European countries were more active in this equation than seemed to be the case at the time. Nevertheless, the end of the Cold War saw the slipping away of the superpower 'overlay' of Europe when it came to security and order, and an apparent fresh set of opportunities to remake this order with new concepts of security.

Since 1989 the Warsaw Treaty Organisation, together with the Soviet Union, has been thrown on the bonfire of history. NATO has expanded its membership and changed its nature. The United States still has a presence in Europe, but one quite different from that of the 1970s and 1980s. The Conference on Security and Co-operation in Europe (CSCE) has turned into the Organisation for Security and Co-operation in Europe (OSCE), and a number of regional organisations have flourished. The European Union has started to develop a defence aspect. Yet there have been the protracted series of conflicts in former Yugoslavia. The Transcaucasian region has suffered civil and inter-state wars, and frontiers have become a source of dispute again. United Nations and multilateral peace operations have been needed on mainland Europe.

If the institutions and the levels of conflict have changed in Europe since the end of the Cold War, what of the concepts of order and security? If the period of Cold War certainty has disappeared, have uncertainties taken its place or are there some new verities? The next section will examine the notion of 'order', placing it in the post-Cold War context. The following section will look at concepts of 'security' and will relate them to these ideas about order.

The concept of order

A dictionary provides several definitions of 'order'. Relevant to this discussion, there is a situation in which 'all components or elements are arranged logically, comprehensibly, or naturally'. This might suggest the opposite of chaos. There is the 'established or customary method or state', especially of society, whereby traditional ways are accepted as given, as opposed to the novel and innovative. Then there is the 'peaceful or harmonious condition of society', when order reigns in the street and there is little disorder or rebellion.[1]

A European security *order* can thus have a number of implications. It can suggest that there is a tidy arrangement of security for Europe, where the elements – the institutions and the policies – are both comprehensive and logical. The aim of policy-makers would thus be to bring order to security arrangements, to tie up loose ends and to prevent overlaps and redundancies. The emphasis is thus on form. It might also suggest the continuation of a hierarchy that is the norm, managing change so that there is as little an upset as possible for those in charge. The stress here is on conformity. Finally, there is the understanding that equates order with peace and harmony, with outcome being the most important element. Emphasis will be placed more on this final definition.

Hedley Bull wrote of 'the nature of order in world politics' and 'order in the contemporary international system' and his writings provide a starting point for any such study. Bull used the term 'order as opposed to disorder', which he defined as 'an actual or possible situation or state of affairs, not as a value, goal or objective'. Furthermore, 'order' was seen by Bull as not the only element that shaped international conduct, nor even the overriding one. There were others such as justice. Order depended on the maintenance of rules, though not necessarily on international law or organisations.[2] Bull defined 'international order' as 'a pattern of activity that sustains the elementary or primary goals of the society of states, or international society'. For him an international society existed when:

A group of states, conscious of certain common interests and common values, form a society in the sense that they conceive themselves to be bound by a common set of rules in their relations with one another, and share in the working of common institutions.[3]

The last part of the sentence is crucial; there must be an element of sharing (the extent of this can be debated) for states, their governments and their citizens, to feel part of a 'society'. This connects the concept of order to a situation whereby states are seen, by themselves and by others, as being bound in a societal relationship by common interests, values, rules and institutions.

Bull sets out goals of the society of states, which need sustaining by a pattern or disposition of activity amounting to international order. These are preservation of the system and society of states itself, 'maintaining the independence or external sovereignty of individual states', the presence of peace as 'the absence of war among member states of international society as the normal condition of their relationship', and the goals of limiting violence, keeping promises and stabilising the possession of property.[4] These goals are fairly status quo and minimalist, and it is easy to see how they may be in conflict with more ambitious and revolutionary goals, especially those associated with concepts of justice. For example, the notion of justice might challenge the very basis of title to property that may have been obtained through the profits of slavery or as the spoils of war.

Hedley Bull distinguished between international order and world order. He described the latter as 'those patterns or dispositions of human activity that sustain the elementary or primary goals of social life among mankind as a whole'. While international order was among states, there was also 'the greater society of all mankind'. The twentieth century marked the stage when global order ceased to be just the sum of the order of the localised political systems and had become the product of a world political system, mainly as a result of the expansion of the European state system across the globe. Indeed Bull, writing in the 1970s, saw a world political system 'of which the system of states is only part' emerging.[5] Since then, a world economic system has emerged, albeit one with regional facets, and there has been a shift to a 'postindustrial order' based on 'the dynamics of technology', especially that associated with the microelectronic revolution.[6]

Two important points need to be stressed here. In writing about international order, Bull accepted that collective action was necessary between states and that this may have to take precedence over the individual needs of states. This already suggests a move away from just describing a pattern of activity, as Bull claimed he was doing, more to identifying a desired outcome or value. Second, Bull established that in normative terms, world society was prior to international order.[7] There is the strong possibility of an increasing clash between the values of international society and those of world society, especially as the elements of world society are seen to emerge and those of international society – with its dominance of the state – are more and more challenged.

Following on from Bull, one can conclude, with K. J. Holsti, that to talk of order in the international system 'implies limits on behavior. In a society of states, these limitations are spelled out in international law, the conventions of diplomacy, the balance of power, and even in war, when it is used to enforce community norms'.[8] This presumes that there is a community and that it has norms that are agreed by a particular process. The assumption of order – as opposed to disorder – in the international system thus leads to subsequent assumptions about the behaviour of states in their efforts to 'manage interdependence' in an anarchic system. On top of this, the development of a world order that is not state based but relies on other forms of social organisation of individuals has meant that there are many cross-cutting integrative strands of economic, environmental and informational activities that can form an order parallel to that of the state-based order. The values and norms of this emerging world society can contradict those of the international society. A world informational society, for example, may have as one of its tenets the freedom of information, which in turn might be opposed by states anxious to defend their military and industrial secrets and also to protect their tax base from companies with a 'virtual' existence.

Another element of conflict between different 'orders' may be seen. States themselves have internal orders, the 'logical' and 'comprehensive' arrangement of their politics, economics and society, which often includes 'the established or customary method' of the peoples and/or the elites (to use two dictionary definitions). The 'peaceful or harmonious condition of society' (to cite a third definition) within a state can probably be graded by a set of criteria (such as civil unrest, amount of crime, number of strikes).

There is no logical causal link between the three levels of order – world order, international order and internal state order – even when the same concept of order is being used. If the values and norms of the elements of world society can conflict with those of international society, so can the values and norms contradict those of any one state's or society's order. If the goals of a society of states are, according to Bull, the preservation of the system and society of states itself, then any state whose internal order aims at the overthrow of that society of states, as the Soviet Union was seen to advocate after the Russian Revolution of 1917, is likely to be outlawed from that society. Likewise, the internal order of a state may be perceived as offending against world order, 'the greater society of mankind'. This does not answer the question of who may define such a 'world order'. A working assumption may be that in particular functional areas, such as the world economy, the hegemonic forces, such as those of transnational industry and banking, together with the leadership of key industrialised countries, might set the primary goals. States and societies whose own goals transgress those of world society, for example by allowing counterfeiting of goods, copying of patented material or confiscation of property without compensation, might either have to fall in line eventually or pay a price (say, in the form of sanctions) for breaking 'the rules'.

If order is seen as the 'peaceful or harmonious condition of society', there again may be little link between the achievement of this at the three levels; global, international and internal. A peaceful international system may be seen as a precursor to the development of a peaceful global system, but this is not necessarily the case, especially if the latter is to be based on concepts of justice resisted by status quo states that live in harmony. Likewise, a system of ordered and internally peaceful states need not produce a peaceful international society, though there is some evidence that states that have in common certain values (especially democratic ones) are likely to benefit from 'an absence of war'.[9]

The existence of at least three levels of order in the world system – a global one, an international one and ones local to particular states or societies – can be seen to have potential consequences for notions of security. Three systems that differ over important values carry the seeds of conflict. Systems of order that are interlocking could potentially create a world with a 'peaceful or harmonious condition' with clear implications for security. What is meant by 'security' first needs closer inspection.

The concept of security: a brief history

Security is a word that has been harnessed to many others: peace and security, collective security, common security, comprehensive security, cooperative security, security communities, security complex, security regime, societal security. These concepts can be studied historically by examining what has been happening 'out there' in the operational environment and what has been understood 'in here' in the psychological environment.[10] The relationship between these two elements is always debatable, especially in the case of security. To what extent is any form of security a condition determined by the operational environment and to what extent does it depend on perception and feeling? For many rationalist writers the relationship is fairly straightforward: rational decision-makers make cost–benefit analyses on the basis of the stated intentions of others, their behaviour and the structures in place to ensure compliance. So security becomes a contractual relationship with 'safeguards . . . to ensure mutual compliance'.[11] A constructivist approach to international relations argues that 'cultural predispositions, institutional affiliations and historical learning experiences tend to define the identity of states and shape their incentives for actions'.[12] For the constructivists, the important element is identity and this can be created (or destroyed) over time, by events and institutions. In the end, the identity of a state (or other collective entity) resides in the minds primarily of its inhabitants, but to have substance in international intercourse it also has to be recognised by those outside the entity.

A good framework to combine the two approaches is provided by Starr in his use of the concepts of opportunity and willingness. He points out that decision-makers' environments 'provide a structure of opportunities, risks, and potential costs and benefits, constraining decision-makers'. Opportunities are guided by what is possible (what exists and is available) and by what is probable, reflecting the unequal distribution of possibilities. The perception of these 'objective' conditions by decision-makers provides the opportunities. Willingness concerns the 'motivations that lead people to avail themselves of opportunities' and is based on perceptions of the global scene and domestic political conditions in the case of decision-makers.[13] A rationalist approach to international relations is one that can answer the sort of possible/probable questions demanded by a study of opportunity and also can deal with willingness in terms of cost–benefit analysis and rational choice theory. However, a constructivist approach can add to an understanding of perceptions of opportunities and of decision-makers' willingness to choose one 'dish from the menu' rather than another. Cultural factors may rule out one set of perceptions and may also privilege one choice over another.

Security studies was traditionally the preserve of the rationalist writers, many of whom accepted the dominance of the sovereign state and of military–diplomatic factors in determining security outcomes. A number of works on deterrence theory showed this approach at its most statist and 'scientific'.[14] Since the end of the Cold War the constructivist approach to security matters in Europe has flourished.[15] The Cold War provided a sort of straitjacket for both the student and the practitioner of international security; the 'menu for choice' was set and limited with only a few dissenting voices seeing possibilities beyond the demands of superpower politics.

The thawing and eventual disappearance of the Cold War has meant a greater range of possibilities and probabilities for the decision-makers and a wider freedom in terms of choosing one option rather than another. Furthermore, this change has not only affected decision-makers; citizens have also been liberated. During the Cold War certain security options were either denied voters and citizens by them not living in democracies or by governments' claims that certain choices (for example, leaving or joining an alliance) were not on the agenda. In post-Cold War Europe, most of these restraints have fallen away and citizens have regarded defence and security policies as areas of wide choice and of much lower saliency than before. Defence expenditure has fallen in almost all European states and a number of issues seen as being more salient to voters – immigration, the environment, international crime – have been placed on the security agenda. The result of this securitisation has not always been desirable for some of those involved, such as immigrants and minorities, but it has meant a greater emphasis on the elements of identity in the study of security, as intangible elements (the perception of particular groups as security threats) have grown in importance. The rest of this section will examine the development of some of the concepts of security in Europe from the Cold War to post-Cold War period.

Perhaps the oldest concept has been that of national security, which normally refers to state security. This is seen as the security of a sovereign state, meaning its ability to survive as such and also to have some basic ability to act within the wider system. National security is defined by governments and elites, and has traditionally been sought through national means (having a national defence) or by alliances and the balance of power. Not only can it exist within an anarchic system; it positively encourages such a system.[16] It also encourages the security dilemma – one state pursues its security often at the cost of the security of another state, which in turn tries to ensure its own security and thus makes the first state even more insecure, and so on.

The concept of order associated with national security is essentially a minimalist, realist one. Much attention is given to the operational environment – capabilities – rather than intentions, as the latter can change overnight. With so much riding on maintaining what is considered to be a proper level of defence (the very existence of a state may be at stake) it is seen to be unwise to trust in the good intentions of other states. Relative gains by other states become more important than absolute gains by one's own state. For example, it is better for a state to increase its number of frigates from four to five while its three neighbours still only have one each than to increase its frigates from four to seven with each neighbour increasing its one frigate to four, three and two, respectively. The prospect of co-operation is narrow, simply because other states cannot be trusted not to cheat. Why help a 'friend' to get richer today when it could be an enemy tomorrow and spend the money on armaments? This view of the world is one where the emphasis is on anarchy and self-help, where international order is minimal and has to give way to the needs of individual states.

The notion of collective security came out of the concert and congress system of the nineteenth century but could be seen at its most institutionalised form in the League of Nations and United Nations systems. The basic notion of collective security is that of the Musketeers Oath: 'All for one and one for all'.[17] There was no longer the assumption that each state would make its own arrangements for security, but that states had an interest in the maintenance of the international system as such and in certain rules in that system. In the League of Nations, the rules were fairly basic: states should not start a war before having tried the League settlement system. This became more complicated with the UN: here the breaking of international peace and security (the two concepts were harnessed together) as defined by the Security Council is the great sin. This allows for a breach of the peace to be defined in terms of what happens internally in a state, such as apartheid in South Africa in the 1970s and 1980s, white minority rule in Southern Rhodesia from 1965 until 1980, and the Iraqi treatment of the Kurds in 1991.

The idea of collective security can be associated with a perception of order that starts to deal with the management of interdependence. At least in military security matters, it recognises that states are part of a collective system whereby a fault in one element affects the system as a whole. Absolute gains start to become more important than comparative ones.[18] Collective action takes precedence over the demands of individual states and anarchy is tempered by the call of common interests, rules and institutions, which may, over time, develop common values. However, the success of any collective security action depends, certainly in the long run, on a perception of the target state as an enemy. This may be difficult if that state is regarded as 'friendly' by the leadership and peoples of key states in the collectivity.

In the immediate post-Second World War period, the division of Europe, and much of the world, by the Cold War was reflected in the creation of alliances that ran on the basis of collective defence. It provided security for the few against a named adversary: in this sense it was opposed to collective security. However, it sought to defend not just sovereign states but also ideologies and ways of life. It was primarily a military method of securing the defence of the state, but it had a strong economic and political element to it. It provided fertile ground for the security dilemma: security for one bloc was purchased at the expense of another.

The neo-realists believed that the emerging European bipolar alliance system had little to do with international society. It was the antithesis of international order, with an emphasis being placed on self-reliance. The notion of 'us' was defined wider than the state but only to include allies who co-operated on military matters in peacetime. Nevertheless, governments were pressed along the road to co-operation by the widening of trust from national defence to allies which allowed defences to be organised collectively both to defend the collectivity against an identified threat and to deter it. The shadow of the future lengthened. An alliance of convenience such as NATO became more institutionalised and more based on a common set of beliefs. It allowed states that had previously been adversaries – such as Germany and France – to build a relationship of trust and interdependence. Nevertheless, this opportunity to construct the elements of society between certain states seemed only possible because of the greater fear of an adversary – the other side of the Cold War divide in Europe.

At the time of the New Cold War, at the start of the 1980s, a fresh concept of security was introduced into international relations: common security. This came out of the Palme Commission,[19] which saw that Europe was being faced with a threat that was collectively greater than the perceived threat seen by each of the blocs – NATO and the Warsaw Pact – in the existence of the other. That threat was the very existence of nuclear weapons and their proliferation in Europe and elsewhere. The idea was to move from the insecurities of the Cold War to a position where both sides would recognise their common need to control the spread of nuclear weapons, limit weapons and forces generally, and deal jointly with economic and environmental issues. However, this supposed an end to each side's demonisation of the other and a reordering of the Cold War priority given to strong military national and alliance defence.

With the advent of Gorbachev's leadership in the Soviet Union, and the events of 1988–90 that led to the end of the Cold War, other concepts came to the fore. Co-operative security was the mechanism by which common security might be achieved and involved co-operation between former adversaries and the various security institutions such as CSCE and NATO.[20] It meant all sides working together in the security field: for example, in the Conventional Forces in Europe agreement, the Open Skies agreement, and with Confidence and Security-Building Measures. Clearly this view of security supposed a willingness by the leaderships of the two Cold War sides to choose a 'non-zero-sum game' approach to their relations.

Comprehensive security involved an understanding of security as reaching beyond the military and diplomatic fields to embrace economic, societal, environmental and cultural aspects.[21] There is a discussion here over the extent to which the concept of security should be comprehensive.[22] Is there not a danger that a wide definition of the term will lead to the securitisation – and the probable militarisation – of civilian policies such as those on refugees and drugs? Nevertheless, a wider definition of the aspects of security policy became more common during the 1990s, in both academic and official literature.[23] As mentioned above, this has partly been the result of the end of the Cold War leading to the opportunity to place different issues on the security agenda and the addition to the international agenda of issues that previously may have been seen as part of the internal order (for example, crime). This is a result of the barriers between states being torn down, not just as a result of the end of the Cold War but also consequent on developments within the European Union (EU) and between the EU and the Central and Eastern European (CEE) countries. As the Single European Market was built and 'Europe Agreements' were signed between the EU and CEE governments, individual states' ability to control certain aspects of life (the flow of goods, money and labour in or out of their country) declined. What had previously been on the domestic law and order agenda – money laundering, organised crime and prostitution – were pushed up to be matters for international security concern.

Later in the 1990s, as the security agenda broadened, a distinction was made between *hard* and *soft* security. One aspect of soft security is civic security. The Danish Foreign Minister made a distinction between these three concepts in 1996 when talking about the European Union:

'Soft security' in this context is understood as all aspects of security short of military combat operations including the defence of the national territory. That is: everything ranging from internal stability to the execution of the Petersberg tasks.[24] 'Hard security' is mainly the territorial defence against an outside aggressor while 'civic security' encompasses the non-military – civic – aspects of 'soft security'.[25]

The Nordic countries had a long tradition of strong elements of civic security, whereby the national defence effort is supported by civilian elements such as civil defence and maintaining the economic infrastructure in times of crisis or conflict.

A connected concept is that of *human* security. Not only does this idea fit into the comprehensive view of security, encompassing issues such as mass migration, organised crime, disease and pollution, it also calls for an approach to using the tools of security in such a way that 'encourages policy-makers to examine the human costs of strategies for promoting state and international security'.[26] Should there be more widespread agreement on this issue, there is the potential for a world order based on an understanding of security that has as one of its norms a consideration of the human cost of loss of life and limbs alongside state and international security interests. This would be a development of the Geneva Conventions as promoted by the International Committee of the Red Cross. These soft security concerns demonstrate a move away from the traditional security ideas by placing an emphasis on the individual as the referent of security (see next section, below), by dealing with a wider range of both threats and risks than before, and by bringing in institutions not previously associated with security (the EU, regional institutions).

The above concepts of security – common, co-operative, comprehensive, soft and human – flourish in an international society of states. They depend on the wish of European states to develop a 'peaceful or harmonious condition of society'. The latter concepts of soft and human security also concern the values of a potential world society. Pursuit of these notions of security accentuates the contradictions of the two types of order, world and international, and their potential to clash with domestic order within states. This can be seen in the case of the OSCE.

Though flourishing in the 1990s, both co-operative and comprehensive security, as Andrew Cottey notes in Chapter 3 of this volume, had been planted in the 1975 Helsinki Final Act which was the basis for the CSCE (now OSCE). This agreement provided an early demonstration of the emergence of elements of international society and world society in Europe, and the contradictions involved in both. The Helsinki Act certainly formed the basis for an emerging international order in Europe by providing the justification for what Bull had called 'a pattern of activity that sustains the elementary or primary goals of the society of states'.[27] It set out a common set of rules for all European states and established common institutions. It would take a decade from the signing of the Final Act for European decision-makers to use the opportunities offered by the institutions and pay heed to the rules and norms. When they did, ambiguities became apparent.

Showing itself to be a precursor to Palme's notion of common security, the Final Act set out in its preamble the recognition of the 'indivisibility of security in Europe'. The Act was also based on the need to recognise the existing order in post-war Europe. It thus accepted, as a guiding principle for relations between the participating states, sovereign equality and the respect for the rights inherent in sovereignty. States were to refrain from the threat or use of force against each other and frontiers were to be inviolable. Other states' territory should not be seized, usurped or made the object of military occupation, though frontiers could be changed 'in accordance with international law, peaceful means and agreement'. States were to refrain from intervening in the internal affairs of other states.[28] These elements, if kept to, would have gone far in reaching the goals of the society of states sustained by international order. All that was needed – and it was too much to expect in the divided Europe of the mid-1970s – was an element of sharing, of a feeling that Europe was 'us' rather than 'them and us'.

There were other elements in the Final Act that owed as much to notions of a world order as to those of international order, using Bull's distinction. The Final Act required states to respect human rights and fundamental freedoms 'including the freedom of thought, conscience, religion or belief' and they were to promote 'civil, political, economic, social, cultural and other rights and freedoms'. National minorities were to be afforded equality before the law. In a section that seemed to cut across the conservative elements in Bull's understanding of international order, the Final Act required states to respect:

> The equal rights of peoples and their right to self-determination . . . all peoples always have the right in full freedom, to determine, when and as they wish, their internal and external political status without external interference, and to pursue as they wish their political, economic, social and cultural development.[29]

This conceptual dynamite can be said to have exploded across Europe as the constraints of alliances weakened, existing states were shown to be fragile and the opportunity arose for new groups to speak – and act – on behalf of various 'peoples'. To the extent that these groups required new states as an expression (in most cases) of their self-determination, the long-term effect may be seen as cementing the international order that had been temporarily fractured. Even so, damage has been done along the way.

The Final Act contained another element that was even less supportive of the international society of states. This was the element that stressed the 'well-being of peoples' and saw, with the establishment of 'Baskets II and III', intensified co-operation across frontiers in the fields of economics, science and technology, the environment, information, culture and education, and between families and citizens. As the opportunities grew for such links and as states lowered their defensive mechanisms against such interchanges, so the foundations of world society (or at least its European basis) – unlimited communications, a global perspective, a freer flow of capital, companies and firms with only weak national ties, a European labour force – began to strengthen.

With these seeds of change planted in the Helsinki Final Act, and with the move from New Cold War to the end of the Cold War by the late 1980s and early 1990s, the concepts of co-operative security and comprehensive security started to take on meaning. The barriers were coming down: first the Berlin Wall, then the 'Iron Curtain' and then the barriers to trade, capital and labour in Western Europe. A new set of opportunities arose for the states in Europe, whereby ideas of security based more on international society, or even on world society, than on coping with international anarchy could be tried.

The notion of comprehensive security allowed for considerations of various sorts of security within this widened span. So the Copenhagen School has talked about *societal* security, thus deepening as well as widening security concepts. Though there is discussion about the definition of the term 'society', Wæver differentiates it from an aggregation of individuals' security and sees it as 'not just a sector of state security, but a distinctive referent object alongside it'.[30] This can mean that particular social groups – nations, religious groups, minorities – may perceive the need to protect themselves and their identity against a number of forces, some of which may represent the state within which they reside. They may look to the elements of a world order that speaks of fundamental freedoms and human rights, minority rights and the right to self-determination, all elements that could undermine the international society of states, at least in the short run. In the long run, such ideas might be used to reconstitute certain groups as states themselves (as in former Yugoslavia, the Baltic states and the Czech and Slovak republics), though that does not guarantee new states from being 'undermined' by similar societal groups within their territory.

Other more global elements might undermine the feeling of security of a society. It might be that the society fears a cultural threat from the export of US mass culture or it wants to resist mass tourism or the effects of overseas investment. Again it may be felt that the state is not sufficiently protecting the society, which could lead either to the government responding positively and trying to resist the globalising elements or the society finding its own methods of protection, one of which may be the creation of a new state.

Analysing security

Ronnie Lipschutz asks two important questions about security, which can be adapted for this chapter. First, what is being secured and by whom? Is the referent the state, a nation, a civilisation, a wider community or something else? Second, what is the condition of security? Is it protection against an external or internal enemy, or insulation against economic pressures?

Or is this condition seen in more positive terms, such as environmental sustainability, economic well-being and democratic government? In other words, when do you think you are secure?[31]

If the referent of much of the security discourse in Europe since 1989 has increasingly been Europe itself (however defined), how has its condition of security been defined? All the various tools of security mentioned above – national defence, collective security, collective defence and co-operative security – have been available, though ideas of co-operative and common security have dominated in the pan-European context.[32] The approach to security has ranged in extent from that concentrating on the purely military to that taking a broader comprehensive security view.[33] The sort of international order that has been emerging, somewhat gingerly, can be described as a security complex, underpinned by a security regime and a security community.

At one end of the spectrum of the academic and official literature considering European security in the post-Cold War context, there is still a fairly traditional view of security being determined by global or continental power considerations, understandable in terms of military–diplomatic power. This approach defines European security in terms of a security complex within which 'major security perceptions and concerns are so interlinked that their national security problems cannot reasonably be analysed apart from one another'.[34] This is a fairly vague notion but it does suggest that there is increasingly in Europe a feeling of 'us' when it comes to security questions. At least at the level of the decision-making elite, there is an acceptance that matters in South-east Europe are of intrinsic concern to, say, the Nordic states, not just because – as in the Cold War – the nuclear stand-off made every potential conflict one of common concern, but because the problems of Europe are felt to be interlinked. This meant that Europe was developing in the security field the sorts of interest, values, rules and institutions that were binding it together in international society.

The notion of a security regime is one developed in the early 1980s by Robert Jervis but it has relevance for post-Cold War Europe.[35] A regime involves 'social institutions consisting of agreed upon principles, norms, rules, procedures and programs that govern the interactions of actors in specific issue areas'.[36] During the Cold War, such a regime as the Conventional Forces in Europe agreement spanned the historic divisions of East and West. Since 1989, such security regimes have become more widespread, covering activities from nuclear arms control to the running of elections. They overlap both in function and area and help to underpin the elements of co-operative security. Such regimes provide the sinews for the international society described by Bull, but their presence in the non-governmental area (for example, in environmental issues, telecommunications and information technology) can also underpin the functioning of the wider global society.[37]

The idea of a security community was developed in the work of Deutsch, where it was seen in the North Atlantic region as eliminating 'war and the expectation of war within [its] boundaries'. Pluralistic security communities, with separate governments maintaining their independence, needed three preconditions to succeed: 'the compatibility of major values relevant to major decision-making', the capacity of each of the political units to respond to each other's 'needs, messages and actions quickly, adequately and without resort to violence' and the 'mutual predictability of behavior'.[38] An emphasis was placed on increased transactions, such as trade, that would bring mutual dependence.

This notion provides a mechanism by which the relationship between two states (and their citizens) can be transformed from that resembling hostility in anarchy to one based on trust within interdependence. This has been seen in particular within the EU where the new set of opportunities provided by the process of integration has in effect decreased the probability of armed conflict between the member states and increased the willingness of decision-makers and publics to use peaceful means in relations within the Union. The concept of a security community is one that has a particular attraction for those concerned with building security without necessarily resorting to armaments. It also has the capacity to bridge the gap between a rationalist approach to international relations, that might concern itself with the interest and transactions aspect, and the constructivist approach, that would emphasise the aspect of values and common identity.

Conclusions

In summary, to talk of security in Europe is no longer to talk of weapons and armies. These are still important factors in any understanding of the term, but since the end of the Cold War in Europe, what was the minor element in the understanding of security – building peace, justice, stability and well-being – has come more to the fore, providing an opportunity for a wider understanding of security that incorporates other elements than just threat, death and destruction.

The end of the Cold War provided Europeans with a set of opportunities to build their security anew. To some extent, their political leaders have taken advantage of these opportunities and the institutions that allow a more positive approach to security than before. A few political leaders have taken up other new opportunities that have allowed the creation of new political entities, sometimes peacefully (as in the Czech and Slovak cases) but sometimes with a terrible cost, as in former Yugoslavia.

A burgeoning international society of states in Europe was already emerging before the end of the Cold War. This has been able to develop even further since 1989. It has not gone unchallenged, nor is there any guarantee that it will not fall into disuse. Furthermore, it is increasingly being challenged by the emerging world society, especially in the economic and technical fields. The states in Europe may find it harder to maintain the institutions and norms of this international society.

Yet there is another possible development within Europe. Increasingly the relations between the states and societies of the European Union are becoming 'non-securitised'.[39] Political interchange will become more like that within a state, with the distinction between traditional security issues and internal security issues becoming increasingly blurred. As the EU extends its boundaries, this area of 'asecurity' (in traditional terms) will expand. Governments and institutions are now discussing how the EU interrelates with the more traditional national defence and NATO. Perhaps of greater interest is the way that the EU will interact both with new members from Central and Eastern Europe and with those states outside any expanded Union. Will new members be rapidly socialised into the security community that the EU is said to represent? Will the relationship with European states outside the EU, not least Russia, be that of a security regime that sustains an international society of states with agreed norms, values and institutions? Even the achievement of this order – rather than an emphasis on world society – would bring a valued prize. For the first time for centuries, Russia would have an uncontested western frontier surrounded by states that did not offer it any threat and whose futures were tied to the peaceful development of Russia.

Notes and references

1 P. Hanks (ed.), *Collins Dictionary of the English Language.* (London and Glasgow: Collins 1979).

2 H. Bull, *The Anarchical Society: A Study of Order in World Politics.* (London: Macmillan 1977), pp. 3–7.

3 *Ibid.*, p. 13.

4 *Ibid.*, pp. 16–20.

5 *Ibid.*, pp. 20–2.

6 J. Rosenau, *Turbulence in World Politics.* (Princeton: Princeton University Press 1990), p. 12.

7 Bull *op.cit.*, p. 22.

8 K. J. Holsti, 'Governance without Government: Polyarchy in Nineteenth Century International Politics' in J. Rosenau and E. O. Czempiel (eds), *Governance without Government: Order and Change in World Politics.* (Cambridge: Cambridge University Press 1992), p. 31. This point is also made in H. Starr, *Anarchy, Order and Integration: How to Manage Interdependence.* (Ann Arbor: University of Michigan Press 1997), especially ch. 1.

9 For an account of the 'democratic peace' argument see B. Russett, *Grasping the Democratic Peace.* (Princeton: Princeton University Press 1993).

10 See H. Sprout and M. Sprout, 'Environmental Factors in the Study of International Politics' in J. Rosenau (ed.), *International Politics and Foreign Policy.* (New York: Free Press 1969), pp. 41–56.

11 D. A. Lake, 'Between Anarchy and Hierarchy'. *International Organization* 50 (1) 1996, pp. 1–33.

12 R. Väyrynen, 'The Security of the Baltic Countries: Cooperation and Defection' in O. F. Knudsen (ed.), *Stability and Security in the Baltic Sea Region: Russian,*

Nordic and European Aspects. (London: Frank Cass 1999), p. 217. See also R. Jepperson *et al.*, 'Norms, Identity and Culture' in P. Katzenstein (ed.), *The Culture of National Security: Norms and Identity in World Politics.* (New York: Columbia University Press 1996), pp. 33–75.

13 Starr *op.cit.*, pp. 13–16. Starr equates willingness with the agent aspect in the international system and opportunity with the structure of the system (*ibid.*, p. 44).

14 See, for example, T. Schelling, *The Strategy of Conflict.* (Cambridge, Mass.: Harvard University Press 1966).

15 See, for example, A. Wendt, 'Anarchy Is What States Make of It'. *International Organization* 46 (2) 1992, pp. 391–425. For a wider appreciation of the approaches towards security issues in Europe see E. Adler and M. Barnett, 'Security communities in theoretical perspective' in Adler and Barnett (eds), *Security Communities.* (Cambridge: Cambridge University Press 1998), pp. 10–15.

16 A classical statement of this traditional state-centric view of international relations can be found in H. Morgenthau, *Politics among Nations: The Struggle for Power and Peace.* (New York: Alfred A. Knopf 1960). A neo-realist or structural-realist approach can be seen in K. Waltz, *Theory of International Politics.* (Reading, Mass.: Addison Wesley 1979). A good account of the differences between these viewpoints and those of the 'liberal institutionalists' is given in J. Grieco, 'Anarchy and the Limits of Cooperation' in D. Baldwin (ed.), *Neorealism and Neoliberalism: The Contemporary Debate.* (New York: Columbia University Press 1993), pp. 118–23.

17 See I. Claude, *Swords into Plowshares* (fourth edn). (New York: Random House 1971).

18 For a discussion of the 'absolute' versus 'relative' gains issue see D. Snidal, 'Relative Gains and the Pattern of International Cooperation' and 'Absolute and Relative Gains in International Relations Theory', both in Baldwin *op.cit.*

19 O. Palme (chairman of the Independent Commission on Disarmament and Security Issues), *Common Security: A Programme for Disarmament.* (London: Pan Books 1982).

20 See K. Möttölä, 'Security around the Baltic Rim: Concepts, Actors and Processes' in L. Hedegaard and B. Lindström (eds), *The NEBI Yearbook 1998. North European and Baltic Sea Integration.* (Berlin: Springer 1998); also N. H. Petersen, 'Towards a European Security Model for the 21st Century'. *NATO Review* 45 (6) 1997, pp. 4–7.

21 B. Buzan, 'Security after the Cold War'. *Cooperation and Conflict* 32 (1) 1997, pp. 5–28.

22 See, for example, D. Deudney, 'The case against linking environmental degradation and national security'. *Millennium* 19 (3) 1990, pp. 461–76.

23 For an account of the academic literature see Buzan *op.cit.* Official sources include NATO's Strategic Concept, for which see *NATO Review* 47 (2) 1999, especially the section on 'Security Challenges and Risks' and 'The Approach to Security in the 21st Century', p. D9. Also, Organisation for Security and Cooperation in Europe, *Lisbon Document 1996.* (Lisbon: OSCE 1996), especially 'Lisbon Declaration on a Common and Comprehensive Security Model for Europe for the Twenty-first Century', pp. 6–9.

24 The so-called 'Petersberg tasks' were formally taken on by the members of the Western European Union in 1992, and more recently by the European Union itself. They cover humanitarian assistance, peacekeeping and tasks of military forces in crisis management.

25 N. H. Petersen, 'Security Cooperation and Integration in the Baltic Region. The Role of the European Union: Soft Security?' in S. A. Christensen and O. Wæver (eds), *DUPIDOK 1996: Dansk udenrigspolitisk dokumentation.* (Copenhagen: Dansk Udenrigspolitisk Institut 1997), pp. 273–8.

26 L. Axworthy, 'NATO's new security vocation'. *NATO Review* 47 (4) 1999, pp. 8–11.

27 Bull *op.cit.*, p. 8.

28 See the reprint of the Final Act in *Survival* XVII (6) 1975, pp. 295–301, and commentary in C. Archer, *Organizing Europe: The Institutions of Integration* (second edn). (London: Edward Arnold 1994).

29 Final Act *op.cit.*, pp. 296–7.

30 O. Wæver, 'Societal Security: The Concept' in O. Wæver *et al.*, *Identity, Migration and the New Security Agenda in Europe.* (London: Pinter 1993), pp. 24 and 27.

31 R. Lipschutz, 'On Security' in Lipschutz (ed.), *On Security.* (New York: Columbia University Press 1995), pp. 1–23.

32 OSCE *op.cit.* (1996).

33 *Ibid.*, paras 9–12.

34 B. Buzan, 'Introduction' in Wæver *et al. op.cit.*, p. 6.

35 R. Jervis, 'Security Regimes'. *International Organization* 36 (2) 1982, pp. 357–78.

36 M. Levy *et al.*, 'The Study of International Regimes'. *European Journal of International Relations* 1 (3) 1995, p. 274.

37 O. Young, *International Governance: Protecting the Environment in a Stateless Society.* (Ithaca: Cornell University Press 1994).

38 K. Deutsch *et al.*, *Political Community and the North Atlantic Area.* (Princeton: Princeton University Press 1957), pp. 66–7. See also Adler and Barnett *op.cit.*

39 P. Joenniemi, *Norden, Europe and Post-security.* (Copenhagen: Copenhagen Peace Research Institute 1998), pp. 18–19.

2 What does it mean to be 'European'?

The problems of constructing a pan-European identity

Robert Bideleux

Introduction

Since the late 1980s the project of European integration based upon the European Union and its antecedents has ceased to be confined to Western Europe and Greece. Most European states are either members or would-be members of the European Union, or else closely associated with it. The rules, laws, institutions, procedures and policies of the European Union increasingly provide the norms, frameworks and templates on which not only the current members but also most of their neighbours base their political, social, economic and environmental activities, rhetoric and endeavours. Pan-European integration is thus passing from pious dream to mundane reality. This raises crucial questions. Does pan-European integration require the construction of an overarching pan-European identity? Can the European Union overcome Europe's continuing East–West cultural divide and help liberate Central and East Europeans from the hazards of ethnic and religious collectivism? And how far south and east should this integrated Europe extend?

Beyond these questions lie deeper ones concerning the relationship between identity, security and order. Some bases of identity are conducive to the peaceful and prosperous coexistence of diverse peoples and communities, whereas others are conducive to intercommunal conflict and to political and economic breakdown. When the bases of identification change profoundly in a region, the effect can be to bring peace to peoples previously locked in conflict, as with the pacification of Central Europe through a pragmatic application of the formula *cuius regio eius religio* after the 1648 Treaty of Westphalia, and Franco-German reconciliation through joint participation in the construction of a supranational European Community since the 1950s. Or it can be to sow the seeds of catastrophic conflict in previously stable and/or harmonious areas – witness the explosive impact of modern nationalist doctrines and identities on the Balkan dominions of the declining Ottoman Empire.

It is often assumed that the bases of identification change in ways that are beyond anyone's control, that such changes 'just happen', and that we must simply live with the consequences – come what may. However, such a stance overlooks the extent to which bases of identification have been manipulated or even manufactured by political and/or cultural elites – and hence the scope for conscious social engineering. For example, the assiduous fostering of an overarching Yugoslav project and identity by the central authorities and cultural elites played a pivotal role in holding the Yugoslavs together during the inter-war era and again from 1945 to the 1970s, just as the equally assiduous fostering of narrow and exclusive ethnic identities among the Yugoslav peoples by the republican political and cultural elites from the 1970s onward paved the way for the bloody disintegration of the Yugoslav Federation during the 1990s.[1] Bases of identification help to set the terms on which people(s) relate to and engage with one another politically, socially and even economically, and are thus among the fundamental determinants of security and well-being. It is therefore incumbent upon those who wish to secure a peaceful, prosperous and united Europe actively to seek, promote and uphold modes of identification which will help to make such a Europe possible, rather than merely to hope that these will emerge spontaneously.

Identity politics, or the staking of claims to self-determination and power on the basis of identity (whether ethnic, national, racial, religious or regional), has acquired enormous saliency in Western Europe since the early 1990s for a variety of reasons. The increasing congruence of bounded territories, governmental functions and shared identities which characterised the European states system in the late nineteenth and early twentieth centuries has been substantially eroded at the national level in recent decades. National identities are fragmenting under the dual pressures of subnational (regional and local) and supranational (macro-regional and global) forces. The European Union is simultaneously moving beyond institutional and policy issues to 'fundamental questions about its nature as a part-formed polity'.[2] Moreover, EU citizenship was established at a time when a number of West European states were belatedly grappling with the implications of the large-scale immigration which mainly occurred during the 1950s to 1970s, the emergence of multicultural societies, and the steady growth of illegal immigration from outside Europe during the 1980s and 1990s. Even the Schengen Agreement, which was originally inspired by primarily economic concerns about the free movement of labour, goods and services across European Union borders, has in practice become increasingly a matter of tightening external border controls against 'non-European' migrants and asylum-seekers. Eruptions of inter-ethnic unrest or conflict in many of Europe's post-communist states have made ethnicity and identity politics even more salient further east.

The growing salience of ethnicity and identity politics represents both a response to and an aggravation of the serious challenges which are currently being posed to democracy and the modern states system. The bonds of national identity which have helped to hold democratic communities and polities together in the late modern era are being weakened by the combined effects of global and regional integration, the cultural fragmentation fostered by the recognition and proliferation of particularistic identities, and the commodification of cultural identities (Irish, Welsh, Scottish, Basque and Catalan identities, for example, have been successfully reinvented through the skilful marketing campaigns of tourist boards, cultural bodies, multinational companies and regional development agencies). In the words of Alain Touraine:

> Squeezed between a globalized economy and aggressively introverted cultures . . . the political space is fragmenting and democracy is being debased – reduced, at best, to a relatively open political marketplace, which no one troubles to defend because it is not the object of any intellectual or affective investment . . . The danger here is that [multi]culturalism, in the name of respect for differences, will encourage the formation of localized power that will impose an antidemocratic authority within particular communities. Should that happen, political society will become no more than a marketplace where communities locked into an obsession with their identities and internal homogeneity enter into loosely regulated transactions.

In time, 'this impoverishment of the democratic idea can only result in the extraparliamentary, even extrapolitical, expression of social demands, protests and hopes'.[3] In the English-speaking world the rhetoric of 'multiculturalism' has acquired very positive connotations and is championed by prominent cosmopolitan-individualist liberal theorists such as Will Kymlicka.[4] However, 'multiculturalism' can also imply acceptance of the group particularism and respect for 'the right to be different' which have been seized upon by the Front National and its 'fellow travellers' on the far right in France as a new basis on which to justify racial discrimination and segregation and the proposed repatriation of immigrants of North African extraction. It is fraught with latent danger.

In October 1999, in publicising a conference on the 'Financing, Resources and Economics of Culture in Sustainable Development', Italian Foreign Minister Lamberto Dini and World Bank President James Wolfensohn argued that the 'self-awareness and pride that come from cultural identity are an essential part of empowering communities to take charge of their own destinies' and that 'development will almost certainly fail without the assertion of identity that culture provides'. Enjoining respect for 'the rootedness of people in their own societies', they called for development practices which will 'conserve and amplify the values, expression and heritage that gives people's lives meaning and human dignity'.[5] However, it is not clear whether such meaning, dignity and empowerment are best achieved by nurturing cultural identity at the local, the regional, the national or the supranational level, or at all four levels at once. None of these levels has an intrinsic claim to primacy. Moreover, while attachment to and freedom to articulate cultural identities may represent deeply felt human needs which it would be dangerous to disregard, we must at the same time remain alive to the even greater dangers posed by the unconstrained expansion of identity politics. The proliferation of claims to self-determination and power on the basis of identity can place all states, boundaries and polities perpetually in question, making it increasingly difficult to sustain any kind of settled, stable, accepted and coherent order that allows us to devote due attention and resources to other matters. In the words of the eminent US legal philosopher Ronald Dworkin, 'self-determination is the most potent – and the most dangerous – political ideal of our time'.[6]

When we have made 'Europe', must we then make 'Europeans'?

In 1861, at the first session of the parliament of the newly unified Italian state, Massimo d'Azeglio famously declared: 'we have made Italy, now we must make Italians'.[7] Is it similarly incumbent upon the proponents of European union to promote an overarching European identity as an integral part of that project?

Some writers, notably the specialist on nationalism Anthony D. Smith, have answered this question by contrasting European integration with the formations of nations and nation-states. Smith has argued that the European project lacks the mythic and symbolic resources and heritage that would allow an overarching European state to supersede Europe's separate nation-states, particularly in terms of affective claims on popular allegiance. In his view:

> national identifications possess distinct advantages over the idea of a unified European identity. They are vivid, accessible, well established, long popularised, and still widely believed, in broad outline at least. In each of these respects, 'Europe' is deficient both as idea and as process. Above all, it lacks a pre-modern past – a 'pre-prehistory' which can provide it with emotional sustenance and historical depth . . . Europeans differ among themselves as much as from non-Europeans . . . Is it possible for the new Europe to arise without 'myth' and 'memory'? Have we not seen that these are indispensable elements in the construction of any durable and resonant collective cultural identity?[8]

However, it is not necessary to assume that the ties that bind together the constituent elements of the European Union must replicate those that hold together nations and nation-states. Instead of basing their aspirations on unpromising historical antecedents, the prime movers of the current European integration project have focused their attentions on the present and the future. As argued by Paul Howe, tangible homogeneity is not among the requisite underpinnings for a community of Europeans . . . A community of Europeans can and probably will be, for some generations anyway, the same rich mosaic of languages, customs and traditions that it is today.

Nevertheless, Howe believes that 'as the European Union acquires some important trappings of statehood – in particular as it starts to confer rights that define people as European citizens – there gradually will develop a more dominant sense of Europeanness'. The prospect, in Howe's view, 'is not that the people of Europe are ready to will themselves to be part of a new nation, but simply that they will acquiesce as the political structures that typically precede such a development are put in place, after which the more organic phase of community-building will naturally run its course'. In the long term, 'a community of Europeans could be strengthened through the gradual accumulation of the more substantive buttresses of resonant communication identified by [Karl] Deutsch[9] (learned memories, symbols, preferences, and so on)'.[10]

Yet, while Howe optimistically dwells on the values and beliefs that many Europeans have in common as the potential bases for benign and harmonious *inclusion*, the existing European Union has become increasingly preoccupied with the *exclusion* of less welcome 'others' – be they Southern and Eastern Slavs, North Africans or Asians. Howe's emphasis on the EU's liberal cosmopolitan founding ideals is thus at odds with its 'systems of discrimination and oppression belying the public sphere of impartiality of norms and equal citizenship', while its 'liberal commitment to the intrinsic worth of all individuals . . . does not seem to square with the idea of exclusionary communities with fortified boundaries and restrictive conditions of membership'.[11]

It would indeed be bitterly ironic if the project of European integration were to overcome the erstwhile racial antagonism and discrimination between peoples perceived to be *European* only to replace them with heightened racial antagonism and discrimination against peoples perceived to be racially or culturally '*non-European*'. This would be internally divisive and a source of internal tension and unrest, as well as exclusionary vis-à-vis 'non-European' migrants. The construction of a Fortress Europe which keeps out 'non-European' economic migrants, refugees and asylum-seekers could be achieving just such a result. According to Andrew Linklater, 'political communities endure because they are exclusive, and most establish their peculiar identities by accentuating the differences between insiders and aliens'.[12] In this respect, the European Union is like any other political community. It is merely taking on the gatekeeping functions formerly exercised by its member states. This is nevertheless rather at odds with its liberal-cosmopolitan rhetoric.

It has also been argued, on quite a different plane, that the creation of a fully democratic and legitimate European Union requires the creation of a European *demos*, which might be seen as involving the replacement of the European peoples by a unitary European people or nation. According to Dimitris Chryssochoou, 'no democracy, small or large scale, has ever existed, exists or ever can exist without a *demos*', for 'democracy implies *ex definitio* the existence of a *demos*. It is on this basis that the case for a European *demos* rests.'[13] However, it is debatable whether the legitimacy of the EU either rests or will ever need to rest upon a European *demos* in an organic ethno-cultural sense, as distinct from a union of separate *demoi*. In committing itself to 'ever-closer union' between distinct and separately respected and nurtured peoples and to the preservation of linguistic and cultural diversity, the EU has in fact set its face against the creation of such a European *demos* and therefore against that route to the creation of a supranational European democracy.

It nevertheless continues to be widely believed that the economic and political projects for European union will only work in a durable fashion if the Union acquires strong cultural and affective underpinnings. Richard Münch proposes that European integration 'means building a cultural identity in terms of a shared view of what Europeans have in common, and what makes them distinct from non-Europeans. It implies the construction of a European world-view, a common definition, shared values, norms, cognitions and aesthetic views.'[14] In the words of Jacques Delors, 'you don't fall in love with a common market; you need something else'.[15] On that occasion, however, Delors was (uncharacteristically) selling the European Union short. It is quite conceivable that public goodwill and allegiance towards the European Union can be maintained by its citizens' accumulation of economic and social rights secured by participation in the Single Market (the EU equivalent of the French *acquis sociaux*) as well as by the 'constitutional patriotism' engendered by common participation in the overarching EU polity. One must beware of the tendency to confuse or conflate the *demos* with an *ethnos*. A *demos* can be simply an association of free and equal citizens living within a single state, which need not be coterminous with a particular ethnic group. In the classic formulation propounded by Abbé Sieyès in 1789, a nation is simply a 'body of associates living under *common* laws and represented by the same *legislative assembly*, etc.'.[16] What really matters is not whether people share a particular ethnic, linguistic or religious identity or identities, but whether they are willing and able to participate in a shared public arena.

'Eastern' versus 'western' nations and nationalism

'The heart of the difference between the two halves of Europe', according to George Schöpflin, has lain in their 'contrasting approaches to citizenship'.[17] In Western Europe (excluding Germany, Austria and Greece), there has been a preponderance of relatively inclusive *ius soli* conceptions of citizenship, whereas in Central and Eastern Europe (including Germany,

Austria and Greece) there has been a preponderance of relatively exclusive *ius sanguinis* definitions of citizenship. In the words of the Croatian
academician Zarko Pukhovski, 'Europe is divided again ... The division
now rests ... on the role and importance of ethno-national sovereignty.
Defining sovereignty in ethnic terms necessarily means exclusion: the
exclusion of ethnic minorities by ethnic majorities.'[18]

Perceptions such as these seem to point to a potential East–West 'clash
of civilisations' in the Huntingtonian sense.[19] However, it needs to be
emphasised that such clashes can occur not only along an East–West axis,
but also *within* Europe's regions and national traditions. Since the early
1990s, elections in Central, East and South-east Europe have been fought
not just on competing economic policies and/or personalistic platforms,
but also on rival conceptions of nationality, citizenship, rights and the
nation. The ascendancy of 'ethnic' nationalism in Central, East and South-
east Europe is being contested in the media, on the hustings and in
academic writing, even if the advocates of more inclusive 'civic' conceptions of citizenship and national identity sometimes appear to be fighting a
losing battle. There are several areas of actual or potential dissonance
and/or incompatibility between current EU norms and those prevalent in
Central, East and South-east Europe. Most pertinently, Article 7 of the
Treaty of Rome states that 'within the scope of this Treaty ... any discrimination on grounds of nationality shall be prohibited'. While the current
member states frequently fall short of this ideal, and while the increasing
'ethnicisation' and 'racialisation' of West European identities and identity
politics since the 1970s should caution West European analysts against
smug complacency over the extent to which their own house is in order,
these lapses and deficiencies pale by comparison with the challenges posed
by the potential admission of states which are in many cases regarded as
being in the exclusive possession of particular ethnic groups and whose
very legitimacy and *raison d'être* have rested on ethnic nationalism and
exclusivity. In almost all the Central, East and South-east European candidates for EU membership, ethnic discrimination and the preferential status
of the dominant ethnic group is not just an unfortunate and regrettable
lapse or aberration, but has been intrinsic to the operation of the state,
democratic representation, public employment and many social, political
and economic rights and entitlements.

It is sometimes argued that the current candidates ought not to be
admitted to the European Union until they have fully understood and
accepted its rules and norms and its cosmopolitan ethos, although it can
be countered that membership would help and encourage them to do so.
Either way, the requisite reorientation will inevitably take some time, as it
will involve profound changes in political and cultural values, mentalities,
attitudes and power structures, and in the ways that Central, East and
South-east European nations and states see and define themselves and
each other. Such changes are more fundamental than the economic re-

forms which receive much greater public attention and are not ones which they really want to make. This contributed to their acute misgivings over the way that Austria was cold shouldered by its EU partners after Jörg Haider's Freedom Party entered the Austrian government in February 2000.

It is not my intention to hold up Western Europe as a paragon of political and moral virtue, as a kind of inner sanctum of perfection from which lesser mortals should be excluded, nor to claim that one ascends some sort of ladder of superiority as one moves from East to West, nor to suggest that Western Europeans are more 'European' than their Eastern neighbours. No part of Europe has a monopoly of either virtue or 'Europeanness'. Nor are these properties synonymous! Not only Russians, Ukrainians, Serbs, Croats, Slovenes, Slovaks, Romanians and Hungarians, but also Bosnians, Kosovars, Poles, Balts, Belgians, Britons, Frenchmen, Germans, Italians, Portuguese and Spaniards have perpetrated appalling crimes against humanity in modern times. What is more, such crimes have often been committed by persons professing belief in the superiority of Europeans over allegedly sub-human or barbaric 'others'. Nor should Central Europeans be allowed to get away with their frequent claims of superiority over (and stronger European credentials than) the Russians, who did more than anyone to save Europe from the Nazi New Order which sprang from the very 'heart of Europe'. Moreover, a noted feature of the high culture of Central and South-east Europe is its particularism, whereas most of the great works of Russian literature and music share the universalism that pervades French and British high culture. This is said not to claim 'superiority' for Russian high culture over its Central and South-east European counterparts, but simply to warn against disingenuous claims about the supposedly innate superiority or greater 'Europeanness' of any one part of Europe.

In Western Europe, nationalism and nation consciousness were mainly fostered as means of identifying citizens with existing states, whereas the modern Central and East European nations were most frequently postulated or 'imagined' as pre-existing and ethnically exclusive cultural entities from which *future* nation-states could be derived. In Western Europe, protonational monarchical states for the most part consciously fostered relatively inclusive nations and national identities as means of reinforcing their political legitimacy and popular allegiance, whereas in Central, East and South-east Europe culturally defined nations have for the most part succeeded in fostering ethnically exclusive nation-states in place of (and in opposition to) previously existing multinational empires. In the process, nationalists in Central, East and South-east Europe 'created, often out of myths of the past and dreams of the future, an ideal fatherland' adorned with characteristics 'for the realisation of which they had no immediate responsibility, but which influenced the nascent nation's wishful image of itself and of its mission'.[20] For example, Vuk Karadzic, the father of the Serb linguistic–literary revival and of the concept of a 'Greater Serbia', argued that 'the Serbs were "the greatest people of the planet", that their culture was 5,000 years old, and that . . . Jesus, too, with his apostles, was a Serb'.[21]

In Western Europe, moreover, the preponderance of relatively inclusive forms of national identity and nation-state owes something to the fortuitous existence of some conveniently placed 'natural frontiers' (seas, mountain ranges) and to the good luck that most of these nations and nation-states had crystallised *before* the popularisation of racial ideas and doctrines during the second half of the nineteenth century. In Central, East and South-east Europe, unfortunately, the topography offered fewer 'natural' national frontiers and most nations and nation-states came to fruition a few decades *later*, under the baleful influence of racial and *volkish* ideas and doctrines and German idealist philosophy. Hence national identities, allegiances and citizenship came to be determined not by birth and/or residence in a particular state or territory (*ius soli*), but by more exclusive Germanic conceptions of the *Volk* and *ius sanguinis*. From 1913 to 1999 German nationality law restricted German nationality to people of German descent, on the assumption that a single German nation had existed independently of any German statehood and would continue to do so. The problems of so-called 'ethnic minorities' have loomed very large in Central, East and South-east European states since 1918, not so much because these states have had more ethnically mixed populations (states such as Spain, France and the UK have been forged out of similarly mixed populations), but because most of the new or expanded 'nation-states' which emerged out of the disintegration of the Central and East European multinational empires were (regrettably) defined in exclusive ethnic terms – and as 'belonging' exclusively to dominant ethnic groups.

During the turbulent inter-war era most of the Central, East and South-east European nations clung fearfully to archaic self-images and Quixotic conceptions of national valour, while nationalists became increasingly messianic and collectivist, claiming rights for the nation rather than for individual citizens and demanding unquestioning loyalty to the nation, which was seen as having an 'historic' or 'God-given' mission or destiny to fulfil. Individuals who rejected national messianism and ethnic or religious collectivism were often pilloried as 'traitors' to their nation. Messianic collectivist nationalism became increasingly illiberal, xenophobic and conducive to various forms of nationalist and fascist authoritarianism. The dominant ethnic groups rejoiced in their new-found 'national freedom' (even though this increasingly took the form of repressive dictatorship) and hegemonically promoted their own languages and cultures, while doing as little as possible (or worse) for the languages and cultures of ethnic minorities. Nationalists like Nichifor Crainic sang the praises of 'the ethnocratic state'.[22]

In Central, East and South-east Europe since 1918, therefore, there has been a relatively limited awareness of the possibility (or even the desirability) of a state which dispenses justice and upholds the law without strongly pronounced ethnic, religious or clannish favour or bias. There has often been one law for minorities and another (often flexible) law for the dominant ethnic and/or religious group. For the most part, 'national intelligentsias' and 'national bourgeoisies' have become 'ethnocracies': servitors, clients and protégés of national states, rather than independent champions of more inclusive civil societies. State patronage, clientelism and the concentration of power and access in the hands of the few have thus been able to develop largely unchecked, to the further detriment of vulnerable minorities. The increasingly *nationalist* orientation of the communist regimes from the late 1950s to the late 1980s merely reinforced these trends, as did the triumphal (re)assertion of ethnic nationalism after 1989. If they are not overcome, these characteristics could compromise the current candidates' participation in the EU, insofar as this requires the ethnically impartial administration of rules, regulations, laws, educational and employment opportunities, social policies, and agricultural and structural funds.

It is sometimes claimed that the differences between Western and Central/Eastern European nationalisms have been greatly exaggerated. Anthony Smith has pointed out that the ways in which Irish, Welsh, Scottish, Norwegian, Finnish, Flemish, Breton, Basque, Catalan, Corsican, Sardinian and Sicilian nationalist movements and identities have been 'mobilised' by writers and intellectuals *against* (rather than *by*) existing states, as well as the ethno-cultural forms of nationalism and national identity which they have fostered, have borne important resemblances to the forms and origins of 'ethnic mobilisation' and 'ethnic nationalism' which have prevailed in Central, East and South-east Europe.[23] However, it can be countered that in Western Europe such manifestations of 'ethnic mobilisation' and 'ethnic nationalism' have often been incubated within (and therefore under the restraining influence of) larger and relatively inclusive 'civic' nations and states, and that they have rarely become the basis of fiercely exclusive 'ethnic-national' states. And, except perhaps in Ireland and Spain, they have rarely exhibited the degrees of intolerance and bigotry that developed within ethnic nationalism in Central and Eastern Europe during parts of the twentieth century.

Admittedly, there have been virulent manifestations of ethnic exclusivism and xenophobia right across Europe at one time or another, and any form of nationalism harbours the potential to degenerate into murderous intolerance, bigotry or authoritarianism. Conversely, some of Europe's 'Eastern' nation-states (e.g. Ukraine and Lithuania) have embraced and implemented relatively inclusive territorial conceptions of the nation and citizenship. Therefore, the Romanian academic Dan Dungaciu is quite justified in warning against the tendency for Western writers to 'essentialise' the differences between 'Western' and 'Central/Eastern' nationalisms and to exaggerate the fanatical propensities of 'Central/Eastern' nationalisms.[24] His list of culprits includes Hans Kohn, Peter Sugar, John Planematz,

Robert Kaplan, Michael Ignatieff and myself.[25] However, while some of these writers have indeed 'essentialised' the more obnoxious characteristics of 'Central/Eastern' nationalisms, I must plead 'not guilty'. Dungaciu quotes my statement that the nationalism fostered in the West by the French Revolution

> had a similarly intolerant and even murderous potential, especially in the hands of a Robespierre or a Saint-Just. But in Western Europe, fortunately, this was counteracted and held in check by the relatively strong development of the rule of law, the separation of powers, liberalism and concepts of limited government.[26]

However, he overlooks my statement that

> we do not believe in the frequently alleged existence of innate differences in the 'ethnic make-up' and 'temper' of the two halves of Europe. That kind of stereotyping borders on racial prejudice and racism. The distinctive political and cultural complexions of the Eastern European nations were, in our view, not innate but structurally determined'.

In other words, I was explicitly repudiating the notion that Central and Eastern European nationalisms are *essentially* different from their Western counterparts. The crucial difference was that 'the structures and contexts within which Eastern European nationalism emerged did not reinforce but came into conflict with the development of tolerance and mutual respect'.[27]

In addition to emphasising structures and contexts, I would now put greater stress on the influence of contingent factors, such as the often almost fortuitous outcomes of political struggles, strategic and diplomatic blunders, and the effects of massive military incursions by Great Powers from outside the Balkans and Central and Eastern Europe. Such circumstances have often inflamed inter-ethnic conflicts which might otherwise have remained largely or even completely dormant – contrary to the Western tendency to see such conflicts as the outcome of 'ancient ethnic hatreds' which were allegedly waiting to erupt at every opportunity or provocation. Powers from outside the region should not be allowed to evade all responsibility for the terrible conflicts that have occurred and for the fearsome inter-ethnic animosities which such conflicts have bequeathed to posterity. The results have indeed been appalling, but it would be a mistake to see them as being either inevitable or intrinsic to the region. Parts of Central, East and South-east Europe have at times been rightly renowned for the relatively peaceful coexistence of peoples with very different ethnic, religious and linguistic identities and affiliations.[28] In any case, Central and East Europeans are not all of one mind. Some are bigoted 'ethnic nationalists', others are more tolerant 'civic nationalists', and some are staunchly anti-nationalist.

Europe's East–West contrasts should therefore be painted in shades of grey rather than in black and white. Largely for contingent rather than intrinsic or 'inevitable' reasons, the twentieth century saw a preponderance of 'civic' nationalisms in Western Europe and a prevalence of 'ethnic' nationalisms in Central/Eastern Europe, but all nationalisms and national identities have contained both 'civic' and 'ethnic' ingredients. The precise balance, far from being rigidly predetermined, has varied considerably within as well as between regions and over time. However, it remains the case that Central, East and South-east European states have tended to place much more emphasis on the perceived collective rights of dominant ethnic and religious groups than on the equal individual rights of all citizens, including minorities and of society as a whole. Most have remained 'ethnocracies', privileging particular ethnic and/or religious groups to degrees rarely to be found in Western Europe.

The continuing tendency to define most Central, East and South-east European states in terms of outmoded, exclusive, inward-looking ethnic and linguistic identities threatens to institutionalise and perpetuate ethnic division and the potential for inter-ethnic conflict and xenophobia and to impair the consolidation of liberal democracy and market economies. Moreover, in the first flush of their hard-won and/or recently regained 'national' independence, most of the Central, East and South-east European states have been unwilling to accept major limitations on their 'national' sovereignty for the sake of the greater harmony, stability, peace and prosperity of their region. The very newness of the successor states of the former Yugoslav and Czechoslovak federations, as also of the former USSR, offered an opportunity to forge new identities and rights of citizenship cast in secular, inclusive, 'civic' moulds. However, states such as Serbia, Croatia, Slovakia, Latvia and Estonia have been slow to recognise and respect the rights of their 'alien' ethnic minorities. They have applied relatively restrictive, exclusive or discriminatory definitions of (and qualifications for) citizenship, in practice if not in law. This has adversely affected the participation of minorities in elections, in acquisition of the homes they have lived in for years, in industrial and agricultural privatisation, and in education, employment and travel opportunities. Unfortunately, the projects which have most effectively aroused and engaged political passions and energies in most of Europe's post-communist states are not liberal democracy and liberal economic reform, but the more primordial projects of nationalism and nation-building. The major challenge confronting the region's statesmen is how to redirect these passions and energies from destructive chauvinism, jealousies, bigotry, xenophobia and vindictiveness towards more tolerant, constructive and inclusive projects of political and economic reform.

In Central, East and South-east Europe, ironically, ethnic identities and exclusive ethnic conceptions of the nation have been reasserted as the basis of states, legitimacy, citizenship and political, social and economic rights and entitlements at a time when the longstanding national basis of polities, governance and citizenship is being fundamentally challenged and eroded in Western Europe as a result of increasing global and regional integration and economic liberalisation. The latter trends have contributed to the growth of nationalist extremism and 'identity politics' in Western Europe, yet (paradoxically) this is occurring at a time when fewer and fewer West Europeans are prepared to fight – let alone die – for their country, 'right or wrong'. The prime targets of 'Western' nationalist sentiment have shifted to the fierce competition for employment, housing and welfare benefits and perceived 'threats to the nation' from the EU and new or longstanding ethnic and racial minorities (rather than from military foes). The current reassertion of nationally bounded and defined citizenries and polities in Central, East and South-east Europe can be regarded as being profoundly at odds with an incipient decoupling of citizenship from identity and the diminishing importance of national polities in Western Europe, resulting from increased transnational mobility, the development of a common EU citizenship and, above all, economic and cultural globalisation.

On the other hand, some analysts argue that, far from being eroded, the links between national and ethnic identity and citizenship in Western Europe are becoming more deeply entrenched by the growth of racist and exclusionary 'ethnic nationalist' movements and sentiments, the tightening of racially and ethnically discriminatory immigration controls, and the adoption in Britain (in 1971 and 1981) and in France (in 1993) of nationality laws based on descent (*ius sanguinis*) rather than place of birth (*ius soli*). If such trends were to persist, the public definition of Britain and France as nations would increasingly resemble the more exclusive 'ethnic' conceptions of the nation prevalent in Greece, Austria and (until 1999) Germany. However, the Jospin government partially reinstated *ius soli* in France, while the nationality laws have been relaxed in Germany with effect from 2000. Moreover, under the terms of the Maastricht Treaty, European Union citizenship is acquired on the basis of the existing *national* citizenship laws of each individual member state: national citizenship confers EU citizenship. 'Even as Western Europe moves towards closer economic union, and perhaps towards political union, citizenship remains a bastion of national sovereignty.'[29] By thus perpetuating large variations in access to citizenship rights, massive anomalies are being created: while several million first-, second- and third-generation immigrants in France and the UK have already gained French, British and hence EU citizenship (and can therefore freely enter Germany as EU citizens), the vast majority of the nearly seven million 'foreigners' resident in Germany have hitherto been denied German and hence EU citizenship (thereby restricting their mobility within the EU). In this regard, the EU states have been laying legal and political minefields which could blow up in their own faces.

The Czech President, Vaclav Havel, has clearly been looking to EU membership to help liberate Central, East and South-east Europe from the tyranny of ethnic exclusivity and collectivism. In the words of his public address at Aachen in May 1996:

> One of the great European traditions – a tradition that Europe increasingly forgot in the first half of the twentieth century – is the idea of the free citizen as the source of all power. After World War II, having learned a lesson from the horrors inflicted by fanatical nationalism, the free part of Europe rededicated itself to this tradition and made it the foundation of reconciliation and co-operation . . . The hope was to bring about a great renaissance of the civic principle as the only possible basis for truly peaceful co-operation among nations. The point was not to suppress national identity or national consciousness, which is one of the dimensions of human identity, but rather to free human beings from the bondage of ethnic collectivism – that source of all strife and enslaver of human individuality.[30]

This theme has been taken up in an important article by Bruce Haddock and Ovidiu Caraiani. They emphasise that the baleful influence of collectivist language, ideologies and mindsets in countries such as Romania neither began nor ended with communist rule, but is deeply rooted in pervasive conceptions of national identity which are yet to be vanquished.

> The threat posed to human rights and individuality by certain styles of nationalist rhetoric is too obvious to require further comment. Yet even (so called) benign forms of nationalism (liberal, civic, reform) implicitly appeal to collectivist principles . . . It is the use of the nation as a political trump . . . that implicitly subordinates claims about rights to questions of identity. Political claims on behalf of the nation are necessarily couched in collective terms.[31]

The requirements of EU membership could strengthen the hands of the liberal cosmopolitans in Central, East and South-east Europe. In order to fulfil its cosmopolitan vocation, however, the EU will have to work harder to live up to its founding ideals and more strongly resist the advancing 'ethnicisation' and 'racialisation' of European identities and polities in the West as well as in the East.

During the early 1990s, as a result of the disintegration of the former Soviet, Yugoslav and Czechoslovak federations, political authority in Central and Eastern Europe was reconfigured along putatively national lines. However, it should be emphasised that this has merely reshuffled rather than resolved the region's long-standing 'national' problems: 'the massive "nationalisation" of political space in the region has left tens of millions of people outside "their own" national territory at the same time that it has subjected the "national" quality of persons and territories to heightened scrutiny'.[32] As a result, nationalism and 'national' calls to arms have again been pressed into service to persuade significant bodies of people to be ready to fight for their embattled nations ('right or wrong'). Slavenka Drakulic famously lamented that

> along with millions of other Croats, I was pinned to the wall of nation-hood – not only by outside pressure from Serbia and the Federal Army but by national homogenisation within Croatia itself . . . reducing us to one dimension – the Nation . . . whereas before I was defined by my education, my job, my ideas, my character – and yes, my nationality too – now I feel stripped of all that.[33]

During the 1990s the Balkans and the Caucasus region spawned virulent forms of nationalism and inter-ethnic conflict which the Hungarian political philosopher G. M. Tamás has characterised as 'ethnarchy' or 'ethno-anarchy', emphasising its volatile, destabilising and anarchic properties:

> Ethnarchy means here that the source of all power is . . . the racially or ethnically pure dominant majority within any arbitrarily given territory . . . Countries, states, nations can be reshaped at will, regardless of their ancient traditions or present interests, regardless of ancient ties . . . Only natural identity counts.

The chief concern of those he calls ethno-anarchists is to establish

> a turf of their own where total identity, total equality, total and magical non-politics reigns supreme. It is a truly radical tendency that . . . has changed the terms of political debate for a long time to come . . . The old rules of diplomacy and warfare do not apply, because the aim is not pre-eminence, advantage, or control of alien territory, but delimitation, distance, exit from the world of politics . . . as we knew it . . . The new ethnarchic power is very frail and volatile, precisely because there are no real arguments there to argue for obedience to authority. After all, anybody within the group is *Us* and can and does lay claim to power . . . What is taking shape is a post-political world . . . The absolute unquestioned power of ethnarchy is apolitical and anti-political.

In contrast to nineteenth-century liberal nationalism, which built states, brought about unifications and fostered high culture, late twentieth-century ethno-anarchism 'destroys states, smashes them into smithereens, and fails to replace them with *anything*. The sheer fact of collective physical existence suffices . . . This is the end of politics as we know it' [emphasis in the original].[34] Indeed, when ethnarchy is viewed in combination with fashionable doctrines of multiculturalism and the far-reaching privatisation of power engendered by globalisation and the neo-liberal counter-revolution in economic policy, the scope for political and cultural fragmentation reaches truly alarming proportions. In the long term, the forces unleashed may be beyond anyone's control, and we may come to look back on the 1990s with nostalgia, as the (relative) calm before the storms to come.

The resurgence of potentially destabilising ethnic nationalism and inter-ethnic tension in some of Europe's post-communist states has mainly been treated as a 'hard security' issue, especially by specialists in international relations and security studies. While not denying that inter-ethnic tensions have been and could again become major sources of political instability or violent conflict within the region's multi-ethnic states, it needs to be emphasised that the problems posed by the prevalence of (mainly collectivist) ethno-cultural conceptions of national identity and citizenship extend much wider and deeper than the focus on 'security hot spots' suggests. Ethnic collectivism severely impedes the full fruition and realisation of liberal conceptions of democracy and individual rights, even in the absence of significant ethnic minorities and/or inter-ethnic tensions. Contrary to claims that narrowly ethnic conceptions of citizenship and national identity pose no real problem in countries such as Poland and Hungary, which have 'achieved' high levels of ethnic homogeneity, it should be recognised that exclusive ethnic collectivism and the illiberal values and mentalities associated with it (including anti-Semitism) can still persist and can be less subject to healthy scrutiny and challenge, even *after* the almost complete elimination of ethnic minorities (which has almost invariably been accomplished at appalling human cost). In the long term, moreover, it is conceivable that a multi-ethnic society such as Romania, with its greater diversity of spiritual and cultural resources, could adapt more successfully to the strained 'civic ideals' and cosmopolitanism of the EU (especially if it can enhance its current internal modus vivendi between ethnic groups) than societies which pride themselves on their supposed ethnic homogeneity. In the words of Lord Acton,

> the co-existence of several nations under the same State is a test, as well as the best security of its freedom. It is also one of the chief instruments of civilisation . . . A State which is incompetent to satisfy different races condemns itself; a State which labours to neutralise, to absorb, or to expel them, destroys its own vitality.[35]

Conclusion: what is 'Europe'?

These issues are of immense importance because Europe is still made up of bounded political communities. The rights, obligations and welfare entitlements of Europeans are conferred by membership of groups (usually nations), although these groups vary greatly in their degrees of inclusiveness and exclusivity. Modern European political thought has tended to assume that bounded political communities are the basic frameworks or 'power containers' within which political, social and economic activity will take place and that the rights, obligations and entitlements of citizens derive from their membership of such communities. Although conceived in increasingly abstract and universalistic terms by liberal rights theorists, the exercise and enforcement of universalistic rights remain tied to specific states and their institutions. Membership, in turn, is closely related to territorial jurisdiction.

> Indeed political territory as we know it today – bounded territory to which access is controlled by the state – presupposes membership. It presupposes some way of distinguishing those who have free access to the territory from those who do not, those who belong to the state from those who do not . . . Only citizens have an unqualified right to enter (and remain in) the territory of a state.[36]

The extreme variability of access to national and EU citizenship, together with the current denial of citizenship rights to some sixteen million 'foreign' inhabitants of the EU, poses profound challenges to liberal democracy and to the operation and standing of the European Union's supranational legal order. Eastward enlargement of the EU will further increase the variations, and hence anomalies, in the conditions on which members of ethnic minorities (whether born within the EU or elsewhere) can acquire the citizenship of an EU member state and hence EU citizenship. That could compromise the future development of the European Union, especially the Single Market and the equal (non-discriminatory) implementation and enforcement of EU rules, regulations and policies. For the EU, as well as for its prospective Central, East and South-east European members, the stakes could scarcely be higher. And it is in these highly charged political and cultural areas, rather than in technical economic, institutional and procedural matters, that the most fundamental problems of eastward enlargement of the EU are likely to arise.

There is space for only the briefest of answers to the question of how far south and east an integrated Europe should extend. Just as one should beware of essentialist conceptions of Eastern and Western Europe, so one should steer clear of essentialist cultural criteria for inclusion in Europe. Unlike Africa, Australia and the Americas, Europe is not a continent bounded by seas or oceans on almost all sides. Nor has it ever been clear cut where Europe ends and Asia begins. 'Geographically, there is no European continent; there is only a European peninsula of the Eurasian continent.'[37] For some, such as Prince Metternich, 'Asia' began on the Landstrasse running eastwards out of Vienna. Poles and Spaniards warm to the notion of a Europe extending 'from Galicia to Galicia'! For others, Asia begins in the Balkans or Transcaucasia or Anatolia or beyond the Urals and the Volga. Though lacking fixed and precise geographical boundaries, Europe's inhabitants have nevertheless developed unusually strong feelings of attachment to place, of belonging to a particular civilisation, and of having a cultural heritage shared with the other inhabitants of their continent. Europeans have had peculiarly sharply etched conceptions of what it means to be 'European', even though the content of those conceptions has changed over time.

In reality, 'Europe' is not a precise geographical expression, but an idea, a states system, a civilisation and a set of values and norms, all of which have been shaped and generated not just by North-western and South-western Europeans but also by Central and Eastern Europeans, Russians, Ukrainians, the Balkans, the Ottoman Turks and, not least, the Moorish kingdoms of medieval Spain. The centre of gravity of European civilisation has repeatedly shifted. North-western Europe, which now regards itself as the chief bastion and custodian of European values and ideals, was long regarded as 'barbarian' by the inhabitants of the Italian peninsula and Byzantium. The equation of Europe with Christendom is unconvincing, because until the Arab and later Ottoman conquests much of what we now think of as the Middle East and North Africa was Christian, just as much of the New World has been since the seventeenth century; and in any case the Muslims of Albania, Kosovo and Bosnia-Herzegovina have as much claim to be Europeans as do the Germans or the French or the Poles or the Czechs or the British. For many people Europe's southern limits are the northern shores of the Mediterranean Sea, but others remind us that the North African littoral was for a long time a core component of the Roman Empire, from which European civilisation claims lineal descent – even though that empire never conceived of itself as 'European'. Latterly the Maghreb states have to all intents and purposes become part of the wider European economy and states system, conducting 70–80 per cent of their trade with the European Union (rather than with other African or Arab states) and being ruled by European-minded Francophones who have sought either formal or *de facto* inclusion in the European Union through various treaties of association, the Euro-Med Partnership (launched in Barcelona in 1995) and, in the case of Morocco, an unsuccessful application for full membership of the EU.

As argued by William McNeill, it is much safer and sounder to define macro-regions and civilisations in terms of networks of communication, contact and trade rather than in terms of the crude and monolithic cultural labels and stereotypes preferred by the likes of Samuel Huntington, which underrate the importance of the contact, exchange and cross-fertilisation that has gone on between adjacent and even some far removed religions, languages, cultures and societies since the beginning of history.[38] Civilisations and macro-regions are not hermetically sealed compartments, nor can they be defined in terms of singular and exclusive criteria, such as religion, race or ethnicity. Europe is a region of intense interaction between peoples and states. The fecundity and adaptability of European civilisation has derived from its multicultural composition and its continual assimilation of ideas and technologies from the Near East, North Africa and more recently the Americas and South and East Asia, rather than from a single dominant or monolithic cultural tradition. Indeed, most of the world's great civilisations have been multicultural rather than monocultural. Those that were not so have tended to stagnate. Therefore, the key to Europe's continued success lies in the accommodation of difference and diversity, rather than in ill-conceived attempts to foster a monolithic European identity of which Europeans have absolutely no need – as they are already unmistakably European without it!

By the same token, 'Europe' should be considered to comprise all who are willing and able unreservedly to participate in and adhere to its prevailing rules, laws, procedures, policies, economic practices and secular values, thereby avoiding the delineation of arbitrary and contentious fixed borders on maps. Insofar as countries such as Morocco, Tunisia, Turkey, Georgia, Armenia, Ukraine and Russia (have) become part of the wider European economy and states system and actively subscribe to its strongly consensual rules, laws, standards and modus operandi, they ought to be eligible for eventual membership of the European Union, whether *de facto* or *de jure*. However, insofar as they resist or reject those rules, laws and standards and the EU's modus operandi, they automatically exclude themselves from 'the European club'. There is a need for clearer criteria for inclusion or eligibility for membership in the European Union, but these criteria should be functional, transactional or interactional, rather than cultural. Cultural criteria will remain indefensibly rigid and contentious externally, in respect of borderline cases such as Turkey, the Maghreb, the Caucasus and even Russia and Ukraine, as well as too divisive of Europe and Europeans internally.

In no other continent have ideals of continental unity been pursued with such fervent commitment as in Europe, yet 'Europe has always been the scene of more or less deep disunity'.[39] It is impossible to discern any coherent essentialist criterion of 'Europeanness', nor has there ever been any foolproof cultural definition of Europe. European identity is always in flux, continually reshaped by interaction and communication between people.

Notes and references

1 A. Wachtel, *Making a Nation, Breaking a Nation: Literature and Cultural Politics in Yugoslavia*. (Stanford: Stanford University Press 1998), pp. 4–5, 8–10, 17.
2 B. Laffan, 'The Politics of Identity and Political Order in Europe'. *Journal of Common Market Studies* 34 (1) 1996, p. 82.
3 A. Touraine, *What is Democracy?*. (Boulder: Westview 1997), pp. 2, 4, 9.
4 W. Kymlicka, *Multicultural Citizenship: A Liberal Theory of Minority Rights*. (Oxford: Oxford University Press 1995).
5 L. Dini and J. Wolfensohn, 'Let's Start Taking the Benefits of Cultural Identity Seriously'. *International Herald Tribune* 6 October 1999.
6 R. Dworkin, *Freedom's Law*. (Cambridge, Mass.: Harvard University Press 1996), pp. 21–2.

7 Quoted in E. Hobsbawm, *Nations and Nationalism since 1870* (second edn). (Cambridge: Cambridge University Press 1992), p. 44.

8 A. D. Smith, 'National Identity and the Idea of European Unity'. *International Affairs* 68 (1) 1992, pp. 62, 68, 70, 74.

9 K. Deutsch, *Nationalism and Social Communication* (second edn). (Cambridge, Mass.: MIT Press 1966).

10 P. Howe, 'A Community of Europeans: The Requisite Underpinnings'. *Journal of Common Market Studies* 33 (1) 1995, pp. 28, 34, 43. Brigid Laffan points out that European integration has been embraced by many nation-states 'as a means of strengthening their existing state identities and as an arena within which to project their state identities . . . The very pliability of nationalism allows national elites to embrace projects like European integration and to sell them to domestic audiences as part of the national project'. See Laffan *op.cit.*, p. 87.

11 T. Kostakopoulou, 'Why a "Community of Europeans" Could Be a Community of Exclusion: A Reply to Howe'. *Journal of Common Market Studies* 35 (2) 1997, pp. 302–6.

12 A. Linklater, *The Transformation of Political Community*. (Cambridge: Polity Press 1998), p. 1.

13 D. Chryssochoou, 'Europe's Could-be Demos: Recasting the Debate'. *West European Politics* 19 (4) 1996, p. 796.

14 R. Münch, 'Between Nation-state, Regionalism and World Society: The European Integration Process'. *Journal of Common Market Studies* 34 (3) 1996, p. 385.

15 Quoted in Laffan *op.cit.*, p. 95.

16 E. J. Sieyès, *What is the Third Estate?* ([1789] London: Pall Mall Press 1963), p. 58.

17 G. Schöpflin, 'Nationalism and Ethnic Minorities in Post-communist Europe' in R. Caplan and J. Feffer (eds), *Europe's New Nationalisms*. (Oxford: Oxford University Press 1997), p. 151.

18 Z. Pukhovski, 'The Moral Basis of Political Restructuring' in C. Brown (ed.), *Political Restructuring in Europe: Ethical Perspectives*. (London: Routledge 1994), p. 215.

19 S. P. Huntington, 'The Clash of Civilizations?' *Foreign Affairs* 72 (3) 1993, pp. 22–49.

20 H. Kohn, *The Idea of Nationalism*. (New York: Macmillan 1944), pp. 329–30.

21 O. Jaszi, *The Dissolution of the Habsburg Monarchy*. (Chicago: University of Chicago Press 1929), p. 264.

22 N. Crainic, 'Programul statului etnocratic' in Crainic, *Ortodoxie si etnocratie*. (Bucharest: Cugetarea 1938), pp. 283–311.

23 A. D. Smith, *National Identity*. (Harmondsworth: Penguin 1991), p. 126.

24 D. Dungaciu, 'Estul si vestul in "oglinda naturii" – este "nationalismul estic" esential diferit de cel "vestic"?' *Polis* (Bucharest) 4 1998, pp. 72–97.

25 Kohn *op.cit.*; P. Sugar and I. Lederer (eds), *Nationalism in Eastern Europe*. (Seattle: University of Washington Press 1969); J. Planematz, 'Two Types of Nationalism' in E. Kamenka (ed.), *Nationalism: The Nature and Evolution of an Idea*. (London: Edward Arnold 1973); R. D. Kaplan, *Balkan Ghosts: A Journey through History*. (New York: St Martin's Press 1993); M. Ignatieff, *Blood and Belonging: Journeys into the New Nationalism*. (London: Chatto and Windus/BBC Books 1993); R. Bideleux and I. Jeffries, *A History of Eastern Europe*. (London: Routledge 1998).

26 Bideleux and Jeffries *op.cit.*, p. 3.

27 *Ibid.*, p. 26.

28 *Ibid.*, pp. 71–8, 127–32, 246–7.

29 R. Brubaker, *Citizenship and Nationhood in France and Germany*. (Cambridge, Mass.: Harvard University Press 1992), p. 3.

30 V. Havel, 'The Hope for Europe'. *New York Review of Books* 20 June 1996, p. 40.

31 B. Haddock and O. Caraiani, 'Nationalism and Civil Society in Romania'. *Political Studies* 47 1999, pp. 272–4.
32 R. Brubaker, *Nationalism Reframed.* (Cambridge: Cambridge University Press 1996), pp. 3, 55.
33 S. Drakulic, *The Balkan Express: Fragments from the Other Side of War.* (New York: Norton 1993).
34 G. M. Tamás, 'Ethnarchy and Anarchism'. *Social Research* 63 (1) 1996, pp. 172–4, 180–3.
35 J. Acton, 'Nationality' in *Essays on Freedom and Power.* ([1862] London: Thames and Hudson 1956), pp. 160–1, 168.
36 Brubaker *op.cit.* (1992), p. 23.
37 R. Coudenhove-Kalergi, *Pan-Europe.* (New York: Knopf 1926), p. 22.
38 W. H. McNeill, 'Foreword' in A. G. Frank and B. K. Gillis (eds), *The World System: Five Hundred or One Thousand Years?* (London: Routledge 1993), pp. x–xii.
39 R. W. Southern, *The Making of the Middle Ages.* (London: Arrow Books 1959), p. 15.

Part II
The institutions

3 The OSCE

Crowning jewel or talking shop?

Andrew Cottey

Introduction

As the Cold War ended in the late 1980s and early 1990s there were hopes of building a new pan-European security order, stretching from the Atlantic to the Urals or even from Vancouver to Vladivostok. The end of the East–West confrontation, progress in arms control and democratisation in Central and Eastern Europe suggested that circumstances might be propitious for the development of a new era of peace in Europe. Soviet President Mikhail Gorbachev's calls for a 'common European home' caught the *zeitgeist* of the time. The Conference on Security and Co-operation in Europe (CSCE)[1] appeared to provide the ideal institutional basis for the development of a new continent-wide security system. The CSCE's membership extended to all 'European' states, including the countries of Western, Central, Eastern and Southern Europe, Turkey, the USSR and the United States and Canada. The CSCE was based on norms adopted by all its member states, embodied the concepts of co-operative and comprehensive security and could claim a successful track record of facilitating East–West détente and, arguably, helping to end the Cold War.

Today, although the CSCE has become the Organisation for Security and Co-operation in Europe (OSCE), extended its membership to the successor states of the former USSR and the former Yugoslavia and developed a wide range of new institutions and policies, hopes of a new pan-European security order remain unfulfilled. The conflicts in the former Yugoslavia, Chechnya, Georgia, Moldova, Nagorno-Karabakh and Tajikistan indicate that the eastern half of the continent continues to face the very real and traditional security problems of war and peace, state-making and state-breaking. The European Union (EU) and the North Atlantic Treaty Organisation (NATO), rather than the OSCE, have become the institutional cores of the new Europe. While there has been substantial progress in consolidating democracy in much of Central and Eastern Europe, in the Balkans and the former USSR there remain severe challenges to – and in some cases gross violations of – the OSCE principles of democracy and respect for human rights. Despite the deepening of co-operation within

the OSCE and other frameworks, relations between Russia and the major
Western powers remain characterised by an uneasy mix of co-operation
and competition, with serious differences over NATO's enlargement into
Central and Eastern Europe and intervention in the former Yugoslavia.[2]

This chapter examines the OSCE's role in post-Cold War Europe. It
begins by tracing the evolution of the OSCE during the 1990s, showing
how the majority of Western and Central and Eastern European states
quickly abandoned hopes of the OSCE becoming the primary European
security institution but arguing that the OSCE nevertheless developed
significant roles in the areas of democracy promotion, conflict prevention
and resolution, and arms control. The chapter then explores whether the
OSCE can be understood as either a pan-European security regime (a set
of norms and institutions facilitating co-operative relations) or an emerging
pan-European security community (a 'zone of peace' where war becomes
inconceivable). It suggests that the OSCE is a limited security regime and
only a potential security community – in both cases because the underlying
prerequisites for such a development (in particular the consolidation of
democracy) remain relatively weak in significant parts of the eastern half
of Europe. The chapter also explores the OSCE's role in addressing the
'southern dimension' of European security (Europe's relations with its
Mediterranean and Middle Eastern neighbours), arguing that the Organisation has only a limited contribution to make in this area. The chapter
concludes by arguing that hopes of the OSCE becoming the crowning
jewel of European security were probably always unrealistic but that criticisms of the Organisation as an 'empty talking shop' are greatly exaggerated. It suggests that the OSCE will continue to have an important if
low-profile role as a framework for Europe-wide diplomacy and in efforts
to promote democracy and prevent and resolve violent conflicts.

The OSCE's roles in the 'new Europe'

The CSCE was born of the Cold War détente of the 1960s and 1970s. The
desire to stabilise the post-war European order led to the opening of
negotiations between thirty-five countries – the United States, Canada, the
USSR and all European states except Albania – in 1972. The resulting 1975
Helsinki Final Act defined ten principles on which all CSCE signatories
agreed to base their relations: respect for each state's sovereignty; refrain-
ing from the threat or use of force; acceptance of the inviolability of
frontiers; respect for the territorial integrity of states; pursuit of the peaceful settlement of disputes; non-intervention in each other's internal affairs;
respect for human rights and fundamental freedoms; recognition of the
equal rights and right to self-determination of peoples; commitment to co-
operation among states; and fulfilment of obligations under international
law.[3] The Helsinki Final Act established three 'Baskets' within which further discussions and co-operation would continue: the military dimension

of security; economics, science and technology and the environment; and humanitarian issues. The Final Act also included military Confidence and Security-Building Measures (CSBMs): notification of military manoeuvres involving more than 25,000 troops and exchanges of observers of military manoeuvres.

Underpinning the Helsinki Final Act was an implicit trade-off. The USSR (and its allies) had a strong interest in consolidating the post-war territorial settlement in Eastern Europe – hence the Final Act's references to the inviolability of frontiers and the territorial integrity of states. The West, however, did not wish to condone Soviet hegemony in Eastern Europe. It therefore insisted that the Final Act include the principles of respect for human rights and fundamental freedoms, recognition of the equal rights and right to self-determination of peoples and a system for reviewing the implementation of these commitments. Thus, the Helsinki Final Act also included provisions for regular 'follow-up' meetings, which took place in Belgrade (1977–8), Madrid (1980–3) and Vienna (1986–9) and resulted in further discussions of human rights and an expansion of the CSBM regime.

Assessments of the CSCE's role in the Cold War are mixed. The CSCE could not prevent the 'second Cold War' of the 1980s and its direct impact on the human rights situation in the Soviet bloc was limited, as were the various CSBMs. The semi-institutionalised CSCE, however, provided a framework for East–West dialogue during the second Cold War and helped to keep détente alive. The CSBMs of the 1970s and 1980s were the precursors of the more substantial conventional arms control agreements which followed (in particular the 1990 Conventional Forces in Europe – CFE – Treaty) and of new forms of security co-operation (such as NATO's Partnership for Peace). The Helsinki process kept human rights on the diplomatic agenda and provided political and moral support to dissidents in Central and Eastern Europe. Some observers argue that by providing support for human rights movements, such as Czechoslovakia's Charter '77, the CSCE played a vital role in making possible the 1989 revolutions in Central and Eastern Europe and the end of the Cold War.

With the end of the Cold War in 1989 the CSCE's time appeared to have come. Across Europe there was consensus that the CSCE should be strengthened as a central part of the new European order, although how this should be achieved was less clear. The November 1990 CSCE summit in Paris capped the end of the Cold War in Europe. European leaders signed the Charter of Paris for a New Europe, which extended CSCE norms and principles to include firm commitments to democracy, free elections and market economics.[4] NATO and Warsaw Pact leaders signed the CFE Treaty, which mandated major reductions in armed forces. New CSCE institutions were put in place: a Council of Foreign Ministers would meet at least annually; the Council would be supported by a Committee of Senior Officials which might also meet in emergency situations; a Secretariat, a Conflict Prevention Centre and an Office for Free Elections would be created (based in Prague, Vienna and Warsaw, respectively); and a Parliamentary Assembly would also be established. More radical ideas – for CSCE security guarantees, peacekeeping forces, a Security Council or the revision of the CSCE's consensus model of decision-making – were, however, not acted upon.

Hopes of the CSCE becoming the core of the new European security 'architecture' rapidly dissipated. Western governments were wary of relying on the CSCE, with its large membership and consensus decision-making (giving the USSR a *de facto* veto), and feared that strengthening the CSCE might undermine NATO, which had for so long been the basis of their security. The crises in the Baltic states and Yugoslavia in 1990–1 highlighted the CSCE's limitations. In January 1991, as Estonia, Latvia and Lithuania pressed for independence from the USSR, the Soviet armed forces intervened to suppress pro-independence demonstrations. The USSR vetoed discussion of the issue and the CSCE was rendered powerless. When war broke out in Yugoslavia in the summer of 1991, the CSCE discussed the issue, offered to send observers and later suspended Yugoslavia's membership, but was unable to end the conflict or agree tougher action. The European Community/Union, the United Nations and NATO subsequently took the lead in international efforts to resolve the Yugoslav conflicts.

The Baltic and Yugoslav crises sharply illustrated the fragility of CSCE norms in parts of Eastern Europe and the constraints imposed by the CSCE's large membership and consensus decision-making. At the same time the growing backlash by Soviet hard-liners against President Gorbachev's reforms, the August 1991 coup against him and the subsequent break-up of the USSR, indicated that neither democracy nor stability could be guaranteed in Russia and the former Soviet republics. Central and Eastern European states rapidly concluded that the CSCE could not guarantee their hard-won independence and sought membership of NATO and the EC/EU. These developments also reaffirmed Western doubts about over-reliance on the CSCE. By late 1991 the early euphoria over the CSCE's potential had largely disappeared. Attention shifted to the development of new roles for NATO and the EC/EU in post-communist Europe.

Since 1991, however, despite its limitations and low profile, the OSCE has gradually expanded its roles in the areas of democracy promotion, conflict prevention and resolution and arms control. Through a series of summits (at Helsinki in 1992, Budapest in 1994 when the CSCE formally became the OSCE, Lisbon in 1996 and Istanbul in 1999), lower-level meetings, ongoing diplomatic negotiations and *ad hoc* responses to specific conflicts, the OSCE has gradually developed new roles and institutions.

A diplomatic framework

The OSCE provides the only diplomatic framework in which all European states participate as equals and which addresses security in its broadest sense (incorporating political, military, human, economic and environ-mental dimensions). Aside from summits of heads of state and government and annual meetings of foreign ministers, the OSCE has, since the early 1990s, included a Permanent Council based in Vienna with ambassadorial level representation of all member states, weekly meetings of the full Coun-cil and regular meetings in other formats (for example, the Forum for Security Co-operation which discusses arms control and *ad hoc* groups addressing particular conflicts). Representatives of all OSCE states also meet in other, usually annual, formats, such as 'human dimension' and arms control implementation meetings and an Economic Forum. As a diplomatic framework the OSCE serves two functions. First, it acts as a channel for dialogue and a form of political confidence-building measure. Second, the OSCE's semi-permanent discussions ensure that many issues (potential conflicts, post-conflict peace-building, human rights, arms con-trol) receive ongoing attention even when they are no longer at the fore-front of the political or diplomatic agenda. Over the 1990s the OSCE has also developed a quite complex institutional architecture supporting its diplomatic and operational work, as Figure 1 illustrates (see p. 48).

Providing Europe's norms

The OSCE provides a set of core norms for international and domestic behaviour agreed by all European states. This role stretches back to the 1975 Helsinki Final Act and was expanded with the commitments to democracy contained in the 1990 Charter of Paris. Since then, all OSCE summits have reaffirmed the commitments made at Helsinki and Paris. Membership of the OSCE thus involves a strong politically (although not legally) binding commitment to the non-use of force in international relations, respect for existing borders and state sovereignty, the pursuit of co-operative relations, democracy and free elections, and respect for human and minority rights. Member states do not always live up to their OSCE promises and some have argued that insensitive attempts to impose international norms on diverse states can be counterproductive.[5] Neverthe-less, no member state has yet rejected the validity of OSCE norms in principle. The various meetings of the OSCE, further, provide a multi-lateral framework in which adherence to OSCE commitments is reviewed and political pressure is brought to bear upon states to improve implementa-tion of these commitments.

Democracy promotion

The OSCE plays a significant role in promoting democracy in post-communist Europe. The origins of this role again go back to the human rights com-mitments established in the Helsinki Final Act and the subsequent 'human dimension' review meetings. With the Charter of Paris commitments to

Summit
Meeting of OSCE heads of state or government

Ministerial Council
Meeting of OSCE foreign ministers

| **Senior Council**
Periodic high-level meeting of political directors and annual Economic Forum | **Permanent Council**
Regular body for political consultation and decision-making (weekly) | **Forum for Security Co-operation**
Regular body for arms control and CSBMs (weekly) |

OSCE Parliamentary Assembly
Copenhagen

Chairman-in-Office
Austria (2000)
Troika
(Norway, Austria, Romania)

Personal Representatives of the CiO

| **Office for Democratic Institutions and Human Rights**
Warsaw | **OSCE Representative on Freedom of the Media**
Vienna | **Secretary General**
Vienna | **High Commissioner on National Minorities**
The Hague |

OSCE Secretariat
Vienna

| **Liaison Office in Central Asia**
Tashkent | **Prague Office** |

OSCE Missions

OSCE Missions in:
- Bosnia and Herzegovina
- Croatia
- Estonia
- Georgia
- Kosovo, Sandjak and Vojvodina*
- Latvia
- Spillover Monitor Mission to Skopje
- Moldova
- Tajikistan
- Kosovo

withdrawn from the field in July 1993

Other OSCE Field Activities

- OSCE Presence in Albania
- Advisory and Monitoring Group in Belarus
- OSCE Assistance Group to Chechnya
- The Personal Representative of the CiO on the Conflict Dealt with by the OSCE Minsk Conference
- OSCE Centres in Almaty, Ashgabad and Bishkek
- OSCE Project Co-ordinator in Ukraine
- OSCE Office in Yerevan
- OSCE Office in Baku

High-Level Planning Group

Planning an OSCE Peacekeeping Force for Nagorno-Karabakh

OSCE Assistance in Implementation of Bilateral Agreements

- The OSCE Representative in the Russian–Latvian Joint Commission on Military Pensioners
- The OSCE Representative to the Estonian Government Commission on Military Pensioners

OSCE RELATED BODIES

| **Court of Conciliation and Arbitration**
Geneva | **Joint Consultative Group**
Promotes implementation of CFE Treaty, Meets regularly in Vienna | **Open Skies Consultative Commission**
Promotes implementation of Open Skies Treaty, Meets in Vienna |

▮▮▮▮ Line of Command
‑‑‑‑‑ Provides Support

Figure 1 The OSCE
Source: Courtesy of the OSCE Secretariat

democracy and free elections and the establishment of the Office for Free Elections (which became the Office for Democratic Institutions and Human Rights – ODIHR – in 1992), the OSCE assumed a greater role. Since the early 1990s the ODIHR (working in conjunction with the OSCE Parliamentary Assembly, the Council of Europe and other international organisations) has monitored parliamentary and presidential elections in virtually all the states of Central and Eastern Europe and the former USSR, making specific recommendations for the conduct of future elections, sharply criticising the conduct of elections in some cases and establishing a reputation for impartiality. Through bilateral contacts with governments and multilateral seminars and conferences, the ODIHR also provides practical advice to post-communist states on various aspects of democratisation such as constitutions, electoral systems, regional and local government, judicial and legal systems, and human and minority rights. Since 1998 the OSCE has had a Representative on Freedom of the Media mandated to support the development of free media, who has worked particularly in the countries of South-east Europe and the former USSR.

The OSCE has also become engaged in a number of democracy-promotion activities relating to specific countries and regions. Following the peace agreements in Bosnia in 1995 and Kosovo in 1999, OSCE missions deployed in both areas have taken the leading role in supporting the organisation of democratic elections and the wider development of democratic institutions and norms. In Belarus since 1997 an OSCE Advisory and Monitoring Group has been engaged in promoting dialogue between the authoritarian regime of President Alexander Lukashenka and opposition groups and more general support for democratic values. Since the late 1990s the OSCE has also been pursuing a strategy of deepening the integration of the Central Asian member states with the Organisation, including promoting democracy.

Conflict management

Since the early 1990s the OSCE has developed a leading role in conflict management, in particular in the fields of conflict prevention and post-conflict peace-building. In response to the growing challenge of complex, ethno-political conflicts the OSCE has developed a number of innovative practices. The Conflict Prevention Centre established at the 1990 Paris summit proved to be relatively ineffectual, lacking a clear mandate or operational role. At the 1992 Helsinki summit, however, the new post of High Commissioner on National Minorities (HCNM) was established. The HCNM is mandated to provide 'early warning' and 'early action' in relation to potential conflicts involving national minorities.[6] Since then the first HCNM, the former Dutch Foreign Minister Max van der Stoel, has been actively engaged in attempting to prevent and resolve ethnic/national minority conflicts in the Baltic states (with regard to the Russian minorities in Estonia and Latvia), in South-east Europe (in Albania, Croatia, Greece, Kosovo and Macedonia), between Hungary and its neighbours (with regard to the Hungarian minorities in Romania and Slovakia), in Ukraine (in Crimea) and in Central Asia (in Kazakhstan and Kyrgyzstan). Through the creative use of visits by the HCNM, recommendations on minority rights, promotion of dialogue and shuttle-diplomacy, van der Stoel is widely credited with having made a major contribution to preventing a number of conflicts.[7]

The OSCE has also developed an extensive network of semi-permanent missions based in areas of potential conflict. By the end of the 1990s, the OSCE had missions (or similar field operations) deployed in (or working in relation to) Albania, Armenia, Bosnia, Croatia, Kazakhstan, Kosovo, Kyrgyzstan, Estonia, Latvia, Belarus, Chechnya, Georgia, Moldova, Tajikistan, Ukraine and Uzbekistan.[8] Through the creative use of low-profile diplomacy and contacts on the ground these missions have been credited with helping to prevent and manage a number of conflicts and facilitating the resolution of some issues (for example, on the withdrawal of Russian troops from Estonia and Latvia in the early 1990s). The post of Chairman-in-Office (CiO) of the OSCE, held by the foreign minister of an OSCE member state on an annual basis, has also taken on an expanding role in efforts to prevent and resolve conflicts through the use of diplomatic visits, the sending of personal representatives and the 'moral authority' associated with the OSCE. The inability of the OSCE to make much progress in resolving the stalemated conflicts in Georgia, Moldova and Nagorno-Karabakh, and the failure of the 1998–9 OSCE Kosovo Verification Mission (KVM), however, illustrate the limits of the OSCE's operational conflict management activities.

In the wake of the peace agreements in Bosnia and Croatia in 1995 and Kosovo in 1999, the OSCE has deployed larger missions in these areas, as well as in Albania. These missions have become involved in a wide range of activities relating to post-conflict peace-building, democratisation and demilitarisation, including the organisation of democratic elections, promoting dialogue between antagonistic political forces, supporting the re-establishment of governmental institutions, encouraging respect for human and minority rights and facilitating arms control agreements.

Arms control and CSBMs

Building on its record during the Cold War, the OSCE continues to play a role as Europe's leading framework for conventional arms control and CSBMs. The original CSBMs agreed in the Helsinki Final Act have gradually been expanded into what is now referred to as the 'Vienna Document'. This includes a range of binding military CSBMs (relating to notification of military exercises, verification and exchange of information on armed forces), as well as a menu of optional CSBMs.

The OSCE's Vienna headquarters also provides the negotiating home for the CFE Treaty (although the CFE agreement is formally separate from the OSCE). Designed to downscale the NATO–Warsaw Pact confrontation, the 1990 CFE Treaty mandated substantial reductions in the offensive military equipment (tanks, artillery, armoured combat vehicles, combat aircraft and attack helicopters) of the two alliances. The CFE Treaty has since been modified in response to the break-up of the USSR in 1991, disputes over force levels in the Caucasus in 1996 and the enlargement of NATO to include the Czech Republic, Hungary and Poland in 1999. Although some critics are inclined to view the CFE Treaty as a relic of the Cold War, it provides an important element of reassurance against the emergence of a renewed East–West military confrontation. In particular, the 1999 CFE revision (which includes further reductions in force levels) indicated the desire of Russia and the West to avoid renewed confrontation despite their differences over NATO's enlargement into Central and Eastern Europe. Whether Russia will remain willing to abide by (or further modify) the CFE Treaty if NATO takes in additional new Central and Eastern European members remains to be seen. Based on the expertise developed over years of CSBM and CFE negotiations, the OSCE also provides the framework for the arms control aspects of the 1995 Dayton peace agreement for Bosnia, which includes CSBMs and CFE-type force limits between Bosnia, Croatia and the Federal Republic of Yugoslavia (FRY).

A pan-European security regime?

In theory, the OSCE ought to constitute an effective pan-European 'security regime'; that is, a set of 'principles, norms, rules, and decision-making procedures' which are accepted by all European states.[9] Under the Helsinki Final Act, the Charter of Paris and other OSCE documents, all European states have, in theory, committed themselves to a set of common norms and principles to govern their international behaviour. During the 1990s they developed more detailed rules, decision-making procedures and institutions to promote compliance with and resolve disputes over OSCE norms.

In reality, the OSCE remains a security regime of limited robustness. As was noted earlier, respect for OSCE norms of democracy and human rights remains weak in parts of post-communist Europe. OSCE commitments to the non-use of force and the peaceful resolution of disputes have been similarly ignored. Despite their OSCE commitments to co-operative security, relations between Russia and the major Western powers remain characterised by elements of competition and balance of power politics.

A number of fundamental problems limit the OSCE's potential as a security regime. Security regimes are inherently difficult to establish.[10] The traditionally 'zero-sum' and competitive approach of states to security, the high costs of failure (i.e., the possibility of war and the destruction of the state itself), the difficulties of determining other states' motivations and of distinguishing between offensive and defensive strategies, and the classical 'collective security' problem of responding to states which 'defect' from agreed norms all encourage states to rely on more traditional strategies of deterrence, alliance and defence, rather than co-operative security regimes. The history of the OSCE illustrates these problems. Even as the CSCE developed, the USSR and the West remained wary of each other's intentions and continued to rely on their existing alliances. Since the end of the Cold War, while security co-operation has expanded in the OSCE and other frameworks, Russo-Western relations have remained shaped by mutual doubts over the other's intentions. Western (and Central and Eastern European) leaders remain unwilling to abandon the 'tried and trusted' NATO in favour of an uncertain OSCE security regime. These problems do not necessarily mean that the OSCE cannot gradually become a more robust security regime for Europe, but they do suggest that such a development will be neither quick nor easy.

The second problem for the OSCE as a security regime is the weakness of respect for OSCE norms in parts of post-communist Europe. The OSCE has always been based on two sets of norms, one relating to international relations (the non-use of force and respect for existing borders), the other to domestic behaviour (respect for human rights and democracy). The latter set of norms was largely imposed on the USSR by the West as a condition for détente and was never fully accepted by the Soviet leadership. After the revolutions of 1989, the new democracies of Central and Eastern Europe committed themselves to Western norms of democracy and market economics in the Charter of Paris and related CSCE documents. Following the break-up of the USSR and Yugoslavia, the Soviet and Yugoslav successor states also accepted these norms as a condition for membership of the CSCE. For many people and leaders in post-communist Europe, this process represented not the imposition of Western values but rather their freedom to express values which they had long supported. Across the region, however, the acceptance of OSCE norms is far from universal. In Belarus, Central Asia and Serbia, post-communist leaders have paid lip-service to OSCE norms, while maintaining authoritarian regimes. In other parts of post-communist Europe, varying degrees of manipulation of electoral processes, authoritarianism and nationalism sit uncomfortably alongside OSCE norms. Similarly, while all OSCE states have in principle committed themselves to respect for existing borders and the non-use of force, the various post-Cold War conflicts have witnessed gross violations of these principles (most obviously in the cases of Serbia/Yugoslavia with regard to Croatia and Bosnia, and Armenia with regard to Nagorno-Karabakh). Most importantly, the future of democracy in Russia is uncertain, as is Russia's commitment to respect for existing borders, the non-use of force and the pursuit of co-operative security. In short, while we may be witnessing the consolidation of a set of broad liberal norms within the

OSCE area, that process is far from complete, there are significant exceptions to the rule and it is not clear that the process is irreversible.

The third problem for the OSCE as a security regime is the existence of tensions, and sometimes outright contradictions, between some of the basic OSCE norms and principles. These tensions, furthermore, relate directly to some of the most severe security problems of the post-Cold War era – ethnic and national conflicts. There are tensions between the principles of respect for state sovereignty and non-intervention in internal affairs on the one hand and those of respect for human rights and democracy on the other. During the Cold War, the USSR emphasised the former and the West the latter, producing repeated disputes over human rights. Since the end of the Cold War, conflicts in the Baltic states in 1990–1, former Yugoslavia, Chechnya and other parts of the former USSR have produced similar disputes over the extent to which the right of the international community (including the OSCE) to intervene in such situations overrides the principles of state sovereignty and non-intervention. There are also tensions between the principles of inviolability of frontiers and the right to self-determination of peoples. Indeed, the majority of conflicts in the former Yugoslavia and the former USSR have pitted existing states against (ethnic) minorities seeking independence. The Chechens, for example, see themselves as a people legitimately seeking self-determination, whereas Russian leaders argue that they are a terrorist minority threatening the integrity of the Russian Federation. The Kosovo conflict similarly pits the right of the Kosovar Albanians to self-determination against the territorial integrity of FRY. In the abstract, one might argue that the OSCE ought to be able to establish mechanisms for resolving disputes over competing principles. In reality these disputes raise some of the most fundamental issues in international politics and are unlikely to be resolved other than on a case-by-case basis. It is notable, furthermore, that disputes over basic OSCE principles have been *de facto* resolved on the basis of power realities. The USSR vetoed CSCE involvement in the Baltic states in 1990–1 and the West was unwilling to intervene; in Bosnia and Kosovo relative Yugoslav and Russian weakness allowed the West to intervene; in Chechnya Russia accepted only tightly constrained OSCE diplomatic intervention and the West was reluctant to intervene more forcefully.

The fourth problem for the OSCE as a security regime is the weakness of its mechanisms for promoting compliance with, let alone enforcing, OSCE norms and principles. The OSCE has gradually developed various mechanisms for reviewing compliance with commitments and responding to violations (the initial CSCE review conferences, the 1991 'Moscow Human Dimension Mechanism' – which allows ten or more member states to appoint a *rapporteur* to report on threats to fulfilment of OSCE human rights and democracy commitments, and the possibility of 'consensus minus one/two' decisions). These mechanisms have been used to varying degrees and do bring political pressure to bear on states. Nevertheless, the various violations of OSCE principles noted above and the difficulty of resolving conflicts within the OSCE space indicate that the Organisation's ability to promote or enforce compliance with its norms remains distinctly limited. There have been proposals for reforming the OSCE's decision-making procedures (for example, by creating an OSCE Security Council or introducing qualified majority voting) and mandating it to impose economic sanctions and deploy peacekeeping or peace-enforcement forces. While such reforms might enhance the OSCE's ability to promote or enforce compliance with its principles, they would not resolve the fundamental problem of enforcing international norms. Iraq's and Serbia's decade-long resistance to international political pressure, economic sanctions and airstrikes illustrates that – short of all-out invasion – the ability of the 'international community' to impose its will on recalcitrant states or leaders faces severe constraints.

Finally, although the OSCE is often also described as a *comprehensive* security organisation, aside from the 'human dimension', the Organisation's role as a comprehensive security *regime* addressing non-military dimensions of security has in practice been limited. Beyond generalised commitments to co-operation in non-military areas and a few relatively limited institutions, the OSCE has not developed detailed normative standards for its member states in areas such as economics and the environment, nor has it developed mechanisms for reviewing or shaping member states' policies in these areas. For most of Europe, the EU rather than the OSCE has emerged as the primary regime addressing economic, environmental and social issues. For both its existing Western European members and its prospective members in Central and Eastern Europe, the EU defines detailed norms in terms of market economics, environmental protection and social policy, backed up by institutions to monitor and enforce compliance and offer financial and technical support in fulfilling the EU *acquis*. Although the OSCE continues to play a role in emphasising a broad understanding of security and addressing some specific issues (such as economic or environmental causes of violent conflict), as a security regime its commitment to comprehensive security is more rhetorical than substantive.

In combination, these factors – the inherent difficulty of establishing any security regime, the fragility of commitments to OSCE norms in parts of post-communist Europe, the tensions between some core OSCE norms, the difficulty of promoting compliance with OSCE norms and the OSCE's limited role in non-military areas – illustrate that the OSCE is not yet a truly robust European security regime and explain why most states are unwilling to rely on the OSCE for their security. It is too easy, however, to dismiss the OSCE entirely. Despite its limitations, the OSCE exhibits many of the features of an international regime and is therefore best understood as a partial or emerging European security regime. The OSCE, furthermore, works not so much by its ability to impose or enforce the will of the 'community of states' directly, but rather by more subtle and long-term forms of political persuasion and low-profile engagement.

An emerging security community?

After the disintegration of the Soviet empire, some hoped that it might be possible not just to build a new security regime in Europe but to go further and establish a pan-European 'security community' – a 'zone of peace' where war would be inconceivable, extending from the Atlantic to the Urals or even from Vancouver to Vladivostok.[11] As the primary pan-European organisation, the OSCE was the obvious institutional framework for such a security community.

A security community has emerged among the countries of Western Europe since the Second World War – a remarkable development given their previous history of war and conflict.[12] The end of the Cold War and the tentative emergence of common values across Europe suggested that it might be possible to expand this security community to include the countries of Central and Eastern Europe and the former USSR. In retrospect such hopes proved overly optimistic. The wars in the former Yugoslavia and the former USSR have shown that these parts of Europe are far from developing into 'zones of peace'. Although Russia and the West have made progress in building new forms of co-operation, war between Russia and NATO is not yet entirely inconceivable – as their divergent positions over Kosovo indicated. Nevertheless, ten years after the fall of the Berlin Wall, the Western security community was extending into Central and Eastern Europe. Paralleling post-war Franco-German relations, Germany's relations with Poland and the Czech Republic have undergone historic reconciliations. Beyond the former Yugoslavia and Albania, the countries of Central and Eastern Europe (as distinct from their eastern neighbours in the former USSR) have all avoided violent conflict, in most cases concluded agreements with their neighbours recognising existing borders and made significant progress in overcoming historic disputes.

One's assessment of whether it may, in the longer term, be possible to establish a pan-European security community extending to the former Yugoslavia and the former USSR depends on one's view of the underlying conditions necessary for the establishment of such a community. The 'democratic peace' hypothesis suggests that the common political values of stable democracies facilitate peaceful relations between states. Others argue that free markets, free trade and economic prosperity underpin peace. Institutionalised co-operation and 'integration', as pioneered by the EC/EU, are also seen as causes of peace. The experience of post-war Western Europe suggests that the combination of these various factors contributed to the development of a security community. The mutually reinforcing combination of successful democratisation, relatively successful market economic reforms and institutionalised co-operation with the West and neighbouring states also appears to have underpinned the integration of states such as Poland, the Czech Republic and Hungary into the Western security community in the 1990s. These developments suggest that there is no reason, in principle, why the existing Western security community cannot gradually be extended further south and east to include the countries of the former Yugoslavia and the former USSR; above all Russia. Given the enormous problems these countries face in establishing stable democracies and viable market economies, however, this process will not be easy.

A parallel understanding of security communities focuses on the *community* (the sense of common identity or 'we-ness') as the basis for stable, peaceful relations. This raises the question of whether sufficient sense of common identity exists – or can be created – in the 'OSCE space' to make a pan-European security community possible. In practice, the OSCE is relatively weak as a community in this sense. Within the OSCE area most people's primary loyalties are probably still to states or ethnic groups. To the extent that people have higher, 'European' loyalties or senses of identity, in Western Europe and Central and Eastern Europe, these are probably associated with the EU or the Euro-Atlantic EU/NATO conglomerate, rather than the wider OSCE. In contrast, countries such as Russia, Ukraine and Turkey are torn between 'European' identities and distinctive (if vague) Slavic or Turkic alternatives. To the extent that identity and community are mutable and socially created, however, the present weakness of the OSCE as an identity community does not preclude the eventual development of an OSCE-wide security community.

These debates raise the issue of the role of the OSCE as an *institution* in promoting the longer-term development of a pan-European security community. The OSCE's combination of common values, co-operative military security, support for democratisation and promotion of a sense of shared identity may contribute to creating the underlying conditions necessary for the eventual emergence of an OSCE-wide security community.[13] The consolidation of democracy in post-communist Europe, however, requires deep and difficult political, economic and social change in the region. The emergence of an OSCE-wide security community may also require deep shifts in identity allegiances. Inevitably, the ability of the OSCE to influence these developments is limited. Nevertheless, the goal of building a pan-European security community should not be abandoned. There is no inherent reason why an OSCE-wide security community cannot be built in the longer term. Despite the horrors of the Yugoslav and Chechen conflicts the long-term trend is towards the gradual expansion of the existing European security community. In this context, Western leaders should perhaps give greater support to the OSCE's democracy-promotion activities and a higher profile to the OSCE as a Europe-wide identity community.

The OSCE, the 'southern dimension' of European security and beyond

This chapter has so far focused on the OSCE's roles *within* Europe. The post-Cold War era has, however, also seen growing debate on the 'southern

dimension' of European security: Europe's relations with its southern neighbours in the Mediterranean region, North Africa and the Middle East. The
OSCE has, since its inception, included a Mediterranean dimension. The
Helsinki Final Act included a chapter on the Mediterranean, which emphasised the close linkage between European and Mediterranean security
and the aim of promoting co-operation with 'non-participating Mediterranean states'.[14] The OSCE has subsequently reiterated this commitment,
Mediterranean states have been informed of OSCE developments and
have the right to make contributions to major OSCE meetings, and the
OSCE has held seminars on a number of Mediterranean issues. This relationship gradually intensified during the 1990s, with Algeria, Egypt, Israel,
Jordan, Morocco and Tunisia being given the status of 'Mediterranean
Partners for Co-operation', and the establishment of an open-ended Contact Group with these states.[15]

The OSCE's Mediterranean dimension has, however, remained low profile and is of central importance neither to the OSCE nor to the Mediterranean Partners. The relationship between the OSCE and its Mediterranean
Partners for Co-operation is essentially one of information-exchange and
dialogue and there has been little enthusiasm to develop it much further.
Despite the fact that many OSCE states have concerns about potential
security problems to their south, there have been no efforts to develop
common OSCE positions towards the Mediterranean or what is sometimes
now referred to as the 'greater Middle East' (the entire region stretching
from the Mediterranean, through the Middle East to the Caucasus and
Central Asia). The competing perspectives of OSCE member states (especially the major Western powers and Russia) over the Middle East peace
process, relations with Iran and Iraq, oil and gas pipeline routes from Central
Asia and the Caucasus, strategic sea routes through the Black Sea and
Mediterranean, and the Balkans, preclude any common OSCE approach
to the southern dimension of European security.

Since the 1970s there has also been debate on how far the OSCE may
provide a model for Mediterranean security co-operation, with periodic
calls for the establishment of a Conference on Security and Co-operation
in the Mediterranean (CSCM). The potential benefits of Mediterranean-
wide co-operation and the need to address military, humanitarian, economic and environmental problems suggested that the Mediterranean
might indeed be able to draw lessons from the OSCE. During the Cold
War, however, US–Soviet naval competition in the Mediterranean and
North African fears of European neo-imperialism prevented progress in
establishing Mediterranean-wide co-operation.

The main outcome of increased concern over Mediterranean security
issues in the 1990s was not the creation of a CSCM, but rather the establishment in 1995 of the EU's Euro-Mediterranean Partnership or 'Barcelona
Process'. The Euro-Mediterranean Partnership draws on the OSCE's experiences, with its inclusive membership (extending to all Mediterranean

states except Libya[16]), commitment to co-operative and comprehensive security and structure of three 'baskets' addressing security, economics and social and human co-operation. The Euro-Mediterranean Partnership, however, differs from the OSCE model in important ways. The EU is the driving force behind the Partnership. Alongside multilateral Mediterranean-wide co-operation, the Partnership is also based on bilateral relations between the EU and individual southern partners (allowing the development of differentiated relationships with each state) and the EU has committed substantial financial resources to support the process. The Euro-Mediterranean Partnership looks set to be the central institutional framework in the Mediterranean in coming decades.

The post-Cold War era has also seen growing debate on 'Europe's' role in wider global security issues. For the most part, this debate has focused on whether the EU can and should assume a global security role, in particular as a partner of the United States in addressing issues such as nuclear proliferation and conflicts in the Middle East, East Asia and Africa. This debate, however, also raises the issue of the OSCE's role in a global context. The OSCE has already developed relations with Japan and South Korea as 'Partners for Co-operation', reflecting both states' interests in developments in the OSCE area and Japan's financial contribution to conflict-management efforts in the former Yugoslavia. These partnerships allow Japan and South Korea to attend OSCE meetings, put forward their views and engage in dialogue with the OSCE, but extend little further. The OSCE, as a 'regional arrangement' under the UN Charter, has also developed relations with the United Nations. This involves regular dialogue between the UN (primarily via its Secretary-General) and the OSCE (through its Chairman-in-Office and Secretary-General), OSCE involvement in UN-sponsored meetings on the role of regional organisations, and operational co-operation in conflict-management activities (especially in the former Yugoslavia, but also elsewhere in the OSCE area).

As with the Mediterranean, some observers have suggested (rather Eurocentrically) that the OSCE might provide a model for regional co-operation in other parts of the world. While there may well be lessons from OSCE experiences, it is notable that Asian leaders have been wary of the imposition of a European model. In contrast to the OSCE, the Association of South-East Asian Nations (ASEAN) has been based strictly on the principle of non-interference in states' internal affairs (and therefore has not addressed human rights issues), and regional co-operation in Asia has emphasised informal consensus in contrast to the more formal decision-making procedures of the OSCE. Nevertheless, enhanced dialogue between regional organisations could be to the benefit of all concerned.

Finally, the global context raises the question of whether the OSCE's member states ever could or should attempt to develop common policies towards global issues or other regions of the world. Within the OSCE, limited progress has been made in developing common principles on the proliferation of weapons of mass destruction and ballistic missiles, the export of conventional armaments and light weapons (small arms) proliferation. Beyond this, there have been no real efforts to develop common OSCE positions or policies on global issues or towards other regions. As with the Mediterranean, the divergent positions of the OSCE's member states, especially its major powers, are likely to preclude such a development for the foreseeable future. In the longer term, should the OSCE gradually become a security community, this development would raise important questions about how far a common OSCE identity might be defined 'against' the non-OSCE world, how far the OSCE should develop common policies towards the rest of the world and whether the OSCE might become the institutional embodiment of the 'North' in an intensifying North–South confrontation. These problems, at least, remain for the distant future, if not forever.

Conclusion

A decade after the end of the Cold War, hopes of the OSCE becoming the crowning jewel of a new pan-European security system have proved illusory. The EU and NATO are emerging as the institutional core of the new Europe. In contrast, most European citizens have probably never even heard of the OSCE. As an all-European security regime the OSCE remains relatively weak. The Western 'zone of peace' may be extending into Central and Eastern Europe, but a genuinely pan-European security community also remains a distant hope – as the conflicts in the former Yugoslavia and the former USSR bear witness. The OSCE's role in addressing the 'southern dimension' of European security remains marginal. The 1999 Istanbul summit, where the OSCE's member states adopted a Charter for European Security which some had hoped would define the new European order but which in practice turned out to be a much more limited document, symbolised the relatively low profile and limitations of the Organisation.

Critics of the OSCE are inclined to dismiss it as little more than an empty talking shop. Such criticisms, however, underestimate the Organisation. The OSCE retains an important role as a pan-European diplomatic and normative framework, defining norms of international and domestic behaviour which all European states have accepted. The OSCE has also developed important operational roles in the areas of democracy and human rights promotion, conflict prevention and resolution, and arms control. In particular, it may be argued that the OSCE's quiet but persistent diplomacy has played a vital role in preventing and managing conflicts in places such as the Baltic states, Ukraine, Macedonia and Albania. While critics are correct to point out that OSCE norms are not always observed and that the Organisation lacks the means to enforce compliance, such criticisms underestimate the more subtle, long-term approach of the OSCE. By providing a set of widely accepted normative standards and working in a low-profile but sustained way to promote those standards, the OSCE makes an invaluable contribution to the consolidation of democracy and stability in post-communist Europe.

Some critics argue that the West should have done much more to exploit the potential of the OSCE as an inclusive security system, in particular as a means of integrating Russia into the new European security order and addressing Russian security concerns. These arguments have been intertwined with criticism of NATO's enlargement into Central and Eastern Europe as an unnecessary and provocative policy. Russia has repeatedly argued that the OSCE should become the primary European security organisation, with an Executive Commission (or Security Council), a central role in peacekeeping and peace enforcement and a *droit de regard* over other security organisations (in particular NATO). While supporting the development of the OSCE, the major Western powers have been reluctant to move in such a direction, fearing a Russian veto over NATO and peace-keeping/enforcement decisions and that the OSCE would simply be an ineffectual collective security system. Western concerns over becoming dependent on the OSCE are, however, perhaps exaggerated. There is certainly a case that the West should do more to promote the OSCE and be more flexible with regard to reforming it – if only to address Russian perceptions of a NATO-dominated Europe.[17] Even if such steps are taken, however, the OSCE is unlikely to be *the* solution to Europe's security problems. While the OSCE may be able to help address some of Russia's security concerns, it will not be able to compensate for Russia's dramatic decline from superpower status or avoid difficult dilemmas about the management of security problems on Russia's periphery. Even if armed with a Security Council and the right to mandate peacekeeping or peace-enforcement operations, the OSCE is unlikely to be able to prevent serious disputes about intervention in conflicts such as those in the former Yugoslavia. Similarly, an OSCE in which an unstable Russia remains a major influence is unlikely to provide an attractive alternative to membership of NATO and the EU for the countries of Central and Eastern Europe.

In these circumstances, the OSCE seems likely to have a continuing but limited role as a pan-European normative framework and in the areas of democracy promotion, conflict prevention and resolution, and arms control. As the countries of Central and Eastern Europe consolidate their democracies and integrate with NATO and the EU, further, the OSCE's attention is shifting south and east to the Balkans, the Caucasus and Central Asia. With the enlarged EU and NATO forming the core of the new Europe, the OSCE's role is likely to be as one component of a broader strategy to promote stability in and build co-operation with the countries outside that core.

Notes and references

1 Member states agreed to a name change to Organisation for Security and Co-operation in Europe (OSCE) at their Budapest summit in November 1994. In

this chapter, therefore, 'CSCE' is used when events prior to that date are being discussed, and 'OSCE' thereafter.

2 See Laura Richards Cleary in Chapter 11 of this volume.

3 Conference on Security and Co-operation in Europe, 1975 Summit, Helsinki, 1 August 1975, Final Act. OSCE website. URL: http://www.osce.org/docs/english/ 1990–1999/summits/helfa75e.htm.

4 Conference on Security and Co-operation in Europe, 1990 Summit, Paris, 19–21 November 1990, Charter of Paris for a New Europe. OSCE website. URL: http://www.osce.org/docs/english/1990–1999/summits/paris90e.htm.

5 See the discussions on South-east Europe by Paul Latawski in Chapter 14 of this volume.

6 Conference on Security and Co-operation in Europe, 1992 Summit, Helsinki, 9–10 July 1992, CSCE Helsinki Document 1992: The Challenges of Change. OSCE website. URL: http://www.osce.org./docs/english/1990–1999/summits/ hels93e.htm.

7 See 'Max van der Stoel, minority man'. *The Economist* 11 September 1999, p. 36.

8 Organisation for Security and Co-operation in Europe, The Secretary General, Annual Report 1999 on OSCE Activities (1 December 1998 to 31 October 1999). OSCE website. URL: http://www.osce.org/docs/english/misc/anrep99e.htm.

9 S. Krasner (ed.), *International Regimes.* (Ithaca: Cornell University Press 1983), p. 2.

10 R. Jervis, 'Security Regimes'. *International Organization* 36 (2) 1982, pp. 357–78.

11 E. Adler, 'Europe's New Security Order: A Pluralistic Security Community' in B. Crawford (ed.), *The Future of European Security.* (Berkley: University of California Centre for German and European Studies 1992), pp. 287–326; L. Reychler, 'A Pan-European Security Community: Utopia or Realistic Perspective?' *Disarmament* XIV 1991, pp. 42–52.

12 K. Deutsch *et al., Political Community and the North Atlantic Area.* (New York: Greenwood Press 1969).

13 E. Adler, 'Seeds of Peaceful Change: The OSCE's Security Community-building Model' in E. Adler and M. Barnett (eds), *Security Communities.* (Cambridge: Cambridge University Press 1998), pp. 119–60.

14 Helsinki Final Act *op.cit.*

15 OSCE Mediterranean Partners for Co-operation. OSCE website. URL: http:// www.osce.org/e/partmedi.htm.

16 Although, since the Libyan regime agreed to extradite two suspects for trial for allegedly planting the 1988 Lockerbie aircraft bomb, EU member states have taken steps to improve relations with Libya. These included inviting the Libyans to begin participation in some aspects of the Barcelona process during 1999.

17 R. Dannreuther, 'Escaping the Enlargement Trap in NATO–Russia Relations'. *Survival* 41 (4) 1999/2000, pp. 145–64.

4 NATO

'West is best'?

Martin A. Smith[1]

Introduction: NATO reinvented

Since the end of the Cold War, the North Atlantic Treaty Organisation has been significantly reoriented and retooled. Broadly speaking this reinvention process has proceeded in four main areas: internal adaptation, external adaptation, peace support roles and, most recently, involvement in crisis management and crisis response operations.

Internal adaptation is NATO-speak for the restructuring and reforms that have focused on rebalancing relations among the member states. Much the most important elements of the internal adaptation process have been the discussions and studies focusing on the possibility of creating procedures and structures whereby European members of the alliance might undertake military operations without the frontline participation of US forces. All members have been committed to this in principle since January 1994 when, at a summit meeting in Brussels, outline agreement was reached to establish so-called 'Combined Joint Task Forces' (CJTF). The idea, as expressed in official NATO statements, was that flexible forces could be deployed on 'non-article five operations'[2] by a 'coalition of the willing'. What this would mean in practice is that not all NATO members would take part, although there was a presumption that all would approve the overall political and strategic goals of the operation.

Over the remainder of the 1990s, the CJTF concept was developed on paper and in official rhetoric to the extent that a potential relationship between NATO and a militarised European Union began to seem both possible and desirable to many. At the NATO Washington summit in April 1999, it was officially agreed that NATO members, including the USA, 'stand ready to define and adopt the necessary arrangements for ready access by the European Union to the collective assets and capabilities of the Alliance, for operations in which the Alliance as a whole is not engaged militarily as an Alliance'.[3] This outline offer was taken as significant encouragement by those in favour of proceeding with the development of an EU military component. Yet, as the discussions by Smith and Timmins and by Rees in, respectively, Chapters 5 and 6 of this volume make clear, most of this remained confined to the realms of paper declarations and planning, notwithstanding the EU's declared intention, later in 1999, to put in place some real military capability by the year 2003. Overall, therefore, the internal adaptation, relatively speaking, has thus far remained the least significant of the four elements of NATO's reinvention in practical terms.

The second area requiring attention here is the *external adaptation* of NATO. This is a term that refers to relations between NATO and non-member states in Europe. It embraces three elements. The overall framework for NATO's external adaptation has, since 1994, been provided by the Partnership for Peace (PfP) process, which is discussed in detail below. A distinct subset of this has been the NATO enlargement process. During the 1990s this enveloped three states – the Czech Republic, Hungary and Poland – which joined NATO in March 1999. By the end of the decade, a further nine states in Central and South-eastern Europe had officially asked to join. However, no guarantees had been forthcoming from NATO that any of them would be invited to open accession negotiations.[4] The final element of NATO's external adaptation is the development of an individual 'special relationship' with Russia. The institutional dimension of this dates from 1997 and was established in the so-called 'Founding Act' which created a 'Permanent Joint Council' as the main forum for ongoing consultation between Russia and the NATO members.[5]

A role in *peace support* and related operations was, in effect, forced upon NATO and its member states by the bloody disintegration of Yugoslavia and, in particular, the civil war in Bosnia in the early 1990s. During the course of 1992 the members stated that they were prepared in principle to support peacekeeping and related operations under the auspices of the CSCE or the United Nations. The UN Secretary-General, Boutros Boutros-Ghali, responded to this offer with alacrity and, over a two-year period from the summer of 1992, NATO collective resources, as well as troops from many of its member states, were deployed extensively in, over and around Bosnia. They have been there ever since, with NATO playing the central role in implementing the military tasks of the Dayton peace accords since the beginning of 1996.[6] A similar NATO-led peace support operation has been ongoing in Kosovo since June 1999, following the coerced agreement of the Yugoslav President, Slobodan Milosevic, in the face of the use of extensive NATO air strikes against Serbia and Serb forces in Kosovo.

When, in March 1999, NATO members launched Operation Allied Force against the Serbs, controversially without seeking a mandate from the UN Security Council, they were confirming *de facto* a fourth major role for the alliance: to be prepared to use military power coercively, as well as for peace support purposes, on non-article five operations. The Kosovo air operation was not the first occasion on which they had done this. Operation Deliberate Force, a campaign of NATO air strikes against Bosnian Serb positions in August–September 1995, had helped pave the way for the end of the civil war there and for the Dayton agreements. Nevertheless, once it became clear that President Milosevic was not going to concede quickly to NATO's demands over Kosovo in the spring of 1999, and that Operation Allied Force would thus have to continue indefinitely, NATO members evidently decided that some *post facto* justification for it was required. They attempted to supply this by formally adopting, at their Washington summit, the new role for NATO of undertaking *crisis management and crisis response* operations.

Whatever the rights and wrongs of individual elements of it, all this activity demonstrates that, contrary to some expectations in 1989–90, NATO has not exhibited significant signs of institutional decline in post-Cold War Europe. As discussed in detail by this author elsewhere,[7] the two key benchmarks by which its continuing institutional vitality can be measured are in the continued commitment of forces by most member states and the continued functioning of its core military force-planning and political consultation regimes.

During the fifty-plus years of its existence, these twin consultative regimes have played key roles in underpinning 'order' in military relations among NATO member states and in creating a 'security community' among them. The essence of this was well captured by Joseph Kruzel, a US former participant in the NATO defence planning process, in 1996:

> Making defense policy in a multilateral context means that each country starts in its national capital and decides on a defense policy. Then each country sends some poor bureaucrat to Brussels to stand in front of this [NATO] group, present the policy, and get rocks thrown at him. However unpleasant that experience is, it means that anyone in NATO who wanted to plan a war against anyone else in NATO would have a hard time doing it because the defense budget and policy processes are transparent. Everyone knows what everyone else is doing.[8]

The discussions that follow in this chapter will explore the proposition that, since the end of the Cold War, NATO's principal contribution to helping with the development of 'security' and 'order' in the wider European context has been through the progressive extension of elements of its established system of transparent and collective military force-planning, and associated 'habits of co-operation', to non-member states. There are two relevant programmes to consider. The first, already mentioned, is the Partnership for Peace initiative. NATO enlargement and relations with Russia are, as noted, two distinct subsets of this. As both have been extensively discussed elsewhere, they will not be considered again in detail here.[9] Currently less developed, but none the less of *potential* importance at least, is NATO's so-called 'Mediterranean Dialogue', which has been under construction since early 1995. Some have seen this as a serious attempt by NATO members to create a 'southern PfP'. Others have viewed it as little more than diplomatic window-dressing.

Extending to the east

At the turn of the millennium, the Partnership for Peace process embraced the nineteen NATO member states and twenty-six partner countries. PfP serves several important purposes for these states. First, it offers both a training ground and a kind of apprenticeship for aspiring NATO members from Central and South-east Europe. Second, it also functions as a kind of consolation or compensation package for states which wish to join NATO but cannot do so in the short-to-medium term, if ever. NATO enlargement has been, as noted above, a distinct process, with no guarantee that any PfP participant will be included in future enlargement rounds.[10] Finally, there is the substance of the co-operative activities undertaken within the PfP framework. These are intended to be worthwhile in themselves and not dependent upon NATO enlargement directly for their utility and value. They can be divided into two related categories. First, there is joint planning, training and exercising of forces from NATO and partner states in preparation for combined peace support operations, as in Bosnia since 1995 and Kosovo since 1999. Second, PfP programmes provide opportunities and forums for the dissemination of Western principles, norms and 'best practice' with regard to the appropriate roles and functions of armed forces in democratic societies.[11]

One of the main stated aims of the PfP from its inception has been to help facilitate and encourage this democratic control of armed forces in partner countries. The PfP Framework Document adopted by NATO members at their 1994 Brussels summit mentioned it specifically.[12] This declared aim was given substance from the autumn of 1994 when NATO members agreed to create a PfP 'Planning and Review Process' (PARP) in deliberate imitation of the conventional force-planning regime which had been established in NATO itself since the 1950s. Anthony Cragg, who as NATO's Assistant Secretary-General for Defence Planning and Policy had day-to-day responsibility for overseeing the workings of the PARP when it came on stream in 1995, wrote that 'the aim of ensuring democratic control of defence forces is served through its accountability to ministers buttressed by working methods which encourage scrutiny by debate in a politico-military forum'.[13] Since that time the PARP has been successively developed to resemble even more closely the 'parent' NATO force-planning regime.

NATO officials have been careful not to allow expectations as to what NATO can and should be doing to be carried too far. Chris Donnelly, NATO's Special Adviser for Central and East European Affairs, has written that 'a national strategy for the transformation of the national defence establishments has to be just that – a national strategy. No external agency, individual or institution can provide an answer', while Marco Carnovale of NATO's Political Affairs Division has pointed out that 'there are no universally accepted definitions or models of democratic control of defence.

NATO itself cannot provide a model, simply because each ally follows its own unique cultural, political and military traditions'.[14] Two particular reasons for such reticence are apparent. One is the natural conservatism of officials and bureaucrats who do not wish to be seen to be promising too much, or raising expectations of what NATO can do too high, for fear of a backlash if high expectations were to be disappointed. Second, NATO officials have been anxious not to leave their institution open to the charge that it is seeking to promote a quasi-imperialist agenda or to establish a hegemony over non-member states by foisting its own values and models on governments and armed forces there. These factors also help to account for the relative equanimity with which NATO officials have viewed – even encouraged – the involvement of other international institutions in 'strengthening democratic control of defence'.[15]

It should not be forgotten that the origins of NATO's eastern outreach programmes in 1990 owed less to any grand design for spreading the perceived benefits of the institution's foundation as a 'community of values' and more to tactical political expediency. The initial impetus was the unanimous wish among the sixteen member states in 1990 to ensure that a united Germany retained its NATO membership. Although the original invitation to form 'liaison partnerships' with NATO in the summer of that year was extended equally to all six remaining Warsaw Pact members (the GDR being about to disappear), the West's key objective was to involve the USSR, and thus pave the way to a final settlement of the German membership issue. The *raison d'être* of the July 1990 NATO summit in London, at least in US and German eyes, was to send a clear signal to the Soviet leadership that NATO was not a threat to Soviet security. The liaison offer was considered to be an important part of that effort.[16] This helped to ensure that little attention was paid, in the summer of 1990, to the possibly distinct agendas of the Central European states. To be fair, there seemed little need as they all appeared happy to take whatever NATO had to offer. All of them moved quickly to identify diplomats in Brussels who would undertake the new liaison function. The success of the London initiative appeared confirmed when, less than two weeks after the summit, President Mikhail Gorbachev told the German Chancellor, Helmut Kohl, that the USSR no longer objected to the principle of NATO membership for the united Germany.

Beyond achieving this immediate objective, was the new liaison process meant to have permanent significance? While it might seem churlish to suggest that it amounted, in Western eyes at the time, to little more than a tactical political device, there are grounds for supporting this view. To begin with, the London Declaration, issued at the summit, was vague about precisely how the new liaison process would work. This reflected the caution of some NATO members, especially France, which harboured strong reservations at that time about involving NATO in East–West engagement to any real extent.[17] Bearing this in mind, it is entirely possible that the

French were persuaded not to block the London agreements by private assurances that the new diplomatic liaison arrangements represented little more than short-term window-dressing.

The liaison process was, furthermore, developed cautiously and in a fairly restricted way on the Western side during the remainder of 1990 and early 1991. The Eastern liaison partners were not allowed unrestricted access to the NATO headquarters. Liaison existed on two levels. First, there were the national delegations to NATO, which were free to develop the process to the degree they saw fit. Second, there was liaison with a relatively small number of 'specified senior people on the NATO International Staff'.[18] Contacts with NATO military headquarters were not at first permitted. Although the whole process was often referred to as 'diplomatic liaison', the CEE personnel who had been assigned to represent their countries at NATO headquarters enjoyed no formal diplomatic status there. NATO members' foot-dragging in this area (agreements to grant such status were not finally approved by them until 1998) is, in itself, another indication that they did not originally intend to establish a significant or enduring institutional relationship between NATO and non-member states. As well as the limited access granted to the Eastern representatives, the quality and scope of the discussions that took place within the new liaison framework also appear to have been fairly limited at the time. An article by the Assistant NATO Secretary-General for Political Affairs, published in August 1990, noted only that 'exchanges of views' and 'briefings' would be taking place within the new framework, rather than any more extensive consultation. He also wrote, rather condescendingly, about the Easterners 'rectifying' previously held views of NATO.[19]

From these limited beginnings, however, something significant was to develop. The whole process of NATO link-building with non-member states in Europe began to acquire its own dynamic and also an increasing value for member states and NATO officials. The watershed occurred during 1994 when the Clinton administration in the USA decided to support NATO enlargement whether or not any military threat to non-member states existed. It did this mainly as a means of reasserting US leadership in NATO and, through that, in European security affairs more generally.[20] In order credibly to decouple NATO enlargement from the existence of an external military threat it was necessary for its supporters to formulate and present other justifications and rationales. The extension of Western values, norms and forms of organisation generally were the major components of these alternative official justifications, as put forward by senior officials from the Clinton administration.[21]

In addition, as the PfP became established from 1994, many NATO officials began to develop a proprietorial interest in its success. They saw it as tangible proof that the institution for which they worked was capable of adapting itself to changing post-Cold War strategic and political realities. In 1996 two members of the NATO International Staff, Michael Rühle and

Nick Williams, wrote that 'PfP has developed a life and value of its own: a NATO without partners has become as unthinkable today as a partnership without the mechanisms of co-operation created by PfP'.[22]

Several potential problems were apparent, however. First, some analysts simply rejected the whole idea that NATO could contribute in any significant way to the spread of democratic norms and values among non-member states. Michael Mandelbaum, a prominent opponent of NATO enlargement, has argued that 'NATO is not only not the most effective instrument for promoting democracy, it is not in *essence* an organization for doing so. Rather, it is a military alliance, an association of some sovereign states directed against others. The "other" in this case is Russia [emphasis in the original]'.[23] It is certainly true that proponents of the extension through NATO of Western norms and values were often vague about what this meant in practice and about the specific institutional requirements and consequences for NATO itself.[24] It could be argued that this is no great problem and may indeed even be advantageous in helping NATO member states to avoid becoming pinned down to irksome commitments. Yet if things are kept too vague and imprecise there is a danger of non-member states becoming dissatisfied with what is on offer. There is also a risk that NATO members may delude themselves into believing that what they are offering is sufficient while in fact their interlocutors are both desiring and expecting something more.

In 1997, Michael Radu identified and discussed a developing mismatch between Western (especially US) desires to decouple NATO enlargement from external security threats and the concerns of most if not all of the CEE states which were then interested in NATO membership. The latter, in Radu's assessment, were very much of the view that at least a potential Russian threat to their security *did* exist. According to Radu, the 'disparity between the motivations of Eastern and Central Europeans on the one hand and western ambiguity on the other has led to confusion, dissimulation, and diminished credibility on all sides'.[25] Like Mandelbaum, Radu was dismissive of arguments that NATO has a useful role to play in extending Western democratic culture eastwards, in the absence of any real military threats. He saw it as 'obvious' that 'without the menacing presence of Russia there would be no need to expand NATO, no pressure to do so, and indeed no need for NATO at all'.[26] In a comparable though more conceptual vein, James Kurth identified what he considered to be an underlying weakness in the NATO enlargement process, and indeed in the post-Cold War adaptation of NATO as a whole. This, he argued, was the lack of a big idea to underpin it:

> the new NATO will not be based upon any vision or idea comparable to the Western civilization of the old NATO . . . The new NATO will lack the old vision and indeed will have no authentic and coherent union at all. It is mostly the product of bureaucratic momentum and political calculations.[27]

Such negative and pessimistic views are not universally shared. Elsewhere, Paul Latawski has put the contrary view to that expressed by Radu:

> The Visegrad group's[28] aim of integration with NATO, it must be emphasised, is not one driven by any clear and present danger. It is grounded in an important lesson Western Europe applied in the wake of the experience of two catastrophic world wars. The Visegrad group, like Western Europe of half a century ago, sees integration as a means of preventing the emergence of future conflict through participation in a community of mutual interest. The foundation of this mutual interest rests on democracy and the free-market economy.[29]

In attempting to determine which perspective is the more credible in this debate it is worth bearing in mind that CEE leaders, most especially those in the Visegrad states, have displayed consistent interest since at least 1993 in acceding to both NATO and the European Union. This suggests a three-fold agenda on their part. One element has undoubtedly been a desire for improved commercial access, and preferably access to the EU's Single Market via membership of that institution. Reassurance against external – that is, Russian – military threats has also been important, as CEE leaders have openly admitted on occasion.[30] An overarching political and cultural desire has in addition been evident; to 'Return to Europe', in the oft-used phrase, by engaging with and ultimately joining whichever of the Western-based institutions are prepared to make membership available.

In assessing the importance of its eastern outreach programmes, one should consider, finally, whether engagement and enlargement have been good for the post-Cold War vitality and relevance of the NATO institution itself. 'Good' in this sense can be measured in the extent to which PfP and associated programmes have enabled the NATO institution to demonstrate adaptability and relevance to post-Cold War security challenges. In this context many, probably most, informed observers would agree with the conclusions of a 1996 report prepared by the North Atlantic Assembly (NAA), a parliamentary forum loosely linked to NATO.[31] The NAA report argued that 'by creating formal links between the sixteen members of the Alliance and twenty-seven "Partner" countries, NATO has become the core vehicle for the enhancement of co-operation, harmonisation and transparency in defence and military affairs across the European continent'.[32] One can also argue that the Clinton administration in 1993–4 was keen to ensure that NATO was not crowded out by other Western-based European institutions in a rush to develop outreach and engagement with countries to their east. Specifically, the argument has been made that President Clinton and his senior foreign policy advisers decided to move ahead with NATO enlargement and enhancements to the PfP from 1994 in response to the in-principle decision of member states to admit (eventually) new CEE members into the European Union.[33]

Extending to the south?

Since its launch early in 1995, NATO's Mediterranean Dialogue has been ignored by most analysts and commentators. Comparatively little has been published about it and the general impression received has been of something that has amounted to not much more than a piece of diplomatic window-dressing. Much scepticism surrounded the beginnings of the Dialogue. It commenced under a cloud as it was launched just after the NATO Secretary-General, Willy Claes, was widely quoted in the media as stating that Islam had replaced Soviet communism as the gravest security threat to the West.[34] The sceptics could also point out that NATO member states seemed to be avoiding difficult issues in deciding to restrict their Dialogue to Egypt, Israel, Mauritania, Morocco and Tunisia (Jordan joined a few months later). It was reasonable to expect Iran, Iraq and Libya (three of the four chief 'pariah states' in Clinton administration foreign policy) not to be invited to take part. But the exclusion of strife-prone Algeria – to the chagrin of the Algerian authorities[35] – seemed to offer clear evidence that NATO and its member states were not really intending to engage seriously with security problems to the south of the Mediterranean Sea. It can also be argued that at least some NATO member states were motivated by a sense of institutional competitiveness rather than a desire to engage seriously with their new southern interlocutors. By early 1995 both the Western European Union and the Organisation for Security and Co-operation in Europe had established co-operative links with North African and Middle Eastern states.[36] European Union members had also agreed to convene an international conference in Barcelona in November of that year at which an EU dialogue and co-operation process with North African and Middle Eastern states was due to be established. The more Atlanticist NATO member states did not wish to see their institution being left behind.

During its first eighteen months, NATO's Mediterranean Dialogue proceeded in a generally desultory way, which seemed to confirm the views of those who had been sceptical about it all along. In 1996 a report issued by the WEU's Parliamentary Assembly argued that 'the endeavours NATO has been making since December 1994 to establish a dialogue with six Southern Mediterranean countries has not achieved the objective of a partnership for peace in the Mediterranean'.[37] Assessing the success or otherwise of the Dialogue in terms of comparing it with the established PfP initiative seemed like a natural thing to do even though, to be fair, NATO member states had not declared that they were trying to create a southern PfP. At this time, they themselves had little to do directly with the process, which consisted mainly of meetings with NATO officials at NATO headquarters for Dialogue partner representatives. NATO officials later admitted privately that often neither side at these meetings really had any clear idea as to what they were supposed to be talking about.[38] For their part, no clear idea existed among NATO member states about what the Dialogue was for either.

Analysts pointed to a lack of consensus between the US and many West European governments over what constituted the key security challenges in the Mediterranean and where the principal focus of their interest should be directed. The USA has been widely perceived as being interested primarily, if not exclusively, in what is sometimes called the 'Eastern Mediterranean'; that is, the Middle East. Southern European members of NATO and the EU have focused more on the Maghreb states in North Africa. They have also been interested principally in softer security issues such as the prospects for economic and commercial co-operation and the challenges posed by migration from North Africa into Southern Europe. It has also been argued that, in terms of their respective approaches to Middle East security issues, the USA has taken an Israel-centric approach while European governments have generally endeavoured to strike a greater balance in their dealings with Israel, the Palestinians and the Arab states.[39] Until there was a greater degree of conceptual consensus – or at least agreement on the focus and scope of the NATO Dialogue – further significant development of the Dialogue seemed unlikely.

Having said that, the picture has improved to some degree since the NATO Madrid summit meeting in July 1997. Although all other summit business was overshadowed by the decision to proceed with eastern enlargement of NATO's membership, the Madrid Declaration on Euro-Atlantic Security and Co-operation issued at the summit did include a section on the Mediterranean Dialogue. The most important element of this was the announcement of the creation of a 'Mediterranean Co-operation Group' (MCG) within the NATO headquarters staffs to take 'overall responsibility' for the Dialogue.[40]

This apparently innocuous announcement belied a more important political development. For the first time, the MCG provided a forum and a means for NATO member governments to have a *direct* input into the Mediterranean Dialogue.[41] Its creation can, therefore, be taken as a signal that NATO member governments were now prepared to try to inject some life into the Dialogue. The main reason why was probably the desire to secure contributions from Islamic states to the multinational NATO-led Implementation and Stabilisation Forces which had been successively deployed in Bosnia, to help implement the Dayton peace accords, from the beginning of 1996. Such contributions, alongside those from NATO members and PfP states, were viewed as being politically important given the ethnic and religious character of the 'entities' that made up the new Bosnian state. Western political leaders and officials set considerable store by the fact that Egypt, Jordan and Morocco all contributed contingents in Bosnia between 1996 and 1999.

Since 1997 the Mediterranean Dialogue overall has become somewhat more structured and focused and it has taken a more important place on NATO's working agenda, even though aspirations to create a southern PfP have continued to be officially disavowed.[42] Annual 'work programmes' have been agreed and implemented by the participants on both sides. This echoes the approach adopted in the early years of NATO's engagement with the CEE states which was managed largely under the auspices of a body called the North Atlantic Co-operation Council (NACC) – in effect the forerunner of the Partnership for Peace. From 1992, the NACC developed annual 'work plans' which were designed to give substance and focus to the co-operation conducted under its auspices while, at the same time, setting parameters to the co-operation and damping down any 'unrealistic' expectations among the Eastern participants.

Because the Mediterranean Dialogue now includes a work programme element, this could open the door eventually to more comprehensive and operationally focused co-operation between NATO and the southern participants. Up to the late 1990s the co-operation had been confined mainly to seminars, attendance on courses and invitations to observe NATO military exercises.[43] The precedent for functional evolution existed in the way in which the NACC's programmes (established from 1991) opened the door to PfP (from 1994) and eventually the enlargement of NATO's membership (from 1997 to 1999). It does, however, remain virtually inconceivable that any of the present Mediterranean Dialogue partners could be invited to join NATO.

By the late 1990s there were some indications that a process of development might, at last, be under way. The MCG had, according to a report published by the NATO Parliamentary Assembly, 'offered a stable forum for extensive political discussions with Dialogue countries, opening the way to multilateralism and military co-operation, especially in the area of peace-keeping'.[44] In October and November 1999 a multinational naval exercise took place, bringing together a cross-section of NATO members with Egypt and Jordan (plus Kuwait). This was the largest such exercise since the 1991 Gulf conflict and, according to some officials, it provided 'a glimpse of how future alliance training efforts may increasingly be cross-regional in nature'.[45] One of the major anomalies in participation in the Mediterranean Dialogue was removed in March 2000 when Algeria's accession was announced.[46]

The progress made in developing and institutionalising the Dialogue should not be allowed to mask the substantial obstacles that remain in the way of a deep and lasting rapprochement between NATO members and countries in North Africa and the Middle East, however. NATO has taken no role in responding to the internal turmoil and bloodletting that has engulfed Algeria, for example. Those influenced by Samuel Huntington's seminal work on civilisational 'fault-lines'[47] might argue that it is difficult if not impossible to develop profound and lasting co-operation between the West and Islamic countries for historical and cultural reasons, and that this has been reflected in the slow and fitful progress in developing the Mediterranean Dialogue to date.

In addition, one should not get carried away by the extent to which NATO member governments have invested fresh impetus in the Mediterranean

Dialogue. A report published by a study group of the NATO Parliamentary Assembly in September 1999 identified three interrelated problems: lack of funding; lack of substantial military input from the NATO side; and, overall, little sense of direction in terms of the future of the Dialogue. The lack of funding raises the question of just how committed NATO governments really are to developing the Dialogue process and investing it with greater substance. The NPA report noted that money had been so tight that 'Dialogue countries, and officials from various governmental offices, do not always have the ability to attend meetings where they are invited'.[48] This problem is reminiscent of the early days of the NACC when Central Asian partners, in particular, often failed to turn up at meetings because they could not justify the expense of doing so. The situation improved following the initiation of PfP in 1994 when NATO members, under US pressure, earmarked resources to fund partner participation in a range of co-operative activities. This has not yet happened with the Mediterranean Dialogue.

The absence of a substantial military component to the Mediterranean Dialogue matters because NATO has remained fundamentally a military security institution. Therefore, the lack of military content can be seen to be indicative of a lack of substance overall. The problem here has been more on the partner than the NATO side. The NPA report cited above argued that 'many Dialogue countries are wary of NATO ambitions in the region, and thus not very enthusiastic about participation in a military dialogue'. Thus far, it noted, 'co-operation has taken shape through courses at SHAPE[49] and various activities at the [NATO] Defense College in Rome. Egypt, Israel and Jordan also sent personnel to observe Partnership for Peace manoeuvres and other activities'.

In summary, in measuring the achievements of NATO's engagement with states to its south, all that can be said with confidence about the Mediterranean Dialogue since 1995 is that it exists. This in itself is a development over and above what was possible during the Cold War. Beyond that, however, the jury must remain out on questions relating to its potential long-term significance.

Conclusions

The discussions in this chapter have focused on the attempts by NATO and its member states to move beyond the institution's Cold War territorial defence remit in order to engage with states elsewhere in Europe and on its southern borders. A key unspoken objective of these endeavours, as with all aspects of NATO's post-Cold War adaptation, has been self-preservation and NATO's survival. In this respect they have succeeded. The observations of Michael Rühle, a senior member of the NATO International Staff, in 1998 bear repeating. He summarises the 'official line' on NATO's continuing importance and roles rather well:

In recent years all major organisations have ceased to be 'single issue' institutions and are engaged in managing . . . wider political processes. NATO remains unique, however, for only it can offer the instruments to bring these processes together in a coherent way. The Alliance's combination of political consultation, military competence and transatlantic vocation make it a unique contributor to the management of the security dimension of the European integration process, the evolution of Russia into a responsible security actor, the maintenance of the transatlantic relationship, and the evolution of crisis management in the Euro-Atlantic area.[50]

Looking at things more objectively, it is difficult to argue against the view that the Partnership for Peace has played a significant role in both developing functional military co-operation and disseminating Western norms and principles on civil–military relations and democratic control of the armed forces to the partner states. The traffic has not been all one way, however. When PfP was established in 1994, most NATO members probably viewed it as a substitute for actual NATO membership for CEE and other states. At the same time they hoped that it might serve as a useful framework for promoting military co-operation.[51] Over the years, as the process developed, NATO and its member states acquired important stakes in its survival and prosperity, most especially because all the other major European institutions had developed their own outreach programmes with non-member states in Europe. Thus, as Istvan Szonyi has demonstrated, a process of 'socialisation' has been apparent among both the NATO and partner states.[52] NATO members have proved willing to offer the partners significantly greater opportunities for co-operation than they originally envisaged. They have, for example, progressively developed the PfP force Planning and Review Process, which, as noted, is based on and now closely resembles the parent NATO force-planning regime. They have also opened up the planning of peace support and related operations to input from involved or interested partner states.

The situation thus far with regard to the Mediterranean Dialogue is much less profound. The Dialogue has not yet developed to the extent where it might begin to affect the attitudes or behaviour of the participants on either the NATO or partner country sides significantly. NATO members have been reluctant to develop the Dialogue as a vehicle for promoting Western norms and values similar to those underpinning the PfP for good and understandable reasons. Even without such an effort, however, the Middle Eastern and North African participants have been suspicious of anything beyond relatively cursory discussions and occasional joint military exercises. NATO has not, therefore, succeeded to date in engaging countries on the other side of the Mediterranean in any meaningful security co-operation. Although the obstacles to doing so have been substantial, one should not overlook the argument that one of the problems has been a relative lack of effort, certainly when compared to the time and resources which have been invested in the PfP. NATO members have apparently concluded, at least implicitly, that the extension of a normative security community is potentially an achievable and desirable goal within the context of a 'wider Europe'. But the parameters of this effort do not extend to the states that face Southern Europe across the thin expanse of the Mediterranean Sea.

Notes and references

1 The views expressed here are personal and should not be construed as representing the views or policy of the British government, Ministry of Defence or the Royal Military Academy, Sandhurst.
2 Article five of the NATO treaty contains the famous security guarantee, that the members will consider an attack against any one of them as being an attack against them all. The term 'non-article five operations' refers, therefore, to any military operation undertaken within a NATO framework for reasons other than responding to a direct attack on one of its member states.
3 Washington Summit Communiqué. NATO website. URL: http://www.nato.int/docu/pr/1999/p99-064e.htm.
4 The nine, whose aspirations were at least recognised at the 1999 summit, were: Estonia, Latvia, Lithuania, Slovakia, Bulgaria, Romania, Slovenia, Albania and Macedonia.
5 The course of relations between NATO and Russia is assessed by Laura Richards Cleary in Chapter 11 of this volume.
6 See M. A. Smith, *NATO in the First Decade after the Cold War.* (The Hague: Kluwer 2000), ch. 5 for a detailed discussion of these issues.
7 *Ibid.*
8 J. Kruzel, 'Partnership for Peace and the Future of European Security' in K. Thompson (ed.), *NATO and the Changing World Order.* (Lanham: University Press of America 1996), p. 34.
9 For a good introduction to the debates on NATO enlargement see R. Asmus *et al.*, 'Building a New NATO'. *Foreign Affairs* 72 (4) 1993, pp. 28–40; M. Brown, 'The Flawed Logic of NATO Expansion'. *Survival* 37 (1) 1995, pp. 34–52; M. MccGwire, 'NATO Expansion: "A Policy Error of Historic Importance" '. *Review of International Studies* 24 (1) 1998, pp. 23–42; M. Mandelbaum, 'Preserving the New Peace'. *Foreign Affairs* 74 (3) 1995, pp. 9–13; J. Morrison, *NATO Expansion and Alternative Future Security Alignments.* (Washington, DC: National Defense University 1995). On NATO and Russia see, in addition to Cleary in this volume, A. Arbatov, 'NATO and Russia'. *Security Dialogue* 26 (2) 1995, pp. 135–46; J. Haslam, 'Russia's Seat at the Table: A Place Denied or A Place Delayed?' *International Affairs* 74 (1) 1998, pp. 119–30; W. Odom, 'Russia's Several Seats at the Table'. *International Affairs* 74 (4) 1998, pp. 809–22; M. Hanson, 'Russia and NATO Expansion: The Uneasy Basis of the Founding Act'. *European Security* 7 (2) 1998, pp. 13–29.
10 On the prospects for further enlargement rounds see K. H. Kamp, 'NATO Entrapped: Debating the Next Enlargement Round'. *Survival* 40 (3) 1998, pp. 170–86; H. Binnendijk and R. Kugler, 'Open NATO's Door Carefully'. *Washington Quarterly* 22 (2) 1999, pp. 125–38; D. Haglund, 'NATO's Expansion and European Security after the Washington Summit – What Next?' *European Security* 8 (1) 1999, pp. 1–15 and M. A. Smith and K. Aldred, *NATO in South East Europe: Enlargement by Stealth?* (London: Centre for Defence Studies 2000), ch. 1.

11 For a good overview of the nature and substance of PfP, written by a NATO staff member, see N. Williams, 'Partnership for Peace: Permanent Fixture or Declining Asset?' *Survival* 38 (1) 1996, pp. 98–110.
12 Partnership for Peace: Framework Document (M-1(94)2). (Brussels: NATO Press Service 1994), p. 1.
13 A. Cragg, 'The Partnership for Peace Planning and Review Process'. *NATO Review* 43 (6) 1995, p. 23.
14 C. Donnelly, 'Defence Transformation in the New Democracies: A Framework for tackling the Problem'. *NATO Review* 45 (1) 1997, p. 15; M. Carnovale, 'NATO Partners and Allies: Civil–Military Relations and Democratic Control of the Armed Forces'. *NATO Review* 45 (2) 1997, p. 32.
15 Carnovale *op.cit.*, p. 34.
16 H. Wegener, 'The Transformed Alliance'. *NATO Review* 38 (4) 1990, p. 1.
17 M. Fortmann and D. Haglund, 'Between Eurovoluntarism and Realism: France and European Security in Transition' in Haglund *et al.* (eds), *NATO's Eastern Dilemmas.* (Boulder: Westview 1994), p. 138; F. Bozo, 'French Security Policy in the New European Order' in C. McInnes (ed.), *Security and Strategy in the New Europe.* (London: Routledge 1992), p. 209.
18 T. Taylor, *NATO and Central Europe: Problems and Opportunities in a New Relationship.* (London: RIIA 1992), p. 15.
19 Wegener *op.cit.*, p. 3.
20 The best insights into the formulation and evolution of the Clinton administration policy on NATO enlargement over this key period are in J. Goldgeier, 'NATO Expansion: The Anatomy of a Decision'. *Washington Quarterly* 21 (1) 1998, pp. 95–9. For the argument that a desire to reassert leadership was the main reason why the Clinton administration adopted NATO enlargement as a flagship foreign policy objective see, *inter alia*, A. Lieven, 'Baltic Iceberg Dead Ahead: NATO Beware'. *World Today* 52 (7) 1996, p. 178.
21 They were, for example, prominent themes in the much-cited article that appeared under the name of US Secretary of State Madeleine Albright in *The Economist* in February 1997. See 'Enlarging NATO: Why Bigger is Better'. *The Economist* 15 February 1997, pp. 21–3.
22 M. Rühle and N. Williams, 'Partnership for Peace after NATO Enlargement'. *European Security* 5 (4) 1996, p. 521.
23 M. Mandelbaum, 'Preserving the New Peace: The Case against NATO Expansion'. *Foreign Affairs* 74 (3) 1995, p. 10.
24 For examples see the article by the former German Deputy Defence Minister Lothar Rühl in *Die Welt* 6 May 1991. Translated in *German Tribune* 1467 19 May 1991, p. 2 and J. Petersen, 'NATO's Next Strategic Concept'. *NATO Review* 46 (2) 1998, p. 18.
25 M. Radu, 'Why Eastern and Central Europe Look West'. *Orbis* 41 (1) 1997, pp. 40–1.
26 *Ibid.*, p. 43.
27 J. Kurth, 'NATO Expansion and the Idea of the West'. *Orbis* 41 (4) 1997, p. 567.
28 The Visegrad group is the name given to a co-operative process bringing together Czechoslovakia, Hungary and Poland and initiated in 1991 with one of the key aims being to press in tandem for closer involvement with and eventual membership of Western-based international institutions. The three became four when the Czechs and Slovaks agreed their 'velvet divorce' in 1993.
29 P. Latawski, 'NATO's "Near Abroad": The Visegrad Group and the Atlantic Alliance'. *RUSI Journal* 138 (6) 1993, p. 40.
30 For example, Czech President Vaclav Havel told a German newspaper in February 1995 that 'for reasons of security, being accepted into NATO is . . . more

urgent for us than being accepted into the European Union. No one knows what the further developments in Russia will be like and whether we will not experience unpleasant surprises there.' Quoted in Morrison *op.cit.*, p. 80.

31 Subsequently renamed the NATO Parliamentary Assembly.

32 'Partnership for Peace: A Basis for New Security Structures and an Incentive for Military Reform in Europe'. North Atlantic Assembly website. URL: http://www.naa.be/publications/comrep/1996/an231dsc.html.

33 The author and Graham Timmins have developed this argument in *Building a Bigger Europe: EU and NATO Enlargement in Comparative Perspective.* (Aldershot: Ashgate 2000), chs 2 and 3.

34 See, for example, 'NATO Turns to the Threat from Islamic Extremists'. *International Herald Tribune* 9 February 1995 and 'Fears over Islam Move'. *Daily Telegraph* 10 February 1995. Claes subsequently tried to backtrack. A commentary published in his name just after the new Mediterranean Dialogue was launched asserted that the question of Islamic fundamentalism 'will not even be on the agenda when NATO talks to these countries. Religious fundamentalism – whether Islamic or of other varieties – is not a concern for NATO'. See 'NATO's Agenda for New European Order'. *Financial Times* 20 February 1995.

35 'NATO Turns Attention to North Africa'. *Financial Times* 24 February 1995.

36 For details of the WEU and OSCE initiatives see 'Security in the Mediterranean Region'. WEU Assembly website. URL: http://www.weu.int/assembly/eng/reports/1543e.html.

37 *Ibid.*

38 Author's interviews with NATO officials conducted in 1995 and 1996. See also 'Arc of Instability'. *Armed Forces Journal International* October 1996, pp. 72–4.

39 See WEU Assembly *op.cit.*; 'Security in the Greater Middle East'. North Atlantic Assembly website. URL: http://www.naa.be/publications/comrep/1998/ar309gsm-e.html; 'Security in the North African Region'. (Brussels: NATO Parliamentary Assembly 1999), pp. 20–1; M. Blunden, 'Insecurity on Europe's Southern Flank'. *Survival* 36 (2) 1994, p. 141 and R. Asmus *et al.*, 'Mediterranean Security: New Challenges, New Tasks'. *NATO Review* 44 (3) 1996, pp. 28–9.

40 See the text of the Madrid Declaration, reprinted as a 'Special Insert' in *NATO Review* 45 (4) 1997, p. 2.

41 See J. Nordam, 'The Mediterranean Dialogue: Dispelling Misconceptions and Building Confidence'. *NATO Review* 45 (4) 1997, pp. 28–9.

42 See A. Carlson, 'NATO and North Africa: Problems and Prospects'. *Parameters* XXVIII (3) 1998, pp. 43–5.

43 For details see A. Bin, 'Strengthening Cooperation in the Mediterranean: NATO's Contribution'. *NATO Review* 46 (4) 1998, pp. 25–7.

44 NATO Parliamentary Assembly *op.cit.*, p. 22.

45 'Exercise Heralds Cross-regional Training for NATO'. *Jane's Defence Weekly* 3 November 1999, p. 2.

46 'Algeria's Participation in NATO's Mediterranean Dialogue'. US State Department website. URL: http://www.state.gov/www/regions/nea/000314_nato_algeria.html.

47 S. Huntington, *The Clash of Civilizations and the Remaking of World Order.* (New York: Simon & Schuster 1996).

48 'Mediterranean Special Group: Meeting at NATO Headquarters Brussels, 17 September 1999'. NATO Parliamentary Assembly website. URL: http://www.naa.be/publications/special/as220gsm9910.html.

49 Supreme Headquarters Allied Powers Europe, NATO's senior military headquarters located at Mons in Belgium.

50 M. Rühle, 'Taking Another Look at NATO's Role in European Security'. *NATO Review* 46 (4) 1998, p. 21.

51 B. Boczek, 'NATO and the Former Warsaw Pact States' in V. Papacosma and M. A. Heiss (eds), *NATO in the Post-Cold War Era: Does it Have a Future?*. (Basingstoke: Macmillan 1995), pp. 214–15; G. Auton, 'The United States and an Expanded NATO' in P. Dutkiewicz and R. Jackson (eds), *NATO Looks East.* (Westport: Praeger 1998), p. 181.
52 I. Szonyi, 'The Partnership for Peace as a Process of Adaptation'. *Journal of Slavic Military Studies* 11 (1) 1998, pp. 18–39.

5   The EU

Coming of age as a security actor?

Martin A. Smith[1] and Graham Timmins

Introduction

The debate surrounding the alleged shift from 'hard' to 'soft' security issues
has pervaded much of the discussion on European security overall since
1989. Notwithstanding a widespread perception that the hard (i.e., military)
dimension of security has become progressively less important, European
Union member states have taken a more sustained interest in the question
of endowing their institution with a military capability than at any previous
point in its history, with the exception of the early 1950s when a plan for a
'European Defence Community' was hatched and aborted. The backdrop
to these political manoeuvres has been the new opportunities made available by the removal of the old superpower 'overlay' which made Europe
(East and West) primarily an object, rather than a subject, in the military
power machinations which took place during the Cold War era.[2] Many,
especially in continental Western Europe, now argue that the European
Union both can and should overcome what they feel is the most significant
outstanding barrier to its emergence as a fully fledged international power.
The first part of this chapter will, therefore, examine the progress made
and the obstacles that remain to the development of a viable EU military
capability.

For the purposes of this investigation, the concept of soft security will
embrace economic, political and social issues. A primary objective of the
European integration process, at least since the 1970s and 1980s, has been
the reduction of socio-economic disparity between and within member
states and the consequent promotion of 'cohesion' among them. The
continuation of the 'wealth gap' in the wider European context could
become a source of tension, instability and conflict and must, therefore, be
addressed if any viable wider European security order is to be achieved.
The extent to which the EU has supported the post-communist economic
and political transformation process in Central and Eastern Europe will be
considered in the second part of this chapter. This will assist in the formulation of overall judgements about the effectiveness of the EU in the soft
security arena in post-Cold War Europe.

From civilian to military power?

A brief Cold War history

A desire for a military security element to the overall European integration process was evident from the outset in the early 1950s. Running in close parallel to the Schuman Plan in 1950, which led to the creation of the European Coal and Steel Community (ECSC), was the Pleven Plan, which proposed the European Defence Community (EDC). The failure of the French National Assembly to ratify the draft EDC treaty in 1954 suggested that creating a European defence system based on common military structures of whatever kind would be a long and difficult haul. Parliamentarians in France had been concerned by the threat to national sovereignty and the UK had refused to participate directly had the EDC been set up, offering instead to negotiate a bilateral alliance with it. A later French proposal for a common European defence system for members of the European Economic Community (EEC) based on an intergovernmental model of co-operation, the Fouchet Plan of 1961, also failed to get off the ground. This was due to Belgian and Dutch concerns about the exclusion of the UK. Germany and Italy were also concerned about the 'anti-US tone' of the proposal.[3]

Thus NATO remained the primary military defence organisation for Western Europe throughout the Cold War, driven by a transatlantic rather than a distinctively European agenda. The Treaty of Brussels signed by the UK, France and the Benelux states in 1948 had agreed on the principle of mutual military assistance but this was rapidly subsumed by the Washington Treaty in 1949, which established NATO. It was, though, to play a role in 1954–5 when the Western European Union (WEU) was formed on the basis of the Brussels Treaty, primarily as a means of facilitating West German rearmament and its integration into NATO.

Despite these setbacks, the idea of a harder security dimension to the European integration project never completely disappeared. A resurrection of sorts came in 1970 with the Davignon Report, which resulted in the European Political Co-operation (EPC) procedure being established. This provided a means by which EEC member states could discuss foreign policy issues and develop a common position where they felt it to be appropriate. However, EPC's role where military security issues were concerned remained peripheral until the draft 'European Act' or Genscher–Colombo Plan, named after the West German and Italian Foreign Ministers, was put forward in 1981. The call for a common European foreign policy was raised as part of a larger push towards political integration and the development of a European security and defence 'identity'. France and the UK were reluctant to support this initiative and it was eventually reduced to a non-binding Solemn Declaration on European Union taken at the European Council summit in Stuttgart in 1983. The EPC was, however, given a treaty base with the signing of the Single European Act in 1985. It was agreed that the member states would 'inform and consult each other on any Foreign Policy matters of general interest so as to ensure that their combined influence is exercised as effectively as possible through co-ordination, the convergence of their positions and implementation of joint action'.[4] But, as Cameron points out, the EPC did not go as far as some member states wished and 'military issues remained out of bounds'.[5]

After the Cold War – quickening the pace?

The European Community's response to the Iraqi invasion of Kuwait in August 1990 offered what seemed to many to be a simultaneous demonstration of both the strengths and weaknesses of the 'civilian power' which it had developed into during the Cold War period.[6] In the immediate aftermath of the invasion, when the principal emphasis was on organising and imposing international sanctions against the Iraqi regime, the EC and its member states were at the forefront of the international response. Once the emphasis began to shift to the military arena, however, the Community was increasingly unable to maintain an important or coherent role. When hostilities finally commenced early in 1991, it was rendered impotent as leading member states responded militarily on a national basis and in bilateral co-ordination with the United States.

Principally because of the Gulf conflict, the period immediately after the end of the Cold War paradoxically saw new demands for the EC to be militarised, notwithstanding the easing of East–West tensions in Europe itself. The European Commission President, Jacques Delors, drew some public conclusions about the lessons of the Gulf conflict as early as March 1991. In a high-profile speech in London, Delors suggested that the conflict had 'provided an object lesson – if one were needed – on the limitations of the European Community'. He then made the argument that:

> In the last resort, security means the ability to defend oneself by force of arms. If the Community is to contribute to the new world order, it must accept that this presupposes participation, where necessary, in forces which are given the task of ensuring respect for international law, when all other attempts to create a basis of understanding and co-operation between nations have failed.[7]

This speech can be seen as a contribution by Delors to the debates which were gathering momentum around the EC's two intergovernmental conferences on economic and political union which were eventually to yield the Maastricht Treaty on European Union signed in December 1991 and finally ratified in November 1993. By the time Delors made his remarks the intergovernmental debate was already well under way. Political battle lines had been drawn between EC 'Europeanists' led by France with support

from Spain and, less wholeheartedly, Germany. These governments believed
that the end of the Cold War made possible the ending of Western Europe's
high degree of dependency on the United States for its military security
needs. Further, some saw a chance to move decisively ahead towards the
'finality' of European integration. On the other side were the 'Atlanticists',
led by the UK with support from the Netherlands and, increasingly, Italy.
Their main concern was to try to ensure that the EC did nothing that
would weaken or undermine NATO or potentially persuade the USA to
reassess its own contribution to that alliance fundamentally. The support
of the Italians for the Atlanticists at this time was something of a surprise.
The Foreign Minister of Italy, Gianni de Michelis, himself citing the frag-
mented response of EC members to the Gulf crisis, had been the first
prominent EC minister to propose that a post-Cold War European Union
be endowed with a military wing. The Italian Foreign Minister had suggested that this could be developed by permitting the EU effectively to take
over the treaty-based commitments and consultative and planning structures, such as they were, of the nine-member Western European Union.[8]

The WEU had started life, as noted, in 1948 under the Brussels Treaty. It
was then known as the 'Western Union', a five-nation pact based on a joint
defence guarantee. Its treaty also committed the members to co-operation
in the economic and cultural spheres. Its life had barely begun, however,
when it was overshadowed, and its putative integrated military structures
taken over, by NATO. This has led most modern-day observers and commentators to doubt that the WEU was ever intended by its creators to
become a serious joint defence arrangement in its own right. Rather, the
dominant view today sees its creation more as a political tactic designed to
help lever the US Congress into supporting a transatlantic defence treaty.
From the early 1950s the WEU, while never officially killed off, enjoyed
only an intermittent existence. It was revived and utilised periodically
when one or more of its member states wished to use it for specific purposes. Such was the case in 1954–5 when the WEU provided an important
part of the overall institutional framework within which West Germany's
accession to NATO and controlled rearmament was managed. Thirty years
later it was 'reactivated' at the suggestion of Belgium and France as a
forum within which distinctly European security concerns could be raised
and discussed. Undoubtedly, for some of its members, the reactivation also
served as a demonstration that the Reagan administration in the USA
could not count on automatic European adherence to what some considered to be its worrying and increasingly wayward policy positions on, for
example, strategic defence and nuclear disarmament.

In the autumn of 1991, it emerged that the Italians and British had
agreed upon a compromise proposal. They envisaged that the WEU would
be reconfigured as a kind of 'bridge' between the new EU and NATO,
while retaining its own institutional identity. In this way, according to the
Anglo-Italian Declaration on European Security and Defence issued in

October 1991, the WEU could act as 'the defence component of the [European] Union and as the means to strengthen the European pillar of the [NATO] Alliance'.[9] The compromise most evident in this joint statement was the Italian one. They had abandoned their previous position supporting the *direct* development of an EU military component. Instead, under the bridge formula, the EU would need to request an autonomous institution to undertake military operations on its behalf. But the UK had also made important concessions, certainly from the rigid opposition to *any* Europe-only military structures that had been displayed by Prime Minister Margaret Thatcher until her fall from power in November 1990. The new government under John Major had, in effect, conceded that an effective NATO monopoly of military security affairs was no longer tenable now that the Cold War was over. Hence the British accepted in principle that the European Union could develop a defence component, albeit indirectly.

The Anglo-Italian bridge formula was accepted virtually word-for-word as the basis of the agreements on defence matters reached at the Maastricht summit in December 1991. Overall, the contents of the Maastricht Treaty were a severe disappointment to those who had favoured decisive progress on the military security front. A declaratory breakthrough was contained in Title V Article J.4 of the Treaty on European Union, where it was stated that, for the first time, the new Union's 'common foreign and security policy shall include all questions relating to the security of the Union'. Previously, under the terms of the Single European Act, only the political and economic dimensions of security had been included, with the military element deliberately left out. On the other hand, Article J.4 was vague in the extreme, noting only an aspiration towards 'the *eventual* framing of a common defence policy, which *might in time* lead to a common defence [emphases added]'.[10]

The subsequent record in practice of the new EU–WEU link was one of severely limited operational achievement. This reflected the lack of consensus among the EU/WEU member states, who overlapped substantially, but not completely,[11] on the deployment of any substantial military forces under the auspices of the WEU. In December 1992 the WEU's Secretary-General, Willem van Eekelen, suggested possible ground-force deployments by WEU member states in Bosnia.[12] This suggestion was ignored. Two years later it was the turn of the French to be rebuffed when they reportedly urged their WEU partners to intervene militarily to try to halt the genocide in Rwanda.[13] During 1994, WEU member states were also castigated by members of the institution's own Parliamentary Assembly, who stated that:

> The theoretical framework exists, but apparently the political will among the changing coalitions of member states to implement a policy to which everybody has agreed is still lacking. The reluctance to act, which is particularly manifest in the time-consuming beating around the bush and procedural battles in the [WEU] Council, is tarnishing

the image of the organisation. This is especially exasperating when it concerns limited operations such as [in the Bosnian town of] Mostar where swift action would be possible with a coalition of the willing.

Member state behaviour was, in short, according to this report, character-ised by 'shuffling, reluctance, and hesitant, slow actions'.[14]

WEU members' collective response to the civil strife in Albania during 1997 also came in for criticism. It would not be fair to say that the WEU did nothing in this instance. It was decided to organise and dispatch a 'Multi-national Police Advisory Element' (MAPE) to the country to help in the reconstruction of the Albanian police forces and their retraining along democratic lines. Only about 100 personnel were assigned to the MAPE in 1998, however, and this prompted criticisms that it represented little more than a token operation. Certainly it was widely felt, from the WEU Secretary-General down, that the reluctance of the institution's member states to consider a military intervention seriously at the height of the fight-ing represented a particular failure. In the event the initiative was taken by the Italian government, which pulled together an *ad hoc* military coalition of mainly Southern European states for a humanitarian relief operation.[15]

In Berlin, in June 1996, NATO Foreign Ministers had formally agreed to a set of guidelines covering institutional and operational co-operation with the WEU. These, they declared, were designed to facilitate the provision of practical NATO support to 'WEU-led operations'. At the time, press cover-age was replete with statements suggesting that a turning point in transat-lantic security relations had been reached.[16] Subsequent, and more sober-minded, scholarly analysis has painted a somewhat different picture, however. Paul Cornish has argued that the agreement would effectively make the WEU/EU dependent on NATO and thus ensure that it was 'most unlikely that a serious rival to NATO could now develop'.[17] Philip Gordon's analysis has led him to the same conclusion. Gordon argues that each of the major NATO member states in Berlin had important domestic and political reasons for seeking to foster what he calls 'the illusion of Europeanization'. Gordon's prediction was that 'the enhanced role for the WEU pronounced after the Berlin meeting' would turn out to be 'hypo-thetical rather than real'.[18] The validity of such analysis appeared to be borne out by the lack of substantial progress after the Berlin meeting. In the spring of 1999, NATO's Secretary-General, Javier Solana, was still feel-ing the need to write that 'the option of drawing upon NATO's assets and capabilities for European-led peacekeeping and crisis-management mis-sions must become real, not remain hypothetical'.[19]

Potentially highly significant developments had, though, been under way from the autumn of 1998. At an Anglo-French summit meeting held at Saint Malo in December of that year, the British Prime Minister, Tony Blair, together with his French counterpart, President Jacques Chirac, put his name to a Declaration which included the statement that 'in order for the European Union to take decisions and approve military action where the [NATO] Alliance as a whole is not engaged, the Union must be given appropriate structures . . . taking account of the existing assets of the WEU and the evolution of its relations with the EU'.[20] Previous British Conservative governments had, as noted, been in the vanguard of opposition to moves towards the European Union developing a military wing of its own. Hence the insistence in 1991 that the WEU maintain its separate institutional identity and equidistance between the EU and NATO under the bridge formula.

Various related reasons can be ascribed to Blair's eye-catching policy shift. In Chapter 9 of this volume, Stuart Gordon suggests that the most significant was a desire to try to avoid the UK being marginalised in Europe following the launching of stage three of Economic and Monetary Union (i.e., the Euro) on 1 January 1999 in which the UK would not participate for the time being. Coupled with this, it was clear by the autumn of 1998 that the WEU was not going to develop into a significant European security institution in its own right. Five years after the ratification of the Maastricht Treaty, nobody had worked out how the British-inspired bridge concept could work effectively in practice.[21] It may also be, *apropos* of this, that Blair was seeking to develop better relations with the French as a means of trying to create a UK–France–Germany triangle in place of the traditional Franco-German duopoly as the powerhouse of EU decision-making.[22]

Whatever the British Prime Minister's motivations, the Saint Malo agreement undoubtedly gave rise to the significant new momentum that produced the Cologne and Helsinki EU summit agreements in June and December 1999, respectively. These two meetings, as noted by Wyn Rees in Chapter 6 of this volume, had the effect of foreshadowing the end of the WEU as a separate international organisation and the setting, for the first time, of concrete targets for the development of an EU military capability. At the same time, Rees notes the significant practical obstacles that remain to these targets actually being achieved. The EU and its member states still have a long way to go before they develop an effective and credible hard security dimension to their institution. There has been positive-sounding talk and promising paper agreements before: at the Maastricht summit in 1991 and in Berlin at the NATO Foreign Ministers' meeting in 1996. Yet these yielded little in the way of tangible capability. This was amply demonstrated by the US domination of Operation Allied Force, the air operation over Serbia and Kosovo between March and June 1999. Taken overall, two main stumbling blocks had become apparent by the second half of 2000. One was institutional and the other may be described as cultural.

The major institutional issues and debates are principally concerned with the development of relations between the EU and NATO. These needed to be worked up from scratch given the Cold War legacy of complete non-contact between the two institutions. A start was made at the EU's summit in Portugal in June 2000 when the creation of four EU–NATO Working

Groups was suggested. These, the EU members agreed, would have specific remits to consider 'security issues, capabilities, goals, modalities enabling EU access to NATO assets and capabilities and the definition of permanent arrangements for EU–NATO consultation'.[23] In November 2000, an initial pledging session was held where EU members made broad offers of forces to help fulfil the 'headline goals' outlined at Helsinki eleven months previously. It was made clear in the agreed declaration that the EU's putative military staff, themselves effectively transferred from the WEU, had drawn upon NATO expertise in preparing an indicative 'force catalogue'. The declaration also stated, when establishing an 'evaluation mechanism' in order to facilitate continued progress towards the headline goals, that

> it will . . . rely on technical data emanating from existing NATO mechanisms such as the Defence Planning Process and the Planning and Review Process . . . via consultations between experts in a working group set up on the same model as that which operated for the drawing up of the capabilities catalogue.[24]

Although these were only relatively limited first steps, their significance should not be underestimated. For the first time during 2000 a real institution-to-institution relationship between the European Union and NATO began to develop. This suggested that fears expressed in the media and by some politicians, most especially in the UK, that any new EU military component would be bound to weaken NATO, were overblown. From the perspective of the EU and its member states it made practical sense to tap into the established NATO force-planning process. As Martin Smith notes in Chapter 4 of this volume, this force-planning process is one of NATO's main institutional strengths. It is also a unique feature in the hard security arena that no other international institution can match.

With regard to what may be called cultural obstacles, that term is used here in the sense of the culture of the institution as a whole. During the Cold War period, the European Community consolidated its international position on the basis of its civilian power economic strength and the exemplary influence accruing from its status as a prototype model of sophisticated and enduring pooling of national sovereignty in key policy areas. Since the member states first began to explore the possibilities of complementing these with a more active role in 'conventional' foreign policy in 1970, a body of opinion has developed which takes the view that this would be a regressive step and that the Community/Union should not become 'just another military superpower'. This viewpoint was trenchantly articulated by Johan Galtung as early as 1973.[25] It has never completely disappeared, notwithstanding the impetus given to those who have favoured the militarisation of the European Union successively by the crises in the Gulf, Bosnia and Kosovo during the 1990s. Potential difficulties were compounded in January 1995 when Austria, Finland and Sweden joined the EU; bringing to four the number of neutral members (with the Irish Republic being the other).

In view of these factors it is significant that, parallel to attempts to develop their military dimension, EU members have also announced a 'non-military crisis management track'. A distinct set of headline goals for this civilian dimension were agreed at the June 2000 summit. They established the same time frame as for establishing the military capability: 2003. By then, the member states agreed, they would have assigned 5,000 police officers for potential 'conflict prevention and crisis management' missions under EU auspices. Within this overall number, a force of 1,000 officers should, they declared, be capable of being deployed within thirty days.[26] In view of this twin-track development it is entirely possible that on future operations and missions the EU will not become directly involved on the military side but will, rather, concentrate instead on the deployment of civilian police officers. A precedent, albeit indirect and limited, exists with the deployment of the WEU's MAPE teams to Albania in 1997 and 1998 where, as noted above, they were involved in the retraining of that country's police forces.

No firm conclusions are yet possible on the likelihood of the European Union developing a meaningful military component. There are certainly substantial difficulties in the way of achieving this goal. On the other hand, the scale of the progress which had already been made by late 2000 should not be underestimated. For the first time in the history of the institution, in its various guises, the member states had collectively agreed to a set of concrete targets covering the scale of potential operations and also a time frame within which to make appropriate forces available. They had followed this up by identifying specific military forces that they would, in principle, be prepared to make available. Perhaps most significantly, a co-operative relationship with NATO had been initiated and EU members appeared to have accepted that in practice no viable military dimension was possible without significant help from Europe's established hard security institution. Thus, the jury remained out and any attempt to predict the ultimate verdict would be a very risky exercise.

Supporting the new democracies?

Operation PHARE: a lighthouse at the end of the tunnel?

The moral imperative behind the creation of a pan-European order has long been a significant factor in debates about European integration. Writing at the outbreak of the Second World War in September 1939, Richard Coudenhove-Kalergi outlined three visions for Europe in the second part of the twentieth century. The first was of 'the joining up of Europe and the Soviet Union as a consequence of social revolution'; the second, 'the establishment in Central Europe of the Third Reich's hegemony, which will then be extended over all of Europe by war or the threat of war'; the third, 'a voluntary union of Europe in a league of free and equal nations'.[27] The triumph of federalism over Soviet communism and national socialism was viewed as the only means by which European states would be able to achieve a lasting, peaceful order. This sentiment was also present following the negotiation of the Treaty of Rome in 1957. Jean Monnet commented then that 'human nature does not change, but when nations and men accept the same rules and the same institutions to make sure that they are applied, their behaviour towards each other changes. This is the process of civilisation itself.'[28]

While it is generally acknowledged today that the burden of post-Cold War system transformation rests on the shoulders of the fledgling democracies in Central and Eastern Europe, the EU states have a significant contribution to make in ensuring the success of this historic process. System transformation is usually interpreted as a dual process of democratisation and marketisation; that is, the creation of a Western-style multi-party democratic system and liberal market economy. The approach taken here is to add an equally important third element: integration. The creation of outward-looking political elites and a functioning economy equipped to cope with the competitive pressures of the global market are in danger of being inhibited if CEE states remain marginalised from the supportive environment of EU membership.

When Soviet General Secretary Mikhail Gorbachev launched his reform programme in 1985 and initiated a process that would sweep away Soviet communism in Central and Eastern Europe by the end of the decade, few observers could have anticipated that any of the CEE states would entertain realistic hopes of EU membership in the near to medium term. The start of accession negotiations in March 1998 came just ten years after Hungary, the most reform-minded of the Soviet-type states, had initiated its programme of economic and political reform. On the other hand, the EU has been heavily criticised for its vacillation in not providing a clear statement regarding prospects for accession for the CEE states until 1993 and for long prevaricating in setting a target date for entry.

The same mixed assessment can be made in relation to the EU's provision of economic support. The idea of a Western assistance programme for Hungary and Poland was first discussed in July 1989 at the G7 summit in Paris. Discussion was broadened out to cover the G24 (comprising the current fifteen member states of the EU, the USA, Canada, Australia, Turkey, New Zealand, Switzerland, Japan, Norway and Iceland) with the European Commission requested to co-ordinate the allocation of the aid. The European Council, under the supervision of the French Presidency, followed up on the Paris G7 summit with the creation of the European Bank for Reconstruction and Development in November 1989 and Operation PHARE a month later, following the Strasbourg European Council. Having initially allocated 300 million ECU, the G24 rapidly expanded

Operation PHARE in 1990 to cover Bulgaria, Czechoslovakia, the German Democratic Republic, Romania and Yugoslavia, with an additional 200 million ECU provided.[29]

Avery and Cameron have described Operation PHARE as 'the largest technical assistance programme in history' and it is indeed an admirable example of multilateral co-operation.[30] The temptation to compare Operation PHARE with the European Recovery Programme or Marshall Plan after the Second World War is evident,[31] but considerable differences existed between the levels and conditions surrounding the economic assistance provided. Whereas Marshall Aid constituted in the region of an average annual contribution of 1.3 per cent of US GNP during 1948–52, which has been estimated to be approximately 50 billion ECU per annum at current prices, Operation PHARE, by the end of 1999, had distributed 11 billion ECU in total. Moreover, as Mayhew notes, financial contributions were subsequently run down as EU accession funding became more prominent and, apart from Japan's continuing financial support, the G24 process is effectively 'dead'.[32] There are other substantial differences between the European Recovery Programme and Operation PHARE. It is difficult to equate six years of wartime devastation with forty years of economic mismanagement and infrastructural neglect in CEE countries.[33] In the 1940s, the West European states were already equipped with established market mechanisms and with the appropriate legal, institutional, political and socio-psychological environments. Today, the CEE states are undergoing a unique system transformation process from the authoritarian, command-economic system imposed under Soviet domination to a broadly Western-style, liberal democratic market economy.

Thus, it is not straightforward to see how assistance is best provided given the more ambitious project of implanting the 'Western Idea' into Central and Eastern European societies. Furthermore, while the Marshall Plan was driven by strong US economic and political self-interest in ensuring the successful reconstruction of the West European economies, questions surrounding the amount and use of the financial aid provided by the PHARE donors were more complicated.[34] In acknowledging the differences of context between 1945 and 1989–90, Pinder concluded in 1991: 'it does not follow that, because the US gave a certain percentage of its GDP in 1948–52, the EC should give the same proportion now'. On the other hand, 'its political leaders would show a shameful lack, not just of generosity, but an ability to grasp the essentials of enlightened self-interest, if they were unable to see that the needs of Eastern Europe may call, over the next five years, for a substantially larger programme than the present one'.[35]

PHARE assistance has been co-ordinated predominantly through national programmes but has also covered multinational and cross-border programmes. Poland has been the largest single recipient through national programmes, receiving 1,022 million ECU during 1995–9 with Romania (649 million ECU) and Hungary (476 million ECU) the next largest recipients in the same period.[36] The objectives and manner in which PHARE has been co-ordinated have also changed over time. Whereas funding was initially directed at transition aid through bilateral or national programmes, a multilateral structured dialogue procedure was initiated at the Essen European Council summit in December 1994 with the objective that aid would be directed more towards accession preparations. As a result, the focus of aid has been shifting from technical assistance initiatives to investment support with a growing emphasis placed on cross-border initiatives.[37] Following an idea proposed by the European Parliament in 1992, PHARE support has also been directed at democratisation projects such as training in parliamentary practices, promoting and monitoring human rights, developing independent media and promoting trade union democracy.

To what extent have the EU assistance programmes really helped to narrow the wealth and prosperity gap between East and West? A cursory glance at the persisting socio-economic disparities between the EU and CEE states demonstrates that much progress still needs to be made. A key debate during the early 1990s was whether 'shock therapy', that is, the sudden exposure to market forces as applied in Poland, or 'gradualism', a more incremental introduction of market forces as applied in Hungary, was the most appropriate means of achieving system transformation in Central and Eastern Europe.

In general, the more industrialised economies of Central Europe are coping better with the transformation process than are the less industrialised states of Eastern Europe. This in itself is not surprising, although caution must be exercised in generalising too much.[38] Growth rates in the region, however, suggest that progress, following an output collapse in the early 1990s, was being made in all states despite occasional setbacks. There should, however, be no doubt about the immensity of the challenge in terms of integrating the economies of the EU member states and those of the CEE states.

The difference in GDP is considerable. Whereas, in 1998–9, EU GDP per capita was $21,833, the 'ins' (minus Cyprus) had a per capita GDP of $3,330 and the 'pre-ins'[39] just $1,716 or 15 per cent and 8 per cent of the EU per capita, respectively. Even using the per capita GDP of the four poorest EU member states (Spain, Ireland, Portugal and Greece) with a combined population of 63.6 million at $12,166, the 'ins', very close in population terms with a combined population of 62.2 million, reached only 27 per cent of this figure. Only Slovenia with a per capita GDP of $8,200 came close to the poorest of the EU member states, Greece, which had a per capita GDP of $8,210.[40]

The comparison is less daunting if the measurement of Purchasing Power Standards (PPS), based on a basket of goods and services, is used. Using these figures, Slovenia had 68 per cent of the EU average at 13,000 PPS, which was not too different to that of Greece (13,100 PPS) and Portugal (13,400 PPS), while the Czech Republic had 63 per cent of the EU average at 12,000 PPS. The CEE average of 7,500 PPS represented 40 per cent of the EU average of 19,000 PPS in 1997. This was a significant rise on the figures in 1995 when the CEE average stood at 6,600 PPS (representing an increase of 14 per cent).[41]

Whatever the basis of the calculation, there is no avoiding the conclusion that closing the economic gap between the EU and CEE states will take a considerable period of time. While the EU states can and should continue to assist the CEE states, their aid programmes are unlikely to make a decisive difference by themselves. The impetus for the necessary reform and restructuring can ultimately only be generated from within the Eastern states themselves. Nevertheless, a strong argument can be made that the EU can help this process, most significantly by enlarging its membership to embrace a progressively larger number of CEE states. It is to this issue that the discussions here now turn.

EU enlargement: on permanent hold?

Virtually all the CEE states have made a 'Return to Europe' – that is, entry into the EU (and NATO) – a key benchmark of success in their overall system transformations. Prospective EU membership is viewed as providing a conducive environment for the creation of compatible economic systems to facilitate trade, for the subsequent amelioration of socio-economic disparities as economic growth accelerates and, finally, for the generation of Western-style political, administrative and legal structures with concomitant value systems. The initial reluctance exhibited by the EU in response to CEE requests for membership and the subsequent unwillingness to set firm target dates for accession have been subject to widespread criticism, as noted. It was not until 1993 that the European Council in Copenhagen first announced its willingness to take applications for membership from Central and Eastern Europe. In doing so it laid down the following criteria:

1 The capacity of the country concerned to assume the obligations of membership (the *acquis communautaire*).
2 The stability of institutions in the candidate country guaranteeing democracy, the rule of law, human rights and respect for minorities.
3 The existence of a functioning market economy.
4 The candidate's endorsement of the objectives of political, economic and monetary union.
5 The candidate's capacity to cope with competitive pressure and market forces within the EU.
6 The Union's capacity to absorb new members while maintaining the momentum of European integration.[42]

The most frustrating aspect of the entry criteria for the applicant states is the condition that the current members are able to 'absorb' the new states.

During the EU's intergovernmental conference of 1996–7, enlargement was highlighted as the major challenge confronting it. However, the resulting Treaty of Amsterdam failed to agree on the institutional and financial reforms necessary to facilitate enlargement and postponed discussion to a further conference that would be held prior to enlargement's commencement. The European Council summit in Amsterdam in June 1997 did agree that accession negotiations would commence in March 1998. It was decided at the Luxembourg European Council summit in December 1997 that accession talks would include all applicant states (except Turkey) but that prospective entry would be limited to the Czech Republic, Estonia, Hungary, Poland, Slovenia and Cyprus. The tensions provoked by the decision to segregate the candidates into these 'ins' and second-tier 'pre-ins' were later acknowledged and at the Helsinki European Council summit in December 1999 the distinction was removed.[43] It does, however, remain the case that entry will be decided according to the ability of each applicant state to meet the 'Copenhagen Criteria'.

In order to prepare the ground effectively for enlargement, institutional reform should be a clear priority for the EU. As Joschka Fischer, the German Foreign Minister, noted in May 2000:

> Enlargement will render imperative a fundamental reform of the European institutions. Just what would a European Council with thirty heads of state and government be like? Thirty presidencies? How long will Council meetings actually last? Days, maybe even weeks? How, with the system of institutions that exists today, are thirty states supposed to balance interests, take decisions and then actually act? How can one prevent the EU from becoming utterly intransparent, compromises from becoming stranger and more incomprehensible, and the citizens' acceptance of the EU from eventually hitting rock bottom?[44]

The concern that Fischer raised is that the 'Monnet method' of gradual 'functional integration' is unlikely to accommodate the clash of national interests as numbers increase. Some have proposed increased 'flexibility' or a 'multi-speed Europe' as an answer to this problem. But the introduction of such differentiated integration, allowing for states to move towards agreed objectives at varying speeds, could give rise to the danger of reducing identity and cohesion. Fischer's own proposed federalist solution is unlikely to receive an enthusiastic reception in many quarters.

The continuing absence of enlargement carries increasing risks of generating an 'expectations gap' between what the EU is prepared to offer and what the CEE states desire. If the gap grows too wide, widespread disenchantment with the EU *per se* could set in among leaders and publics in the CEE states. The *Central and Eastern Eurobarometer* of public opinion, which is published by the EU Commission on an annual basis, suggests that this danger was present in the late 1990s. In 1998 only Romania among the ten CEE applicant states registered a majority having a positive image of the EU (51 per cent). Only four of the ten states registered a majority in favour of membership if there were to be a referendum on the issue. The average result came out at only 45 per cent in favour (40 per cent if the Romanian result of 85 per cent in favour is removed).[45] These figures supported what had been reported on an anecdotal basis for much of the 1990s. This was that the EU was increasingly considered to be 'closed' and fundamentally protectionist in nature. Polish President Lech Walesa warned in 1991, for example, that the Iron Curtain was in danger of being replaced by a 'silver curtain' between the rich and poor states of Europe.[46]

Institutional enlargement is a vital element in any attempt to extend the established Western-based security community eastwards. From a European integration perspective, enlargement is also intended to serve the objective of spreading economic prosperity. These two together can create order. That said, the EU has so far maintained a cautious position on the question of further enlargement, with the first entrants from Central and Eastern Europe expected to join at some point around the year 2005. Also, it should not be forgotten that enlargement, far from extending order, may provoke disorder if it is handled badly.

Conclusions

The European Union's track record as both a prospective hard and expanding soft security actor in post-Cold War Europe is open to criticism. The question as to whether it will, or should, develop the means to employ military power effectively and cohesively is still open. Its overall effectiveness was undoubtedly limited during the Gulf War and in dealing with the collapse of Yugoslavia during the 1990s because it was not able to go beyond the application of diplomatic and economic instruments. The jury is also still out regarding the long-term impact of Operation PHARE on the economic transformation process in Central and Eastern Europe. The evidence assembled above suggests, however, that targeted technical assistance will not be enough by itself to close the socio-economic gap between members and non-members of the EU in Europe and hence contribute significantly to the effective extension of order.

Hence the crucial importance of enlargement. The dangers of a growing expectations gap in Central and Eastern Europe are now apparent. However, the ability of the EU to absorb new members is as big, if not a bigger, uncertainty as the ability of the applicant states to meet the entry criteria set out in Copenhagen in 1993. Furthermore, the manner in which the EU deals with outsiders – Russia in particular – will provide a big challenge for the future.

Observers can be forgiven a degree of scepticism, even cynicism, regarding the prospects on all these fronts given the gap between rhetoric and reality that existed during the 1990s. As Jean Monnet predicted in the

1950s, European integration has been an incremental and not always steady process. The question is whether events will allow the EU, which only came on the scene in its present form in November 1993, the time to work its way through a sometimes painful post-Cold War adolescence.

Notes and references

1 The views expressed here are personal and should not be construed as representing the views or policy of the British government, Ministry of Defence or the Royal Military Academy, Sandhurst.
2 On the concept of 'overlay' see, *inter alia*, B. Buzan, *People, States and Fear* (second edn). (London: Harvester-Wheatsheaf 1991), pp. 219–21.
3 F. Cameron, *The Foreign and Security Policy of the European Union*. (Sheffield: Sheffield University Press 1999), p. 16.
4 The Single European Act (subsequently amended by the Treaty on European Union). EU website. URL: http://europa.eu.int/abc/obj/treaties/en/entr14a.htm#C_Single_European_Act.
5 Cameron *op.cit.*, p. 19.
6 This term was coined and the concept articulated by François Duchene in the early 1970s. See F. Duchene, 'Europe's Role in World Peace' in R. Mayne (ed.), *Europe Tomorrow*. (London: Fontana 1972), ch. 2 and Duchene, 'The European Community and the Uncertainties of Interdependence' in M. Kohnstamm and W. Hager (eds), *A Nation Writ Large? Foreign Policy Problems before the European Communities*. (London: Macmillan 1973), ch. 1.
7 J. Delors, 'European Integration and Security'. *Survival* 33 (2) 1991, pp. 99–102.
8 'Rome Says EC Should Consider Forming its own "Army for Defence"'. *Independent* 19 September 1990.
9 *Declaration on European Security and Defence.* (London: UK Foreign and Commonwealth Office 1991), p. 2.
10 Treaty on European Union Article J.4. EU website. URL: http://europa.eu.int/abc/obj/treaties/en/entr2f.htm#Article_J.4.
11 Of the fifteen EU members in 2000, only ten were also full members of the WEU. Austria, Denmark, Finland, Ireland and Sweden have contented themselves with observer status.
12 'WEU Urged to Intervene in Bosnia Conflict'. *Financial Times* 9 December 1992.
13 'France Calls for Europe to Act over Rwanda'. *Daily Telegraph* 18 June 1994.
14 *A European Defence Policy.* (Paris: WEU Assembly 1994), pp. 23–6.
15 See the WEU Assembly report 'Public Perception of WEU's Contribution to Stabilising Democracy in Albania'. WEU website. URL: http://www.weu.int/assembly/eng/reports/1650e.html.
16 See, *inter alia*, 'Shedding of US Ties Satisfies NATO Members'. *Independent* 4 June 1996 and 'NATO Acquires European Identity'. *The Economist* 8 June 1996, pp. 43–4.
17 P. Cornish, 'European Security: The End of Architecture and the New NATO'. *International Affairs* 72 (4) 1996, p. 764.
18 P. Gordon, 'Does the WEU Have a Role?' *Washington Quarterly* 20 (1) 1997, pp. 131–4.
19 J. Solana, 'Growing the Alliance'. *The Economist* 13 March 1999, p. 24.
20 Saint Malo Declaration. UK Foreign Office website. URL: http://www.fco.gov.uk/news/newstext.asp?1795.
21 See Stuart Gordon, Chapter 9 in this volume.

22 On this see C. Grant, *Can Britain Lead in Europe?* (London: Centre for European Reform 1998), pp. 80–1.
23 'Santa Maria Da Feira European Council, Presidency Conclusions'. EU website. URL: http://ue.eu.int/en/Info/eurocouncil/index.htm.
24 *Military Capabilities Commitment Declaration.* (Brussels: Council of the European Union 2000).
25 J. Galtung, *The European Community: A Superpower in the Making?* (London: Allen & Unwin 1973).
26 'Santa Maria Da Feira Presidency Conclusions' *op.cit.*
27 R. N. Coudenhove-Kalergi, *Europe Must Unite.* (Glarus: Paneuropa Editions 1939). Extract reprinted in A. G. Harryvan and J. van der Harst (eds), *Documents on European Union.* (London: Macmillan 1997), p. 33.
28 J. Monnet, 'A Ferment of Change'. *Journal of Common Market Studies* 1 (1) 1962. Extract reprinted in B. Nelsen and A. C.-G. Stubb (eds), *The European Union: Readings on the Theory and Practice of European Integration.* (London: Lynne Rienner 1994), p. 24.
29 A. Mayhew, *Recreating Europe: The European Union's Policy towards Central and Eastern Europe.* (Cambridge: Cambridge University Press 1998), pp. 14–16.
30 G. Avery and F. Cameron, *The Enlargement of the European Union.* (Sheffield: Sheffield University Press 1998), p. 19.
31 Both J. Pinder, *The European Community and Eastern Europe.* (London: RIIA 1991) and G. Denton, *A New Europe? Prospects for the Reintegration of East and West.* (London: Her Majesty's Stationery Office 1991) raise the issue of comparison. The leading text covering the European Recovery Programme is A. S. Milward, *The Reconstruction of Western Europe 1945–51.* (London: Methuen 1984).
32 Mayhew *op.cit.*, pp. 133–4.
33 Pinder *op.cit.*, pp. 96–7.
34 See W. Reinicke, *Building a New Europe: The Challenge of System Transformation and Systemic Reform.* (Washington DC: Brookings Institution 1992); M. Hughes, 'Can the West Agree on Aid to Eastern Europe?' *RFE/RL Research Report* 1 (11) 1992 and Mayhew *op.cit.*, p. 133.
35 Pinder *op.cit.*, p. 99.
36 'The PHARE Programme'. EU commission website. URL: http://europa.eu.int/comm/enlargement/pas/phare/index.htm.
37 Mayhew *op.cit.*, pp. 138–43.
38 See G. Blazyca, 'The Politics of Economic Transformation' in S. White *et al.*, *Developments in Central and East European Politics* (second edn). (London: Macmillan 1998), ch. 10.
39 The distinction which the EU formerly drew between the 'ins' and 'pre-ins' is explained below.
40 These figures are based on the discussions in M. A. Smith and G. Timmins, *Building a Bigger Europe: EU and NATO Enlargement in Comparative Perspective.* (Aldershot: Ashgate 2000), pp. 129–31.
41 See Eurostat Press Release No 68/98. (Brussels: European Commission 1998).
42 *Bulletin of the European Communities* 6 1993, p. 13.
43 As at autumn 2000 the applicant states were: Bulgaria, Czech Republic, Estonia, Hungary, Latvia, Lithuania, Poland, Romania, Slovakia, Slovenia, Turkey, Cyprus and Malta.
44 J. Fischer, 'Reflections on the Finality of European Integration'. German Foreign Ministry website. URL: http://www.auswaertiges-amt.government.de/6_archiv/index.htm.
45 *Central and Eastern Eurobarometer 1998.* (Brussels: European Commission 1998).
46 *RFE/RL Report on Eastern Europe* 2 (1) 1993, p. 35.

6 The WEU

Eliminating the middleman

Wyn Rees

Introduction

At the beginning of a new millennium, the Western European Union (WEU) is in the position of disappearing as an international organisation. Although it survived for over fifty years, this fact should not come as a great surprise as its role has always been an uncertain one. During the Cold War the WEU existed in a state of almost suspended animation. It served occasionally as a mechanism to dissipate some of the centrifugal forces between Western Europe and the United States but even its most fervent supporters would have struggled to describe its work as essential.[1]

During the 1990s, it received renewed attention because the European security environment had been transformed by the ending of the Cold War. As an inner defence 'club' among the European states, it found itself at the heart of a debate about the most appropriate structures for providing security: on the one side, an adapted NATO under US leadership and, on the other, a circle of European states seeking to do more for themselves. The WEU has been located at the fulcrum between these two approaches and has been buffeted by the turbulence surrounding the attendant debates. The role assigned to the WEU has been dependent on a range of processes that have been external to the organisation: notably progress in European integration; crises such as in Bosnia, Albania and Kosovo; and the post-Cold War transformation of NATO.

By the end of the 1990s greater clarity had emerged about the future of the WEU. The aspirations of those who had hoped that a European defence identity would arise to eclipse the role of NATO have not been fulfilled. Meanwhile, the Atlantic Alliance has proved its capacity to adapt to new roles such as peacekeeping and peace enforcement and to enlarging its membership. But the alliance still leaves unsatisfied the wishes of some of its European members to be able to act in situations where the United States' interests are not engaged. The European Union has eventually found the requisite consensus to develop a military capacity under its own aegis, enabling it to dispense with the former system of subcontracting defence matters to the WEU. Considering that the EU and the WEU comprise basically the same set of states, this rationalisation of organisations is long overdue.

The evolution of WEU in the 1990s

The WEU in the 1990s embodied the desire of a group of West European states to develop a muscular military capability that would provide an alternative to reliance on NATO. As Martin Smith and Graham Timmins have noted in Chapter 5 of this volume, it was agreed in the Treaty on European Union, in 1992, that the WEU would serve both as the defence arm of the EU and as the European identity within NATO[2] – a kind of middleman equidistant between two more powerful organisations. The EU would 'request' (and later, in the 1997 Amsterdam Treaty, 'avail') this organisation to act on its behalf when the use of military forces was required in furtherance of its Common Foreign and Security Policy (CFSP). This inelegant compromise shrouded a difference of approach among its architects. On the one side were those countries that believed that the process of European economic and political integration should be accompanied by a capacity for military action, that autonomy in defence matters was an essential complement to a political union. On the other side were countries that pointed out the continuing divergences of interest between European states and feared that any duplication of NATO's role could alienate the United States from the security of the continent.[3]

Those states that sought to constrain the EU–WEU nexus, most notably the United Kingdom, were in a powerful position because the intergovernmental nature of decision-making made it impossible to develop either organisation without unanimous support. Hence elaborating the WEU's relationship with the EU proved to be a slow process. Through much of the 1990s there was little sustained contact between the organisations and inadequate sharing of information; all of which was symptomatic of a deep malaise. In addition, attempts to improve the modest military capabilities of the WEU, to render it more operationally capable, remained limited. Certain military forces from among its member states which were already committed to NATO were also made available to the WEU (a process known as 'double-hatting'): a small Planning Staff was made operational in 1993 and this was subsequently complemented by the creation of a Situation Centre in the headquarters in Brussels. A satellite interpretation facility was set up in Torrejon in Spain.[4]

The development of the WEU was further constrained by the absence of political will that was manifest in the CFSP. The Second Pillar of the EU lacked the requisite instruments to make it effective and the European Commission proved to be reluctant to challenge the preserve of national governments by exercising its right of initiative. The resulting CFSP initiatives were timid in nature and the EU proved to be unwilling to task the WEU with operations on any significant scale. The experience of the EU's weakness in the face of the conflict in former Yugoslavia served to under-mine its confidence and the WEU was left to languish on the sidelines. The WEU only undertook a series of relatively minor tasks. One was the joint conduct of embargo operations in the Adriatic with NATO; a second was monitoring an embargo on the River Danube; a third was a police opera-tion in the Bosnian city of Mostar; and a fourth was a mine-clearing assist-ance mission in Croatia.[5] During the crisis in Albania in 1996–7, when anarchy was enveloping the country, the WEU was passed over in the choice of an interventionary force in favour of an *ad hoc* grouping of European states, led by Italy. It was only called upon to provide a Multinational Police Advisory Element (MAPE) once the process of reconstruction in Albania was under way. Although intervention operations had been viewed as poten-tial opportunities for WEU to make a contribution to European security, the political sensitivity of the organisation in the eyes of some national cap-itals led to it being deliberately paralysed.

The failure of the Europeans to build an autonomous military capacity made it imperative that a way be found to reconcile European aspirations with NATO. The Clinton administration facilitated this in January 1994 by embracing the idea of a European Security and Defence Identity (ESDI) constructed inside the Atlantic Alliance and putting forward the concept of Combined Joint Task Forces (CJTF) to make Europe-led operations a real possibility. The USA offered to make some of its national military assets available to its European partners through NATO, so as to remove the need for them to duplicate the alliance's existing capabilities. NATO was being offered as a 'separable but not separate'[6] structure for the con-duct of military operations in which flexible coalitions of states might take the lead. It was envisaged that in the event of a military operation in which US interests were not engaged, the Deputy Supreme Allied Commander in Europe (D-SACEUR) would designate a NATO Multinational Command and appropriate military resources to undertake a mission under the aus-pices of the WEU Council. This apparent generosity disguised a desire by Washington to ensure a *droit de regard* over European actions that might lead to the involvement of the USA. NATO thereby enshrined its right to choose whether to lead in a future crisis.

The French government held out against the CJTF initiative on the grounds that European reliance on the USA was being accentuated. Yet the Chirac government finally acquiesced at the North Atlantic Council meeting in Berlin in June 1996.[7] The absence of a realistic European defence alternative and the experience of the need for US military power in the crises in the Balkans meant that this was the only credible way forward for the ESDI. NATO, under US leadership, had asserted its pri-macy in European security. It had successfully adapted to new roles, such as peacekeeping and peacemaking, and it had also taken the lead in the process of organisational enlargement to the east. A programme of 'Europeanising' NATO was offered to the USA's allies in terms of developing their voice within the alliance and reallocating some of the positions in its command structure. Nevertheless, it was hard to avoid the conclusion that the aspiration for an ESDI, that had been so influential in the first half of the 1990s, had failed to bear fruit. This had resulted from an absence of political will among the European states, especially in relation to spending money on defence, as well as a determination from certain countries, such as the UK, not to put at risk the central role of NATO.

WEU absorption into the European Union

In the 1997 Treaty of Amsterdam (ToA) there was little substantive progress in developing the defence dimension of the EU and, more specifically, drawing the WEU closer to the Union. Although in the lead up to the intergovernmental conference which produced the draft ToA, nine WEU members favoured its eventual integration into the EU, the tenth, the UK, was opposed.[8] The result was that the WEU retained its autonomy and the European Council was denied the right to instruct the organisation. Nevertheless, there were some important signals at Amsterdam that went some way towards compensating for the absence of substantive progress. First, the treaty referred to the objective of 'fostering closer relations'[9] between the two organisations and joint presidencies were called for when a WEU member was in line for the presidency of the Union. Second, the WEU's 'Petersberg Tasks', of humanitarian operations, peacekeeping and the employment of combat forces in crisis management,[10] were formally integrated into the EU's Second Pillar. Third, the WEU was to be fully involved in the setting up of an EU Policy Planning and Early Warning Unit, which was to work on plans on behalf of the CFSP.

The disappointing outcome of the Amsterdam Treaty was subsequently overtaken by a succession of important developments on the European defence scene. At the Cologne and Helsinki European Councils, of June and December 1999, respectively, it was agreed that the WEU would be integrated into the EU and that for an interim period Javier Solana (a former Secretary-General of NATO) would serve as both the High Representative of the CFSP and as the Secretary-General of the WEU. The aim would be for the EU to enjoy 'the capacity for autonomous action, backed up by credible military forces'.[11] A mechanism for deciding upon the commitment of military forces would be placed within the EU's Ministerial Council in order that the CFSP would enjoy access to the full range of instruments, including military force. The Helsinki communiqué declared the EU's intention to strengthen its Common European Security and Defence Policy (CESDP) by creating a Rapid Reaction Force of corps size to be available for deployment by 2003. This force will be capable of being dispatched within sixty days and will be sustainable for a year. It is also intended that appropriate civilian resources for crisis management and post-conflict reconstruction will support the EU's military formations. At the end of the Portuguese presidency of the EU it was announced that the member states had pledged a force of 5,000 police officers to be made available for conflict prevention and crisis management tasks.[12]

The catalyst for this transformation of the EU into a defence actor reflected a perception of European weakness rather than strength. This was particularly the case for the British, whose experiences of the conflicts in the Balkans had resulted in a reassessment of their strategic priorities. Transatlantic relations had been stretched to crisis point by the differing policies advocated by Washington and European capitals in relation to resolving the conflict in Bosnia between 1992 and 1995. The breach in co-operation had been masked by the decisive leadership of the USA, in the summer of 1995, that led to the bombing of the Bosnian Serbs and their subsequent decision to agree to a negotiated peace agreement at Dayton, Ohio. But in 1998–9, a similar difference in transatlantic attitudes arose in relation to Western strategy against the Milosevic regime in Belgrade over the crisis in Kosovo. The US fear of incurring casualties in a ground invasion of Kosovo left NATO with a military plan that was totally reliant upon air power to force the Serbian government to withdraw its military and paramilitary forces. At the same time, the relative military weakness of the Europeans limited the influence that they could exert on the Clinton administration. The British derived the lesson that US–European interests could diverge fundamentally in such post-Cold War crises. In the light of increasingly unpredictable US attitudes towards transatlantic relations, the British became convinced that Europe needed to be capable of doing more in the face of military crises. This factor, together with those discussed by Stuart Gordon in Chapter 9 of this volume, was instrumental in promoting a reappraisal of the UK's approach towards European defence.

The British shift coincided with France's disillusion over its limited success in securing a major restructuring of NATO. Whereas the two states had traditionally differed in their attitudes towards the continental defence debate, a confluence of interests arose in which both desired to build a more powerful military capability within Europe. The result was that the two most important military states on the continent were able to lay the foundations for the Cologne and Helsinki initiatives. The UK, in an unprecedented *volte-face*, signalled its willingness to contemplate the demise of the WEU and entertain a defence role for the EU, at an informal meeting of EU leaders at Pörtschach in October 1998. This was followed in December by the Anglo-French Saint Malo Declaration, which called for an autonomous European military capability that remained compatible with NATO.[13]

The EU was eager to affirm that its intended defence capability would be designed to underpin and not to detract from NATO. The US government was not easily convinced and required numerous reassurances that the Europeans were neither duplicating nor decoupling the alliance. US NATO Ambassador Alexander Vershbow cautioned that greater European efforts should not be achieved at the expense of weakening the US–European relationship. He stated that 'we want the EU to be . . . clear that the development of [a military] capacity will complement and strengthen NATO and not emerge at the expense of the transatlantic link. The EU . . . could bring more clarity to this point.'[14] These fears were symptomatic of a traditional schizophrenia towards European integration in the military sphere. The USA has for a long time berated the Europeans for bearing an insufficient share of the burden in defence, yet conversely becomes agitated about the prospect of losing influence when a concrete European initiative is launched.

The reality of the situation is quite different. The concept of European autonomy continues to be limited by dependence on the USA. NATO remains the cornerstone of collective defence and would be the only organisation capable of conducting major military operations. Consistent with the 1996 Berlin decisions, the USA and its European allies would have to decide how to react to a crisis and whether the alliance would be in charge of the operation. In all but the most limited of Petersberg tasks, if the Europeans take the lead, they will still require US assistance such as logistical, intelligence and communications support. Such a scenario would necessitate two decision-making processes to operate in parallel, one in the European Council and the other in the alliance's North Atlantic Council. Both of these processes will be subject to decision-making by unanimity and will be susceptible to national vetoes.

Building a defence structure within the EU

Having taken the decision in principle to phase out the WEU, the EU has set about modelling its own internal structures to incorporate defence. The Union requires politico-military advice to be available to ministers in a crisis situation as well as prepared plans and inventories of military assets that can be tailored to the demands of specific situations. Based on the Cologne decisions, it appears likely that a dedicated Defence Council will be formed, consisting of Ministers of Defence, rather than the existing General Affairs Council meeting on special occasions with Ministers of Defence in attendance. Within the Council structure a Political and Security Committee (PSC), consisting of political directors from member states, will provide the requisite expertise on how to handle a crisis. A Franco-German proposal was put forward for the CFSP High Representative to hold the presidency of the PSC. Specialised military knowledge will be forthcoming from a Military Committee (MC) comprising national Chiefs of Defence Staff, or their representatives, and a Military Staff (MS) will serve as the secretariat.

All of these structures will draw heavily upon their WEU forerunners: the WEU Council, the Political–Military Group, the Military Committee and the Military Staff (formerly the Planning Cell). In addition, the EU will be able to benefit from the generic planning that was generated within the former WEU Planning Cell. The WEU has provided a source of expertise for the EU during its own process of constructing defence structures. Thus, for example, the WEU Military Staff helped to generate the 'force catalogue' against which EU member states' initial offers of forces for potential EU operations in November 2000 could be measured.

However, the problems of realising even a modest CESDP should not be underestimated. First is the undeniable reality that the EU is moving into an unknown domain. Some analysts have argued against the EU developing a defence competence on the grounds that its civilian character, which can be interpreted as a unique source of strength, would be compromised.[15] It will certainly take some time before the EU will build up its own body of experience in defence matters, even though its WEU inheritance will speed up the transition process. Nor can it be discounted that there will be tensions within the structures designed to take defence decisions. For example, it is possible that friction will develop between the PSC and the EU's Committee of Permanent Representatives (COREPER), the latter having traditionally been the filter for all advice ascending to the Council.[16] The lines of demarcation between the two bodies are insufficiently clear and the PSC may seek to circumvent COREPER, particularly in a time of crisis. There are also grounds for anticipating problems arising between the culture of a Military Staff working alongside a civilian Council secretariat.

A second area of controversy surrounds the article five collective defence guarantee embodied in the 1954 Modified Brussels Treaty. This guarantee, more robust even than that of NATO, underpinned the WEU for its entire history but it was operationalised through NATO. The process of absorbing the WEU into the EU presents a thorny political problem of what to do with the redundant article five. Only France, thus far, has argued for this to be included in the EU's Second Pillar: governments in Paris have long been opposed to the idea of NATO being the sole guarantor of collective defence in Europe. A second option would be to leave article five in a state of suspended animation. This would have the benefit of avoiding the need to dismantle an important political symbol and it would leave the way open for the guarantee to be resurrected at a possible future date.[17] The final option would be to attach the article five guarantee to the Second Pillar of the EU as an optional protocol. This would enable those states that wish to be committed to its provisions to sign, while other countries could stand apart.

The diverse membership of the European Union presents a third area of difficulty. There are states within the EU – Austria, Ireland, Finland and Sweden – which have long been committed to a policy of armed neutrality. Yet these states now find themselves within a Union that is evolving a significant defence dimension. Denmark, although not a neutral state, is also uneasy about the new developments because it has always opposed duplicating the NATO framework. By confining the changes to Petersberg tasks these five states have been able to accept the new arrangements. But the neutrals have been given influence over military issues that they did not enjoy in their old status as WEU observers and there are potential implications for the ten WEU full members that any broadening of defence tasks could be constrained by the attitudes of the neutrals.

A fourth problem concerns states outside the EU that fear being excluded by the new defence provisions. Among the non-EU members of NATO, Turkey in particular has expressed disquiet at the prospect of being sidelined from the mainstream discourse. It has received support for its views from the United States.[18] Turkey has pressed for EU decision-making on defence matters to involve the non-EU members of NATO, in order to ensure that its own interests are not neglected in favour of those of its rival, Greece. It has a potent source of influence in that its status in the North Atlantic Council grants it a veto power over the release of alliance assets in a CJTF operation. By the time of the Feira EU summit in June 2000, Turkey (as well as Norway) had formally expressed its interest in offering military capabilities to an EU intervention force, but expressed disquiet that the EU was asserting its autonomy of decision over defence matters in relation to the non-EU NATO members.[19]

A related problem has been the fear expressed by the WEU's 'associate partner' states in Central and Eastern Europe at the prospect of losing the high level of intimacy on security matters that they had become accustomed to through this relationship with the WEU. For instance, military representatives from the associate partners attended the Military Committee of the WEU, they participated in the Planning Cell and they enjoyed representation at the Torrejon Satellite Centre. Not only are such states concerned at the prospect of being sidelined on security matters but they are also wary of the potential impact on the accession process to the EU. The inclusion of defence within the Union might be employed as a further factor to slow down the enlargement process or even contribute towards the creation of a multi-tier European Union. While the December 1999 Helsinki communiqué went some way towards reassuring these countries that the EU was mindful of their concerns, there is no doubt that many of the associate partners remained anxious about their future.

A final problem relates to the need to ensure accountability in the area of the CESDP. Financial accountability is one area of concern. Although the new decision-making structures within the Council can be financed within the existing budget, the prospect of catering for operational tasks will demand additional resources. If access to the EU budget is to be sanctioned then this raises the question of the level of oversight that will be granted to the Union's institutions – something which countries like the UK and France have regarded as anathema. A second topic for concern is the democratic accountability of the new arrangements. The ability of national parliaments to hold their governments to account is limited: they can usually only instigate *post facto* investigations of crises, with reports appearing many months later. They are unable to make inputs into the development of policy. National parliaments are likely to experience difficulties with the proposed new arrangements due to the presence of 'variable geometry': decision-making in the military sphere could take place partly within the context of the EU but partly within NATO. There is also likely to be some differentiation with member states participating to varying degrees in some measures but not in others.

All the above factors, coupled with the inherent secrecy that accompanies defence decisions, render accountability problematic. No additional powers have been granted to supranational organs to maintain scrutiny over the CESDP. The European Commission, in the light of its track record in CFSP, is likely to play only an ephemeral role in the area of defence and is concentrating its focus upon contributing to civilian crisis management tasks. The European Parliament possesses only limited powers of accountability in foreign and security policy. It has the right to be consulted but has no direct input into decision-making. The European Parliament has also found itself engaged in a struggle with the WEU Parliamentary Assembly over accountability issues in relation to the CESDP. The WEU Parliamentary Assembly has sought to perpetuate a role for its members by creating a European Security and Defence Assembly to continue after the demise of the WEU. In all, therefore, the modalities for ensuring accountability over defence matters, which are increasingly being undertaken in the name of 'Europe', remain problematic.

Military capabilities for European defence

The core issue in the development of a meaningful European security and defence policy remains the military capabilities that the member states can generate during a conflict and their political will to place their personnel in harm's way. One of the characteristics of the continental defence debate during the 1990s was its preoccupation with organisational architectures and the drafting of declarations – at the expense of enhancing actual military capabilities. As a result, when crises have occurred, a persistent gap has been apparent between the situational demands of a conflict and what Europeans have been able and willing to do. Military weakness has served to undermine the credibility of Europe's determination to act.

Enhancing Europe's capacity to act will require additional defence spending at a difficult time politically. It is hard to ratchet up defence expenditure during a period in which domestic audiences do not perceive there to be significant military threats to security. The expectation in the post-Cold War period has been for defence budgets to decline and, in the case of countries such as Germany, military expenditure has fallen to only 1.5 per cent of the gross national product. Until 1995 France was the only European nation to resist the temptation to reduce its defence spending but since the Chirac presidency even France's defence budget has declined. In the light of the new EU defence initiative, France and the UK have argued that a form of convergence criterion should be established in order for common Europe-wide efforts in defence to be agreed and then periodic reviews undertaken to measure progress.[20] Such targets would create peer pressure for improvements to be implemented and would address the problem of sharing burdens more equitably. The French presidency of the EU, during the second half of 2000, witnessed the first of what may become a series of Capabilities Commitment Conferences in which states pledge themselves to attain specific military goals. The first conference, in November 2000, was dedicated to fulfilling the broad Helsinki 'headline goals' within the agreed timescale (i.e., by 2003).

The objective in the CESDP has been to underpin the new defence structures with muscular military capabilities. The British, drawing on the experience of their Strategic Defence Review in 1998, have been at the forefront of defining European force priorities. In the words of British Defence Secretary, Geoffrey Hoon, the EU must pursue the goals of greater 'deployability, sustainability, flexibility, mobility, survivability and interoperability'.[21] The focus is on joint force packages, experienced in working together, that can be transported to crisis zones at short notice. Once in a theatre of operations, these forces must be able to respond to a variety of demands across the spectrum of conflict and possess the necessary logistical support to remain *in situ* until the mission is completed. The experience of the Implementation Force/Stabilisation Force and Kosovo Force missions in the Balkans has reinforced the lesson that large numbers of personnel on rotational deployments can be required for indefinite periods of time in peacekeeping operations.

The current reliance of many EU states on force structures configured around conscription is one issue that has been highlighted for remedial action. US Deputy Secretary of State Strobe Talbott stated in December 1999 that 'too many allies have too many men and women under arms focused on missions of the past'.[22] Professional armed forces, staffed by experienced personnel, are considered more appropriate to the types of tasks that can arise, ranging from the evacuation of civilians from an internal conflict to a peacemaking operation demanding high-intensity warfare. The EU commitment to develop a 'headline' rapid reaction capability of 50,000–60,000 personnel is an attempt to provide the nucleus of a European intervention force. Countries such as France, Italy and Spain have begun the process of phasing out conscription, but this will take many years to complete. Germany, on the other hand, remains committed to preserving a system of national service for socio-political reasons that owe much to its own history. US Defense Secretary William Cohen called upon Germany to reconsider its position over professionalisation during a speech to senior officers in the Bundeswehr in December 1999, indicating that this would be a leitmotif for his government in determining the seriousness of Europe's intent.[23] A government-sponsored panel of inquiry on reform of the German armed forces, chaired by former President Richard von Weizsäcker, recommended a dramatic reduction in the future size of the intake of conscripts, from 130,000 to 30,000.[24] Whether Defence Minister Rudolf Scharping will prove to be as radical as this in his decisions on the long-term future of conscription in the Bundeswehr remains to be seen.

Determining where conflicts may occur and possessing the means to deploy at short notice are other factors exercising the minds of European military planners. Members of the EU have long been aware of their deficiencies in power projection assets, such as long-range air- and sea-lift capabilities, but little progress has been made in addressing these weaknesses. In some crises, European states have been forced to hire transport aircraft from countries such as Ukraine to remedy their own shortfall, and under an initiative on future mobility, European states have been considering the use of commercial air- and sea-lift resources in crises. The Future Large Aircraft programme, built around the A400M heavy lift transport aircraft from the Airbus consortium, continues to be the best hope for a comprehensive enhancement of Europe's ability to deploy forces to distant theatres. France and Germany have signalled their intention to procure this aircraft and, in a step designed to demonstrate solidarity with its allies, the British government announced in May 2000 that it would purchase twenty-five A400M transporters for the Royal Air Force. In the meantime, until those aircraft have been manufactured, the UK will hire four US C17 Globemaster aircraft to meet its immediate requirements.[25]

The experience of the Kosovo conflict reminded the Europeans of their need to invest in high-technology military goods. The USA provided the bulk of the combat aircraft and the precision-guided munitions in the air operations against Serbia. For their part, the Europeans found that some of their aircraft were unable to bomb with pinpoint accuracy, that their stockpiles of munitions were rapidly exhausted and that their communications systems were of an insufficient standard. The prowess of the US military capabilities was not the result of mere good fortune, but of high levels of spending and targeted research and development. US spending on high-technology research, for instance, accounts for 30 per cent of its defence budget, a figure which far exceeds that of Europe.[26] European allies need to think strategically about their high-technology research, for example in areas such as electronic warfare capabilities and intelligence satellites. In the case of the latter, while the WEU's satellite facility at Torrejon will provide a welcome source of information for EU decision-makers in the future, it is only an interpretation centre. Torrejon does not have the ability to task its own dedicated satellites and has relied upon commercially available imagery, which could be denied to it during a crisis.[27] In the early 1990s France sought to persuade partners like Germany that European satellite programmes, such as Helios and Horus, were vital facets of European independence. At a Franco-German summit in Mayence in June 2000, the two countries reopened the question of procuring an independent European satellite capability.[28]

Efforts to develop a more muscular European military capability inevitably extend to the issue of realising a common European armaments market. If arms could be procured rationally on a Europe-wide basis, with economies of scale and the possibility of national specialisations, then spending power might be substantially increased. Allies have continued to fund multiple programmes even in the case of very expensive weapon platforms. For example, Germany, Italy, Spain and the UK have invested in the European Fighter Aircraft (EFA), while France has developed the Rafale and Sweden has brought into service the Gripen. National projects have continued to duplicate each other as governments have attached a premium to preserving their own defence industrial base, ensuring employment and protecting technological vitality. Countries have remained wedded to the principle of *juste retour* in dealings with their neighbours.

Amid this situation defence companies in the commercial world have undertaken their own programmes of closures and mergers in the face of the shrinking markets for defence goods. Intergovernmental progress in procurement, however, has been limited and all initiatives have taken place outside of the EU. One initiative was the West European Armaments Group (WEAG), comprising the WEU states plus Denmark, Turkey and Norway; another was the Joint Armaments Co-operation Structure (JACS) which has attempted to create a common industrial strategy among a key group of states. What is needed is a top-down strategy, driven from within the EU, which seeks to rationalise defence industries and harness them to the evolving military demands of the member states. There would be nothing to prevent the Union from importing and further developing the existing procurement initiatives,[29] which could be placed under the remit of a European Armaments Agency – a declaratory goal of the EU since the signing of the Treaty on European Union. Speaking to the French Senate in June 2000, CFSP High Representative Javier Solana stated that 'the Union's security and defence policy must be able to take support under every circumstance from an autonomous capacity for arms supplies'.[30]

Future developments

The EU has embarked on a process in which its destination is uncertain. While it has agreed to build a military decision-making capacity within the Union along with dedicated armed forces under its control, it is unclear where this may lead in the longer term. What is apparent is that there are differences of opinion among the key actors about the nature of this process. At one end of the spectrum is the United States, standing apart from the mechanics of the process, yet with a vital interest in how it develops. It remains suspicious of a process that it cannot influence directly and that risks diminishing America's primacy in European defence matters. Towards the middle of the spectrum stands the UK, with a desire to enhance European military capabilities but prevent any actions that could undermine the NATO alliance. At the far end of the spectrum are countries such as France which possess a more ambitious goal for the CESDP. The reconciling of these different attitudes will determine the path and the extent of the success of the EU's defence initiative.

The British government's priorities in relation to a prospective European Rapid Reaction Force are illustrative of its wider attitudes towards the future of the CESDP. The British regard the most likely role of the force as a European contribution to a NATO-led military operation. If European interests during a crisis prove to be coterminous with the United States', then the UK would advocate the employment of NATO rather than rely on a European framework. The UK regards the EU initiative as a means to galvanise the efforts of its allies and attaches much less emphasis to its independent value – except as a last resort. In March 2000, Defence Secretary Geoffrey Hoon argued that the granting of a defence status to the EU will have the principal benefit of ensuring that the Union is an 'intelligent customer' of NATO's military resources, rather than a military actor in its own right.[31]

Consistent with this approach, the UK has argued for NATO operating procedures and planning guidelines to serve as the model for the European defence capability. This would guarantee compatibility with the NATO Defence Capabilities Initiative, an agenda for improving the military resources of the alliance which was launched with US backing at the fiftieth anniversary summit in Washington in April 1999. The UK insisted that the Cologne summit communiqué contained words that decried the objective of duplicating NATO and instead committed the EU to 'full mutual consultation, cooperation and transparency with the Alliance'.[32] The UK envisages that the existing NATO military representatives will be double-hatted to serve on the EU Military Committee, so that complementary advice will be available to the two organisations. Such measures as these would contribute to the development of an efficient interface between the EU and the alliance, thereby facilitating rapid and co-ordinated action in an emergency.

France, on the other hand, has tended to place greater emphasis on institutional structures and has long believed that a European defence identity should be an equal, rather than subordinate, pillar in the alliance. France is likely to be more ambitious about the roles that a European defence capability should perform.[33] It believes that the Rapid Reaction Force should provide the kernel of a larger European military capability and has proposed that an additional force should be established for the North Mediterranean area.[34] After all, European states possess nearly two million people in uniform and so the target of establishing a single corps is modest in relation to potential capabilities. France is desirous of higher defence spending among its allies in order to realise this goal. There is an expectation within France that the emergence of a European capability will generate its own momentum and will reduce the traditionally dominant position of the USA on defence questions. For practical and political reasons it stresses the concept of EU autonomy in military capacity and decision-making. The French government has expressed its opposition to British desires for EU defence planning to be based on NATO guidelines. It would prefer the Union to adopt its own separate format in order to assert its separation from US oversight and it is suspected in some quarters of contributing to 'foot-dragging' within the EU over establishing an interface with the alliance.[35]

The real test, as far as French officials are concerned, will arise over whether the USA will be prepared to stand aside in some crises and grant the EU the opportunity to act as the lead organisation. Only as a result of such situations will the EU have the chance to build the requisite experience and self-confidence. Since the early 1990s Europe has possessed an independent military force of corps size, the Eurocorps, consisting of France, Germany, Belgium, Spain and Luxembourg. Its weakness has lain in the fact that the UK and Italy have not been members and that Germany remained constrained in its capacity to deploy troops outside of its territory. As a result, the Eurocorps was never used in a crisis situation and remained a largely symbolic force. Yet France has advocated the use of European-led forces in the past; such as the deployment of the WEU in Croatia in September 1991, the European 'Extraction Force' to rescue OSCE monitors in Kosovo in 1998–9 and the employment of the Eurocorps headquarters to command KFOR in Kosovo from April 2000.[36] This attitude is likely to resurface in its approach towards the future use of the European Rapid Reaction Force.

As for the United States, it remains ambivalent about the EU initiative and will want to keep a watchful eye on progress. On the one hand, it welcomes efforts by its allies to improve their military capabilities and shoulder a larger share of the defence burden. It constantly berates some of its partners for what it perceives to be their inadequate contributions. Yet, on the other, Washington has long been fearful of a European caucus emerging within the alliance in which decisions would be taken and then presented to the USA as agreed positions. It is also wary lest Europe treat defence as a stage on which to posture and the rhetoric about robust military capabilities fails to be translated into increased spending. This could lead to a worst-case scenario, from a future US President's point of view, in which a more assertive and complacent Europe could become involved in a regional crisis and then expect the United States to intervene to extricate it if things went wrong.

Nevertheless, in spite of US anxieties, the experience of the last decade shows that the greater danger to the US–European relationship lies in the Europeans failing to enhance their military effectiveness. A Europe that can make only a limited contribution to NATO military interventions and proves incapable of independent action will only become the object of US derision in the longer term. An unsatisfactory division of effort was discernible during the 1990s: the USA provided the firepower for an operation (albeit as long as US lives were not put at risk) and the Europeans provided the bulk of the financial resources for post-conflict reconstruction. Furthermore, the United States will be likely to become increasingly dissatisfied with European allies that call for its leadership in all levels of crises on the continent and simultaneously fail to respond to US calls to contribute more to shared global security concerns. Such a recipe will lead to dissent and recrimination within the alliance, with the attendant risk that the two sides of the Atlantic will drift apart.

Conclusion

A balanced assessment of the potential inherent in the Common European Security and Defence Policy is difficult at this stage because the process is in its infancy. The reactions of its most trenchant critics, who hailed it as the creation of a 'European Army', were clearly exaggerated.[37] The CESDP does not represent a 'communitarisation' of defence activity within the EU. No substantial powers have been granted to either the European Commission or the European Parliament over defence and the decision-making bodies and military staffs will all reside within the intergovernmental Council. The countries that have driven the initiative thus far, the UK and France, are the firmest advocates of preserving defence as an intergovernmental area of activity. Indeed, it can be argued that the initiative has served to reaffirm an intergovernmental approach within the Union, because it has imported an issue area into the EU that will be managed by national governments.

For those committed to the process of further European integration, there is hope to be found in the CESDP. An important psychological barrier has been breached by embracing hard security within the EU: one need only refer to the controversy surrounding the Treaties of Maastricht and Amsterdam, over defence, to verify this fact. Alongside the processes of monetary union and enlargement, making a military instrument available to the CFSP adds a further dimension to the process of drawing Europe closer together. Furthermore it reopens a debate that was started after Maastricht about the development of a common European defence policy. The Cologne and Helsinki summits may come to be viewed in retrospect as the start of a decisive phase in defence co-operation.

Yet for those confident that such a period of co-operation lies ahead, words of caution are appropriate. The problems attendant on building momentum in the defence field should not be underestimated: the experience of the last decade should be sufficient to cool the ardour of all but the most visionary. Rhetoric tended to exceed military realities, crises occurred and Europe proved incapable of action and defence budgets spiralled downwards. The future development of the CESDP will not be smooth; it will be subject to the usual disagreements, frictions and differences in priority. Its progress will depend upon the leadership role played by those European states in the vanguard of developments and their ability to reconcile differences of view between themselves. In particular, a close working relationship will need to be forged between the EU and NATO. The principal European countries will need to work hard to reassure Washington that progress in defence matters will not be achieved at its expense. Without this, EU developments are likely to be paralysed and damage will be done to the transatlantic relationship.

Notes and references

1 For details of the past roles performed by the WEU see A. Deighton (ed.), *Western European Union 1954–1997: Defence, Security, Integration.* (Oxford: European Interdependence Research Unit, St Antony's College 1997) and G. W. Rees, *The Western European Union at the Crossroads: Between Transatlantic Solidarity and European Integration.* (Boulder: Westview 1998).

2 Treaty on European Union. Article J.4.2, Title V.

3 National perspectives among European states on defence and security issues are thoroughly explored in J. Howorth and A. Menon (eds), *The European Union and National Defence Policy.* (London: Routledge 1997).

4 B. Molard, 'The WEU Satellite Centre: Just Five Years on'. *NATO's Sixteen Nations* (special supplement) 1998, pp. 18–22.

5 A. Massiroli, *CFSP: Defence and Flexibility (Chaillot Paper 38).* (Paris: WEU Institute for Security Studies 2000), pp. 17–18.

6 Declaration of Heads of State and Government. (Brussels: NATO Press Service 1994).

7 Ministerial Meeting of the North Atlantic Council, Berlin 3 June 1996: Final Communiqué. (Brussels: NATO Press Service 1996).

8 *WEU Contribution to the EU Intergovernmental Conference of 1996.* (Brussels: WEU 1995).

9 Treaty of Amsterdam. Article 17.

10 These were first agreed and articulated in the Petersberg Declaration. (London: WEU 1992).

11 Presidency Conclusions, Cologne, 4–5 June 1999. (Brussels: Council of the European Union 1999).

12 Presidency Conclusions, Santa Maria Da Feira, Portugal, 19–20 June 2000. (Brussels: Council of the European Union 2000).

13 Joint Declaration on European Defence. (London: Foreign and Commonwealth Office 1998).

14 Alexander Vershbow, speech at Wilton Park Conference Centre, 26 January 2000. US Embassy Text.

15 K. Smith, 'The Instruments of European Union Foreign Policy' in J. Zielonka (ed.), *Paradoxes of European Foreign Policy.* (The Hague: Kluwer Law International 1998), pp. 78–9.

16 I am indebted to Professor Jörg Monar for this point.

17 French Defence Minister Alain Richard has argued that article five remains an important political commitment that could be developed in the future. See his remarks on the French presidency of the WEU in *Agence Europe* 7718 17 May 2000, p. 6.

18 US Deputy Secretary of State Strobe Talbott, speech to NATO Foreign Ministers, Brussels, 15 December 1999. US Embassy Text Service, London, EUR307.

19 Presidency Conclusions, Santa Maria Da Feira, Portugal, 19–20 June 2000 and 'Turkey is Not Pleased with Arrangement Decided in Feira for European but non-EU NATO Allies'. *Agence Europe* 7744 24 June 2000.
20 See A. Massiroli, 'European Security and Defence: The Case for Setting "Convergence Criteria"'. *European Foreign Affairs Review* 4 (4) 1999, pp. 485–500.
21 Speech by UK Secretary of State for Defence Geoffrey Hoon, 'The Headline Goal: Backing up Words with Actions'. European Defence Conference, 28 March 2000. *Official Texts* 266.
22 Talbott *op.cit.*
23 US Defense Secretary William Cohen, speech to Bundeswehr Commanders Conference, Hamburg, 1 December 1999. US Embassy Text Service, London, EUR411.
24 J. Hooper, 'German Government Faces Split over Reform of Armed Forces'. *Guardian* 24 May 2000.
25 M. Evans, '13,000 Jobs Bonus in £5bn order by MoD'. *The Times* 17 May 2000.
26 K. Schake *et al.*, 'Building a European Defence Capability'. *Survival* 4 (1) 1999, p. 26.
27 For example, the WEU has used Russian imagery in the past, which might be denied during an emergency.
28 'At Mayence Summit, progress on IGC and on Cooperation over Armaments'. *Agence Europe* 7736 13 and 14 June 2000.
29 Massiroli (2000) *op.cit.*, p. 37.
30 'Solana Stresses Indispensable Nature of Military Instrument for Effective and Credible Foreign Policy'. *Agence Europe* 7743 23 June 2000.
31 Hoon *op.cit.*
32 Presidency Conclusions, Cologne *op.cit.*
33 I am indebted to Professor Jolyon Howorth for this point.
34 Jacques Chirac, President of the French Republic, speech to the Presidential Committee of the WEU Parliamentary Assembly, Elysee Palace, Paris, 30 May 2000.
35 US Ambassador to NATO Alexander Vershbow, speech at Transatlantic Forum, Paris, 18 May 2000. US Embassy Text.
36 M. Evans, 'Nato Passes Kosovo Baton to Euro Force'. *The Times* 15 April 2000.
37 P. Webster and T. Baldwin, 'Thatcher Launches Attack on Euro Army'. *The Times* 8 December 1999.

Part III

National and regional perspectives

7   The United States

Strategic vision or tactical posturing?

James Sperling

Introduction

American debates over NATO and EU enlargement have been lopsided. The initial debate over EU enlargement only emerged insofar as it related to NATO enlargement. The Clinton administration generally established *ad hoc* linkages between the two, but a consensus eventually emerged within the administration and Congress that NATO enlargement should precede EU enlargement owing to the stabilising function of NATO, the inherent difficulty of EU enlargement itself, and a belated unwillingness to cede the initiative in reshaping the European security space to the EU. The Clinton administration and influential members of Congress only became wary of the diplomatic and military-strategic consequences of EU enlargement as the NATO ratification process drew to a close. This response raises the question posed in the title of this chapter: was American policy towards the two enlargements informed by a compelling strategic vision or was it simply the sum of unconnected tactical posturings? In this chapter I address this question, the answer to which is central to an understanding of the enlargement debates within the United States and also provides insights into the expectations placed on Europe in the post-Cold War security order.

International institutions in the US foreign policy calculus

International institutions have played an important role in the post-Second World War US foreign policy calculus. The institutions initially constructed to govern the European security space, particularly the European Recovery Program and NATO, were devised as mechanisms for imposing US economic and security preferences on the Western Europeans. Institutions were not constructed in accordance with a strict universalism that would have subordinated US self-interest to a 'common Atlantic interest'. Rather, the institutions of the post-war period are better understood as mechanisms which allowed the United States to participate in the evolution of the European security space, to shape and constrain the policy choices (if not preferences) of its allies, and to legitimise the role in Europe that the United States eventually assumed.

While the United States expected its European partners and allies to act within and according to multilateral norms, the United States itself retained a preference for unilateralism in its foreign policy actions on many issues of direct interest to the Europeans. Examples include the unilateral cancellation of the Skybolt missile system which compromised the British nuclear deterrent; the abrupt abandonment of the Multilateral Force which contributed to the downfall of the Erhard government in the Federal Republic of Germany; the resupply of Israel from Bremerhaven during the Yom Kippur War in 1973, which compromised the German policy of neutrality and its oil supply; and the failed economic boycott of the USSR by the Reagan administration in the early 1980s. This pattern has continued into the post-Cold War period. The decision to enlarge NATO was largely imposed on the Europeans by the Clinton administration, the United States exercised a unit veto over which Central and Eastern European (CEE) states were to be admitted to NATO, and the timetable for enlargement was of US design. The long post-war burden-sharing debate, US unilateralism within and outside of NATO, and the tenor of the debates over NATO enlargement all suggest that the United States still views NATO as an institution for imposing US preferences on the Europeans and legitimising the US role as chief architect of the European security order.

The United States has been a rhetorical champion of the European Union, and its predecessor institutions the European Economic Community (EEC) and the European Community (EC), since the original European Coal and Steel Community (ECSC) was founded in 1952. Arguably, the ECSC and the EEC reflected US economic and strategic preferences. Economically, a revived Europe was expected to become a better customer for US goods; and strategically, a wealthier Europe would be better able to assume the burden of the common defence against the USSR. Consequently, the United States lent its prestige and encouragement to the project of European integration. Yet over time conflicts of economic interest emerged as the requirements of European integration collided with the requirements of a more open Atlantic economy: protection of French farmers against their more efficient US counterparts was the price the more free trade-oriented Germans had to pay for the protection of German industrial goods within Europe and the desired political rapprochement with France.

The United States has given rhetorical support to the long-term objective of European political union and the further 'deepening' of the EU, but has also tended to view the EU as an economic actor in the Atlantic economy; initially as a trading bloc and now as a monetary bloc. In the military and, to a lesser extent, diplomatic contexts the EU has been largely written off as ineffectual. On military and strategic issues, the United States assumed that NATO and the individual member states remained the proper addresses for negotiation. This assumption carried over into the post-Cold War environment, although the United States encouraged the Europeans to create a European Security and Defence Identity (ESDI) *within* NATO to effect a more equitable sharing of both the financial costs and strategic risks of governing the European periphery. A number of developments suggest that the EU is developing into an actor with which the United States will be increasingly forced to negotiate on issues imping-ing on the evolution of the European security space. Its Common Foreign and Security Policy (CFSP) attained constitutional status in the Maastricht Treaty (1991) and was strengthened with the Amsterdam Treaty (1997). Progress towards a Common European Security and Defence Policy (CESDP) appears to have overtaken the ESDI. Finally, the EU has created a High Representative for Foreign Policy who jointly serves as the Secretary-General of the Western European Union and has an *ex officio* place at the NATO high table.

NATO and the EU have had divergent roles in the US foreign policy calcu-lus. Both institutions underpinned the US strategy of double-containment; viz, containing Soviet power in the East and providing security for and from Germany in the West.[1] NATO provided a transatlantic alliance that extended the Western Europeans a unilateral US security guarantee and a reassuring framework for European co-operation on economic and military security issues. The institutional design of the containment strategy allowed the Europeans to prosper economically and promised larger European defence expenditures that would lessen the burden placed on the United States to maintain global equilibrium. NATO provided the framework for a Euro-pean 'second pillar' that might eventually serve as a partner in leadership in the Atlantic area. The EU and NATO made possible the Franco-German reconciliation that formed the basis of a powerful axis, which has pushed forward European integration, and NATO possessed the instrumental value of establishing a legitimate US role in the governance of the European security space. But most importantly, the United States expected a right to lead and the unquestioning loyalty of its European wards.

Even though the EEC and EC flourished within the US protectorate, the progressive loss of relative power by the United States in the Atlantic area in the 1950s and 1960s was matched by a corresponding European willing-ness to challenge US policy prescriptions and leadership. This develop-ment was particularly marked in the area of monetary and trade relations after 1960 and began to erode US prerogatives in defence as well by the mid-1970s. The post-Cold War context gave the Europeans additional degrees of freedom in seeking to place a European stamp on the emerging security architecture. Arguably, the EU promise of an eastward enlarge-ment at its Copenhagen summit in 1993, and the initial German prefer-ence for the Conference on Security and Co-operation in Europe to emerge as the key European security institution, drove the United States both to ensure that NATO would not be displaced by the CSCE and to prevent the Western Europeans from usurping the US leadership role in Europe.[2]

The double enlargement of the EU and NATO will have divergent con-sequences for the United States. Arguably, the enlargement of NATO will have a salutary effect on the US position within Europe. Increasing the membership of NATO with states diplomatically committed to the United

States may help perpetuate US leadership as the EU becomes more self-confident and competent in the area of defence; and the expansion of NATO's tasks 'out of area' will lessen the relative cost of meeting global threats. The deepening and enlargement of the EU will create a Europe that is better able to resist US demands for support and thwart US designs to act in ways that are judged by the Europeans to be against the European self-interest.

One source of potential conflict within the transatlantic area is the emergence of a European identity that will lead to a definition of interest that is in opposition to the transatlantic identity preferred by the United States. Put somewhat differently, can the United States be treated as a European power by the Europeans, with a legitimate interest and role in the evolution of Europe, if the emerging European identity by necessity excludes the United States? This danger was present in the 'European pillar' concept animating US policy since the Kennedy administration, but it has emerged with renewed vigour in the changed post-Cold War context. Although the Clinton administration recognised the danger that deepening the EU, particularly the progress towards a CFSP, could eventually pose to US–EU co-operation, it was generally assumed that the United States and Europe have essentially congruent interests globally that will strengthen co-operation despite this danger.

The enlargement and deepening of the EU will increase its heterogeneity of purpose and interest, at least in the short term. If the decision-making structures of the EU cannot mute that heterogeneity, the progress towards political integration could be undone and the EU would become an impotent and undependable economic or military partner for the United States. More problematically, an enlargement of the EU that does not overcome the institutional barriers to effective decision-making would disrupt the integration process and could in turn undermine the cohesiveness of NATO. For that reason, the United States has implicitly moved towards an understanding of the EU as a potential competitor in the security field.[3] Prior to the Cologne and Helsinki summits in 1999, the Clinton administration treated the EU as an actor with economic and diplomatic interests not dissimilar to those of the United States. After those summits, it became clear that the EU had the potential to emerge as a security actor with capabilities independent of NATO and the United States. The US fear that the CESDP could create an EU security identity outside of or in opposition to NATO suggests that the United States now accepts the French logic that US leadership is not easily reconciled with a politically mature and diplomatically capable EU.

The US conceptualisation of security

The post-Cold War international system has witnessed a reinterpretation of security in the European context. This change was particularly marked in the German context, where the post-war inability (or unwillingness) to employ the military instrument outside the narrow compass of NATO Europe created an intellectual orientation that focused on conflict prevention as well as deterrence and a reconsideration of the non-military elements of power. As recently as the mid-1990s, Ronald Asmus could argue:

> Many Europeans have also come to assume a division of labor whereby they take on a leading role in terms of 'soft power', leaving the lion's share of 'hard power' burdens in international security to the superpower. They are comfortable with the notion of Europe as a 'civilian power' . . . Many Europeans have managed to convince themselves of the merits of such a division of labour, neglecting or overlooking the fact that the US has never agreed to it and that most Americans – if asked – would find such an arrangement offensive and unacceptable in moral, political and economic terms.[4]

In the aftermath of Bosnia and Kosovo, however, it is no longer accurate to argue that the Europeans are content with a 'civilian' role in Europe. The progress towards a CESDP and the rhetorical embrace of NATO's Defence Capabilities Initiative (DCI) in 1999 suggest that the EU states are no longer content to concede the prerogatives attending 'hard power' to the United States. Likewise, the United States now understands that threats to its security or interests cannot be adequately remedied or deterred by an over-reliance upon the military instrument. What remains true, however, is that the US security strategy places greater reliance upon the military rather than the economic or diplomatic elements of power.

The Bush and Clinton foreign policies of the 1990s had objectives in Europe that echoed those of earlier administrations.[5] First, both administrations made an effort to establish a new division of labour within the Atlantic Alliance that shifted the burden and responsibilities for regional stability on to the United States' NATO partners without forgoing US political predominance. Second, there was conditional support of European efforts to create an autonomous defence identity as a part of the Atlantic Alliance. Yet both the Bush and Clinton administrations were keenly aware of the potential role Europe could play as competitor to the United States and consistently hedged their support for greater progress towards a European security identity with the caveat that NATO must remain the pre-eminent security institution. Third, both administrations sought a linkage between the economic and military dimensions of the Atlantic Alliance to lighten the burden of leadership without forgoing its prerogatives. The rhetoric of the Bush and Clinton administrations, while it differed at the margin, effectively rehearsed the debate of the early 1970s: how does the United States retain its leadership role in Europe at a lower cost?

With the end of the Cold War, the Bush administration announced that the United States needed to move beyond containment. Yet the administration none the less remained committed to preventing 'any hostile power or group of powers from dominating the Eurasian land mass'.[6] US interests were conceived within an intellectual framework that combined a traditional military-based understanding of security while acknowledging the interdependence of economic power and national security. Even under the aegis of fostering democracy and the market economy, the security strategy emphasised the desire to 'maintain stable regional military balances to deter those powers that might seek regional dominance' and an interest in maintaining the institutional primacy of NATO.[7] As the Bush administration focused on the requirements of facilitating the transition to democracy in the CEE states, the US security strategy increasingly appreciated the importance of the non-military instruments of diplomacy. While this appreciation was linked to the idea that market-oriented democracies were more likely to share the values and interests of the United States, it was the Clinton administration that modified the US reliance upon the military elements of power.

The Clinton strategy of engagement and enlargement had four key elements. First, a new division of labour would need to be established within the Atlantic Alliance. Second, the United States must retain (and be granted) a leadership position within any Euro-Atlantic security order. Third, the deepening and widening of the European Union, particularly in the development of a Common Foreign and Security Policy, was to be encouraged so long as it produced a more equitable sharing of the burdens and risks within the alliance without encroaching on US policy prerogatives. Finally, the future security of the Euro-Atlantic region depended upon the successful transitions to democracy and the market economy in the CEE states and the republics of the former USSR, particularly the Russian Federation.[8] The Clinton administration's strategy of engagement and enlargement built upon its predecessor's strategy of engagement and leadership. The change was more than cosmetic and it obscured as much as it revealed.

The Clinton administration went much further than the Bush administration in adopting the policy strategies favoured by the Europeans and demonstrated a greater willingness to employ the non-military instruments of diplomacy to achieve US objectives in either half of Europe. This tendency has emerged most clearly in the evolution of the objectives and achievements of the New Transatlantic Agenda (NTA) of 1995 as well as the US material and diplomatic support of the EU's Stability Pact in 1999.[9] The administration focused on two tasks: enlarging the number of market-oriented democracies in the European political space and ensuring the continued credibility of NATO and the EU as the core institutions of European security. Obscured by the new rhetoric, however, was the unwillingness of the Clinton administration to abdicate either the leadership position enjoyed by the United States or the leverage attending Europe's dependence on the US unilateral security guarantee. Perhaps as important, there was a recognition that the security threats facing the United States had changed qualitatively: the threats posed to the United States were no longer solely military in nature and transnational phenomena were expected to dominate the future security agenda.[10] Yet a military definition of interest still dominated the foreign policy calculus of the first Clinton administration.

The Department of Defense produced a 'Europe Strategy Report' in 1995 that gave content to the strategy of engagement and enlargement. The report identified the fundamental objectives of US security policy in Europe as preventing the renationalisation of foreign and defence policies, defending the territory of NATO member states, preventing the proliferation of weapons of mass destruction and maintaining the pre-eminent role of NATO in, and US leadership of, the European security architecture. These goals, and hence the content of US security concerns, largely reflected US preoccupations in Europe over the course of the entire postwar period.[11] Yet by 1999 the Clinton administration had identified a number of threats to US security that are often best addressed by recourse to the 'softer' elements of power. These included transnational threats, such as terrorism, criminal organisations and cyber vandalism; the proliferation of dangerous technologies to rogue states and non-state actors; and environmental or health threats (irreparable damage to regional ecosystems or epidemics).

A second change in the strategic objectives of the United States emerged between 1995 and 1999. In 1995, the Clinton administration echoed the Bush administration's concern about preventing another hegemon from developing on the European continent; and administration officials still spoke of the need to ensure 'a continent free from domination by any power or combination of powers hostile to the United States'.[12] At the century's end, the Clinton administration adopted a security strategy for Europe that shared two assumptions of a 'civilian power'. These were, first, that peace in Europe is contingent upon continent-wide political and economic stability and, second, that security threats today are diffused throughout the international system and can be best addressed in multilateral fora.[13] While the United States appears to have moved towards a redefinition of security that depends upon the exercise of 'soft power', it is doubtful that multilateralism still means much more than the Europeans following the US lead inside and outside of Europe.

Both the *National Security Strategy of Engagement and Enlargement* (1995) and the *National Security Strategy for a New Century* (1999) identify three categories of interest that justify the calibrated use of US armed force: vital national interests, important interests and humanitarian interests. Vital national interests are defined as 'interests which are of a broad, overriding importance to the survival, security and vitality of our national entity including our commitments to our allies'. Important interests justify the use of limited force 'reflecting the relative saliency of the interests we have at stake' and humanitarian interests might result in the employment of the armed forces in non-combat roles. This categorisation of security threats, developed during the tenure of William Perry as Secretary of Defense, points to future difficulties in arriving at a joint definition of security within the Atlantic area. It is clear that threats are defined in a 'national' rather than 'common' or even 'transatlantic' frame of reference; and that the likely US and European rank-ordering of threats will differ not only in degree but in kind.

Even though a common set of security threats remains elusive, the emergence of a common frame of reference has been facilitated by the evolution of the New Transatlantic Agenda. The NTA reflected the European desire to strike a new transatlantic strategic relationship to fill the conceptual vacuum left by the end of the Cold War. Neither containment nor the simple division of labour between the United States and the EU could sustain co-operation where the 'new security agenda' required cross-issue linkages politically and conceptually.[14] It also reflected the European calculation that in the absence of a new strategic bargain, the United States would either turn inwards or its attention would shift to the Pacific Rim, an area considered in the mid-1990s as the gateway to the United States' future. In either case, a premature US withdrawal or the collapse of co-operation between the EU and the United States would not serve the European interest. A new transatlantic bargain was also desired by the Clinton administration for reasons similar to those of the EU. The United States sought a framework document that would legitimise the US role in Europe and guarantee a US voice in the evolution of the European security order. A new bargain would provide the basis for creating a transatlantic market place that would open the European market to US finance and commerce. Finally, it might also provide a mechanism for drafting European resources, diplomatic and financial, into the support of US diplomacy outside the NATO area.[15]

The NTA has pushed forward co-operation on the various elements of the new security agenda, a development that undoubtedly helped reshape the US definition of security in the late 1990s. The concrete successes of the NTA have been located primarily in those areas that are strictly matters of traditional political economy, particularly the reduction of non-tariff barriers to trade. Perhaps the most important of those agreements struck within the NTA framework has been the Transatlantic Economic Partnership (TEP) signed in 1998. The TEP is the fullest statement of the US–EU goal of creating a new transatlantic market place. The agreement identifies not only the traditional preoccupation with liberalising commercial policy, but includes investments and the challenges of the 'new economy'.[16] The NTA has also registered concrete successes where political economy intersects with traditional security concerns, as in the case of the Balkan stabilisation plans, particularly the EU-sponsored Stability Pact, and coping with the problems of nuclear safety in Russia and Ukraine.

It is also clear that the NTA has broadened co-operation between the EU and the United States across the new and old security agendas, a development that could dampen the identity conflict inherent in the European preference for creating a pan-European identity and the US insistence upon strengthening the transatlantic identity.[17] Yet the debates over NATO enlargement and the consequences of EU enlargement for the United States suggest that there is a fundamental incompatibility between the construction of both a pan-European and a transatlantic identity.[18]

US debates over EU and NATO enlargement

Explicit parallelism between EU and NATO enlargement emerged at the May 1995 Noordwijk aan Zee ministerial meeting of the NATO Council. At that time, NATO enlargement was viewed as complementing 'the enlargement of the European Union, a parallel process which also . . . contributes significantly to extending security and stability to the new democracies in the East'.[19] The emphasis on parallelism was located in the shared strategic interests of the EU and NATO as well as the renewed interest in building a viable European pillar of the alliance, an aspiration that found form in the Combined Joint Task Force (CJTF) concept. The officially endorsed *Study on NATO Enlargement* in 1995 reaffirmed the complementarity and desired parallelism in EU and NATO enlargement, although that position was qualified with the proviso that the enlargements 'will proceed autonomously according to their respective internal dynamics'.[20] Parallel enlargement was further qualified in March 1996 when it was acknowledged that there could 'not be a parallelism in time'.[21] The progressive disengagement of the enlargement processes reflected an unwillingness to leave NATO enlargement hostage to the enlargement of the EU, a process expected to face significant delays owing to the need for internal reform. By the time of the NATO Madrid summit in July 1997, parallelism had been abandoned and has since disappeared from NATO rhetoric. What remains of critical importance, however, is the continued official insistence that NATO and the EU 'share common strategic interests'.

The NATO enlargement debate in the USA

The parallel enlargements of NATO and the EU became a US policy preference once the decision was taken to enlarge NATO. In an early policy statement, the Department of Defense treated the enlargement of the EU as an integral part of the European security architecture, a role qualified by the 'need for complementarity with the process of NATO enlargement'.[22] An important rationale for complementary enlargements was located in the desire to 'erase the outdated boundaries of the Cold War' and 'extend eastward the same structure of values and institutions that enabled Western Europe to overcome its own legacy of conflict and division'.[23] A further argument embraced a division of labour approach: while only NATO could effectively extend a credible security guarantee to the CEE states, only the EU could provide the economic component of the post-Cold War process of transition: especially direct foreign investment and foreign markets for CEE industrial and agricultural goods.[24] Hence, a necessary condition for prosperity and democracy in the CEE states was NATO membership.[25] Another rationale was provided by Senator Pete V. Dominici, who argued that the NATO and EU enlargements were linked by 'a complicated intersection of economics and foreign policy' underlined by the progress towards Economic and Monetary Union in the EU. Former Secretary of State James Baker endorsed the view that EU enlargement was as critical to the stability and security of the CEE states as it was to NATO enlargement; and that membership in NATO was not a substitute for membership in the EU.[26] Despite the strategic interdependence of the EU and NATO enlargements, those who favoured NATO enlargement generally avoided making any direct linkage between the two in testimony before the Congress. That debate was only engaged after the EU's efforts to replace the NATO- (and US-) sanctioned ESDI with an autonomous CESDP.

There were three NATO enlargement debates in the United States: within the Clinton administration before NATO enlargement became policy, the defence of the enlargement decision by the administration and the public debate over NATO enlargement that took place in the Congress after the enlargement decision was taken. James M. Goldgeier has argued persuasively that the Clinton administration foreign policy team rarely read off the same page between 1993 and 1994. It was also clear that President Clinton's preferences dominated the decision-making process once the enlargement issue captured his attention.[27] Yet the debate that took place within the administration foreshadowed the public debate over NATO enlargement.

The Clinton administration was initially divided on NATO enlargement. Those in the Department of Defense were particularly wary of enlargement, while those in the White House and State Department were generally in favour of it, with the important exception of a sceptical Strobe Talbott. The proponents of enlargement fell into two camps. The first consisted primarily of those like National Security Adviser Anthony Lake who believed that the United States had to find an alternative strategic concept: the policy of containment was *passé* given the changed international context and had to be replaced by a policy of enlargement.[28] Lake embraced the 'democratic peace' argument: the view that, since mature democratic states do not fight each other, the spread of democracy is intimately linked to the promotion of peaceful international relations. Further to this, Lake believed that European security was best served by the enlargement of NATO. He found allies in those who focused on the strategic requirements of Germany and the centrality of Germany to NATO and European security in the post-Cold War era.[29] The importance of Germany was located not only in its desire to reinforce its strategic position with an eastward extension of NATO's boundary and its desire to consolidate its reconciliation with Poland, but also in the historical lessons drawn from the failure of the Weimar Republic.

Those opposed to NATO enlargement presented three sets of arguments. The Pentagon questioned the military–strategic consequences of NATO enlargement and doubted the suitability of the likely CEE candidate states for NATO membership; and it feared that NATO enlargement would jeopardise important arms control agreements with the Russian Federation without enhancing NATO security. At the State Department, Strobe Talbott argued persuasively that enlargement would cause irreparable damage to US–Russian relations and undermine reform in Russia. These concerns led Secretary of Defense Les Aspin to develop the Partnership for Peace (PfP) programme as a means for deferring NATO enlargement until the CEE states could demonstrate that they could meet the military requirements of the alliance.[30] Although the PfP was successful in engaging the former Warsaw Pact countries, it did not forestall the pressure for enlargement. Yet the concerns expressed by the Pentagon were translated into the criteria for NATO enlargement. The concern with Russian sensibilities and the manifest importance of the arms control agreements with the Russian Federation that constituted an important part of the emerging European security architecture produced a two-track enlargement strategy; viz, that the eastward enlargement of NATO would be complemented by an enhanced relationship between NATO and the Russian Federation.

Preserving NATO's pre-eminent role in the emerging European security architecture figured prominently in the Clinton administration's defence of the enlargement decision. Administration officials portrayed Europe as the most important region of the world for US security and NATO as the key institution for guaranteeing the security of the continent. Consequently, the vital importance of NATO to US security implied that the United States could not allow NATO to be eclipsed by another institution; neither the EU nor the OSCE. Moreover, administration officials believed that the success that NATO had had in the post-war period in denationalising defence policies in Europe should continue in the post-Cold War period. Continued NATO dominance required enlargement; it legitimised and guaranteed US leadership in Europe on security affairs. Enlargement was also viewed as a method for adapting the alliance to the likely tasks that it would face in the future; viz, the tasks of crisis management and peacekeeping out of area.[31]

The administration also provided persuasive strategic rationales for NATO enlargement. The first and most consistent argument was that NATO enlargement would prevent the emergence of a 'buffer zone' or 'power vacuum' in Central and Eastern Europe that could become a source of competition between the United States and Russia or between Germany and Russia.[32] The enlargement of NATO was also held to enhance the prospects for stability in Europe because it would serve to deter conflicts that might have otherwise occurred. Secretary of State Madeleine Albright argued that a 'larger NATO will make us safer by expanding the area in Europe where wars simply do not happen'.[33] This line of reasoning reflected the contextual role played by NATO in facilitating the Franco-German reconciliation in the post-war period; and the institutional role NATO has played in preventing the outbreak of war between Greece and Turkey over Cyprus. A final argument in favour of NATO enlargement focused on securing the peace in Europe in order to free the United States to pursue its foreign policy interests in more unsettled areas of the world, particularly in Asia.[34]

Its proponents ascribed three general categories of benefit to NATO enlargement. Some pointed to the benefits attending an improved geostrategic position for the United States; others emphasised NATO's potential contribution to nation-building in the CEE states, particularly the consolidation of the market and democracy, or the institutional transformation of NATO that would leverage US interests outside of Europe. While proponents of enlargement outside the Clinton administration generally echoed the rationales put forward by the administration, the geostrategic arguments in favour of enlargement merit discussion.

Enlargement was seen by many to advance the geostrategic interests of the United States, particularly with respect to Germany and Russia. In testimony before the Senate Committee on Foreign Relations, Henry Kissinger and William E. Odom argued that NATO expansion made geostrategic sense because it would resolve the German question. Odom provided four reasons why NATO enlargement had to occur. First, NATO enlargement would prevent the Anglo-French enmity towards Germany from developing into a competition for influence over a Central Europe in a security vacuum. Second, since the political elites in Germany were convinced that enlargement was necessary and desirable, it was in the US interest not to disappoint Germany. Third, the CEE fears of Germany and Russia could only be allayed by NATO membership. Finally, if the Central and Eastern European states were to be barred from NATO, it would force Russia into a 'strategic competition with Germany over hegemony in Central and Eastern Europe'.[35] Kissinger, in his Senate testimony, focused on the strategic relationship between Russia and Germany in the nineteenth and early twentieth centuries. He believed that without NATO enlargement (and a strong US presence in Europe), 'NATO would thus risk either collision or collusion between Germany and Russia'. Predictably, perhaps, Kissinger was preoccupied with the adverse consequences of a security vacuum in Central and Eastern Europe. The rationale presented by Kissinger advised a continuation of the post-war strategy of double-containment – the containment of Russian power in the East and German power in the West – complicated by an international context encouraging a great power competition in Central Europe between them.[36]

Opponents of enlargement detailed four categories of unacceptable costs. These were a worsened geostrategic outcome for the United States, a diluted and ineffective NATO, unacceptably high financial costs that would unfairly burden the US taxpayer and NATO's inability to deliver to the

CEE states what they most needed to consolidate markets and their economies. The first two objections proved to be the more compelling.

The dominant geostrategic critique of NATO enlargement focused on the irreparable harm that would be done to US relations with the Russian Federation. Some argued that the United States broke an informal agreement with Mikhail Gorbachev in 1990: that in exchange for allowing a unified Germany to remain in NATO, there would be no eastward expansion.[37] These individuals believed that NATO enlargement would reduce the security of the European area, because enlargement would undermine reformists within the Russian government, bestow a greater legitimacy upon nationalist factions within the Duma and military and make it difficult to forge a parliamentary coalition to support future arms control treaties. Opponents also noted that enlargement lacked strategic purpose and was likely to decrease the overall security of the European space. This objection carried with it concerns over unnecessarily provoking the Russian Federation and setting in motion a desire to reclaim a part of its lost empire along its periphery, encouraging the creation of a Sino-Russian coalition to offset the European–US coalition symbolised by NATO and transforming a wary partner into a certain enemy.

The second important line of argument against NATO enlargement focused on the negative impact that a larger membership would have on the alliance as an institution of collective defence. Some supporters of enlargement, like Senator Jesse Helms, believed that enlargement would be against the United States' interest if NATO were to move towards collective security and abandon its core function of collective defence.[38] Opponents also believed that enlargement would reduce the credibility of the article five guarantee and perhaps more importantly renew doubts about the credibility of the US nuclear guarantee in the event of a hostile, renascent Russia. Enlargement also raised concerns that NATO would not retain its cohesiveness in the face of divergent interests along Europe's widened periphery, would lack sufficient resources to support the integration of the accession states into the alliance, and would be forced to broker, and possibly physically mediate, ethnic conflicts in the new member states. Moreover, the provisions of the Founding Act with the Russian Federation created concerns in the Congress.[39] Many believed that the effort to assuage Russian sensibilities with the creation of the Permanent Joint Council undermined the alliance itself by giving Russia an implied *droit de regard* over future enlargement decisions, the disposition of nuclear weapons and conventional forces in the new member states and any other issue that came before the NATO Council.[40]

Still, these objections to NATO enlargement are not as powerful as they may appear and gloss over arguments in favour of enlargement. The impact of NATO enlargement on the Russian Federation is questionable in two respects. It is difficult to judge what role, if any, NATO policy plays in the domestic political calculations of the Russian Federation; and it is also questionable that the long-term evolution of Russian foreign policy has been appreciably affected by the decision taken to enlarge the alliance in July 1997. Moreover, NATO enlargement removes the temptation of a unified Germany to renationalise its security policy to secure its eastern flank; a policy development, were it to occur, that would certainly bring it into conflict with the Russian Federation and unnerve its partners in the EU.

Fears that the enlargement of NATO will weaken the cohesion and security guarantees afforded by the alliance as well as the concern that the Founding Act has transformed the Russian Federation into a *de facto* member of NATO are not easily dismissed. Although Secretary Madeleine Albright and other members of the Clinton administration insisted that NATO remained a collective defence organisation, the administration had pushed NATO to take on tasks normally ascribed to a collective security organisation. The cohesion of NATO and the credibility of the US security guarantee have always been in question. Yet most of those testifying before the Congress believed that the Czech Republic, Hungary and Poland were likely to increase rather than decrease the cohesion of the alliance, an expectation reflected in the active roles played by these states in Bosnia and Kosovo. While the Founding Act does not give Russia any standing in the North Atlantic Council, the creation of an institutional foundation for Russian–NATO co-operation does provide Russia with an opportunity to influence NATO decisions. In this context, however, influence is not likely to be a one-way street; something enlargement critics ignored or underestimated.

The EU enlargement debate in the USA

The US debate on the eastward enlargement of the EU has generally been restricted to complaints about the inability or unwillingness of the EU to enlarge in a timely manner. RAND analysts in particular have also expressed concern that a heterogeneous slate of membership candidates could create 'backdoor' security guarantees to the new EU states that were members of the Western European Union but not of NATO.[41] This specific concern arose owing to the presumptive right of EU member states to join the WEU, an alliance with an automatic mutual security guarantee. Congressional testimony during the NATO enlargement ratification debate did not go far beyond these concerns; official Washington discounted heavily both the political aspirations of the EU and the willingness of the EU member states to pool their sovereignty in the area of security and defence policy.

The EU debate in the United States was not fully and systematically engaged until the Anglo-French Saint Malo Declaration in December 1998. At Saint Malo, the British accepted that the EU 'must have the capacity for autonomous action, backed up by credible military forces, the means to decide to use them, and a readiness to do so in order to respond to international crises'. In what proved an important policy departure, France and the UK agreed that Europe required guaranteed access to the appropriate military capabilities 'pre-designated within NATO's European pillar or national or multinational European means outside the NATO framework'.[42]

At the time of the Saint Malo summit, there was still some concern over whether the WEU was to remain outside or be absorbed by the EU. The European Council summit at Cologne in June 1999 settled that question relatively unambiguously. Once the Europeans were able to agree on how to absorb the WEU functions that were necessary for the EU to 'fulfil its new responsibilities in the area of the Petersberg Tasks . . . the WEU as an organisation would have completed its purpose'. Notably, the Council restricted the defence ambitions of the EU to the Petersberg Tasks[43] and also added the caveat that any EU decision would be taken 'without prejudice to actions by NATO'. The Council stated that the ability of the EU to play 'its full role on the international stage' required a CFSP 'backed up by credible operational capabilities'. Those operational capabilities, in turn, were to lead either to EU-led operations using NATO assets and capabilities or to EU-led operations without recourse to NATO assets or capabilities.[44] A second Anglo-French declaration in November 1999 elaborated upon the Saint Malo and Cologne agreements. Both governments agreed that the EU required an 'autonomous capacity to take decisions and, where NATO as a whole is not engaged, to launch and then to conduct EU-led military operations'. Moreover, the French and British agreed that the EU should be able to deploy between 50,000 and 60,000 personnel for crisis management tasks. Both Anglo-French recommendations were accepted verbatim by the Helsinki European Council in December 1999.[45]

By the end of 1999 significant changes had occurred in the balance of responsibilities between Europe and the United States, the institutional manifestation of the European pillar of the Atlantic Alliance, and the character of the European pillar. The Europeans met the US challenge to assume greater responsibility within the European security space and explicitly delineated a new division of labour within the alliance. Europe is responsible for the Petersberg Tasks within Europe while relying upon NATO and the United States for article five obligations and conflicts 'out of area'. The WEU is no longer the 'hinge institution' mediating the relationship between NATO and an EU with foreign and defence policy ambitions. Instead, the EU and NATO are now direct partners. This development foreshadows a change in the character of the European pillar: instead of talking of an ESDI within NATO, the focus will increasingly shift to the evolution of a CESDP that is compatible with NATO. The emergence of a credible CESDP backed by an integrated European defence base promises a changed balance of power within NATO. An autonomous EU foreign policy identity will inevitably delegitimise US dominance within NATO and perhaps undermine the US commitment to European security as well.

As late as 1998 the State Department discounted EU defence capabilities, reiterated the longstanding US position that only NATO could guarantee

European security and viewed the EU primarily as 'the economic partner we must have for the next century'.[46] The Anglo-French concordance on the need for an EU defence policy, however, led to the acknowledgement of an EU defence role by NATO at the April 1999 Washington summit. The administration had not fully factored in the consequences of the WEU's potential demise on alliance cohesion.[47] None the less, the United States agreed that the EU would have ready access to the 'assets and capabilities of the Alliance'.[48] As Washington acceded to a more prominent role for the EU in security affairs, it also gained agreement to the Defence Capabilities Initiative introduced by Secretary of Defense Cohen in September 1998. The DCI was intended to ensure that the Europeans redressed their demonstrable operational shortcomings and were prevented from substituting rhetoric and a new layer of bureaucracy for the acquisition of credible military capabilities.

The Clinton administration tried to construct a European defence capability that would comply with the 'three Ds': no duplication of NATO structures; no de-linking from NATO's core missions; and no discrimination against non-EU members of NATO.[49] These criteria have been augmented by Lord Robertson, Secretary-General of NATO, to include the 'three Is': indivisibility of the transatlantic link; improvement of capabilities; and inclusiveness of all allies. These injunctions were codified in the Senate's 'Roth Resolution' of 1999. The Clinton administration and the Senate had similar views. Both believed that the key was to be found in improved European defence capabilities rather than in new institutions, that the CESDP should not 'promote a strategic perspective on transatlantic security issues that conflicts with that promoted by NATO', and the CESDP should not 'promote a decline in the military resources that European allies contribute to NATO'.[50]

The Roth Resolution was subsequently revised to take into account the changes in EU policy at Cologne. Senate Resolution 208 focused on the ramifications of the EU intention to absorb the WEU. The Resolution reflected an unstated concern; viz, the fear that an 'EU caucus' within NATO would challenge US leadership. The Resolution's key stated concern was that the Europeans had to improve the military capabilities of the alliance and refrain from creating 'new institutions outside the alliance'. The Resolution, while recognising the EU's desire to attain an autonomous defence capability, none the less expressed the Senate's concern that the EU only undertake a mission after NATO had referred the mission to it. The Resolution also encouraged the EU states to acquire military capabilities enabling them 'to deploy forces over long distances, sustain operations for extended periods of time, and operate jointly with the United States in high-intensity conflicts'.[51] The discomfiture with an autonomous Europe within NATO reflects the US desire to sustain the post-war relationship between Europe and the United States within NATO; and the emphasis on acquiring force projection capabilities indicates the US desire for the EU states (and NATO) to assume global responsibilities. Two observations are in order. First, the EU is not a transatlantic institution but an institution that aspires to European political identity that may very well have interests that diverge from those of the United States inside and outside Europe. Second, the United States seeks an institutional solution to the emergence of a European defence identity located outside NATO in order to minimise the risks of the occurrence of what Peter Rodman called 'the contingency that dare not speak its name',[52] when the Europeans want to act where the United States does not want them to do so. The emergence of an EU moving towards political union, however haltingly, is likely to generate that contingency at some point in the future.

Conclusion

The post-Cold War environment has seen renewed US efforts to cajole the European allies into assuming greater responsibility for their own military and economic security and into paying a higher price for the changed and hedged US security guarantee. Yet the United States has sought to retain the prerogatives of a leadership poised between dominance and hegemony. The post-Cold War environment has also complicated the US security strategy. Given the ambiguities of the changed strategic context in Europe, it should perhaps not come as a surprise that the Clinton administration's position towards NATO and EU enlargement was driven as much by tactical concerns over perpetuating US leadership in Europe as by the strategic requirements of a stable European security order.

This assessment is consistent with both the domestic debate over the enlargement of NATO and the response of the US Congress and the Clinton administration to the EU's first steps towards a CESDP. Tactical concerns are more marked in the US positions taken towards the evolution of an EU security and defence identity, but even the US position towards NATO was tactical in two senses. First, the Clinton administration's decision to enlarge NATO reflected in part an effort to overcome the short-term diplomatic difficulty of finding a place for the CEE states in the transatlantic security order and, second, the Clinton administration correctly understood that the United States could force the pace and chart the direction of NATO enlargement, whereas it could only cajole the EU to enlarge.

Until 1999 the US positions taken towards EU enlargement were almost exclusively tactical. Some understood that divergent enlargements of NATO and the EU posed the danger of extending backdoor security guarantees that would commit NATO to non-member states. Others understood that the successful completion of monetary union would inevitably have foreign and defence policy ramifications that NATO would have to contain if it were to retain its centrality to the European security order. But many who favoured EU enlargement over NATO enlargement were indifferent to or unaware of the potential consequences that enlargement and deepening would have on the political character of the EU and the US role in Europe. Still others believed that the CEE states would remain unable to meet the criteria for EU membership in the medium term and consequently looked to NATO as a second-best mechanism for integrating those states into the transatlantic security order of US design.

The Congress and Clinton administration only fully appreciated the strategic consequences of an autonomous EU security and defence policy after the Anglo-French concordance at Saint Malo. The WEU had been viewed as the firewall between an autonomous EU and NATO. The prospective emergence of a European Security and Defence Identity that is not mediated by the WEU poses the potential for a strategic challenge to a US-designed and dominated security architecture in Europe. It suggests an inevitable recalibrating of the balance of power within NATO between the United States and an EU possessing a coherence of purpose and self-interest.

The successful launch of Economic and Monetary Union in 1999 began the process of recalibrating the balance of power between the United States and Europe. Accordingly, this change in the relative power positions of Europe and the United States, in combination with a changed geostrategic context, requires a 'new Atlanticism' displacing the old Atlanticism played out in the idiom of power politics and bloc competition. While the content of the new Atlanticism has long been codified in the NTA, the form of co-operation between Europe and the United States remains contested. The United States, particularly in the realm of security and defence, appears reluctant at this juncture to treat Europe or the EU as an equal either within or outside of NATO. Likewise, the steps taken at Cologne and Helsinki must be understood as an EU effort to achieve defence autonomy from the United States. Autonomy does not imply opposition. Autonomy does imply an effort to become a partner with equal power in the transatlantic community. It remains to be seen whether an Atlantic community long dominated by the United States can accommodate the inevitable equality of its two pillars.

Notes and references

1 The concept of double-containment is found in W. F. Hanrieder, *Germany, Europe, America: Fifty Years of German Foreign Policy.* (New Haven: Yale University Press 1989).
2 For an argument which links the Copenhagen decision and subsequent US policy in this way see M. A. Smith and G. Timmins, *Building a Bigger Europe: EU and NATO Enlargement in Comparative Perspective.* (Aldershot: Ashgate 2000), ch. 2.
3 On the disabilities facing the EU after the Amsterdam summit see J. Peterson and E. Bomberg, *Decision Making in the European Union.* (London: Macmillan 1999). On the challenges facing EU–US co-operation in security and defence see 'NATO and the EU's European Security and Defense Policy'. Hearing before the subcommittee on European Affairs of the Committee on Foreign Relations, United States Senate, 106th Congress, Second Session, 9 March 2000. (Washington, DC: Government Printing Office 2000).

4 See R. D. Asmus, 'NATO's Double Enlargement: New Tasks, New Members' in
C. Clemens (ed.), *NATO and the Quest for Post-Cold War Security.* (New York: St
Martin's Press 1997), p. 81.

5 There are close parallels with the Nixon foreign policy. See R. Litwak, *Détente
and the Nixon Doctrine: American Foreign Policy and the Pursuit of Stability 1969–
1976.* (Cambridge: Cambridge University Press 1984).

6 *National Security Strategy of the United States.* (Washington, DC: The White House
1990), p. 1.

7 *Ibid.*, pp. 2–3, 10–12.

8 For a critique of this 'Clinton Doctrine' see R. Haass, 'Paradigm Lost'. *Foreign
Affairs* 74 (1) 1995, pp. 44–5.

9 For details of the Stability Pact see Paul Latawski, Chapter 14 in this volume.

10 In 1995 the Clinton administration stated that 'not all security risks are immediate or military in nature. Transnational phenomena such as terrorism, narcotics
trafficking, environmental degradation, natural resource depletion, rapid population growth and refugee flows also have security implications for both present
and long term American policy'. *National Security Strategy of the United States.*
(Washington, DC: The White House 1995), p. 1.

11 'United States Security Strategy for Europe and NATO'. Department of Defense
website. URL: http://defenselink.mil/pubs/europe/chapter–1.html.

12 *National Security Strategy* (1995) *op.cit.*, p. 25. See also D. Hamilton, 'Creating the
New Atlantic Community' in J. Gedmin (ed.), *European Integration and American
Interests.* (Washington, DC: AEI Press 1997), p. 91.

13 See *National Security Strategy of the United States.* (Washington, DC: The White
House 1999), p. 29.

14 See J. Peterson, 'Security Cooperation with the United States: Establishing a
True Transatlantic Partnership' in F. Algieri *et al.* (eds), *Managing Security in
Europe: The European Union and the Challenge of Enlargement.* (Gütersloh:
Bertelsmann Foundation 1996), pp. 125–6.

15 See Secretary of State Warren Christopher, 'A New Atlantic Community for the
21st Century'. 6 September 1996, Stuttgart, Germany. Also Undersecretary of
State for Economic, Business and Agricultural Affairs Joan E. Spero, 'The New
Transatlantic Agenda: Setting the Course for US Cooperation with Europe'.
13 May 1996, New York. Text available from the Information Research Centre,
US Embassy, London.

16 'The Transatlantic Economic Partnership'. Statement released following the
US–EU summit, Birmingham, United Kingdom, 18 May 1998. For a statement of
the US economic objectives in this context, see Assistant Secretary for European
and Canadian Affairs Marc Grossman, 'The European Union, Austria, and the
Future of Central Europe'. Address at the Woodrow Wilson School of Public and
International Affairs, 1 May 1998, Princeton University, Princeton, New Jersey.
Text available from the Information Research Centre, US Embassy, London.

17 See: Undersecretary of State for Political Affairs Thomas R. Pickering, 'Remarks
at *Europe* Magazine Forum'. 22 May 1998, Washington, DC; The Bonn Declaration released at the US–EU summit, Bonn, Germany, 21 June 1999; Assistant
Secretary for European and Canadian Affairs Marc Grossman, 'US–European
Security beyond Kosovo'. Address at Washington Semester Program, American
University, 15 October 1999, Washington, DC. Text available from the Information Research Centre, US Embassy, London.

18 Note the introductory comments of Senator Gordon H. Smith before the Senate Committee on Foreign Relations: 'we are in trouble on both sides of the
Atlantic if the purpose of this effort in the EU is to differentiate Europe from
the United States, if the common policies consist of a lowest common denominator and if common security is to be provided by a separate and autonomous

entity outside of NATO ... There are many in the US Congress who would welcome the opportunity to shed European security obligations, especially now.' See 'NATO's 50th Anniversary Summit'. Hearing before the Committee on Foreign Relations, United States Senate, 106th Congress, First Session, 21 April 1999. (Washington, DC: GPO 1999), p. 5.

19 *Ministerial Meeting of the North Atlantic Council, Noordwijk aan Zee, 30 May 1995.* (Brussels: NATO Press Service 1995), para. 4.

20 *Study on NATO Enlargement.* (Brussels: NATO 1995), p. 8 and G. von Moltke, 'NATO Moves towards Enlargement'. *NATO Review* 44 (1) 1996, p. 5.

21 K. Voigt, 'NATO Enlargement: Sustaining the Momentum'. *NATO Review* 44 (2) 1996, p. 16.

22 'US Security Strategy for Europe and NATO' *op.cit.*, p. 7.

23 Secretary of State Warren Christopher, 'A Democratic and Undivided Europe in Our Time'. 20 March 1996, Cerin Palace, Prague, Czech Republic. Text available from the Information Research Centre, US Embassy, London.

24 'Prepared Statement of Dr F. Stephen Larrabee'. 'NATO's 50th Anniversary Summit' *op.cit.*, p. 38. In earlier testimony, Larrabee stated that 'membership in the European Union (EU) will contribute to enhancing stability in Eastern Europe. But EU integration alone is not enough. EU integration must be complemented by a security framework and that framework could only be supplied by NATO.' See 'Prepared Statement of Dr F. Stephen Larrabee'. 'The Debate on NATO Enlargement'. Hearings before the Committee on Foreign Relations, United States Senate, 105th Congress, First Session, 7, 9, 22, 28, 30 October and 5 November 1997. (Washington, DC: GPO 1998).

25 See Secretary of State Madeleine Albright, 'Prepared Statement before the Senate Armed Services Committee', 23 April 1997. State Department website. URL: http://secretary.state.gov/www/statements/970432.html, p. 4.

26 'Prepared Testimony by Chairman Pete V. Dominici'. Hearings before the Committee on the Budget, United States Senate, 105th Congress, First Session, 23 October 1997. (Washington, DC: GPO 1998) and 'Prepared Statement of James A. Baker III'. *Ibid.*

27 J. M. Goldgeier, *Not Whether but When: The US Decision to Enlarge NATO.* (Washington, DC: Brookings Institution 1999), pp. 152ff.

28 *Ibid.*, p. 38.

29 The primary Clinton administration proponent of the 'Germany first' position was Richard Holbrooke, then Assistant Secretary of State for European and Canadian Affairs. See Goldgeier, p. 171.

30 The criteria later established by Secretary of Defense William Perry included the following: those states seeking membership in NATO had to demonstrate that they would not detract from the credibility of the alliance, demonstrate a commitment to collective defence, demonstrate a commitment to consensus decision-making and strive towards the interoperability of their armed forces and doctrine with those of NATO. 'US Security Strategy for Europe and NATO' *op.cit.*, p. 5.

31 See Secretary of Defense William Cohen, 'Statement before the Committee on Foreign Relations, United States Senate', 24 February 1998. URL: http://www.fas.org/man/nato/congress/1998/98022411_tpo.html, pp. 4–5.

32 Secretary of State Warren Christopher, 'A Democratic and Undivided Europe' *op.cit.* 'Prepared Statement of Franklin D. Kramer, Assistant Secretary of Defense for International Security Affairs'. 'The Debate on NATO Enlargement' *op.cit.*, p. 94.

33 Secretary of State Madeleine Albright, 'Statement before the Senate Appropriations Committee', 21 October 1997. State Department website. URL: http://www.secretary.state.gov/www/statements/971021.html, p. 2.

34 *Ibid.*
35 'Statement of William E. Odom, Lt. Gen.'. 'The Debate on NATO Enlargement' *op.cit.*, p. 240.
36 'Statement of Hon. Henry A. Kissinger'. *Ibid.*, p. 184.
37 'Prepared Testimony by Susan Eisenhower'. Senate Budget Committee, 29 October 1997. URL: http://web.lexis-nexis.com/congcom ... 8e0289e09bdc2757fcc7ba&taggedDocs=, p. 6.
38 See testimony of Senator Jesse Helms, 'The Debate on NATO Enlargement' *op.cit.*, p. 3.
39 On the content and record of the Founding Act and Permanent Joint Council see Laura Richards Cleary, Chapter 11 in this volume.
40 For the Clinton administration's rebuttal of these concerns, see testimony by Secretary of State Madeleine Albright. 'The Debate on NATO Enlargement' *op.cit.*, p. 11. For the Senate's concern about this issue, see testimony by Senator John Kyl. 'NATO's 50th Anniversary Summit' *op.cit.*, p. 10.
41 R. Kugler, *Enlarging NATO: The Russia Factor.* (Santa Monica: RAND 1996), p. 3.
42 For analysis of the importance of the Saint Malo Declaration and the shifts in UK policy see Stuart Gordon, Chapter 9 in this volume.
43 For the Petersberg Tasks see Wyn Rees, Chapter 6 in this volume.
44 'European Council Declaration on Strengthening the European Common Policy on Security and Defence' (the Cologne European Council, 3 and 4 June 1999). *Internationale Politik* 1 (1) 2000, pp. 114–15.
45 See 'Joint Declaration by the British and French Governments on European Defence, at the Anglo-French Summit on November 25, 1999, in London'. *Internationale Politik* 1 (2) 2000, p. 132 and 'Presidency Conclusions at the Helsinki European Council, 10 and 11 December 1999'. *Internationale Politik* 1 (1) 2000, p. 139.
46 Undersecretary of State for Political Affairs Thomas R. Pickering, 'A Transatlantic Partnership for the 21st Century'. 8 December 1998, Columbia University, New York City. Text available from the Information Research Centre, US Embassy, London.
47 The Washington communiqué insisted that defence co-operation with the EU would be mediated by the WEU and that operations under the CJTF concept would be led by the WEU. See 'Washington Summit Communiqué'. *NATO Review* 47 (2) 1999, p. D4.
48 *Loc.cit.*
49 'Prepared Statement of E. Anthony Wayne (Principal Deputy Assistant Secretary of State, Bureau of European Affairs). The European Union: Internal Reform, Enlargement, and the Common Foreign and Security Policy'. Hearing before the Subcommittee on European Affairs of the Committee on Foreign Relations, United States Senate, 106th Congress, First Session, 24 March 1999. (Washington, DC: GPO 1999), p. 13.
50 Senate Resolution 175. 106th Congress, First Session, 5 August 1999. Section 1 (b) (6, 7, 9 and 10).
51 Senate Resolution 208. 106th Congress, First Session, 3 November 1999. Section 1 (b) (1, 2, and 4). See also 'Statement of the Hon. Franklin D. Kramer, Assistant Secretary of Defense for International Security Affairs. NATO and the EU's European Security and Defense Policy'. Hearing before the Subcommittee on European Affairs of the Committee on Foreign Relations, United States Senate, 106th Congress, Second Session, 9 March 2000. (Washington, DC: GPO 2000).
52 'Statement of Peter W. Rodman'. 'The European Union: Internal Reform, Enlargement, and the Common Foreign and Security Policy' *op.cit.*, p. 41.

8 France

Willing the means to the end?

R. E. Utley

Introduction

'From 1945 to 1989, the great glaciation of the Cold War was beneficial for France . . . In the Cold War, France found comfort and flourished.'[1] Indeed, the bipolarity of international relations in Europe during the Cold War provided an environment exploited by successive French leaders from Charles de Gaulle onwards to engineer a particularly 'French' course in external relations. The superpower standoff, backed by well-armed, opposing alliance blocs, and centred on a divided Germany, facilitated the French approach. Based on ideas of national rank, status and autonomy, characterised by the development of a national nuclear deterrent capability and withdrawal from NATO's integrated military system, France pursued ostensibly independent external policies in the search for a 'third force' position in international affairs. It was semi-detached from the Atlantic Alliance, often critical in relations with the United States, more positive towards the USSR and a driving force for West European co-operation.

The end of the Cold War thus removed many of the perceived constants of French external policy calculations. The division of Europe was ended, Germany was reunified, the USSR collapsed and the Atlantic Alliance found itself without an adversary as the Warsaw Pact dissolved. New states emerged in Europe, tensions were rife in the former Soviet republics, and significant questions were raised regarding the value of nuclear deterrence in meeting the new challenges.

In the face of such upheaval in the foundations of France's security, it took some time for new directions to be defined by the leadership. However, certain distinct strands could be seen. France, although unsettled by the end of the Cold War, was unlikely to surrender hopes for rank, status and a degree of independence in her external relations. She was similarly unlikely to alter the fundamentals of her relations with the United States, and was likely to remain at best a critical friend. And concern over the residual capabilities and emerging instabilities of the USSR/Russia was prominent. One of the clearest strands of post-Cold War French external policy, however, emerged as the construction of Europe. Not only would this give an element of continuity with previous policy direction, in a rapidly changing external environment, but it would also provide a framework to manage the capabilities of the newly reunified Germany and to maintain a strong French role in European affairs. French advocacy of closer European relations quickly extended beyond previous efforts for economic and political co-operation, to include defence and security – areas where the bases of previous French international calculations had been most shaken by the end of the Cold War and its consequences.

Therefore, the end of the Cold War brought into sharp relief the redundancy of previous French security calculations, and the difficulties France would face in adapting to the demands of a new era in international security. Prioritising European co-operation, France sought to promote concert and collaboration primarily among the West European states themselves. However, facing suspicion and reticence on the part of certain European partners, France's focus shifted towards the search for European security within the context of the Atlantic Alliance. After years of distance from NATO's integrated security structures, though, France was little more satisfied in this path than she had been in the prior European framework. However, as Europe stumbled reluctantly towards the security conception preferred by France in the last years of the twentieth century, practical impulses to enhance co-operation came from the experience of the war over Kosovo, and political advances were made in terms of France's relations with the UK. Paris is well aware that the journey is far from over, but at the beginning of the twenty-first century the signs are perhaps more encouraging for France than they have ever been.

France, security and Europe

The theme of European security runs like a thread through France's post-1945 external policies. The Brussels Treaty (which created the Western European Union) and the Atlantic Alliance in the 1940s; debates over West German rearmament and the European Defence Community in the 1950s; the Franco-German Elysée Treaty in the 1960s; attempts to revive the Western European Union (WEU) under Pompidou in the 1970s; and François Mitterrand's revitalisation of Franco-German security co-operation, as a prelude to wider European efforts (initially again through the WEU), in the 1980s; all attest to the importance of European security concerns in the French polity. Such concerns became still more acute in the aftermath of the Cold War: in the fundamentally altered strategic circumstances of the 1990s, the European dimension came to dominate security debates in France. But what was understood by security? Who is European? And how is European security to be achieved?

Undoubtedly, in the Cold War period security in France was understood primarily in its military sense, and predominantly in relation to the national territory. However, in the 1990s France (in common with many other Western states) adopted a more expansive understanding of security, in terms of geography and potential threats. As Prime Minister Edouard Balladur argued in France's 1994 *Livre blanc* (White Paper) on defence:

> France's defence [was] no longer applicable only at her immediate borders. It depend[ed] on the maintenance of international stability, and on the prevention of crises, in Europe or outside Europe, which would place [France's] interests and [her] security in danger if they degenerated.[2]

If a threat from the East remained, in the shape of residual Russian military capabilities and uncertainty as to future political developments in the former USSR, France was equally conscious that her security could be called into question throughout Central and Eastern Europe; into the Mediterranean and the Middle East; and to Africa and beyond, incorporating potential threats to overseas departments and territories. Moreover, if France's new thinking on security encompassed more clearly an extended geographical vision, it was similarly expansive on the new types of threat envisaged. The *Livre blanc* recognised the security challenges of proliferation of weapons of mass destruction and their means of delivery; terrorism; religious extremism and nationalism; drug trafficking and organised crime; and the destabilising effects of the growth in world population and uneven economic development.[3] To these were added, by President Jacques Chirac in 1996, the fragility of numerous states in the post-Cold War world, the assertion of new international actors, and potential clashes of interest between ambitious regional powers.[4] France, then, was well aware that a wide range of potential threats could emerge from the uncertainties of the new security era.

None the less, given the immediate practical challenges to security and stability perceived by France in the 1990s (the break-up of Yugoslavia and its consequences, primarily, but also crises in the Middle East and Chechnya, for example), and their significant military aspects, the concept of security has remained closely linked to questions of defence. In contrast to the Cold War years, however, national responses to potentially multifaceted security challenges are no longer favoured. It is widely recognised that national actions, in the majority of cases, have become not only impractical, but also unfeasible. As it was increasingly acknowledged that France was no longer a great power,[5] it was recognised that in the majority of cases the country did not possess sufficient political, financial and military capabilities to effect an assertive national role in international affairs. Consequently, France completed something of a sea change in considerations of external defence and security issues. The traditional Gaullist watchwords of autonomy and independence in external affairs were more shelved than scuppered, but the emphasis was firmly shifted towards multilateral and co-operative approaches to the management of international security challenges. Multilateralism was envisaged in a number of contexts, from *ad hoc* bilateral arrangements at the one extreme through to formalised NATO or UN operations at the other. Nevertheless, building on France's determined political and diplomatic efforts of the 1980s, the preferred context for co-operation has been Europe. As Chirac reiterated:

> Europe can and must assert itself again as one of the world's great actors. First of all it must assure peace and security on its own territory. To guarantee these, a new security architecture must be built . . . Europe must also contribute to global stability, as its history, its level of development and its interests command. It must therefore have a real common foreign and security policy.[6]

Europe, however, holds particular connotations in French political minds. While de Gaulle regularly espoused the creation of Europe from the Atlantic to the Urals, subsequent French conceptions have been much more restrained. 'Europe' means Western Europe, largely through the framework of the European Union. Especially in the realm of defence and security, it has become focused on a core of France, Germany and, increasingly, the United Kingdom.[7]

If the end – a European security capability based on the primary co-operation of Paris, Berlin and London – is therefore clear, the means to that end have been distinctly less clear in recent years. In the last decade France has made heavy diplomatic investments in all of the European security institutions considered in Part II of this volume. Initially favouring the CSCE/OSCE as a pan-European institution, particularly in terms of managing any residual Russian threat to European security, before becoming disillusioned by its weaknesses, France thereafter privileged the European Union and pursuit of a Common Foreign and Security Policy (CFSP) for Europe. In such a context the WEU again returned to prominence. However, the major difficulty for France has been NATO: having originally toyed with supplanting NATO in the early post-Cold War years with a European security capability not involving the USA, successive governments in Paris found that their alliance partners were far from keen to trade uniquely European options for Washington's political and military might. Thus French strategy changed from seeking a European security order without NATO to achieving that order in the context of Alliance reform from within. This has the added benefit, of course, of preserving a US commitment, which France may not like, but which contributes to French security as much as it does to any of the other NATO members. As Jacques Baumel[8] argued quite frankly, 'the maintenance on the Old Continent of a certain American military presence and solid political commitment [was] the only real counterweight to the serious threats that Europe could yet face'.[9]

Common security through the European Union

> The European Union is an economic giant, which has still not suc-
> ceeded in equipping itself, on the international stage, with a political
> influence in line with its economic and financial strength. The devel-
> opment of the CFSP is therefore a crucial question for the very future
> of European construction. The development of the CFSP is equally
> critical in order that the European Union fully asserts itself in the
> reconstruction of Europe after the end of the Cold War, in meeting
> the new threats which have emerged with the disappearance of the
> bipolar world and in the readjustment of international relations now
> dominated by one sole superpower.[10]

The importance of a common European position on security questions is
plain to see in French political thinking, in terms of the European Union
itself, and the potency of the EU on the world stage. France sought in the
1990s to cement European security co-operation in the Treaty on European
Union concluded at Maastricht (1992), and in subsequent amendments
incorporated at Amsterdam (1997).[11] However, the French polity has been
struck as much by the shortcomings as by the successes of this approach.

On the plus side for France, Maastricht made significant progress in
establishing the notion of a CFSP for Europe. Together with related provisions envisaging a common defence, linked to the role of the WEU, and
affording primacy in CFSP decisions to intergovernmental institutions,
Maastricht seemed to fulfil many French objectives. CFSP was elevated on
the European agenda, common defence – and the means to implement it
without the USA – was foreshadowed, and national control over any such
developments was retained as decision-making powers remained with the
governments of member states. Accordingly, Prime Minister Pierre
Bérégovoy described progress towards European security at Maastricht as
'the most dazzling'[12] of all the developments affecting French security
since the end of the Cold War.

However, French hopes for Maastricht and CFSP soon appeared to have
been misplaced. CFSP proved controversial among EU member states, on
at least three counts. First, it was difficult to argue in the early 1990s that
there was any common vision among the partners on questions of foreign
and security policy, as shown by their massively divergent positions in
response to the Yugoslav crisis.[13] Second, there were fears among several
member states regarding a potential dilution of sovereignty in CFSP and a
common defence. This was particularly a British concern.[14] Third, there
was significant discord over the means by which CFSP and a common
defence would be implemented, with the treaty preference for WEU con-
flicting with the positions of EU members who also held membership of
NATO, and those who were neutral, and thus could not adhere to the
mutual defence clauses associated with WEU.

CFSP was not assisted by its association with France and Germany, and with French preferences in particular. From early in the post-Cold War period, many suspicions were raised – particularly in Britain – regarding France's motives and objectives in advancing this course. Margaret Thatcher, referring to wider Franco-German initiatives towards European Union, captured something of the mood when she referred to 'the Franco-German juggernaut'.[15] Proposals from Paris and Bonn for a Community-wide Common Foreign and Security Policy had emerged as early as 1990. Mrs Thatcher was immediately sceptical about such a plan.[16] The proposals were complemented by regular calls for the development and enhancement of a European security architecture, by implication at least downgrading the role and significance of NATO. Britain's opposition to this was shared to varying degrees, at various times, by Italy, the Netherlands and Portugal. Franco-German concepts were bolstered in 1991 by plans to convert the Franco-German Brigade, constructed in the 1980s, into a Franco-German Corps, later the Eurocorps, in which other European partners could participate. Presented as constituting the 'embryo of a European army',[17] and as such almost guaranteed to cause alarm among states who perceived a potential erosion of NATO (Britain and Italy, notably, in this respect),[18] the corps was strongly perceived to be 'Mitterrand's Trojan horse, an instrument to hijack the Alliance'.[19]

If France's security achievements at Maastricht soon came under challenge outside France, the disappointment inside France also mounted. It was recognised that realisation of CFSP, if it happened at all, would take much time: 'the old nations of Europe [would] not easily renounce the prerogatives which [were] at the heart of their sovereignty'.[20] The problems faced by France's vision of CFSP were increased as there was no founding political concept common to all the EU's member states.[21] In the three years from the treaty's conclusion, it was noted that European security and defence co-operation hardly progressed at all.[22] If integration in general, and a unified common security policy in particular, was to succeed, 'France . . . must convince her partners and give them her vision of the future European status.'[23] Maastricht effectively constituted unfulfilled promise: as Jacques Chirac was well aware in 1996, 'the most part remain[ed] to be done'[24] in European security.

After the optimism that had surrounded the signing of the Maastricht Treaty, the treaty concluded at Amsterdam was rated in France as a qualified success, at best, for European defence and security.[25] On the plus side, CFSP was reaffirmed, the decision-making powers of the European Council were substantially reinforced, and, at French insistence, a High Representative for Common Foreign and Security Policy was to be appointed, to enhance the perceptions and effectiveness of CFSP on the world stage.[26]

Less positively, however, clear concerns arose in France as to the shortcomings of the Amsterdam Treaty. Although progress had been made in addressing institutional weaknesses in the Maastricht Treaty, the main focus had been on points of economic and monetary stability, and the continued absence of a common vision on foreign and security policy among the European partners meant further advances in this area were unlikely. Moreover, the value of CFSP agreements that had been concluded was entirely dependent on their confirmation in practice. In addition, problems over voting and weighting in the EU were unresolved: France held reservations about the extent of voting still required to be unanimous, and the limited range of areas where qualified majority voting could be implemented. This was potentially compounded by concerns for 'balance' between smaller and larger members of the EU, especially as it entered a phase of enlargement. Paris had no wish that concerted action, if desired by the principal member states (France, Germany and the UK, for example), could be prevented by groupings of smaller or neutral states, and would thus have preferred to see greater weightings given to the voting positions of those principal members.[27] Last, France was disappointed by limitations on the role of the High Representative for Common Foreign and Security Policy – commonly referred to as 'Monsieur PESC' (from *politique étrangère et de sécurité commune*). In this respect, the treaty was perceived to fall 'somewhat short of French demands',[28] as 'Monsieur PESC' was considered to have insufficient scope for independent, autonomous action, thereby reducing the value of his role. For Prime Minister Lionel Jospin in 1997, the Amsterdam Treaty provisions, so 'laboriously'[29] agreed in security and defence, were inadequate: '[France] must go much further again and give back to European defence co-operation indispensable political momentum.'[30] Both Maastricht and Amsterdam, it was argued, were most prominently characterised by their 'timidities',[31] and France's conception of European security would not be achieved by timidity.

Maastricht and Amsterdam, therefore, were profoundly disappointing for France in terms of the application of their provisions on common security. However, Paris remained undeterred as to the final goal, and employed a significant degree of diplomatic pragmatism in order to achieve the end by other means. As the extent of EU members' opposition to a European security capability without the USA was emphasised in the negotiations and aftermath of Maastricht (and as France's own security needs were considered realistically), Paris changed tactics, and the focus of French attention in creating an effective European security effort switched to the Atlantic Alliance.

Common security through NATO

As the Cold War ended, NATO in its then form was distinctly not, for France, the preferred structure for a European security order. Defence Minister Jean-Pierre Chevènement argued that NATO doctrine had effectively been bankrupted by the end of the Cold War,[32] and this view gained ground as the role of military alliances was increasingly called into question.

However, as the obstacles to attaining an effective, autonomous European capability outside NATO increased, the prospect of achieving it from within the Alliance became more attractive.

For France, the enhancement of the European pillar of the Atlantic Alliance offered numerous advantages. Not least, it would maintain an effective Alliance (read US) role in European security, from which France had benefited for over forty years – notwithstanding her withdrawal from NATO's integrated military structures in 1966. In addition, while maintaining US involvement in European security, it offered arguably the best prospects for reducing US preponderance in the Alliance, a preponderance which was no more easily reconciled with French political priorities in the 1990s than it had been at any time since the Second World War. This would provide the opportunities to increase French influence in the resultant Alliance. Moreover, if a European security capability was to be achieved at all, attainment from within the Alliance represented perhaps the only workable means to the end.

Consequently, France sought to enhance the role and status of the European partners within NATO. Working with Germany, she gained acceptance by Washington of the principle of a European Security and Defence Identity (ESDI) at NATO's London summit in July 1990, and quietly increased French participation in NATO decision-making processes and military activities.[33] France became more overtly co-operative with NATO under the right-wing *cohabitation* government of 1993–5, helping to police the NATO-controlled no-fly zone over Bosnia and extending political participation in the Alliance, for example, while bringing firmer pressures to bear for a stronger, potentially autonomous European pillar of the Alliance. Positive results were seen at NATO's Brussels summit of 1994, which introduced the principles of Combined Joint Task Forces (CJTF). Small, responsive and highly mobile, CJTF in theory could be exclusively European in composition, and could be placed under European (WEU) command if necessary.[34] Thus, at least potentially, the CJTF concept could constitute a clear contribution to the development of an effective European pillar within the Alliance.

Under the new presidency of Jacques Chirac from May 1995, relations between France and NATO ostensibly continued to improve. In December 1995, Foreign Minister Hervé de Charette unexpectedly announced a series of measures extending French participation in the Alliance. France's Defence Minister was to participate regularly in the work of the Alliance; France would take her full seat on the Military Committee; Paris would participate in the NATO Defence College, the Oberammergau School and NATO's Situation Centre; and working relations between France and SHAPE (Supreme Headquarters Allied Powers Europe) would be improved.[35] Indeed, de Charette held out the prospect of further improvements in France–NATO relations, if greater progress was made towards 'the emergence of a visible European identity, both on the military and political level, within the Alliance',[36] strengthening the role of the WEU and building on the concessions to European capabilities characterised by the CJTF principles. Moreover, the new French approach appeared to be generating results. In the conclusions of the NATO Foreign Ministers' meeting in Berlin in June 1996, the European element was prominent.[37] The allies agreed on prior designation of command, control and support structures to be used in the event of WEU-led CJTF operations. The European deputy to the US Supreme Allied Commander Europe (SACEUR), it was further agreed, would serve as WEU supreme commander in charge of European operations, and the right of NATO to influence European operations was minimised. For Prime Minister Alain Juppé, the incorporation of such specific provisions in support of the European Security and Defence Identity was the meeting's 'principal achievement'.[38]

However, it would be wrong to suggest that French rapprochement with NATO, in pursuit of both national and European objectives, was either very successful or very comfortable. On the contrary, France–NATO relations – and in this context particularly Franco-US relations – were difficult, and neither party was satisfied with the course of developments. The divergence between Paris and Washington by the time of the NATO summit in Madrid, in July 1997, was such that discord surrounded almost every issue, from NATO enlargement to the allocation of commands in NATO's new command structure. All prospect of full French reintegration into NATO was withdrawn. The rapprochement had lasted for a year and a half.

Difficulties had emerged, in fact, as early as 1990, as France began to seek reform of NATO to reflect her own national and European priorities. Although the London summit of that year accepted the principle of ESDI, it also agreed to rely more heavily on multinational corps in future operations, and moved towards acceptance of an out-of-area capability for the Alliance.[39] Increased reliance on multinational formations implied increased military integration, even as France argued that the end of the Cold War reduced the need for integration. An out-of-area capability suggested yet wider US influence in and beyond Europe. France was therefore opposed to both initiatives. Further rejection of excessive US weight in NATO, relative to that of the Europeans, was apparent in attempts to limit the powers of NATO's US SACEUR.[40] The benefits of US involvement in European security were recognised, but France showed clearly her perception that the end of the Cold War meant a reduced role for Washington, and a clearer role for France, and Europe. It was thus a position unlikely to appeal to the United States.

The improvement in relations between France and NATO under Balladur's *cohabitation* government was accompanied by continued pressures for reform, and by further criticisms of military integration and the role of SACEUR. Moreover, French disquiet was exacerbated, rather than alleviated, by NATO's stance on CJTF at the 1994 Brussels summit and thereafter. France had secured agreement on CJTF by means of a compromise involving Paris's support for the Partnership for Peace (PfP) programme, strengthening links with Central and Eastern states with a view to extending NATO's membership. Little was formalised at Brussels regarding CJTF and, especially, their use in European frameworks under European command. While PfP subsequently pushed on apace,[41] little progress was perceived in Paris on defining CJTF, giving rise to strong perceptions that US commitment to a European pillar of the Alliance was questionable.[42] By early 1995, French political opinion had become clearly dissatisfied with progress on the Brussels objectives for Europe: reinforcement of WEU to allow fulfilment of its new roles was declared a priority, and, with regard to CJTF, France fervently – and publicly – hoped that the issue '[could] pass from the stage of concept to that of practical reality'.[43]

The rapprochement of Chirac's early presidency was similarly accompanied by tensions and divergence in France–NATO and Franco-US relations. Encompassing a range of issues, in the context of the European security capability they again came to focus on arrangements for European deployment of CJTF, and the relationship these missions would bear to NATO's integrated military system. Although matters were eventually resolved, with much difficulty, largely in favour of French positions,[44] the issue had led to real differences with Washington. Nor did that prove to be the end of divergence. As NATO negotiated a reformed command structure in 1996–7 the problems over implementing a 'real' European pillar resurfaced. In discussions on the reallocation of NATO commands, it emerged that France still believed the USA retained an excessive number of posts. France not only sought to reduce this number, and to redistribute US responsibilities among the Europeans, but also to achieve a similar share of the command structure for herself as was occupied by Britain and Germany. In particular, France demanded European control of NATO's Southern Region command, ultimately meeting headlong with a point-blank US refusal.[45] This was not the only area of divergence as NATO's Madrid summit loomed: Paris and Washington also disagreed over the scale of forthcoming NATO enlargement.[46] However, the question of the Southern command proved critical. In the face of US refusals to cede what France perceived to be adequate recognition of, and responsibility to, NATO's still-nascent European pillar, Paris announced that notwithstanding its reforms, France would not reintegrate into NATO's military command structures.[47]

Therefore, by the later 1990s it seemed that both of France's strategies for securing a European security identity and capability had failed. The EU-based approach had shown significant limitations, as France's partners were reluctant to countenance the creation of a European security and defence stance independent of the United States. The alternative approach, working to construct such a position within the Alliance, had proved equally limited as French and US interests collided.

A way out of this predicament for France emerged in 1998–9. Ironically, as the security situation in the Balkans deteriorated, with large-scale Serb repression of Kosovar Albanians, France found a new path towards effective European security co-operation.

Common security: a precedent set in Kosovo?

As fragile Balkan stability deteriorated from 1997, this time in Kosovo, the European Union again faced a challenge to its security and stability on its very borders. France was closely involved in efforts on all fronts – EU, OSCE, UN, international Contact Group and NATO – to resolve the crisis, out of preference through diplomacy, but through the use of force if necessary. There were numerous reasons for France's prominent role, including humanitarian concerns and international law; conceptions of a historic French role in the Balkans; and inclinations to maintain prestige and status in international affairs. There was also a fourth reason: Europe. It was vital in French perceptions that through concern for European unity, and particularly through concern to advance the prospect of a European security capability, a strong European element should be maintained in resolving what was, after all, a European crisis.

France's political leaders were explicit about the linkage between the Kosovo crisis and the opportunities it provided to advance France's European security and defence ideal. President Chirac, in particular, was overt in the connections he established. In a speech of April 1999, he insisted that 'faced with this conflict on European soil, the European Union must indeed play its full role'.[48] He reiterated his view a week later: 'it was indispensable that the European Union play[ed] its full part in the political resolution of a crisis which was unfolding at its door'.[49] As Prime Minister Lionel Jospin argued before the National Assembly as NATO air strikes began, 'What [was] at stake . . . [was] a certain idea of Europe.'[50]

However, France's pursuit of the European ideal in the context of the Kosovo crisis overall demonstrated a degree of flexibility and pragmatism which had been missing in earlier efforts to achieve a European security capability. Thus it was noteworthy that the EU was not the institution charged with implementing crisis diplomacy, after its failures earlier in the decade to resolve the Yugoslav civil war. Rather, French efforts were channelled through the diplomatic processes of the international Contact Group, on the one hand, bolstered by the threat of military action by NATO on the other. None the less, the 'European' criterion was apparently maintained. Not least, four of the six Contact Group members were leading members of the European Union – France, Germany, Italy and the UK – and three of these constituted France's ideal core of any European security capability. In addition, all these four would be significantly committed to NATO action alongside the USA if diplomacy failed. Therefore, if precedents could be set for effective diplomatic co-operation, and for coordinated military action if diplomacy failed, the prospects for a European security and defence capability could be significantly enhanced. After

France's disappointment with the Amsterdam Treaty, Kosovo offered an opportunity to kick-start European security co-operation.

Paradoxically, Kosovo also offered the prospect of relaunching the second strand of France's European security plans – that of working through NATO. In this sense the timing of the conflict was critical. The diplomatic process at Rambouillet collapsed in February 1999, NATO air strikes were launched in March, and NATO's fiftieth anniversary summit and agreement on a new Strategic Concept took place in April. Therefore, a solid French presence in NATO's military action could, again, serve both national and European ends. Not only could it reassert French claims for a leadership role in a reformed Alliance, it could also provide firm foundations for recognition of a capable, and credible, European pillar within the Alliance.

This position on Europe dominated France's approach to the negotiation of NATO's new Strategic Concept. The French position was encapsulated by Chirac in his message on the Alliance's anniversary:

> the Alliance today must take into account the profound strategic changes on the continent of Europe. Among the trends, two [were] critical: first, the consolidation of the European Union which [would] allow the Europeans to take on an increasing role, while strengthening the Alliance overall and, secondly, the creation of a European defence identity within the Alliance. This [was] a prerequisite for a revitalised transatlantic link based on a balanced dialogue between the United States and the European Union.[51]

As the basic position remained largely unchanged, so too did areas of particular French concern. For France, the new Strategic Concept should explicitly recognise developments towards a European defence capability, and should allow the utilisation of NATO support, in a non-NATO framework, by the European members of the Alliance, as and when necessary. It also required acceptance of the facts that European military capabilities were essentially limited, and that European states could not afford, and mostly did not want, the luxury of maintaining separate forces for NATO and non-NATO military actions. Codification of the European Security and Defence Identity in NATO doctrine represented the only way that, realistically, it could be achieved. NATO, then, remained largely a convenient means to a long-standing European end for France.

So how successful was France in advancing the cause of European security through the experience of the Kosovo crisis? In the field of practical European co-operation, assessments in France were mixed. The perception was strong in France during the war that Europe was missing a historic opportunity. It had been missed diplomatically, as non-EU bodies had undertaken primary responsibility in crisis diplomacy; it had been missed militarily, as NATO's role clearly demonstrated. Even among Chirac's own party, 'the fact that [NATO found] itself in the front line show[ed France] how far [she] still [had] to go for Europe to be free'.[52] For many, the crucial point was this: Europe 'did not have the means for its diplomacy';[53] it was a 'military dwarf'.[54] None the less, as the war ended the French government's portrayal of European achievements was markedly more positive. Europe, meaning the EU, had emerged as a real political force on the continent. Its capacity to act was reiterated in the post-war arrangements for the troop commitments in Kosovo (in the context of NATO's Kosovo Force). In composition, command assignation and subsequently in plans for command to be exercised by the Eurocorps, the emphasis was firmly placed on Europe. Moreover, NATO's new Strategic Concept made regular reference to ESDI and the prospects for an increased European pillar in the Alliance.[55] French authorities therefore had some cause for satisfaction in the precedents set by the Kosovo crisis for the future of the European security capability.

Common security: into the new century

If recent developments prove to be reliable indicators of future progression, it seems that French objectives in relation to a European security capability are indeed on the way to fruition. The experiences of Kosovo, bolstered by developments in defence and European security between France and the UK, and to a lesser extent France and Germany, and emphasised by the achievements of the Cologne and Helsinki European Council meetings, all represent a revitalisation of France's search for a new European security capability to meet the challenges of a new era. None the less, there are also signs of realistic pragmatism in France's positions. Paris is fully cognisant of the challenges that remain to be faced along the path to France's preferred European security order, and in general is not expecting rapid progress.

Perhaps the single most promising development for France has been the significant improvement in relations between the UK and France since the centre-left governments of Tony Blair and Lionel Jospin came to power in May and June 1997. More openly favourable towards the enhancement of European unity than his predecessors, including in the field of foreign, security and defence issues, Blair has gone further than any of his recent predecessors in establishing co-operative and constructive relations with France even on such potentially sensitive questions.

Primary among the achievements, in the French view, is the agreement concluded at the Anglo-French summit in Saint Malo in December 1998. Firm in tone, the declaration called for the European Union to have an 'autonomous capacity for action, supported by credible military forces, with the means to decide to use them, and a readiness to do so in order to respond to international crises'.[56] Combined with a Letter of Intent also signed at Saint Malo by UK Defence Minister George Robertson and his French counterpart Alain Richard, designed to improve the UK–French co-operation in crisis management and military operations, the political desire to improve UK–French military relations was clear. Moreover, the value of the declaration to France, in terms of advancing the goal of European security, was enhanced when German weight was added at the conclusion of the subsequent Franco-German summit in Toulouse.

The emphasis on renewed progress towards European defence was accentuated for France by UK–French co-operation in the diplomatic and military phases of the Kosovo crisis, in negotiations to incorporate ESDI into NATO's new Strategic Concept and particularly at the EU summit in Cologne in June 1999. In a declaration on the reinforcement of a Common European Security and Defence Policy, incorporating much of the phraseology of the Saint Malo Declaration, EU leaders undertook to equip the European Union with the means and capabilities to assume its security and defence responsibilities, to enhance its conflict-prevention and crisis-management capacities, to improve European military forces at all levels, and to incorporate the WEU into the EU by the end of the year 2000.[57] The new vitality of European security co-operation was underlined at the subsequent EU summit in Helsinki in December 1999. In line with calls made at the Anglo-French summit of November 1999, the Helsinki meeting agreed on the formation of a European Rapid Reaction Corps (50,000–60,000 strong), deployable within sixty days, and sustainable for at least a year.[58]

Despite such progress, however, France retains a degree of uncertainty, and elements of dissatisfaction, regarding achievements to date and prospects for their continuance. Relations with the UK, while viewed with much satisfaction, are also perceived to depend largely on Tony Blair and his Labour government.[59] Regarding the decisions of the Cologne European Council, they are argued in France to have been 'still lack[ing] in real substance and incorporat[ing] many ambiguities'.[60] Helsinki, for all its positive achievements, in the French view, was but a 'staging post'[61] on the way towards European defence, and the inability of the EU members to agree on the best way to encourage Russian moderation in its battles in Chechnya was not thought to bode well for CFSP even at this advanced stage.

In conclusion, it can be seen that a European security order, predicated as much on EU strengths as possible, remains a clear French goal at the beginning of the new century. However, if the objective was clear, the means to the end were much less so. France will thus continue to show determination in pursuit of her European security ideal, and will continue to deploy pragmatism and flexibility to attain a conclusion as near to her own preferences as possible. Progress will not necessarily be rapid, and achievements may not be complete, but Paris's course is set, and no significant redirection is likely in the foreseeable future.

Notes and references

1 F. Bujon de l'Estang, formerly a foreign policy adviser to Jacques Chirac, cited in J. Laughland, *The Death of Politics: France under Mitterrand.* (London: Michael Joseph 1994), p. 229.

2 *Livre blanc sur la Défense, 1994.* (Paris: La Documentation Française 1994), p. 3.

3 *Ibid.*, pp. 21–2, 26–7, 30–1.

4 J. Chirac, 'La politique de défense de la France'. *Défense Nationale* 52 (8/9) 1996, pp. 7–18.

5 The 1990s witnessed an extensive debate in France on the country's status as an international power. For a useful discussion see P. Boniface, *La France est-elle encore une grande puissance?* (Paris: Presses de la Fondation Nationale des Sciences Politiques 1998).

6 Chirac *op.cit.*, p. 8.

7 On the importance of this trilateral approach, see, *inter alia*, L. Le Hégarat, 'Union politique et défense européenne'. *Défense Nationale* 49 (8/9) 1993, pp. 75–85; P. Moreau Defarges, 'L'Union européenne après six mois, ou le rêve évanoui'. *Défense Nationale* 50 (5) 1994, pp. 79–88.

8 French Senator, former Minister and President of the Defence Commission of the WEU.

9 J. Baumel, 'La France, l'OTAN et l'Europe'. *Défense Nationale* 51 (3) 1995, p. 85.

10 A. Barrau, *Rapport d'Information sur la Politique Etrangère, de Sécurité et de Défense Commune de l'Union Européenne* 2254. Assemblée Nationale 16 March 2000. URL: http://www.assemblee-nat.fr/2/2cra.htm.

11 The Consolidated Version of the Treaty on European Union, incorporating the Amsterdam amendments, can be accessed through the website of the European Union. URL: http://www.europa.eu.int.

12 P. Bérégovoy, 'Construction européenne et intérêt de la France'. *Défense Nationale* 48 (11) 1992, p. 20.

13 Critical in this respect was the divergence of France and Germany over recognition of Slovenian and Croatian independence at the turn of 1991/2. Given that the primary impulses towards CFSP had come from France and Germany, their failure to agree was particularly damaging.

14 J. Major, *The Autobiography.* (London: HarperCollins 1999), pp. 273 and 279.

15 M. Thatcher, *The Downing Street Years.* (London: HarperCollins 1993), p. 762.

16 *Ibid.*, p. 761.

17 D. Colard, 'Le couple franco-allemand après l'unification'. *Défense Nationale* 50 (6) 1994, p. 106.

18 G. Schöllgen, 'Putting Germany's Post-unification Foreign Policy to the Test'. *NATO Review* 41 (2) 1993, p. 20.

19 E. Foster, 'The Franco-German Corps: A 'Theological' Debate?' *Journal of the RUSI* 137 (4) 1992, p. 64.

20 H. Conze (ingénieur générale de l'armement), 'La défense de l'Europe: pourquoi attendre?' *Défense Nationale* 49 (5) 1993, p. 75.

21 Le Hégarat *op.cit.*, p. 79.

22 Baumel *op.cit.*, p. 87.

23 P. Vougny, '1996: Une année vitale pour l'Europe'. *Défense Nationale* 52 (1) 1996, p. 9.

24 Chirac *op.cit.*, p. 12.

25 H. de Bresson and A. Franco, 'Les Quinze ont échoué à réformer les institutions de l'Union'. *Le Monde* 19 June 1997.

26 Unsigned, 'Les principaux points du traité d'Amsterdam, qui fait suite au traité de Maastricht'. *Le Monde* 19 June 1997.

27 Barrau *op.cit.*, pp. 11 and 14.

28 A. Barrau, *Rapport d'Information sur des Propositions pour la Présidence Française de l'Union Européenne* 2138. Assemblée Nationale 3 February 2000. URL: http://www.assemblee-nat.fr/2/2cra.htm.

29 L. Jospin, 'La politique de défense de la France'. *Défense Nationale* 53 (11) 1997, p. 13.

30 *Ibid.*

31 X. de Villepin, 'Souveraineté et système européen de défense'. *Défense Nationale* 54 (12) 1998, p. 5.

32 D. Jeambar and C. Makarian, 'Jean-Pierre Chevènement, ministre de la défense: "Non-accès de l'Allemagne aux armes nucléaires"'. *Le Point* 8 January 1990.

33 French compliance allowed the formal adoption by NATO of non-article five missions, such as peacekeeping, at the June 1992 meeting of Alliance foreign ministers. A three-way agreement between France, Germany and NATO was signed in January 1993 allowing the Eurocorps to come under NATO's operational control in the event of a crisis. From December 1992 French officers were authorised to participate in NATO military staff work to consider a potential United Nations mandate to implement a Bosnian peace settlement. From April 1993 the head of France's mission to the NATO Military Committee began to participate with a 'deliberative' rather than a 'consultative' voice (observer status) in discussions of peacekeeping activities.

34 Unsigned, 'M. Léotard approuve le projet américain de forces interarmées combinées'. *Le Monde* 8 January 1994 and J. Isnard, 'Les états-majors vont concevoir des forces combinées interarmées'. *Le Monde* 13 January 1994.

35 See 'France Increases its Participation in the Transformation of the Alliance'. *NATO Review* 44 (1) 1996, p. 16.

36 *Ibid.*

37 L. Delattre and D. Vernet, 'L'Alliance Atlantique se donne une dimension européenne'. *Le Monde* 5 June 1996.

38 A. Juppé, 'Une défense inscrite dans une perspective européenne et internationale'. *Défense Nationale* 52 (11) 1996, p. 7.

39 Unsigned, '"L'OTAN doit offrir son amitié à ses anciens adversaires"'. *Le Monde* 8/9 July 1990.

40 See A. Menon, *France, NATO and the Limits of Independence, 1981–97: The Politics of Ambivalence.* (London: Macmillan 2000), ch. 2.

41 For more on PfP see Martin A. Smith, Chapter 4 in this volume.

42 A. Juppé, 'La France et la sécurité européenne'. *Défense Nationale* 51 (4) 1995, p. 7.

43 *Ibid.*, p. 8.

44 Delattre and Vernet *op.cit.* and C. Millon, 'Vers une nouvelle alliance'. *Le Monde* 11 June 1996.

45 See Menon *op.cit.*, p. 56.

46 For an indication of the scope and ill-feeling of the dispute see J. Isnard, 'La France tente d'obtenir un grand commandement régional de l'OTAN'. *Le Monde* 21/2 July 1996; J. Isnard, 'Les Etats-Unis et l'Europe se disputent le commandement sud de l'OTAN'. *Le Monde* 22/3 September 1996; Unsigned, 'Les Américains sont décidés à conserver le commandement de l'OTAN en Méditerranée'. *Le Monde* 1 October 1996; Unsigned, 'OTAN: blocage franco-américain sur la question du commandement sud de l'Alliance'. *Le Monde* 24/5 November 1996; D. Vernet, 'Jacques Chirac a engagé son autorité sur l'affaire du commandement sud'. *Le Monde* 12 December 1996; and L. Rosenzweig and D. Vernet, 'La France risque de se trouver isolée lors du sommet atlantique de Madrid'. *Le Monde* 4 July 1997.

47 In a joint communiqué issued by the Presidency and the Prime Minister's office on 2 July 1997, before the Madrid summit began. See Unsigned, 'Les conditions . . . ne sont pas réunies'. *Le Monde* 4 July 1997.

48 Unsigned, 'M. Chirac: "Une honte pour l'Europe et le monde"'. *Le Monde* 14 April 1999.

49 Unsigned, 'M. Chirac: "Mener le combat à son terme et le gagner"'. *Le Monde* 23 April 1999.

50 Unsigned, 'Lionel Jospin: "L'action militaire n'est pas une fin en soi"'. *Le Monde* 27 March 1999.

51 J. Chirac, Message to *NATO Review* 50th Anniversary Commemorative Edition 1999, p. 31.

52 J.-M. Aphatie, 'Une partie des responsables français contestent le cadre et les modalités de l'action de l'OTAN'. *Le Monde* 27 March 1999.

53 Unsigned, 'L'OTAN: l'enjeu de Washington'. *Le Monde* 24 April 1999.

54 Unsigned, 'Un nain militaire'. *Le Monde* 6 June 1999.

55 See 'The Alliance's Strategic Concept'. *NATO Review* 47 (2) 1999, pp. D7–D13.

56 'Déclaration Franco-Britannique sur la Défense Européenne, Saint-Malo (4 December 1998)'. URL: http://www.elysee.fr/mag/london11.htm.

57 'Déclaration sur le Renforcement de la Politique Européenne Commune en matière de Sécurité et Défense, Conseil Européen de Cologne (4 June 1999)'. URL: http://www.elysee.fr/mag/london09.htm. See also 'Presidency Conclusions, Cologne European Council, 3 and 4 June 1999'. URL: www.europa.eu.int/Newsroom.

58 See 'Presidency Conclusions, Helsinki European Council, 10 and 11 December 1999'. URL: http://www.europa.eu.int/Newsroom.

59 J. Baumel, 'L'Identité européenne de défense et de sécurité face à l'OTAN' in P. Pascallon (ed.), *L'Alliance Atlantique et l'OTAN, 1949–1999: un demi-siècle de succès.* (Brussels: Bruylant 1999), p. 94.

60 P. Lemaître, 'La naissance officielle de l'Europe de la défense a été proclamée Cologne'. *Le Monde* 5 June 1999.

61 P. Lemaître and L. Zecchini, 'Helsinki: élargissement, défense commune . . . et Tchétchénie'. *Le Monde* 11 December 1999.

9 The United Kingdom

Between a rock and a soft place?

Stuart Gordon[1]

Introduction

The UK's 1998 *Strategic Defence Review* (*SDR*) concentrated on a broader range of threats to British 'security' than had been the case throughout much of the Cold War period. It drew attention away from 'hard' security threats to the UK's sovereignty and territorial integrity and, instead, focused more upon 'the consequences of the break up of states' and 'ethnic and religious conflict, population and environmental pressures, and crime'[2] as fundamental sources of insecurity. This represented a broadening of the term 'insecurity' to encompass 'instability' posing a threat to the British economy, multiculturalism and wider British interests.

Furthermore, the removal of the all-encompassing threat posed by the USSR did not lead the UK into either a form of isolationism or an overriding sense that threats to security in geographically remote areas are now in some ways 'divisible' from threats to UK security. The *SDR* clearly reinforced this: 'Britain's place in the world is determined by our interests as a nation and as a leading member of the international community. Indeed the two are inextricably linked because our national interests have a vital international dimension.'[3]

British security policy has increasingly and overtly recognised the general indivisibility of systemic and British 'security' and appears firmly to underwrite the idea that the UK should be 'willing and able to play a leading role internationally'. Furthermore, it identifies that the UK has 'an important wider interest in supporting international order and in promoting freedom, democracy and prosperity'. British policy therefore appears to recognise not only a broader definition of the term 'security' but also a general commitment to international regimes, organisations, norms and principles that promote systemic and broader aspects of regional stability. Both the *SDR* and the 1999 Defence White Paper recognise continuing broad commitments to NATO, the UN and 'a wide range of other institutions' that have a 'major part to play in the development and reinforcement of European security' and the 'maintenance of international order and in promoting freedom, democracy and prosperity'.[4]

Nevertheless, not everything has changed. More traditional 'national interests' circumscribe these policy impulses. British commitments to crisis management are not universal, and underwriting 'systemic order' is not simply a product of blind enthusiasm for what Noam Chomsky describes as the 'New Military Humanism'[5] or what has also been described as the UK's 'Ethical Foreign Policy'. Instead, systemic stability is a component of social and economic stability *within* the UK. Hence, even the moral debate can be framed in terms of British 'self-interest' and the requirement to underwrite systemic stability where there are no headline national interests at stake still requires the engagement of the electorate's interest and support. In combination with material limitations on British power projection capabilities, this latter fickle and fragile requirement sets obvious limitations on British involvement in the maintenance of systemic stability. Equitable 'burden-sharing' among allies, moral compulsion and easily communicated (to the electorate) 'self-interest' all serve as means for legitimising this greater orientation towards the maintenance of systemic stability. Nevertheless, the difficulty of engaging these factors and 'legitimising' foreign policy objectives does set profound limitations on the UK's contributions to the maintenance of systemic stability.

The principal means through which the UK makes a material military contribution to systemic and regional order is through NATO and its developing crisis-management capabilities. However, increasingly British leaders have seen the need to develop capabilities through European institutions. This chapter therefore charts the changes in British attitudes to transatlantic and European security structures. In particular it examines British attitudes towards the rebalancing of the transatlantic relationship within NATO; NATO's evolving roles; and the European Security and Defence Identity (ESDI).

Rebalancing the transatlantic relationship

The end of the Cold War has changed the UK's relationship with both Europe and the USA. This has been manifest most clearly in the rebalancing of the transatlantic relationship within NATO. The Cold War saw the USA assuming a leadership position within the Alliance, reflecting obvious asymmetries in power. For Europe the advantages of this were clear: it provided both 'mass' in terms of defence and served to reduce decision-making transaction costs between the allies as a consequence of clear US leadership. The end of the Cold War has reduced the benefits of such a structure both through the dissolution of the Soviet threat and because the USA is becoming more selective about the nature and terms of its engagement with security crises than it has been since the end of the Second World War. It has also precipitated a reduction in the automaticity of European acceptance of US hegemony.

The reduction in the scale of the US military commitment has caused the UK to take more seriously the balance of power within Europe. Specifically, without a clear willingness on the part of the USA to balance Franco-German influence, the UK needs to take action to do this herself. In many ways this is a continuation of the UK's traditional policy of maintaining the balance of power in Europe, a policy with a considerable lineage. Furthermore, as several authors have noted, the UK is most useful to the USA when she is playing a leading role in Europe. Hence, without a reconfiguration of the UK's relationship with its European partners in order to provide it with this role there is a risk that it will become comparatively marginalised even within NATO.[6]

The crisis in Bosnia, prior to 1995, highlighted the fact that the USA and the Europeans would respond in different ways and at different times to crises. Without the rallying focus of the Soviet threat these differences have threatened the coherence of the North Atlantic Alliance. There is also an increasing tendency for the USA to pursue its interests unilaterally in a variety of circumstances – when it has become frustrated with its allies, disillusioned with the limited operational competence and decision-making gridlock of the United Nations and when it is fired with an urgency to take on international problems, such as the proliferation of weapons of mass destruction within Iraq and North Korea. This has had an increasing impact on NATO's strategic environment, and has shaped the terms of debate within the Alliance about the future of the 'transatlantic bargain', burden-sharing, military structures and new roles for the Alliance. NATO's response has been to work towards reconfiguration around a new self-image; that of 'separable but not separate' capabilities for the European and North Atlantic allies. Yet this represents a dangerously narrow tight-rope, particularly for the UK.

US foreign policy has obviously had to adapt with the ending of the Cold War. The USA has increasingly, although not exclusively, focused upon what could be described as the projection of 'soft' interests – democratisation, 'good governance' and liberal values as opposed to the 'hard' strategic interests of the Cold War period. In effect this is something of a foreign policy in 'soft focus'. Nevertheless, the USA has proven much more willing to use 'hard' military means, albeit limited to the use of airpower, than the majority of its European partners in terms of its policy responses to pariah regimes in both Belgrade and, since 1991, Baghdad.

The Europeans have also been forced into taking military action but more as a consequence of geography than predilection. However, their responses have been more geographically constrained and less prone to being violent. The Europeans, faced with the dissolution of Yugoslavia and uncertain that the USA will intervene in the Balkans or the Southern Mediterranean or, if it does, that it will do so in a way that is entirely consistent with European national interests, are being forced to consider mechanisms that will enable a European response in the absence of an appropriate US one. In a sense this represents the combination of geopolitical entrapment and a limited US disengagement forcing the militarily prominent European states into a rebalancing of the transatlantic relationship and an examination of the prominence of the ESDI within the European Union.

To some extent the European foreign policy positions have reflected the absence of a capability to intervene in a militarily credible way as well as the profusion of different foreign policy responses. While the emerging mechanisms for ensuring the effectiveness of the EU's Common Foreign and Security Policy (CFSP) deal with the latter problem the recent reinvigoration of the ESDI is, arguably, driven by the former and serves to increase the degree of European military autonomy. This has far less to do with the ideology of European integration and more to do with the requirement for pragmatic, effective European responses where a US presence cannot be guaranteed. It has been the main motivating factor behind changing British attitudes towards the ESDI.

Post-Cold War military engagements have served continuously to underline the weakness of European military capability in comparison with that of the USA. Within NATO, the European powers account for more than 60 per cent of the Alliance's population and a similar proportion of its armed forces personnel. While collectively spending some 60 per cent of the Pentagon's budget on defence, European capabilities are as little as one-tenth those of the USA.[7] This paucity of military capability is partly a product of the duplication of military capabilities between European states; itself largely unavoidable in a Europe populated by several states that have sought to deal with European integration in a way that seeks to preserve national sovereignty on hard security issues. There are therefore both political and military elements to Europe's incapacity. This was highlighted most graphically by Europe's troubled response to the dissolution of the former Yugoslavia from 1991. Without addressing both the military and political elements of Europe's incapacity the Europeans will be left overly dependent upon the USA. The Assembly of the Western European Union is among those that have recognised the problems inherent 'in a situation of dependence and imbalance that is extremely disadvantageous to Europe and even to our American partners'.[8]

British policy towards the rebalancing of the transatlantic relationship and the reinvigoration of the ESDI is undergoing a period of profound change. Yet UK security policy remains delicately balanced between its commitments to Europe and to the USA in a way that is reassuringly familiar. Nevertheless, it is a tightrope that is becoming ever more difficult to walk. A number of issues between Europe and the USA are either new or of increased and increasing salience. At best they represent fault lines, or areas of friction; at worst they require the type of choice that British foreign policy has, hitherto, sought to avoid. Increasingly the debate over NATO's evolving role, the 'mandate issue' and the future evolution of the ESDI will force security policy choices to be made by the UK in a way that, thus far, has not been required of policy formulators.

The UK and the legitimacy of NATO out-of-area action

The British debate over the legitimacy of NATO's evolving roles has possessed two main strands. First, there is the extent to which the North Atlantic Treaty supports roles geographically and functionally beyond those implied or specified by article five, which states that an attack on any one member state shall be considered an attack against them all. Second, there is the issue of the nature of NATO's relationship with other international institutions.

The focus of UK security policy on expeditionary operations[9] has led policy-makers to reconsider the geographical extent to which British troops and those of NATO can be employed. This debate has been mirrored throughout NATO and is the subject of much controversy. For some, particularly in the more globally orientated USA, the adoption of a global role for NATO would serve to legitimise the projection of US power in circumstances where a UN Security Council resolution was not always forthcoming. However, such a global role, with its overtones of great power neo-imperialism, may be unpalatable for many within Europe. Former British Prime Minister Edward Heath has, for example, described the idea of a NATO global peacekeeping role as a 'new imperialism to replace that banished after the Second World War'.[10]

The North Atlantic Treaty is quite clear on the extent to which NATO can act in pursuit of article five guarantees. Article six identifies 'the territory of any of the member states in Europe or North America, the territory of Turkey and the islands under the jurisdiction of any of the Parties to the Treaty in the area North of the Tropic of Cancer'. Furthermore, article five applies to the forces, vessels and aircraft of any of the member states 'when in or over these territories or any other area in Europe in which occupation forces of any of the Parties were stationed [in 1949] or the Mediterranean Sea or the North Atlantic area North of the Tropic of Cancer'.

Having said this, beyond the geographical restrictions placed on article five operations there are no restrictions relating to other areas in which signatory states may opt to co-operate militarily. The treaty itself allows for a wider interpretation of the geographical scope of NATO's non-article five roles. In the preamble to the treaty, signatories pledge to 'seek to promote stability and well-being in the North Atlantic area'. The 'North Atlantic area' is not defined geographically. Article four makes the rather open-ended stipulation that member states 'will consult together whenever, in the opinion of any of them, the territorial integrity, political independence or security of any of the Parties [to the treaty] is threatened'.[11]

With increasing willingness to define 'security' in broader terms than has traditionally been the case, the possibilities for constraining NATO through the North Atlantic Treaty itself appear to recede if the political will exists to broaden its remit. Nevertheless, the British view on this matter is best characterised as 'non-prescriptively pragmatic'. The British government's instinct will be to leave the definition of NATO's area of operations as it is at the moment: very flexible. In foreshadowing the April 1999 NATO Washington summit, the UK Ministry of Defence's Policy Director told the House of Commons Select Committee on Defence that the new NATO Strategic Concept would:

> Give . . . a clear flavour of where NATO sees its prime interests as being, which is in European security . . . what it will not do is lay down precise limits . . . for a number of very good reasons, one of which is [that] we want to avoid the slight mistake of the last Strategic Concept of writing down something which looks really quite sensible today but looks dated only two or three years later.[12]

This lack of prescription is also reflected in official British attitudes towards the mechanisms for legitimising military action.

The mandate question

The declaratory British government position on the process and mechanisms for legitimising military action is that:

> All NATO operations must have a basis in international law. The legal basis required in any particular case will depend on the particular circumstances. Article 51 of the UN Charter recognises the inherent right of self-defence, which includes the right to seek aid from elsewhere; friendly nations can give such aid individually and collectively. In other cases, a UN Security Council Resolution under Chapter VII of the UN Charter may be necessary to authorise the use of force.[13]

Securing proof of compliance with the laws of armed conflict and the more general body of international law is relatively straightforward. In practice, however, the debate is much more narrowly defined in terms of whether a specific Security Council resolution is required or simply desirable in order to authorise and legitimise NATO military action beyond article five-type operations. Again the British position can be characterised as non-prescriptive pragmatism; somewhat different from its European allies and, arguably, much more in line with the USA. Both France and Germany have attempted to limit NATO action beyond (geographically and in terms of role) article five operations, to those conducted with an express mandate from the United Nations or the Organisation for Security and Co-operation in Europe. This contrasts with the clear autonomy (i.e., a right to take action on a case-by-case basis without specific UN Security Council authorisation)[14] demanded for NATO by elements within the

Clinton administration and US Congress during the 1990s. This paralleled the rise of US disenchantment with two aspects of the functioning of the UN: first, the decision-making paralysis within the Security Council caused by the exercise of the veto by China, Russia and to a lesser extent France; second the USA has become increasingly frustrated at the UN Secretariat's lack of operational capacity, particularly in the more challenging peace support operation environments of the 1990s. The British position is very similar. In 1998, Foreign Secretary Robin Cook told the NATO Council that 'I am not sure that it would be wise to limit ourselves by writing a legal base, rather than by making sure that as an organisation we have the flexibility to respond to problems in the real world'.[15]

Events in the former Yugoslavia appeared to sharpen the UK's resolve to maintain the autonomy of NATO non-article five action. The 1999 air strikes on the Federal Republic of Yugoslavia were conducted without a specific UN Security Council resolution. In fact the Security Council was largely marginalised by the UK and USA as a result of the anticipated Russian and Chinese opposition to the air campaign. The actions were legitimised by reference to the democratic nature of the nineteen NATO member states conducting the operations as well as the scale of the atrocities allegedly perpetrated by the Yugoslav (Serb) authorities. The latter factor, in particular, was claimed to draw the operations within the realm of both international law and respectability.

Yet this establishes the potential for a precedent; a case which was argued within the USA and hotly contested by several other allies. The European allies and those states with a position to protect on the UN Security Council are unlikely to desire the translation of this process from a unique event to one establishing precedential law. The new NATO Strategic Concept, unveiled at Washington in 1999, pledged that NATO would operate 'within international law'. The failure to mention specifically the requirement for a UN Security Council resolution can therefore be seen as something of a fudge, avoiding the difficult issue of whether a UN/OSCE mandate is specifically required under international law. The British position remains, as noted, flexibly pragmatic and strives to maintain the maximum freedom of manoeuvre without sacrificing too much in the way of legitimacy.

The UK and NATO enlargement

NATO enlargement offers the prospect of compounding the difficulties of decision-making within NATO as well as providing obstacles to the 'deepening' of European integration through the ESDI. Potentially, it will also dilute the UK's voice within an enlarged NATO. Nevertheless, the UK does appear to be reasonably enthusiastic about the idea of enlargement. Arguably this is because the prospect of further enlargement remains relatively remote (at least within the medium term). Since the accession to membership of the Czech Republic, Hungary and Poland in March 1999, there appears to be little consensus within the Alliance over either the scope or the timing of any future enlargement. Jonathan Eyal makes this point cogently when he states that 'it is difficult to see how a new consensus could be created for another enlargement in a few years, how the US Congress could be persuaded to ratify another wave, and how the Russians could be persuaded that, yet again, this should not threaten their interests'.[16] The declaratory position of the UK government on further enlargement is as flexibly pragmatic as on the other issues. It is that it 'supports further enlargement when the Allies collectively judge that further invitations would strengthen European security and the Alliance itself'.[17]

In effect the UK considers that NATO is a security organisation comprised of security producers rather than simply security consumers. Thus, the benchmark for NATO candidacy is that membership will add to NATO's military effectiveness and will not seriously destabilise European security. Foreign Secretary Cook emphasised this point at Sintra in 1997 when he stated that NATO must not admit new members whose security could not be guaranteed or whose military could not meet NATO's standards.[18] Yet a straight application of these criteria would almost certainly rule out further expansion. Russian antipathy towards NATO enlargement ensures that any future enlargement may well jeopardise the stability of Europe. Certainly it is the case that few, if any, of the candidate countries could add to NATO's military effectiveness at present.[19] However, while military capability is important, it is also the case that NATO has never been an alliance of military equals. Other political considerations have often prevailed over the requirement for NATO to be a group of security providers. The British approach therefore provides flexible criteria, which, when strictly applied, limit expansion yet are sufficiently flexible to allow political considerations to prevail over military ones in the overall quest for security in the Euro-Atlantic area. In 1998 the House of Commons Select Committee on Defence recognised this when it concluded that, for NATO's forthcoming enlargement, 'the benefits of increased stability in Central and Eastern Europe outweigh any potential military costs'.[20]

The UK's relative enthusiasm for enlargement is tempered by a number of other factors. Not least of these is that a great deal of work has yet to be done with the Czech Republic, Hungary and Poland before they attain NATO military standards in many areas. Until they are effectively 'digested' it is unlikely that member states will risk further enlargement. Furthermore, at the NATO summit in Madrid in 1997 there were clearly three candidates that stood out from the crowd of potential NATO members. There is currently nothing approaching even this degree of consensus on future applicants. In effect, the UK can afford to sound relatively enthusiastic about something that is unlikely to occur in the short to medium term. The UK has sought to draw attention away from the debate on a second wave of enlargement through the revitalisation of both its own bilateral and NATO's multilateral 'outreach programmes'. This also serves to regularise relations with both Ukraine and, less successfully, Russia.

British 'outreach' is described as 'defence diplomacy' and was transformed into a specific mission of the Ministry of Defence through the *SDR*. The UK also sought to place greater emphasis on 'partnership' and outreach at NATO's Washington summit, securing their place as core NATO activities and reflecting positively on the *SDR* itself. Outreach has also provided the vehicle through which a relatively coherent foreign policy towards Ukraine has been constructed. The UK supports the NATO–Ukraine Charter established at Madrid as well as the enhanced Partnership for Peace and economic/technical nuclear assistance programmes. In effect, this policy amounts to the 'Finlandisation' of the Ukraine – support for its sovereignty but a rejection of strategies that destabilise the UK's relations with Moscow.

A similar approach has been adopted in terms of bilateral British and multilateral NATO relations with Russia. The enhanced PfP, the NATO–Russia Founding Act and the Permanent Joint Council represent a form of 'appeasement by smoke and mirrors'; attempting to build the perception of 'partnership' with Russia but offering little in concrete terms. It could even be argued that these measures serve broadly to legitimise Russia's marginalisation from involvement in security issues in Europe and elsewhere.

The UK and the evolving European defence capability

The ending of the Cold War has seen various efforts to reinvigorate the Western European Union. In 1991 an Anglo-Italian Declaration on European Security and Defence proposed that the WEU should act as a 'bridge' between the EU and NATO.[21] While the Italians had clearly made a concession in their agreement to stop pushing for a direct EU military component, the British concessions were greater. Certainly, with Margaret Thatcher as Prime Minister until November 1990, it was inconceivable that the UK would agree to *any* European-only military structures. John Major, in contrast, 'conceded that an effective NATO monopoly of military security affairs was no longer tenable now that the Cold War was over. Hence the British accepted in principle that the European Union could develop a defence component; albeit indirectly.'[22]

This Anglo-Italian understanding formed the basis of the 1991 Maastricht Treaty agreements on defence. These referred to the WEU as an 'integral part' of the development of the European Union and requested the WEU to elaborate and implement decisions and actions of the EU that had 'defence implications'. The treaty also included an agreement on the development of the Common Foreign and Security Policy, which potentially included the 'eventual framing of a common defence policy which might in time lead to a common defence'.[23] This hardly smacked of real commitment, however.

At the EU's Amsterdam summit in July 1997 the new British Labour government initially continued the Conservatives' opposition to a role for the WEU that took it beyond that of a European pillar for NATO. While several EU members pushed for a closer institutional relationship between the WEU and the EU, the UK delegation continued to resist the idea of a 'common defence' and the merging of the EU and the WEU. The Treaty of Amsterdam was something of a compromise, but one which did not go far beyond the Maastricht Treaty. It reconfirmed the EU's ability to engage in dialogue with the WEU, yet it provided it with no powers of direction over the WEU.[24] It did place real limits on the way in which the ESDI could develop: 'a certain line was drawn under [the ESDI] at the Amsterdam summit, largely at British instigation, by preventing the merger of the WEU and the EU'.[25] In effect, it represented something of a high-water mark for the concept of an ESDI embodied through the WEU.

The *Strategic Defence Review* in 1998 did 'nothing to clarify or advance the development of the European Security and Defence Identity'[26] and, if anything, reiterated the commitment to the pre-existing transatlantic NATO arrangements. Specifically the *SDR* stated that:

> Our security is indivisible from that of our European partners and Allies. We therefore have a fundamental interest in the security and stability of the continent as a whole and in the effectiveness of NATO as a collective political and military instrument to underpin these interests. In turn this depends on the transatlantic relationship and the continued engagement in Europe of the US.[27]

In fact the *SDR* contained little evidence of a move towards a more European approach to the issue of defence, although there had been rhetorical nods in the direction of Europe from several ministers. Then Defence Secretary George Robertson, for example, made a special point of referring to the defence relationship with Germany in the course of a speech to the English Speaking Union.[28] Nevertheless, the UK continued to insist that the WEU version of the ESDI should not be formally and institutionally swept into the EU. Despite its prominence in this debate the UK was not alone. Apart from the other Atlanticist states, Finland and Sweden both lobbied hard in opposition to the emergence of a defence arm for the EU for fear that it would compromise their long-held neutrality.

The UK at the crossroads: 'the times they are a-changing'

As a result of the disagreements between the Atlanticist states and the other Europeans the ESDI remained a rather ambiguous idea, caught between competing visions. One was for an ESDI that was separate from NATO but associated, in undetermined ways, with the EU; while the other was, in effect, a means of strengthening NATO through increasing the salience of the European pillar. However, British policy towards the ESDI began to change as a consequence of the very disagreements that threatened NATO's cohesion. It became increasingly clear that there might be circumstances in which the UK identified a requirement to react militarily yet the USA did not. This presented the British with a tightrope to walk. The ESDI needed to be sufficiently meaningful to enable an effective European response to crises but not so strong that its existence represented a challenge to NATO itself. In a way this offered a means of strengthening the Alliance and avoiding the politically bloody disputes that had arisen between the UK and France, on the one hand, and the USA, on the other, over the use of airpower in Bosnia. It was both a practical necessity and a means for ensuring a more balanced transatlantic relationship. The change in British attitudes also appeared predicated on a recognition that the Clinton administration felt assured that an enhanced ESDI would not weaken NATO or marginalise the USA and may even serve a useful purpose in refocusing the burden-sharing debate.

In October 1998, Prime Minister Tony Blair announced at the informal EU summit at Portschäch a willingness to move the development of an ESDI up the EU agenda. This was an attempt to improve the new government's European credentials at a point when most other EU members were joining the new monetary union, yet the supposedly pro-European new British government was not. It was also clear that the appointment of an EU High Representative for CFSP matters, particularly a former NATO Secretary-General, Javier Solana, would have the effect of 'sharpening' the EU's foreign and security policies. The shadow of the Bosnian crisis, and a divided and less than credible EC/EU response, was still cast over responses to the developing crisis in Kosovo. The need to enable Europe to punch at a level appropriate to its political weight was therefore increasingly clear.

A more profound shift in the tone of British policy towards the ESDI was contained in the text of the Saint Malo agreement with France in December 1998. The Saint Malo Declaration was a watershed. It removed long-standing British objections to the absorption, by the EU, of the WEU's putative military tasks and planning structures. It also called upon the EU to 'have recourse to suitable military means' to respond to international crises. The Declaration made the point that:

> In order for the European Union to take decisions and approve military action where the [NATO] Alliance as a whole is not engaged, the Union must be given appropriate structures . . . without unnecessary duplication, taking account of the existing assets of the WEU and the evolution of its relations with the EU.[29]

Saint Malo thus raised the possibility of military action outside of the framework of the NATO Alliance. The Declaration called for the European

Union to 'have the capacity for autonomous action' in order to respond to international crises. Yet 'autonomy' is not a finite or absolute but a relative term and consequently exists in degrees. The Declaration's failure to cast light on the extent to which 'autonomous' action would be possible or the impact this would have upon the transatlantic Alliance is both a masterpiece of diplomatic language and a potential hostage to fortune. While the inclusion of such phrases is an obvious necessity if pressure is to be maintained on the USA in order to develop the ESDI in a meaningful way within NATO, it also raises the real danger of rivalry developing between the ESDI and transatlantic NATO.[30] At the very least it may mean different things to the parties to the Saint Malo Declaration.

While the language on these issues was rather vague, on the nature of defence decision-making it was more precise. It made it clear that the British and French authorities agreed that both defence and a CFSP must remain 'intergovernmental'. Certainly the British interpretation was that they were embarked upon a project which would establish capacity for military action in accordance with a common, not a single, foreign policy while 'acting in conformity with our respective obligations in NATO'. As such Saint Malo represented neither a threat to the transatlantic bargain nor the process of managing defence and foreign policy through intergovernmental rather than federal mechanisms. However, this last assumption is questionable.

The Declaration made it clear that the EU Council must be able to take decisions on 'the whole range of activity set out in Title V of the Treaty on European Union'; that is, the Maastricht Treaty. Title V of the treaty represents both the protection of and potential challenges to the intergovernmental process of decision-making.[31] It contains an undertaking not 'to prejudice the specific character of the security and defence policy of certain member states' as well as other measures which serve to maintain national vetoes over both defence and foreign policy formulation in the context of the EU. In particular article twenty-three restricts qualified majority voting on issues that have defence or foreign policy implications. These measures clearly strengthen the intergovernmental approach.

However, article two requires signatories to refrain from 'any action which is contrary to the interests of the Union or likely to impair its effectiveness as a cohesive force in international relations', thereby implying a *requirement* for consultation on major foreign and security policy action by member states. Furthermore, article fourteen calls upon the EU Commission to ensure 'the implementation of joint action' while article eighteen calls upon the EU presidency to 'represent the Union' and 'be responsible for the implementation of decisions'. Article twenty-one identifies the European Parliament's right to be informed by the presidency of decisions with foreign and security implications. Title V of Maastricht thus represents two potential paths: one an intergovernmental approach to defence and foreign policy issues; the other a more federal approach. The

British government remained publicly committed to representing Saint Malo as a firm commitment to the former yet it is clear that Title V does not represent the watertight guarantees on the issue of sovereignty that the British have claimed.[32]

The timing of the Saint Malo Declaration was revealing. It preceded both NATO's Washington summit and the start of the EU's single currency on 1 January 1999. The launch of the Euro without UK participation both offered the prospect of deepening Franco-German hegemony within the EU and risked emphasising the UK's continued marginalisation. Saint Malo thus offered an opportunity to change such perceptions before they were reinforced. The NATO summit offered a rare opportunity for progress in terms of NATO support for the changing ESDI as well as affording obvious publicity opportunities. Furthermore, Saint Malo headed off criticism before it arose. Despite some political investment in the institutional development of the WEU, by 1999 it was clear that it was never going to be invested with sufficient political will for it to become a significant security institution in its own right. The British-inspired 'bridge' concept had demonstrably failed and a new policy needed to be developed before this once more became a motif of British obstructionism within Europe.

Beyond Saint Malo

At their Cologne summit in June 1999, EU member states agreed to begin preparations to absorb the WEU's tasks and structures by the end of the year 2000. This agreement was reached as Javier Solana was appointed as the first EU High Representative for CFSP. The creation of a new EU Political and Security Committee was also intended to provide a degree of coherence and consistency to the EU's CFSP and its new Common European Security and Defence Policy (CESDP), the follow-on to the ESDI.

The Kosovo crisis had also spurred on the UK's continuing policy change. NATO's Defence Capabilities Initiative, the 1999 WEU audit of European military capabilities and the Kosovo 'lessons learned' process increased pressure on European governments to improve their military capabilities. At the Anglo-French summit in London in November 1999, and again at the EU's Helsinki summit in December of that year, discussions continued on the creation of a European Rapid Reaction Force. The plan did not envisage a new European standing army. Instead, it involved addressing the shortfalls identified in the WEU's capability audit by creating logistical, command and communications structures that would be capable of deploying and sustaining the equivalent of an army corps supported by sophisticated air weapons. At Helsinki the EU endorsed the 'headline goals' that member states should be able, by 2003, to deploy within sixty days and sustain in theatre for at least one year military forces up to 60,000 strong.

Despite its apparent new enthusiasm for the CESDP, the UK government went out of its way to explain that it did not support the idea of EU involvement in responding to a direct attack on any of its member states, and that no standing force was being created. The new NATO Secretary-General, George (now Lord) Robertson, reinforced this in stating that 'if you assume that the European contribution to the Kosovo air campaign could have been raised from 15 to, say, 30%, the EU is still not going to be able to start World War Three on its own'.[33]

A further assumption on the British part was that a European-led set-up would still, almost certainly, involve NATO in some way, shape or form.[34] NATO's Deputy Supreme Commander, who is always a European, is likely to provide the senior military commander for any EU-led operations. So what is being created is a mechanism for mobilising a coalition of Europeans in the event of a crisis. The troop-contributing nations of the Eurocorps[35] are pushing for this formation to provide the foundation of the future force. They gained agreement for the Eurocorps headquarters element to take over command of the Kosovo Force from the German-led NATO LANDCENT headquarters in spring 2000.[36] Yet British policy-makers, off the record at least, are not at all keen on the elevation of Eurocorps. While some British misgivings can be explained in terms of the paucity of its capability, particularly in terms of mobility, it is also clear that London has little real influence over this organisation and the invigoration of Eurocorps represents a reanimation of the threat to NATO from an 'alternative' force. Nevertheless, the 'overstretch' being endured by the British armed services ensures that even this is preferable to the UK assuming a heavier and longer-term commitment to the Balkans than it already has. However, the British offer to provide its Northwood-based Permanent Joint Headquarters as a means of providing strategic military direction to any EU-led force, such as Eurocorps, may well be a way of attempting to offset the difficulties the rise of the Eurocorps may pose.

While the supporters of the CESDP are confident of further developments, it is easy to exaggerate their likelihood. Recent events can be seen as a direct product of experience in Kosovo and while it should be expected that developments will continue as a consequence of this 'Kosovo effect' it is likely to wear off, and a renewal of friction may, once more, retard progress. This could come from a number of sources. Many European states may not want to increase, or even stop cutting, their defence budgets to make the vision achievable and few states would currently countenance any degree of defence specialisation that the project may entail. However, a CESDP comprising allies joining on a comparatively equal basis would, at the very least, require some states to restructure their defence forces and this is likely to lead to short-term increases in several states' defence budgets, particularly in order to acquire strategic air- and sea-lift, deployable medical services, and the type of restructuring necessary to ensure sustainability. Those states that have generated too deep a peace dividend are going to be forced to face the prospect that they will either have to spend more or they will find themselves, to some extent, marginalised from the process. Both the British and the French governments appear to recognise the inevitability of this,[37] yet other states' enthusiasm may well be tempered by this realisation. The military burden-sharing debate is thus likely to continue but to become one with an intra-European as well as a transatlantic dimension.[38]

Conclusion

The UK's attitude to European defence clearly altered with the change of government in 1997. There is a fundamental question at the heart of British policy towards both the transatlantic Alliance and the CESDP. This is whether the transatlantic relationship and a CESDP are entirely compatible. Perhaps strangely, the most consistent proponents of a belief in their compatibility are from the USA. From the Marshall Plan onwards, successive US administrations have generally been enthusiastic supporters of an increasing economic, political and even military role for Europe. Urged on by Congress and the momentum of the burden-sharing debate, the UK has been pushed into a Europe that does more, and pays more, in terms of defence. The US commitment to NATO is itself rooted in a paradox. The US presence has been a consequence of European dependence on US military prowess. However, an entrapped USA resents the burdens of this relationship. The challenge for the UK has been to walk a tightrope effectively at a time when there is an increasing premium on developing a capacity for an effective, albeit still relatively limited, European military capability.

For the USA, the ideal is for the Europeans to have a degree of operational but not strategic 'autonomy'. Since late 1999, Americans have been calling more vocally for assurances from the Europeans that NATO will be given the first option on any crisis. However, if the Europeans provide them, the EU will be turned into an organisation of last resort. It is difficult to see how France, in particular, will accommodate such a policy.

Nevertheless, there are real practical limitations on the autonomy that any CESDP is able to exhibit. Practical dependence on US strategic assets such as intelligence and strategic lift ensures that the United States has a practical veto. While the French may still decry this as unwarranted US hegemony it may be the price to pay for continued US commitment to European defence.

It is clear that for the UK support for the CESDP is not a means for creating a 'European superstate'. It is the action of a middle-ranking power no longer able to pursue objectives alone. As such it is a genuine attempt to create capabilities in order to provide political options beyond an unpredictable dependence on the USA. For as long as it avoids choosing definitively between the United States and Europe, the UK is caught between a rock and a soft place.

Notes and references

1 The views expressed here are personal and should not be construed as representing the views or policy of the British government, Ministry of Defence or the Royal Military Academy, Sandhurst.

2 1999 Defence White Paper. (London: Her Majesty's Stationery Office 1999), p. 8.

3 *Strategic Defence Review.* (London: Her Majesty's Stationery Office 1998), para. 17.

4 1999 Defence White Paper *op.cit.*, p. 7.

5 N. Chomsky, *The New Military Humanism: Lessons from Kosovo.* (London: Pluto 1999).

6 For a fuller development of this argument see J. Sharp (ed.), *About Turn, Forward March with Europe.* (London: Institute for Public Policy Research 1996).

7 For example, the European NATO members have some two million men under arms, a force twice the size of that of the USA, but have only 250,000 combat-capable troops.

8 Assembly of the WEU's Draft Plan for Action, *A Time for Defence.* Quoted in House of Commons Select Committee on Defence, *Third Report Session 1997–98.* (London: Her Majesty's Stationery Office 1999).

9 Resulting from the *SDR*. See C. McInnes, 'Labour's Strategic Defence Review'. *International Affairs* 74 (4) 1998, pp. 823–45; M. Chalmers, *The Strategic Defence Review: What Does it Tell us about the Foreign Policy of the New British Government?* Paper presented to the BISA conference, Leeds University, 16 December 1997.

10 Edward Heath quoted in A. Hyde-Price, *European Security beyond the Cold War.* (London: Sage 1991), p. 202 fn. 14.

11 Quotations from the NATO Treaty are taken from the text reprinted in *The North Atlantic Treaty Organisation: Facts and Figures.* (Brussels: NATO 1989), pp. 376–7.

12 Richard Hatfield in evidence to House of Commons Select Committee on Defence. See *Third Report op.cit.*

13 *Ibid.*, para. 89.

14 *The NATO Summit and its Implications for Europe.* Report by Tom Cox MP submitted to the Assembly of the WEU. Author's copy.

15 Speech to the NATO Council, 8 December 1998. Author's copy.

16 *Third Report op.cit.*, para. 100.

17 *Ibid.*, para. 91.

18 Robin Cook cited in the *Financial Times* 30 May 1997.

19 *Third Report op.cit.*, para. 92.

20 *Ibid.*, para. 52.

21 Declaration on European Security and Defence. (London: UK Foreign and Commonwealth Office, 1991), p. 2. See also T. Taylor, 'A British Perspective' in M. J. Brenner (ed.), *Multilateralism and Western Security.* (New York: St Martin's 1995), pp. 84–5.

22 M. A. Smith, 'European Security – Without NATO?' (Unpublished paper 1999), p. 4.

23 The Treaty on European Union. Article J. 4.1.

24 *Third Report op.cit.*, Q. 2881.

25 *Ibid.*, Q. 1630.

26 House of Commons Select Committee on Defence, *Eighth Report Session 1997–98.* (London: Her Majesty's Stationery Office 1999), para. 140.

27 *Strategic Defence Review op.cit.*, p. 7.

28 G. Robertson, 'Building European Security and the Role of Defence Diplomacy'. UK MoD website. URL: http/www.mod.uk/speeches/sofs4–9.html.

29 For the full text of the Saint Malo agreement see Declaration on European Defence. UK Foreign and Commonwealth Office website. URL: http://www.fco.gov.uk/news/news.

30 See also the Final Declaration of the Franco-German summit. Potsdam, 1 December 1998, para. 4. (London: German Embassy 1998).

31 For an excellent critique of the 'dangers of Title V' see A. Judd, 'The Devil's in the Detail – and the Detail Calls it a European Army'. *Daily Telegraph* 28 February 2000. The author would like to thank Dr Edmund Yorke for these points.

32 However, this is not necessarily intrinsically bad. See G. Howe, 'Sovereignty and Interdependence: Britain's Place in the World'. *International Affairs* 66 (4) 1990, pp. 675–95. Howe argues that sovereignty is 'not some pre-defined absolute' but 'a resource to be used'.

33 'Forward March for Europe'. *Financial Times* 25 November 1999.

34 Prime Minister Blair has also made it quite clear that increasing Anglo-French collaboration is 'not an attempt in any shape or form to supplant or compete with NATO. We are all quite clear on this, which is why NATO welcomed the European defence initiative at the Washington summit earlier this year. It is about strengthening Europe's military effectiveness and capabilities in a way which will both reinforce and complement the NATO Alliance . . . whilst enabling Europe to act effectively in situations where the Alliance as a whole is not engaged.' See *Conclusions of the Anglo-French Summit.* (London: Foreign and Commonwealth Office 1999).

35 In 2000 the states which had earmarked troops for possible deployment with the Eurocorps were France, Germany, Spain, Belgium and Luxembourg.

36 It should be noted that agreement was reached to enable the Eurocorps to be deployed under NATO authority in January 1993. See C. M. Kelleher, *The Future of European Security: An Interim Assessment.* (Washington, DC: Brookings 1995), pp. 59–60.

37 In 1996 President Chirac announced a process of reorientation of the French armed forces which will lead to their professionalisation and restructuring along what can be described as 'expeditionary' lines. British defence structures began a similar process through the *SDR* in 1998, as noted.

38 The intra-European burden-sharing debate is unlikely to be clean cut. Germany, while spending considerably less on defence in comparative terms than the UK and France, has contributed substantially to 'soft' security. Its financial payments in lieu of troop contributions to the Gulf War, its role as the largest net contributor to the EU and to the emerging democracies of Central Europe and its hosting of Balkan refugees can all be cited as equivalent contributions to European security to those of France and the UK. Denmark, Norway and the Netherlands can also point to their contributions to development and emergency relief assistance.

10 Germany

A new vision of order?

Graham Timmins

Introduction: what kind of power?

Speaking to the crowds in Berlin following the opening of the Berlin Wall in November 1989, former West German Chancellor Willy Brandt argued that 'nothing would be the same again'. Events within Europe since then have demonstrated the accuracy of this statement. For Germany, Europe and the world as a whole, the end of the Cold War prompted an epoch-defining reassessment of the international order. In September 1990, the two Germanys – the (western) Federal Republic of Germany (FRG) and (eastern) German Democratic Republic (GDR) – together with the allied powers of the USA, USSR, France and the UK, signed the '2 + 4' treaty. A significant chapter in the West German foreign policy agenda was brought to a conclusion. The treaty provided the formal international sanctioning of German unification and one month later, in October 1990, the Federal Republic absorbed the five states that had previously comprised the GDR.

The thawing of the Cold War order and its formal end, announced at the CSCE summit in Paris in November 1990, removed the need for West German preoccupation with protecting its eastern border from the threat of Soviet aggression. The dissolution of the USSR one year later in December 1991 further reduced German concerns. However, as many observers have noted, a clear, military security *threat* from the East has been replaced by myriad increasingly non-military security *risks*. The changing nature of the European security agenda has been discussed, in conceptual terms, by Clive Archer in Chapter 1 of this volume and it is clear that European states now find themselves confronted with a more complex set of issues. Reflecting on the significance of the ending of the Cold War from a Western perspective, one German observer concluded that 'we have slain a large dragon, but we now live in a jungle filled with a bewildering variety of poisonous snakes'.[1]

Given the proximity of that jungle to Germany's eastern border, it is to be expected that Germany would want to play a major role in developing a new European security order both in its hard and soft dimensions. Germany has long been referred to in terms of its being a 'civilian' rather than military power. This description springs from the constraints imposed in the post-Second World War context on its ability to develop a military role and, arguably, the pacifist tendencies that this also produced within German society. Hanns Maull argues that civilian power is based upon a specific role concept, 'a complex bundle of norms, beliefs, attitudes and perceptions that tells a state (or, more precisely, its decision makers) how to behave'.[2] Civilian power is manifested in an attempt to 'civilise' international relations through the negotiation of an agreed order, which is articulated through international law and operationalised via international institutions. This 'civilised political order', taken as being akin to the conduct present within democratic states, is described by Maull in terms of a 'civilisational hexagon of interrelated principles and objectives'.[3] These are: '(a) the effective control of private violence through the [state] monopolisation of force; (b) a culture of non-violent resolution of political disputes; (c) the rule of law; (d) development of social division of labour and institutions; (e) participation in decision-making by those affected by them; and (f) social justice'.[4]

In order to address these issues it is necessary to outline the German foreign policy agenda in the post-Cold War era. Broadly speaking, German priorities can be placed into four categories:

1 *Deepening*: a continuation of European integration beyond the Maastricht Treaty and the commencement of a 'constitutional' debate within the European Union.
2 *The Franco-German relationship*: maintenance of the core European relationship between France and Germany driving the deepening agenda forwards.
3 *Widening*: support for an early enlargement of the European Union into Central and Eastern Europe.
4 *An overlapping and multilateral security architecture*: continuation and enhancement of a European security architecture that provides a key role for the USA and facilitates a pan-European dialogue.

Germany is arguably well placed to take the lead in defining a new European security order, a shift towards economic security issues seemingly playing to German strengths. It is, however, unlikely that the hard security dimension will develop in such a manner that Germany can ignore the expectations being placed upon it. Even assuming that Europe develops a durable security order, the need to address external concerns will remain valid. Following on from this, key issues for discussion in this chapter will be the development of the German, European and wider foreign policy agendas during the 1990s.

Unification: a changing Germany in a changing Europe

When, in October 1990, German unification was completed, the FRG's population grew from 64 million to 80 million, and with it came optimism about new markets and growth of the German economy. While unification appeared to be an occasion for celebration, it also became a cause of some consternation for Germany's neighbours. This was highlighted by the British Prime Minister Margaret Thatcher's Chequers seminar during the summer of 1990, where the question was discussed as to 'whether the Germans could be trusted'.[5] The fear that existed regarding Germany was twofold. First, with renewed access to its traditional East European markets, there was a fear that Germany could be tempted to revise its western orientation in favour of an eastern focus. What implications would this have for the European integration process and, in particular, the proposals for political union that were creeping up the agenda? Second, would Germany's economic strength become such that it would begin to destabilise socio-economic conditions in neighbouring states? Added to this, would Germany begin to flex its political muscles as its economic strength increased? These questions commanded significant attention during the early 1990s. Morgan's assessment was that, akin to the UK after 1945, Germany would be faced with overload in its foreign policy agenda and would be required to make difficult decisions.[6]

The assumption behind this view was that the end of the Cold War would result in a growing renationalisation of Western European foreign policies and that Germany, if it were to become a 'normal' state, would indeed start flexing its political and military muscles. Ash, on the other hand, suggested that Germany would continue to pursue a multilateral agenda across all four issue areas outlined above, rather than making choices. The consequence of this would be that Germany would find itself failing to address any of them fully.[7] In arguing this case, Ash draws our attention to a significant issue. Fears surrounding Germany have tended to focus upon a scenario of German domination. Taking a different perspective, there is an equally worrying scenario of German *indecision*. As the foreign policies of both the George Bush Senior and Clinton presidencies in the 1990s suggested, Germany, as the largest economic power in Europe, and given its geopolitical importance at the heart of the European continent, would be expected to take a leading role in defining the post-Cold War European order. A key question would be how and where the boundaries between leadership and domination were to be defined.

Germany and the European Union

The European integration agenda in the early 1990s was dominated by three key issues. These were, first, the difficulties of ratifying the Maastricht Treaty following the Danish negative referendum decision in 1992 and, following the second Danish referendum, implementing it in the face of the growing Eurosceptic lobby in the UK and elsewhere. Second, there was the pressing need to address European security in light of the growing

Balkan crisis. Finally, there existed growing moral pressure on the European Union to open its doors to membership applications from Central and Eastern European countries.

The ratification of the Maastricht Treaty in Germany was not as straightforward as observers may have expected. Chancellor Helmut Kohl had on several occasions attempted to placate its neighbours by reiterating the view that German unification and European integration were two sides of the same coin. However, Germany became the last of the twelve member states to complete ratification in 1993; waiting until the German Constitutional Court had ruled that Maastricht was compatible with the Basic Law. Germany during the 1990s, for the first time, began to exhibit some of the awkwardness towards the EC/EU that France and the UK had demonstrated at various times during the post-Second World War period. Having agreed to Economic and Monetary Union, a public debate began to emerge which suggested that many Germans were more reluctant to give up their beloved Deutschmark than had been anticipated. Moreover, Germany incurred the political wrath of its neighbours when the Bundesbank increased interest rates to fund the spiralling costs of unification, a move that provoked similar increases across Europe, placing many economies under severe pressure. When the Finance Minister, Theo Waigel, unilaterally cancelled a meeting with his French counterpart in 1993 as a protest against growing public pressure from France on Germany to lower interest rates, the result was an unaccustomed disruption of the usually harmonious Franco-German relationship. Similarly, when Kohl, in a seemingly spontaneous outburst in Brussels, demanded an increase in Germany's number of votes within the Council of Ministers in recognition of its disproportionate contribution to the EU budget and when Martin Bangermann, a German EU Commissioner, launched a symbolic protest in refusing to respond to correspondence not written in German, there seemed to be an accumulating number of indications that Germany could no longer be viewed as a submissive partner.

Germany's initial involvement in the Western response to the Balkan crisis, too, did little to endear it to its neighbours. Calls by Hans-Dietrich Genscher, the German Foreign Minister, on his EC/EU counterparts to recognise the breakaway states of Croatia and Slovenia as soon as possible, and the threat that Germany would do so unilaterally unless they did, provoked criticism and was viewed as a contributing factor to the escalating descent into violence in the region. Genscher's view was not too far away from those previously expressed by Willy Brandt, Chancellor from 1969 to 1974. During the negotiations with Moscow and East Berlin to find a mechanism for establishing diplomatic relations between the two Germanys, Brandt had argued that it was necessary to recognise the realities of the present in order to shape the future. The German government saw little point in attempting to hold together the crumbling Yugoslav Federation. That it had been prepared to push its position so forcibly had taken its

Western partners by surprise, however. Where Germany took the most obvious lead was in calling for an early enlargement of the EU into Central and Eastern Europe. When Kohl announced in Warsaw in the summer of 1994 that Poland could expect a closer relationship with the EU by the turn of the century, he did so without any prior discussion with the other EU states. The French government again voiced its criticism, arguing that deepening had to be the main priority for the EU ahead of enlargement.

From Lamers to Fischer: a German model for Europe?

During the latter part of 1994, Germany held the EU presidency and used the opportunity to articulate its position on the European integration agenda. It did so via an internal paper produced in September 1994 by Karl Lamers, parliamentary spokesman for the ruling Christian Democratic Union, and Wolfgang Schäuble, who became Helmut Kohl's (short-lived) successor as leader of the CDU in 1999. Its status was nothing more than an unofficial discussion document and Chancellor Kohl was able to distance himself and the government from the contents. It was, however, clear from the absence of internal discussion that the views it expressed were shared throughout the party. The paper pointed to a number of issues that had provoked difficulties in the integration process:

- The failure to implement institutional reform to take account of enlargement in the 1970s and 1980s, which had caused an 'overextension of the EU's institutions'.
- The 'growing differentiation of interests' between the member states, which had been exacerbated by socio-economic developments and threatened to 'obscure the commonality of interests' being pursued as part of the integration process.
- The differing internal and external policy priorities that resulted from a European Union that now stretched from 'the North Cape to Gibraltar'.
- The systemic crisis of post-industrial change throughout the European Union that had resulted in widespread unemployment; generating tensions within social welfare systems.
- The increase in 'regressive nationalism' provoked by internal socio-economic difficulties and exacerbated by immigration trends.
- The 'highly debilitating effect' of governmental overload being experienced throughout the EU.
- The need to address the rising issue of enlarging the EU into Central and Eastern Europe.[8]

The paper recognised Germany's central geopolitical position within the continent and stressed the need for multilateralism in building a post-Cold War order in Europe. Unlike the UK and French positions, which at the time argued that deepening and widening could not effectively be achieved simultaneously, Lamers stressed the connection between the two processes. He argued that 'deepening [was] a precondition for widening', with the clear implication that both agendas would need to be addressed at the same time. He identified a need to develop 'public acceptance of European integration', implement measures to 'combat organised crime, establish a common policy on migration, fight unemployment, establish a common social policy, ensure Europe's continued competitiveness and protect the environment'. Five specific proposals were forwarded as a means of realising this German agenda:

- Further development of the EU's institutions, the implementation of subsidiarity and a retransfer of power.
- The strengthening of the EU's hard core.
- A raising of the quality of the Franco-German relationship.
- The improvement in the EU's capacity for effective action in foreign and security policy.
- Enlargement of the EU into Central and Eastern Europe.[9]

The further development of the EU's institutional framework was aimed at strengthening 'the EU's capacity to act and to make its structures and procedures more democratic and federal'. The controversy that this paper would provoke throughout the European Union was anticipated and explains why it was released officially as nothing more substantial than an internal discussion paper.

Most controversial was the proposal for a 'variable geometric' or 'multi-speed' approach to integration. The opt-out clauses of the Maastricht Treaty obtained by the UK and Denmark threatened to fragment the 'Community' or 'Monnet' method of integration, whereby all member states moved together in unison. Variable geometry would be a means by which member states could implement common agreements according to their ability and willingness and thus prevent a 'multi-track' Europe from developing.[10] The UK was hostile to this proposal, particularly given the argument that 'it is essential that no country should be allowed to use its right of veto to block the efforts of other countries more able and willing to intensify their cooperation and deepen integration'.[11] The British government feared that variable geometry would marginalise the UK from the integration process. Italy, too, was concerned that the 'hard core' envisaged in the area of monetary policy would exclude it from the single currency. Adding to UK concerns was the suggestion that monetary integration would need to be accompanied by similar moves in the areas of fiscal, budgetary, economic and social policy. When the Social Democrats came to power in the federal elections of September 1998, Oskar Lafontaine, the Finance Minister, reaffirmed the German view that fiscal harmonisation would be the logical continuation from Economic and Monetary Union. In doing so he earned himself the title of 'the most dangerous man in Europe' from the tabloid press in the UK. The special European Council summit, called by the German EU presidency in 1999 to discuss budgetary issues, further underlined Germany's commitment to addressing both the monetary and fiscal dimensions of the European integration process.

It should not be forgotten or overlooked that Germany is a federal state. This means that resistance to the concept of a European order based on federalism is much less pronounced than is seen in unitary state systems such as the UK. The possible framing of a constitutional document setting out the powers and responsibilities of the EU and national governments was raised in the Lamers paper. It was presented there as a means of entrenching the use of 'subsidiarity' and was an idea that was taken up by the SPD government in the lead-up to the Nice European Council summit in December 2000. Foreign Minister Joschka Fischer, speaking at the Humboldt University in Berlin in May 2000, articulated this proposal in a radical perspective on the future of the European Union. Although speaking in a personal capacity, he set out a vision of an increasingly federal European system and called for a constitutional debate:

> enhanced cooperation means nothing more than increased inter-governmentalism under pressure from the facts and the shortcomings of the 'Monnet Method'. The steps towards a constituent treaty – and exactly that will be the precondition for full integration – require a deliberate political act to re-establish Europe.[12]

Highly critical of the manner in which subsidiarity had been implemented within the EU context, 'a subject that is currently being discussed by everyone and understood by virtually no one', Fischer argued that integration would not succeed if the process was perceived to be undermining national government institutions. He further argued that it would require a clear division of sovereign responsibilities between the European federation and the member states.[13]

In 1999, Lamers and Schäuble subsequently returned to the issues outlined in their paper of five years earlier. They, too, argued that a constitutional debate was necessary:

> The framework of a constitutional treaty should be drafted under the auspices of the European Parliament and European Council by a group of eminent persons who must include representatives of the first tranche of acceding countries. Written and reasoned in clear language, and addressed to a European public, it would give structure to, and provide direction for, what is currently a fragmented debate. It would then become clear that terms such as 'the European superstate', 'a federal Europe' or 'the United States of Europe' are unsuitable in defining the innovative nature of Europe's legal framework. There will be as little sole, ultimate or overall responsibility at European level as there

currently is at national level. What is crucial is not the terminology we use but that Europe should be democratic and capable of effective action. Now that the territorial principle of power has become out-dated, a new organisational principle will give rise to new legal con-structs. The new type of federal system established by economic and monetary union is an illustrative example of this. Our European future is not merely a continuation of our national past.[14]

In the aftermath of the EU's Nice summit in December 2000 it appeared that Germany had succeeded in prompting an intergovernmental confer-ence on a potential EU constitution to be convened some time around 2004. This would fit in with the German preference for opening up the EU to its first Central and Eastern European members during 2003.

Both the call for a constitutional debate and the support for early enlarge-ment have placed strains on the Franco-German relationship. It nevertheless remains apparent that Germany is firmly committed to maintaining good relations with its Western partner. Writing in 1994, Lamers and Schäuble stressed that 'the quality of Franco-German relations must be raised to a new level if the historic process of European unification is not to peter out before it reaches its political goal'.[15] In making this call it was recognised that tensions had started to emerge during the early 1990s, particularly over French concerns that enlargement would weaken Germany's commit-ment to the process of deepening and shift the balance of political power eastwards. Lamers and Schäuble suggested that the 'core of the core' within the EU is the Franco-German partnership and, upon returning to their reflections in 1999, were critical of the Schröder government, accusing the SPD–Green coalition of having neglected the partnership.[16] Expectations were rife in 1998 when Schröder came to power that Germany would begin to shift its strategic allegiance away from Paris and more towards London, such was the influence that Tony Blair's New Labour had exercised on the SPD during the election campaign. However, while it is inevitable that Schröder and Blair would have much in common on internal policies, there has been little indication that the Franco-German partnership has suffered as a consequence. Indeed, Foreign Minister Fischer went out of his way in his May 2000 speech to stress the continued importance of the relationship, arguing that every stage of the European integration process had depended upon 'the alliance of Franco-German interests'.[17]

New military security roles?

The end of the Cold War and of the bipolar division of international relations had immense significance for Germany's prospective global roles. No longer divided, the two Germanys were able to complete their unifica-tion in a manner that would have been inconceivable during the Cold War. Moreover, Germany's central geopolitical position gave it an obvious interest in the future European 'security architecture'. During the Cold War, West Germany prioritised its membership of NATO as the bedrock of its military security policy. This, nevertheless, did not prevent it from playing a central role in attempts to generate a distinctly European 'security identity' and in the creation of the Conference on Security and Co-operation in Europe in 1975. The question that emerged in the early 1990s, therefore, focused on the extent to which Germany would maintain the priority of its transatlantic orientation via NATO, or push the Western European (EC/EU) or pan-European (CSCE/OSCE) security dimensions. The answer has proven thus far to be 'all of the above'. This will doubtless perturb those who have argued that, with the end of the Cold War, Germany should make foreign policy choices. Even those who have argued this, however, have conceded that in reality its leaders are likely to continue to avoid doing so.

For a time between 1990 and 1992, it seemed as if German policy was moving towards embracing the idea that the pan-European CSCE should supplant both NATO and the Warsaw Pact as the principal, and perhaps sole, European collective security organisation. Since then, however, this view has fallen from favour among policy-makers in the main parties and groupings. The proponents of a stronger CSCE took a battering during the course of 1991 when it was unable to halt the onset of the civil war in Yugoslavia. Perhaps more importantly, the CSCE was widely seen to be an irrelevance during the period of the anti-Gorbachev *coup d'état* in the USSR during August of that year. This event marked a turning point in attitudes towards the CSCE and NATO. Thereafter, Central European leaders who had henceforth expressed support for proposals to develop the CSCE as the basis for a new all-European security community largely abandoned these ideas and instead began to articulate an interest in NATO membership for their countries. In Germany, too, support for the view that the CSCE might become a significantly more important hard security institution began to ebb.[18]

In retrospect, the decision of Germany's long-serving Foreign Minister to retire in the spring of 1992 can be seen as having dealt a fatal blow to the prospects of Germany continuing to support a significant beefing-up of the CSCE. As McKenzie has noted, 'Germany's CSCE policy was largely a product of Hans-Dietrich Genscher'.[19] Since his departure the CSCE/OSCE has lacked a champion of comparable influence and stature in the German and wider Western political spectrums. The CDU/CSU parties have evinced relatively little interest in the OSCE; and have not entertained ideas that it might replace NATO, even in the long term. Perhaps more surprisingly, the German Social Democrats, since coming to office, have not really pushed for a more positive approach to the CSCE/OSCE. In 1996 the SPD's foreign policy spokesman, Karsten Voigt, wrote that:

> Anyone who proclaims the strengthening of the OSCE as a substitute
> for the eastward enlargement of NATO and of the WEU rather than as

a supplementary measure supports in reality the abandonment of an intensified integration with and between those states which are willing and able to effect an intensified multilateral integration of their foreign and security policies. In the foreseeable future, the OSCE will not be able to develop into the system of collective security in the narrower sense recurrently discussed in Europe.[20]

Germany remains committed to NATO and US involvement in Europe. Although its interest in NATO enlargement into Central and Eastern Europe has been less pronounced than in the case of EU enlargement, it was the then Defence Minister, Volker Rühe, who first publicly raised the issue in 1993.[21] He later played a supportive role as the USA under President Clinton pursued enlargement at the Madrid summit in 1997. Germany by this time had started to articulate its military priorities in the Central and Eastern European region. Handl, Longhurst and Zaborowski have summarised these as being:

- To contribute to the security of Germany and her allies, to enhance confidence through partnership and co-operation and to strengthen crisis prevention and crisis management.
- To add another important dimension to the web of ties with the Eastern countries which create growing confidence in their relations.
- To contribute to the transformation of the armed forces and defence administrations in the post-communist states.
- To share German experience and models in the military sphere that should increase democratic stability, political control and transparency of military structures.
- To create a solid basis for permanent ties with countries and to increase their understanding of German policy.
- To increase co-operation in arms procurement and production, and enhance, therefore, the chances of German and European arms production programmes in competition with the USA.[22]

Germany is equally committed to the development of the EU's Common Foreign and Security Policy and has fully endorsed the decisions taken at Cologne and Helsinki in 1999. These have, potentially at least, paved the way for the creation of an EU Rapid Reaction Force, as discussed by Smith and Timmins in Chapter 5 of this volume. Indeed, during the 1980s Germany had played a key role in the reactivation of the Western European Union and the initial generation of moves towards a European Security and Defence Identity that spawned the Franco-German brigade and corps. These, in turn, formed the basis for the creation of the Eurocorps in 1992 and 1993.

The most striking development in German security policy during the 1990s was the shift in attitudes – both elite and mass – regarding 'out-of-area' activities. The German Basic Law had debarred West Germany from deploying troops except where they were involved in NATO defensive operations. Upon this basis, Germany had argued that it was effectively prohibited from military involvement in the Gulf War in 1991. In doing so, it had incurred the criticism of its NATO partners, most especially in the USA, who in the post-Cold War era have expected Germany to take a more active role in hard security operations. During the early 1990s Germany began to inch towards a compromise by deploying non-armed military personnel in crisis zones around the world: in Croatia, Kenya, Somalia, Cambodia and Kuwait. It was, however, the decision taken in 1994 to deploy German aircrew as part of the NATO operation to support the UN-mandated 'no-fly zone' over Bosnia that first saw German personnel on active military service in a combat zone. The full participation of the German airforce and armed infantry in the NATO interventions in Kosovo during 1999 represented the final completion of Germany's transformation; or the 'normalisation' of German foreign and security policies, as it has been called.[23] Jeffery and Paterson point to three main explanations for Germany's watershed involvement in Kosovo. First, there was a desire to demonstrate loyalty to its Alliance partners. Second, there were the humanitarian arguments in the face of Serbian 'ethnic cleansing' and potential genocide and the historical memory of national socialism which these provoked. Finally, there was pragmatic concern over preventing large migratory flows of refugees westwards.[24]

Conclusion

What is clear from the discussions in this chapter is the continuing importance that Germany places on institutional order and the role of multilateralism in underwriting this. The image of an 'overlapping security architecture' based on the EU, NATO and, to a lesser extent, OSCE is congruent with Germany's desire to maintain good relations with its European neighbours to the west and the east as well as with the USA and Russia. This is also indicative of the extent to which Germany has thus far managed to avoid having to make the choices envisaged by Morgan and others at the start of the 1990s. It is consistent with the close links that German leaders draw between the hard and soft dimensions of security in the post-Cold War context. Germany, however, still finds itself saddled with the expectations of leadership while attempting to avoid suspicions of hegemony.

Notes and references

1 J. Müller, 'The Catastrophe Quota'. *Journal of Conflict Resolution* 38 1994. Quoted by Adrian Hyde-Price in G. Smith *et al.* (eds), *Developments in German Politics* (second edn). (London: Macmillan 1996), p. 173.

2 H. W. Maull, 'German Foreign Policy Post-Kosovo: Still a Civilian Power?' *German Politics* 9 (2) 2000, p. 14.

3 *Ibid.*

4 *Ibid.*, pp. 14–15.

5 See C. Powell, 'The Leaked Chequers Memorandum: What the PM Learnt about the Germans' in H. James and M. Stone (eds), *When the Wall Came Down: Reactions to German Unification.* (London: Routledge 1992), pp. 233–9.

6 R. Morgan, 'Germany in the New Europe' in C. Crouch and D. Marquand (eds), *Towards Greater Europe? A Continent without an Iron Curtain.* (Oxford: Blackwell 1992).

7 T. G. Ash, 'Germany's Choice'. *Foreign Affairs* 73 (4) 1994, pp. 65–81.

8 K. Lamers and W. Schäuble, 'Reflections on European Policy'. CDU/CSU Parliamentary Faction, Bonn, 1 September 1994. Reprinted in K. A. Lamers, *A German Agenda for the European Union.* (London: The Federal Trust for Education and Research/Konrad Adenauer Foundation 1994), pp. 11–12.

9 *Ibid.*, p. 14.

10 See C. Deubner, *Deutsche Europapolitik: Von Maastricht Nach Kerneuropa?* (Baden-Baden: Nomos 1995), p. 184 for the origins of the variable geometry proposal. See A. C.-G. Stubb, 'A Categorisation of Differentiated Integration'. *Journal of Common Market Studies* 34 (2) 1996 and Stubb, 'The 1996 Intergovernmental Conference and the Management of Flexible Integration'. *Journal of European Public Policy* 4 (1) 1997 for a detailed discussion of enhanced co-operation, or 'flexibility', to which the proposal is now more commonly referred.

11 Lamers *op.cit.*, p. 16.

12 J. Fischer, 'Reflections on the Finality of European Integration'. German Foreign Ministry website. URL: http://www.auswaertiges-amt.government.de/6_archiv/index.htm.

13 *Ibid.*

14 W. Schäuble and K. Lamers, 'Reflections on European Policy II'. Bonn, 3 May 1999. Christian Democratic Union website. URL: http://www.cdu.de/englisch/eulamers.htm.

15 Lamers (1994) *op.cit.*, p. 18.

16 Lamers and Schäuble (1999) *op.cit.*, p. 11.

17 Fischer *op.cit.*

18 See M. McKenzie, *Germany and the Institutions of Collective Security in Europe.* (PRIF Report No.36). (Frankfurt: Peace Research Institute 1994), p. 28.

19 *Ibid.*, p. 31.

20 K. Voigt, 'German Interest in Multilateralism'. *Aussenpolitik* 47 (II) 1996, p. 112.

21 He did so in a high-profile lecture to the IISS in London. See V. Rühe, 'Shaping Euro-Atlantic Policies: A Grand Strategy for a New Era'. *Survival* 35 (2) 1993, p. 135.

22 V. Handl *et al.*, 'Germany's Security Policy towards East Central Europe'. IGS Discussion Paper 12. (Birmingham: University of Birmingham 2000), p. 17.

23 By, for example, Philip Gordon. See his 'The Normalization of German Foreign Policy'. *Orbis* 38 (2) 1994, pp. 225–43.

24 C. Jeffery and W. E. Paterson, 'Germany's Power in Europe'. IGS Discussion Paper 10. (Birmingham: University of Birmingham 2000), pp. 40–1.

11 Russia

Caging the bear?

Laura Richards Cleary

Introduction

The impetus for the development of new security architecture has come from the West, through the initiatives of either NATO or the European Union. Although not couched in such obvious terms, the aim has been to secure the West's victory in the Cold War by promoting democracy and capitalism to its former enemies. It must be acknowledged that the states of Central and Eastern Europe have, for the most part, been willing recipients, with the exception of Russia.

Between 1991 and 1993 it was strongly suggested that if a truly pan-European security order was to be built, Russia would need to form a cornerstone of that structure. Thus Russia should be incorporated, on a gradual basis, into the political, economic and security institutions which would form the interlocking framework of security. While the Clinton administration argued for Russia's inclusion during the 1990s, it has become increasingly clear that neither the institutions nor Russia itself have been quite as keen.

Sense can be made of the contradictory statements issued by Russian politicians, and the inconsistent policy positions adopted by the government, if they are viewed within the context of the larger search for Russian identity. This is the central argument of this chapter: that so long as Russia remains uncertain about its identity it will not enjoy particularly close relations with either NATO or the EU. Under the current set of conditions, membership of NATO or the EU means more than joining a military or economic alliance, it means ascribing to a particular identity. Russia's full participation within a European security framework will only be achieved if government and institutions can accommodate diversity.

There are essentially three competing themes within Russian/NATO/EU relations. These are enlargement, encirclement and empire. While enlargement makes sense from a Western perspective, and indeed from that of many Eastern applicants, to many Russians the process looks increasingly reminiscent of the encirclement which occurred during the Cold War. Russia views the West as triumphant and seeking to contain its former enemy rather than treat it as it would an equal partner.

Russia has lost status and territory and its culture is currently under threat from lack of funding and support and the onslaught of globalisation. Its very identity has been undermined. Thus Russia is resorting to defining itself purely in opposition to the West. So long as this remains the case Russia will remain aloof from those institutions which seek to secure the Western identity.

With hindsight, the Cold War era appears to have been marked by an unprecedented level of certainty. The 'enemy' was easily identified and the divisions between the two opposing blocs were clearly demarcated. There was a recognised order to international relations. In the post-Cold War era the only certainty has been the degree of uncertainty in terms of identifying either enemy or type of threat.[1] From this situation has arisen a desire to move beyond a traditional security order. In drafting the blueprints for the new security architecture, however, three issues will need to be addressed. First, security will need to be redefined; second, a European identity will have to be established; and, finally, the two must be consolidated within a framework that is mutually supportive.

Creating order out of chaos

The Cold War generated a high degree of stability within international relations because the concepts of security and identity were defined and achieved within two distinct systems. Within international relations 'order' is created out of 'chaos' through a variety of means: an organising principle, an ideology, an institution, or, more generally, by a combination of these factors. As noted by Clive Archer in Chapter 1 of this volume, there is an element of sharing implicit within these principles, structures and relations. This was certainly the case during the period of the Cold War when territorial sovereignty was enshrined in state constitutions and in international agreements such as the Helsinki Final Act. The United States, the USSR and the institutions that they led advanced the competing ideologies of democracy and communism. In the West, political and economic stability were generated through, first, Marshall Aid and, subsequently, the European Community. Political and military security was furthered by the creation of NATO, an alliance of democratic states committed to the establishment and perpetuation of democratic institutions. In the East, the communist variant of political and economic stability was created through the auspices of COMECON and secured by the counterpoint to NATO, the Warsaw Treaty Organisation. The institutional arrangements of NATO and the Warsaw Pact were of critical significance in the promotion of the respective ideologies, the generation of identities, and the maintenance of the larger security system.

The disbanding of the Warsaw Pact in April 1991 and the dissolution of the USSR on 25 December of the same year marked the end not only of an institution and of a state but also of the larger European security order.

Since 1991 NATO and the European Union, through different means, have attempted to fill the void. NATO has undergone a significant shift away from the static defence posture required to support a policy of nuclear deterrence, towards more flexible and rapidly deployable forces. In the absence of a direct threat, member states have significantly reduced the size of their armed forces, the level of procurement and other defence outlays. This in turn has meant a change of tactics for NATO. It is no longer the sole guarantor of security in Europe. Through the new Strategic Concept, made public at the Rome summit in 1991, and updated in 1999, NATO has sought to place itself at the core of a framework of interlocking institutions which includes the European Union, the Organisation for Security and Co-operation in Europe and the United Nations.

Despite the streamlining of operations and a renewed emphasis on the political function of the Alliance, Central and Eastern Europe and the republics of the Former Soviet Union (FSU) remain the focus of attention for NATO planners. Their aim is, as Secretary of State Madeleine Albright explained in 1997, 'to do for Europe's east what NATO did fifty years ago for Europe's west: to integrate new democracies, defeat old hatreds, provide confidence in economic recovery and deter conflict'.[2] Fifty years ago the security arrangements provided by NATO were offered in conjunction with the new economic order created by the Marshall Plan. The provision of security now offered by NATO to the states of Central and Eastern Europe is in conjunction with the European Union's proposals for the development of a new economic order created through the provision of immediate financial aid in the form of loans, TACIS and PHARE assistance programmes and the promise of eventual inclusion in the EU.

This chapter will concentrate primarily on Russia's relations with NATO rather than those it has with the EU. This is for the simple reason that much of Russia's current foreign policy is determined on the basis of prevailing threats, specifically of a military nature. To adopt a more positive, proactive foreign policy, one focused on political, diplomatic and economic co-operation and gain, would require a level of direction and co-ordination within the Russian government not currently achievable due to the larger societal instability. Thus, Russia has viewed the EU as being, if not a benign actor in international relations, then at least one which does not pose an immediate threat to Russia's territorial integrity. NATO, on the other hand, is viewed with a high degree of suspicion by politicians and public alike.[3] This despite NATO's attempts since 1991 to downplay its military function and reassert its political nature.

Securing an identity

The USSR was both the catalyst for and the victim of the collapse of the Cold War system. The implosion of the communist order started a chain reaction that resulted in the loss of Russia's great power status, the dissolution of the empire and a crisis in national identity. While Russia may in time come to terms with the facts that her status has been revoked and that her empire is a thing of the past, she cannot survive as a state unless she resolves the question of identity.

Any state that is insecure about its own identity will pose a threat to the security of those states that surround it. Thus Russia's identity crisis may continue to pose problems for its immediate neighbours as well as for an enlarged NATO. The latter is especially true if the European identity is still in development. Edward Moxon-Browne has argued that a comprehensive sense of security in Europe can only be achieved once a viable European identity has been created.[4] As Robert Bideleux argues in Chapter 2 of this volume, while such an identity is in development and the EU is acting as a catalyst in its evolution, it remains in an incomplete state. A working definition of the term 'European political identity' has been offered by Moxon-Browne in which he suggests that Europeans 'accept among themselves a redistribution of resources and an equitable pattern of rights and duties that can be upheld by common institutions responsible for the authoritative allocation of values',[5] a view broadly shared by Bideleux. That identity is defined as much by national and transnational institutions as it is by comparison with a sense of 'other'. Two distinct 'others', the American and Russian identities, are recognised. While it is relatively easy to characterise American distinctiveness,[6] the character of Russia is more difficult to sketch.

It could be argued that this is nothing new. As every student of Russian history has learned, there is within Russia, and within Russians themselves, a constant battle between Westerners and Slavophiles. The former have tended to look towards Western Europe for their inspiration, believing that Russia has, by some twist of fate, been diverted from the path of European development. The incorporation of Western values and the implementation of Western institutional practices would enable Russia to rejoin the fold. In contrast, the Slavophiles believe that Russia's future lies within its past, that the distinction of being Russian is in itself a virtue and that Western mannerisms should not be aped.[7] In essence, this conflict is not over something as specific as civil rights or civic identity, but something far less tangible: an attitude to that which is solely defined as Russia or Russianness. Despite dissent over the best approach to any specific reform, modernisation programme or foreign policy, the overriding concern of any politician or citizen always has been the primacy of 'Mother Russia'.

Mother Russia has herself been either more or less expansive at different points in history. Within the Russian context, the state and its ideology essentially 'create' the nation. Thus during the Tsarist period Russia was united by an ideology which combined Christian orthodoxy and imperialist tendencies. Soviet Russia was bound together by communist ideology and the same need for imperial expansion. In the post-communist era a unifying ideology has been notable by its absence. Members of the Russian elite have toyed with elements of liberalism, yet failure to apply these wholeheartedly and consistently has meant that reform has borne insufficient fruit. Liberalism, as a result, has been abandoned. As Russia gropes for a new ideology her politicians increasingly reflect on past glories as a great power and look forward to renewed imperial expansion as a means of reuniting the nation and reaffirming national identity.

A historic argument, and one which is receiving renewed favour, is that there are three levels to that identity. Russian consciousness must be developed simultaneously at all levels if the state is to survive.[8] At the core of that identity is *ethnic* Russia, with *historic* Russia, including Belarus and Ukraine, forming the second layer and *imperial* Russia, incorporating other ethnic groups overcome during the periods of Tsarist and Soviet expansion, forging the third.

When the USSR dissolved at the end of 1991, Russia was stripped bare of two of its mantles, leaving a federation which was not a pure Russian state. Alexander Tsipko has described the Russian Federation as 'an artificial entity, a kind of remainder after the subtraction of the rest of the Soviet republics'.[9] The Russian Federation is smaller than pre-revolutionary Russia, but larger than old Muscovy. In its present form it has retained a considerable part of Russia's imperial and colonial possessions, yet these possessions make it difficult to equate an ethnic core with a territorial mass. Efforts by Chechens or Tatars to acquire statehood fuel insecurity and the desire to reunite with the 'like-minded' groups of historic Russia, the Belarussians, for example, to create a more stable core for Russia.

There has been a great deal of rhetoric regarding the states of the 'near abroad', the former Soviet republics. A broad array of leaders – Zhirinovsky, Primakov, Yeltsin and Putin – have made statements in which they have expressed the desire for 'a closer union' with Russia's neighbours. Implied within this is either the assertion of direct control over neighbouring states, a controlling interest in the affairs of the near abroad or a relationship of slightly less than equal partners. Tsipko has argued that the democrats of the late Soviet period paid scant regard to the effect that their actions might have on the stability of the union. The dissolution of that union was viewed as a necessary means by which to achieve a new civic nation. The politicians of the new Russia would now argue that a civic nation has not emerged from the ashes of the union and, further, that any sense of stability or security has become illusory. A civic nation, it is concluded, is of less importance than stability and security. These can be achieved by renewing links with the states of the near abroad.

Since 1994, and the election of Alyaksandr Lukashenka as President of Belarus, Russia has been moving closer to part of its historic core. In 1995 a joint customs union was created. In 1996 Yeltsin and Lukashenka signed a unity pact and in 1997 Yeltsin proposed a full merger with a single government controlling a joint budget, with common currency and unified fuel and energy systems. Throughout 1998 the two governments worked towards that goal, achieving a *de jure* union of the two states in 1999. At the time of his proposal Yeltsin was perceived as playing the nationalist card. The actions in Chechnya (discussed below) demonstrated how poorly manned and trained the Russian armed forces were. That meant that reintegration must occur at the political and economic levels. Any attempts to do so within the framework of the Commonwealth of Independent States (CIS) have proven limited. Given the above-outlined approach to defining Russian identity, and the state's current capabilities, it is understandable that politicians, purporting to be nationalists, would view NATO enlargement as a direct threat.

The view from inside the cage

Since 1985 Russian reactions to the European security order and to NATO in particular have fluctuated dramatically. When Mikhail Gorbachev came to power in March 1985 it did not appear that US–Soviet relations could get any worse. President Ronald Reagan's frequent references to the 'Evil Empire' and the promotion of 'Star Wars', the Strategic Defense Initiative, marked the height of rhetoric and the low point in US–Soviet relations. Through the promotion of 'New Thinking' in foreign policy (1985–91), which placed a renewed emphasis on disarmament and a co-operative approach to common problems, Gorbachev sought to reduce the level of international tension. This he accomplished through the signing of a series of disarmament agreements and by engaging in discussions with the leaders of Europe for a 'Common European Home'. By the end of the Cold War, Western leaders, and particularly US President George Bush, were doing what they could to support Gorbachev's government and reform programme. Despite their efforts, and perhaps even because of them, the Soviet government faltered and was rejected by the republican governments of the union in 1991. Although a new phase in East–West relations officially began when the union was dissolved in December 1991, the policies initiated in the late Soviet period remained essentially unchanged. As the largest successor state, Russia remained the primary focus of Western attention. Despite a high degree of political and economic incompetence, the West supported the Yeltsin government, in all its incarnations. In terms of the political rhetoric emanating from Moscow, this support was not always reciprocated.

Between 1991 and 1993, Yeltsin and his Foreign Minister, Andrei Kozyrev, pursued a pro-Western foreign policy. Their reaction to calls for a new security regime in Europe was quite favourable, although they preferred the Conference on Security and Co-operation in Europe to NATO as the cornerstone for that new architecture. Nevertheless, Yeltsin appeared fairly magnanimous when he conceded the participation of former Warsaw Pact members in the political framework of NATO. Russia also adopted a relaxed attitude towards NATO's Partnership for Peace programme when the concept was first tabled in late 1993. Both the political and military establishment believed that PfP would be a 'waiting room' for CEE and FSU states, since it did not appear at that time that NATO was seriously considering expansion.

From late 1993 onwards Russia's response to NATO proposals for enlargement became erratic. It was not unusual for Yeltsin to state publicly that Russia had no objections to Poland establishing closer relations with the Alliance, and then for the Foreign Ministry to outline the objections to such a relationship the following day, or for Kozyrev to declare his support for NATO's role in Europe only to be denounced by the Duma, the lower house of the Russian parliament. Yeltsin's declining health was initially cited as the cause for such policy blunders, but it became increasingly apparent that the root causes of this tug of war ran much deeper. Three specific reasons can be identified. First, at the very moment when NATO was pushing ahead with PfP it was becoming evident that the liberal agenda adopted by the Yeltsin team was not going to provide the remarkable transformation of society which had been promised in the time stated. The challenges to Russian society's security in the economic, political and cultural spheres could not be met by the existing political institutions. Second, because the liberal agenda had been advocated by the USA and the other members of the Group of Seven (G7), politicians began to turn away from Western prescriptions and promote a Russian or Eurasian antidote. As nationalist fervour increased among all political parties, so too did more insular viewpoints. The success of communist and nationalist forces in the parliamentary elections of 1993 and 1995 made the adoption of a pro-Western foreign policy much more problematic for the Yeltsin administration. Finally, despite NATO assurances that expansion was not 'threat-driven' and that Russia was viewed as a partner in, rather than an enemy of, security, Russian political and military elites continued to believe that the process of enlargement was aimed at Russia.

From a Russian perspective, NATO's deeds do not match its words. Successive invasions throughout the ages, by among others the Mongol hordes, the Poles, the Swedes, the French, the Germans, the British and the Americans, have all left their mark on the Russian national psyche. As a result, Russia has always favoured the creation of a buffer zone to ensure its security. With the inclusion of the CEE and FSU within NATO activities Russia effectively becomes encircled. As a number of senior Russian military personnel have stressed to this author, one need only look at a map of Russia. If the process of enlargement continues then Russia will be confronted by NATO to the west and to the east, since the United States is a mere fifty miles away. It is for this reason that Russia has become increasingly vociferous in its objections to enlargement. There are two issues of particular concern to the Russian establishment: the inclusion of the Baltic states within NATO and the gravitation of Ukraine into the Alliance's sphere of influence.

Lithuania, Latvia and Estonia were the first republics to petition the Soviet government for their sovereignty and independence. Despite the associated problems of disentangling the communist-era economic network and dealing with a sizeable Russian population within the region, the Baltic states have made integration into the political, economic and military security institutions of Western Europe one of their top priorities. To this end, they were among the first of the former Soviet republics actively to pursue closer ties with NATO, believing that the security guarantees offered by that institution would provide sufficient protection from a revanchist Russia. The Baltic states have been active in the PfP since its inception and have worked diligently on addressing questions of democratic control of the armed forces, border security and transnational crime: issues which NATO feels to be of paramount importance in the new security regime. While forging new links with NATO generates a sense of security within the Baltic states, it creates the opposite feeling in Russia. Were Lithuania, Latvia and Estonia to become full members of the Atlantic Alliance, Russia could be denied access to the Baltic Sea, an access right which it has struggled throughout history to maintain. For this reason, Deputy Defence Minister Nikolai Mikhailov announced in December 1998 that troops in Kaliningrad *oblast* would act as the spearhead of Russia's deterrent against NATO. This is, however, a fairly hollow threat, since Kaliningrad is considered to be one of the most unstable regions in Russia; territorially isolated from the motherland, dependent upon imported goods for 80 per cent of its consumption and with increasing levels of unemployment. If EU enlargement proceeds, it could become encircled by EU member states that are also members of NATO.[10]

Russian feelings of insecurity are heightened by Ukrainian moves towards Western institutions, particularly NATO. The member states of NATO view an independent, stable and democratic Ukraine as being of strategic importance for the development of the continent as a whole; Ukraine in turn views NATO as the most capable and reliable pillar of European security. It also views co-operation with and integration into the institutions of Europe as a means by which it can assert its own identity and independence from Russia. Thus Ukraine has been keen to participate in PfP, participating in several joint exercises, and to provide peacekeepers for the Stabilisation Force (SFOR) in Bosnia. While the Ukrainian government is working towards full-scale integration into European and transatlantic security structures it realises that it is not yet ready to achieve that goal. Its political and military institutions must develop further. Continued involvement in a variety of regional associations should help to secure the reform process, while the establishment of closer relations with Poland provides it with a 'representative' within Western institutions. Ukraine is aware, however, that it is trying to perform a difficult balancing act. Closer integration with the West is necessary for its long-term security and prosperity, but too rapid pursuit of that course will jeopardise that self-same security. At each step it must appease Russia.

Russia wants to be appeased, because by receiving supplicants it maintains an aura of its former status. Increasingly, however, that is the only way in which its status can be maintained. If power is determined by political stability, economic potential, availability of natural resources, population and the ability to provide for defence, then Russia has been failing on all counts. Russia has the trappings of democracy in the sense that it holds regular elections, yet stability is absent when politicians and journalists are kidnapped, imprisoned and executed on a regular basis. It has the semblance of a market economy, but the Russian rouble has been in frequent freefall and the banking system in the process of collapse. Russia holds an abundance of natural resources, but they cannot be easily exploited because of outdated technology. Russia used to have a population on a par with that of the United States, now the birth rate is declining and the mortality rate is increasing. Russia's armed forces were once respected and feared. Now, as a result of underfunding, undermanning and political infighting, not even Estonia is afraid of Russia. If Russia is to avoid being pushed to the periphery of European interests it needs to develop a stable working relationship with NATO.

This truth is recognised at some levels, but not at others. In the absence of any clear programme for transforming Russia, politicians have recreated an old 'enemy' in order to unify society. That enemy is NATO. Initially, it appeared that this was a tactic adopted by politicians to score cheap political points. There was relatively little support among the general populace for the adoption of such a stance. As the political and economic situation in Russia has deteriorated, however, adherence to such a worldview has grown.[11] Despite the rhetoric, the military as an institution, elements of the Foreign Ministry and some members of the Yeltsin government recognised that a modus vivendi was required. So, like the other members of the CIS, Russia has participated in PfP, and contributed to SFOR. On 27 May 1997 the NATO–Russia Founding Act was signed. Russia, reflecting on past glory as a superpower, had long demanded a veto over NATO actions. This was a right which neither NATO nor the USA was ever likely to grant. The Founding Act does, however, establish the basis for a permanent security partnership. Crucial to this is the statement that NATO and Russia do not consider each other as adversaries.[12] The mechanism for consultation and co-operation is the Permanent Joint Council, which meets at various levels: foreign ministers, defence ministers and ambassadorial. Varying degrees of co-operation can be noted at the different levels. The participation of Russian forces in SFOR, the interaction of military personnel within NATO and their attendance at various seminars on civil–military relations led to the development of a stable working relationship with their NATO counterparts. Within NATO's Supreme Headquarters Allied Powers Europe (SHAPE) there exists a reasonable, functioning relationship. At the ambassadorial level of the Permanent Joint Council, however, political posturing limited the effectiveness of the body. This differentiation was indicative of Russian–NATO relations as a whole.

Between 1997 and early 1999 a functioning relationship existed between Russia and NATO. This was achieved in part because Russia chose to work with the United States rather than the USA's alliance. During the Cold War, Russia and the United States enjoyed equal status as superpowers, with the Warsaw Pact and NATO as their respective alliances. Stripped of its supportive alliance, Russia was left on an unequal footing with NATO. With regard to the United States it has continued to view itself as an equal partner.[13] Russia was willing to participate in SFOR, but only if Russian troops were placed under US, rather than NATO, command. Thus participation in operations at ground level allowed Russia to maintain a sense of equal partnership and a belief that it was contributing to the European security order in a fundamental way.

Two events in 1999 – NATO's campaign in Kosovo and Russia's own in Chechnya – succeeded in rocking the emerging European security order and Russia's belief in its equal status within that to their very cores. The stated reasons for engagement in Kosovo and Chechnya were laudable in both instances; however, they were undermined by the actual military action undertaken. In the case of Kosovo, Western political leaders advocated the pursuit of an 'ethical foreign policy', the provision of humanitarian aid to Kosovar Albanians, and the cessation of ethnic cleansing in the territory of the former Yugoslavia.

The Russian government agreed in principle with these political aims but disagreed strongly with the way in which NATO hoped to achieve them. Russian objections to NATO policy centred on four issues:

1   In referring to Yugoslav President Slobodan Milosevic as a new Hitler, and focusing solely on atrocities conducted by the Serbs while ignoring those performed by Albanians, NATO failed to resolve any of the tensions within the region and indeed contributed to ethnic conflict by promoting anti-Serb/anti-Slavic tendencies.

2   NATO's, and particularly the USA's, reluctance to engage in anything other than an air campaign, and that conducted at a height of three miles, resulted in a failure to provide humanitarian aid (a stated objective) and an increase in the number of refugees.

3   NATO failed to treat Russia as an equal member within the European security framework. Russian Defence Minister Sergeev contended that NATO viewed Russia as unfit for anything other than peacemaking operations carried out by the Alliance. Understandably, Sergeev disagreed with this view, arguing that it deprived Russia of 'its own independent policy aimed at stabilising the situation in the region'.[14]

4   Finally, Russia argued that NATO's actions in the former Yugoslavia were 'out of area' and therefore in contravention of the principles of collective defence and of international law since NATO acted without the consent of the UN.

Many of these objections were also voiced in the West and were generally dealt with through normal diplomatic channels. In Central and Eastern Europe there was a good deal of concern over NATO's actions, and support for the first, second and fourth objections noted above was in evidence. In the interests of harmony and concern over future inclusion into NATO and the EU, CEE governments attempted to tolerate opposition. They were assisted in this by NATO's decision not to place too strenuous demands on these governments for military support. In the case of Russia, however, politicians of varying hues and the general public became more vociferous in their opposition to NATO as an institution and its proposals for enlargement. The ascendancy of nationalists and communists in the parliament, coupled with the Yeltsin administration's inability to do anything other than react to pressure from below, resulted in the severance of ties between Russia and the Permanent Joint Council. This was accompanied by an increase in the number of Russian mercenaries willing to fight on behalf of Serbia.

It is perhaps ironic that Russian mercenaries should choose to fight for the concept of a greater Slav brotherhood when they were generally unwilling to defend Mother Russia from various internal uprisings. The Russian Federation consists of 21 republics, 49 *oblasts* (provinces), 1 autonomous *oblast*, 6 *krai* (territories) and 10 autonomous *okrugs* (districts), which demonstrate varying degrees of loyalty to Moscow. Since 1991 relations between Moscow and the constituent units of the Federation have fluctuated in accordance with the economic fortunes of the Federation as a whole. When the economy has been in freefall the republics and regions have demanded greater autonomy to manage local economies. One of the greatest challenges for Yeltsin and Putin has been to bring the regions to heel.

With its declaration of independence in November 1991, Chechnya became the first republic within the Russian Federation to assert itself. Russia could not accept this declaration for a number of reasons. Given the arguments noted above, it was crucial for Russia to maintain its territorial integrity. Further, acknowledgement of the right to self-determination for one group could lead to a flood of claims from other minority groups (of which there are over a hundred).[15] Between 1991 and 1994 attempts, of both a political and military nature, were made to bring the Chechen Republic back into the fold. All failed. On 7 December 1994 the Russian Security Council voted to send Russian troops into Chechnya in force. The 1994–6 campaign was fought on the basis of maintaining the territorial and cultural integrity of the state by denying the Chechen independence movement its goal and opposing the spread of Islamic fundamentalism. Little, apart from a stalemate, was achieved by the conclusion of the campaign in 1996. Relations between Moscow and Grozny, the capital of Chechnya, remained strained, and it has been suggested that the government and military were simply waiting for another excuse to intervene in the region and 'resolve' the crisis once and for all.

In 1999 the abduction of Interior Ministry General Gennadii Shipgun and a series of bombings throughout Russia, allegedly orchestrated by Chechen separatists, provided the government with the rationale for a renewed onslaught against the recalcitrant republic. The emphasis had now changed, becoming one against 'bandits, terrorists and extremists'. Again, in principle, there is nothing wrong in seeking to maintain state sovereignty or combat terrorism. Every national security concept and doctrine purports these to be their aims. The difficulty arises in the way in which these policies are implemented. In both the first and second Chechen wars the Russian army has been indiscriminate in its targeting. There are no civilian 'safe areas' in Chechnya. NATO, the European Union, the OSCE and the Council of Europe have grown increasingly concerned about human rights abuses in the region. NATO's Supreme Allied Commander Europe (SACEUR), General Wesley Clark, stated that Russia's targeting of civilian populations was inappropriate. The EU threatened sanctions and a reduction in the amount of aid available through TACIS.[16] OSCE observers were denied access to the war zone, and the Council of Europe started the procedure to suspend Russia from membership. Russia has tended to be fairly dismissive of all criticism, claiming, in light of the objections noted above to NATO's conduct of its Kosovo campaign, that the Western allies were merely hypocritical. The EU's objections drew little public response.

The EU has adopted a 'softly, softly' approach to Russia, as it is aware that for eastward enlargement to succeed Russia should be neither antagonised nor isolated. Like NATO, the EU has sought to engage Russia in a number of frameworks and activities, thus giving the semblance of a cooperative working relationship. The main legal framework for EU–Russian relations is the Partnership and Co-operation Agreement (PCA) that came into force in December 1997.[17] It is explicitly conditional on Russia continuing on the path of political and economic reform in the belief that a democratic and free-market-orientated Russia is essential for long-term regional security. Most of the PCA's provisions cover economic relations. The objective is to encourage Russia's increasing integration into the European market by progressive trade liberalisation and the harmonisation of Russia's laws with those of the EU's Single Market on such matters as customs regulations, standards and certification, competition and the environment.

This framework clearly seeks to promote the concepts of political and economic security. In Russia, the EU has not been widely viewed as a major foreign policy actor in the traditional sense. The steps taken at the Cologne European Council summit in June 1999 may eventually change that view. The 'Common Strategy on Russia' which was adopted at that session reflects the EU's greater political ambitions for contributing to regional security by establishing a 'strategic partnership' with Russia. It is based on what is called 'the vision of the EU' for its partnership with Russia:

> A stable democratic and prosperous Russia, firmly anchored in a united Europe free of new dividing lines, is essential to lasting peace on the continent. The issues that divide the whole continent can be resolved only through ever-closer co-operation between Russia and the European Union.[18]

It is envisaged that the EU and Russia will work closely together on a wide range of 'challenges to security on the European continent', including international organised crime, money laundering, drugs, illegal immigration, trafficking in people and environmental dangers. There was also the suggestion that Russia might be asked to participate in the WEU's 'Petersberg Tasks' of peacekeeping, humanitarian assistance and crisis management, and this has been repeated in the EU's 1999 proposals for a Common European Security and Defence Policy (CESDP). Potentially, therefore, Russia could be constructively engaged in a wide range of initiatives designed to enhance security and promote constructive interaction with states in the region, through its programmes of co-operation with both the EU and NATO.

Although Russia has been dismissive of criticism in the past, it is by no means indifferent to the developments occurring within Europe. If anything, since the assumption of power by Vladimir Putin in December 1999, Russia is even more focused on Europe. Putin was very active in the first half of 2000, courting UK Prime Minister Tony Blair, making renewed overtures to NATO by inviting Secretary-General Lord Robertson to Moscow and stating that future membership remained a possibility, addressing an EU–Russia summit, and offering interested European states an alternative to the proposed US national missile defence system against 'rogue' states. At the time of writing it is unclear whether Putin can best be classed as a Westerner or Slavophile. He has stated on a number of occasions in very different forums that Russia 'was, is and will be a European country by its location, culture and its attitude toward economic integration'.[19] Geographically and culturally Russia is most assuredly part of Europe. If, however, a European identity is determined predominantly by the sharing of certain political values then Russia cannot be considered part of Europe. Russia appears to be concerned less with the development of democratic norms than the need to reassert state power in order to combat terrorism and extremism. This perspective was reflected in a number of policy initiatives in 2000. In January Putin signed a revised national security concept, the most notable clauses of which centred on the conditions under which Russia would resort to first use of nuclear weapons and the shift in emphasis from purely criminal to political terrorism. In April, Russia began to implement a common defence policy with Belarus. Finally, throughout 2000 steps were taken to rebuild and strengthen the Russian armed forces and military-industrial complex. It is clear that Russia considers itself to be in a position in which only it can guarantee its security.

Conclusion

The Cold War is generally viewed in terms of the standoff between NATO and the Warsaw Pact. The system that ensued focused the world's attention on the need to achieve a specific form of security that could be defined in terms of defence against a military onslaught, conventional or nuclear. Yet it is important to remember that the original intentions behind the formation of the Atlantic Alliance were not solely to act as a counterbalance to the USSR. Each participant had a different motivation. Some wished to constrain Germany, others to maintain the link between the USA and Europe, and all wanted to prevent the revival of the 'balance of power' game.[20] The Alliance was successful in achieving all of these goals, and under the umbrella of protection that it provided, new forms of security developed. Markets flourished, Europe was rebuilt, and the political identity which Moxon-Browne and Bideleux have described took shape.

For the West, this is the legacy of the Cold War. We are secure in our cultural and political identities. For much of Central and Eastern Europe this is a legacy in which they would wish to partake. In doing so they would be reclaiming a lost heritage. For Russia, whose developmental path has always veered away from that of the West, this type of security seems a distant prize.

Russia is as aware as the West that military force has lost its utility, and that comprehensive national security requires a priority provision of economic, social and ecological conditions.[21] Russia is also aware that the threats to that security include ethnic and religious conflict, transnational crime and terrorism. What separates Russia from the Western members of NATO and the EU is that it is having to deal with all of these problems within its own territory without benefit of established political or economic institutions. As Odom declares, 'we are dealing with a very weak regime trying to rule a Russia that has never existed before, the residual centre of a former empire that has yet to define itself politically or territorially'.[22]

Whether he is a Westerner or a Slavophile, President Putin is a pragmatist above all else. His first actions, following his election as Russia's President in March 2000, suggested that he believed that the immediate salvation of the Russian state lay in the reassertion of authority and authoritarian methods of control. The long-term threat to Russia is the onslaught of globalisation, a process that even in the most stable of states highlights social tensions and inconsistencies. Russia cannot afford to adopt a long-term isolationist policy. It needs, as Odom has suggested, a seat at the table.[23]

The enshrining of a 'special relationship' within the NATO–Russia Founding Act provides Russia with at least one forum. It now appears that Russia is interested in regaining its seat, yet full integration will be contingent upon NATO's own transition from a military to a political-based organisation. While significant progress was made on that front between 1991 and 1999, the Kosovo campaign made it clear that the military component is not yet a thing of the past. As a result, Russia will continue to cast a critical eye over both NATO's words and its deeds. It is also likely that Russia will use its seat at the table in the same way as it has used its position as one of the leading nuclear powers, as a platform from which it can express its dissatisfaction over other international events. While all members and partners of NATO are free to express differing opinions on any international event, the lack of support for the US–British bombings of Iraq in 1998 being an example, NATO as an institution must give the appearance of acting as a cohesive whole. In its very public displays of opposition, Russia acts the part of the rogue player on the team.

NATO may seek to encourage political and military stability within Europe, but it will not fully succeed unless the EU achieves the stabilisation of the economies of Central and Eastern Europe and the FSU. While Russia is aware that the nature of security has changed, it has not yet recognised that there are alternative methods of achieving it. In the recent past Russia has viewed the EU as an institution solely in terms of its provision of financial and technical assistance. Overtures to member states have been made when Russia has seen an opportunity to drive a wedge between the EU and the United States. The divide and rule methods employed during the Cold War are in evidence again. Russia has not yet realised that the EU is a major component, if not the engine, in the drive towards a new European identity. Nor have Russian leaders realised that identity is the key to security.

In the past decade some have concluded that Russia should participate fully in NATO because to do so would be the 'right thing' or 'good for Russia'. One could extend this argument to encompass Russia's relations with the EU. To argue in such a manner in either case would, however, be to miss the point. Participation in NATO or the EU means more than joining a military or economic alliance, it means ascribing to a particular identity. To do that a state must be convinced that the identity is appropriate for its political culture. Russia is a proud nation suffering a difficult transition. NATO and the EU are undergoing their own transformations. Whether by default or design NATO has become a hybrid entity that is both a wider security organisation and a defence alliance.[24] The EU is an economic alliance with ambitions, post-Kosovo, to become a defence alliance also. While it is unlikely that Russia will return to a Soviet-type political system, it is also unlikely that she will adopt a liberal democratic system in the Western sense. It can be guaranteed that the system that emerges, no matter where it is on the political spectrum, will have a particularly Russian character. Russia's full participation within the emerging European security framework will only be achieved if both her government and the international institutions can accommodate diversity.

Notes and references

1 The British government's *Strategic Defence Review* (1998), for example, reflects a shift away from the nation-state as the dominant force in international affairs.

Over the next twenty years it is predicted that risks to international stability will come from ethnic and religious conflict; population and environmental pressures; competition for scarce resources; drugs; terrorism and crime.

2 M. Albright and D. Obey, 'Does NATO Enlargement Serve US Interests?' *CQ Researcher* 7 May 1997.

3 M. Light *et al.*, 'A Wider Europe: The View from Moscow and Kyiv'. *International Affairs* 76 (1) 2000, p. 80.

4 E. Moxon-Browne, 'Eastern and Western Europe: Towards a New European Identity?' *Contemporary Politics* 13 (1) 1997, p. 33.

5 *Ibid.*, p. 29.

6 *Ibid.*, p. 30.

7 This description of the tensions between Westerners and Slavophiles is by necessity overly simplified, for the Slavophiles' approach is informed by reference to elements of Western nationalism, particularly of the German variety. For a more detailed account see P. Truscott, *Russia First: Breaking with the West.* (London: Tauris 1997), pp. 9–34.

8 R. Solchanyk, 'Russia, Ukraine and the Imperial Legacy'. *Post-Soviet Affairs* Oct.–Dec. 1993, p. 349.

9 A. Tsipko, 'Dialectics of the Ascent of a New Russian Statehood' in O. Ieda (ed.), *New Order in Post-Communist Eurasia.* (Hokkaido: Slavic Research Center, Hokkaido University 1993), p. 187.

10 For further discussion see Jackie Gower, Chapter 12 in this volume.

11 Light *et al. op.cit.*, p. 80.

12 Founding Act on Mutual Relations, Cooperation and Security between NATO and the Russian Federation. NATO website. URL: http://www.nato.int/docu/basictxt/fndact-a.htm.

13 F. Lewis, 'Why NATO – Not the United States – Frightens Moscow'. *Transition* 2 (4) 1996, p. 50.

14 *RFE/RL Newsline* 4 (62) 2000.

15 Truscott *op.cit.*, pp. 39–40.

16 The EU took the decision to slash funding from 150 million Euros to 34 million Euros at the Helsinki summit in December 1999. By June 2000 the EU was reconsidering this decision. EU Commission President Romano Prodi suggested that the TACIS programme should be 'consolidated to strengthen cooperation between Russia and the EU'. See *RFE/RL Newsline* 4 (104) 2000.

17 Council and Commission of the EU, 'Agreement on Partnership and Cooperation between the European Communities and their Member States and the Russian Federation'. *Official Journal* L. 327 November 1997.

18 *Presidency Conclusions: Cologne European Council of the European Union*, Annex II. (Brussels: Council of the European Union 1999).

19 *RFE/RL Newsline* 4 (103) 2000.

20 W. Odom, 'Russia's Several Seats at the Table'. *International Affairs* 74 (4) 1998, pp. 809–13.

21 V. Mizin and S. Oznobishchev, 'Security after the Cold War'. *International Affairs* (Moscow) 8 1993, p. 8.

22 Odom *op.cit.*, p. 817.

23 *Ibid.*, p. 809.

24 G. Williams, 'The Legacy of the Cold War – The Security Debate: From Euphoria to Hangover' in *The Atlantic Alliance: NATO's 50 years of Peace, 1949–1999.* (London: International Systems and Communications Ltd 1998).

12 The Baltic states

Bridge or barrier to the east?

Jackie Gower

Introduction

The three Baltic states (Estonia, Latvia and Lithuania) feel particularly vulnerable as very small, newly independent states with extremely limited military resources located in close proximity to Russia, which has historically regarded them as integral parts of her empire. The presence of large Russian-speaking minorities in both Latvia and Estonia and the sensitive issue of transit rights from the Russian *oblast* of Kaliningrad across Lithuania inevitably mean that Russia continues to regard the Baltic states as a legitimate sphere of special interest. Although there is no reason to fear that the present Russian government has any plans to try to reincorporate the Baltic states into a 'greater Russia', there have been periodic warnings that it would be prepared if necessary to defend its interests in the region, and in the Duma and mass media the use of force has been raised as an option.[1] On the basis of any realistic assessment of even the collective capabilities of the Baltic states, they would be unable to defend themselves effectively[2] and so from the very beginning they have regarded NATO and EU membership as the only viable guarantee of their independence. Their security strategy has therefore been to attain full membership of both the EU and NATO as soon as possible and their domestic and foreign policies since their independence in 1991 have been centred on these overriding goals. Russia's reaction has been to differentiate sharply between EU and NATO enlargement to the Baltics, with acquiescence bordering on positive support for the former and implacable opposition to the latter. Although both organisations vigorously deny any suggestion that Russia should influence their membership policies, it does now seem almost certain that all three Baltic states will join the EU within the next five years, whereas there is uncertainty still about their prospects of attaining NATO membership. Indeed, it seems to be hoped in some circles at least that the 'soft security' offered by the EU may suffice and the Baltic states might be persuaded to accept a similar security status to Finland and Sweden, and thus avoid upsetting the regional balance of power and alienating Russia.

This chapter will chart the developments over the past decade with respect to both EU and NATO enlargement to the Baltic states and consider the prospects for both their national security and the wider security interests of the Baltic/North-eastern Europe region. It will also consider the potential role that the Baltic states themselves may play in the creation of a collective security community. Although they have tended to regard EU and NATO membership as providing a protective barrier against possible threats from their neighbours to the east, there is increasing interest in their potential to provide a bridge, particularly through increased trade and social and cultural interaction. They might come to play a pivotal role in the development of co-operation and partnership between the European Union and Russia, converting the latter's interest in the Baltic region from a potential source of tension into a positive incentive to engage constructively with her neighbours. The Baltic region will be one of the key testing grounds for the emerging European security order and Baltic–Russian relations within the context of an enlarged European Union may hold the key to its success.

The quest for membership of the EU and NATO

The historical context

The background to the Baltic states' sense of insecurity and hence determination to integrate themselves into Western institutions stems from their historical memories of being pawns in the geopolitical contests of their very much larger neighbours. They enjoyed a brief period of independence in the inter-war years, but in 1939 their fate was sealed by the notorious Molotov–Ribbentrop non-aggression pact in which Germany and the USSR secretly carved up Central and Eastern Europe between themselves.[3] In 1940 Moscow-dominated governments in Estonia, Latvia and Lithuania formally requested that their states should be incorporated into the USSR, only to be invaded by the German army in the following year. After three years of German occupation, 'liberation' for the Baltics in 1944 meant their return to Soviet rule as three of the fifteen republics of the USSR. The Soviet annexation was never formally recognised by the international community, but it rapidly became part of the Cold War order and the Balts understandably felt abandoned by the West. This experience, too, clearly shapes their perceptions of their security needs today and explains their determination to obtain specific 'hard security' guarantees, above all through article five of the NATO treaty.[4]

Although the standard of living in the Baltic states was above the Soviet average, the intense Russification, including large-scale colonisation, was bitterly resented and played a major part in the emergence of national independence movements in the late 1980s. The presence of very large Russian-speaking minorities in both Estonia and Latvia is an enduring legacy of the Soviet period and a major component of the Baltic security challenge. Lithuania was the first Soviet republic to declare its independence on 11 March 1990, followed swiftly by Estonia and Latvia. Boris

Yeltsin, President of the largest of the Soviet republics, Russia, supported their bid for freedom[5] and within months the USSR had disintegrated. In September 1991 the Baltic states were admitted to the United Nations as independent sovereign states. However, having attained their own freedom, many Russians, both among the policy-making elite and the general public, found it difficult to come to terms with the realities of Baltic independence and this was undoubtedly the most serious problem facing the new states.[6] The immediate objective of their new governments was therefore to avoid isolation by integrating into as many international organisations as possible and to seek practical assistance for the rebuilding of their economies and creation of independent defence forces. As former republics of the highly integrated and centralised USSR, the Baltic states faced considerably greater challenges than the other Central and Eastern European states, needing not only to dismantle the political and economic communist systems but to establish independent administrative structures, including those for the management of the economy and defence.[7]

NATO

Perceptions of their strategic vulnerability have inevitably meant that NATO membership has been the most important and urgent goal for all three Baltic states and yet it seems likely to prove the most difficult to achieve. In part this is a result of NATO's reluctance to extend its hard security guarantee to states that are widely regarded as 'indefensible' on the basis of their geography, small populations and proximity to Russia. When the problems of unresolved borders and transit rights through Lithuania from Kaliningrad are also considered, it is not surprising that NATO enlargement to the Baltics is seen as a much greater challenge than to the Czech Republic, Hungary or Poland.[8] It is also plain that Russia's objections to the prospect of NATO enlarging beyond Poland into former Soviet territory is regarded as a significant factor in the calculations on the security gains and losses of Baltic membership of the Alliance. This does not mean that Russia has a veto on Baltic membership, but NATO members will undoubtedly be extremely cautious about the timing, and possibly even the principle, of their admission. However, they are also sensitive to the danger of creating a 'grey zone' of uncertainty and ambiguity along the shores of the Baltic between Poland and Finland that would clearly weaken security in the whole region. Therefore, in all official communications from both NATO and the Baltic states, their membership of the Alliance is presented as a technical question dependent on them meeting such requirements as the settlement of all disputes with neighbours and being in a position to contribute to the collective security guarantee.

In practical terms the Baltic states are already quite well integrated into the broader framework of the Atlantic Alliance, sending representatives to the Euro-Atlantic Partnership Council and participating in a wide range of activities under the Partnership for Peace programme, including military exercises on Baltic soil. They have also been associate partners in the Western European Union since 1994 and could participate in a Combined Joint Task Force if required. They have received considerable assistance from their Nordic neighbours in equipping and training their new security forces and have participated in the Nordic peacekeeping brigade in Bosnia. Military assistance has also been provided by individual NATO and non-NATO states to support a number of initiatives to encourage Baltic co-operation to enhance their collective defence capabilities: BALTBAT is the Baltic peacekeeping battalion, BALTRON is the naval squadron and BALTNET the air-surveillance and control network which will be linked to NATO facilities through Poland.[9]

However, despite all these initiatives, the Baltic states' sense of insecurity remains and their determination to attain full membership of NATO has in no way diminished. Prior to the NATO summit in July 1997 they lobbied vigorously for at least one Baltic state to be included on the invitation list for membership. Lithuania had high hopes that it might be the trailblazer for the others, particularly as it was expected that Estonia might be offered that role in the EU enlargement strategy due to be outlined later that month. The Madrid summit was therefore an enormous disappointment despite the formal assurances that 'NATO remains open to new members ... No European democratic country whose admission would fulfil the objectives of the Treaty will be excluded.'[10] Some comfort was derived from the acknowledgement of the progress made towards greater stability and co-operation by the states in the Baltic region 'who are aspiring members' and at the Washington summit in 1999 their candidature was again explicitly recognised. A Membership Action Plan (MAP) was launched for all the candidates as evidence that 'the door to NATO membership under Article 10 of the Washington Treaty remains open'[11] and candidate countries were encouraged to adopt national programmes of specific activities designed to prepare them for membership. However, as the MAP contains no timetable for accession and indeed no guarantee that it will lead to membership, some commentators have seen it as 'a device for delay'.[12]

It would seem that one of the major problems facing the Baltic states is that, unlike the Czech Republic, Hungary and Poland, they lack strong European sponsors within NATO (Denmark is their main advocate) and the support of the USA has been balanced by its desire not to antagonise Russia. President Clinton was quite sympathetic to their security needs and at least partly compensated for the disappointment of Madrid by signing the US–Baltic Charter of Partnership in January 1998 which contains the significant statement that 'Europe will not be fully secure unless Estonia, Latvia and Lithuania each are secure'.[13] All the Baltic states remained officially optimistic that at the next NATO summit they would finally achieve their goal but Russian anger over NATO action in Kosovo in 1999 has not improved the general political environment for further

NATO enlargement.[14] It also remains the case that while Russia is opposed to any further NATO enlargement, it is the proposal to include the Baltics that arouses the greatest hostility.[15] Membership of the EU is coming to be seen as a more realistic prospect.

The European Community/European Union

In 1991 the European Community extended its PHARE programmes of technical assistance to the three Baltic states, significantly affording them the same status as the other CEE states and thereby endorsing their desire to redefine their geopolitical position. Apart from the value of the financial aid itself, this decision was to prove a major turning point in the political history of the Baltic states since it subsequently became clear that the EC was already differentiating between those post-communist states it regarded as potential future members and those that it did not. All the other former Soviet republics, including Russia, received EC aid under a separate programme, TACIS, and were subsequently offered Partnership and Co-operation Agreements.[16] The Baltic states, however, like the other CEE states, were able to negotiate association or 'Europe' agreements which are much more comprehensive in both their political and economic provisions. Even more significantly, on the basis of the Copenhagen European Council decision in June 1993, the Europe Agreement states are promised membership of the EU as soon as they are able to meet the political and economic conditions required.[17] The Europe Agreements were signed in June 1995 and Latvia submitted its application for EU membership in October, followed by Estonia in November and Lithuania in December. The European Commission prepared a detailed assessment of the political and economic conditions in each applicant state and measured their progress in meeting the Copenhagen criteria, which were that:

> Membership requires that the candidate country has achieved stability of institutions guaranteeing democracy, the rule of law, human rights and respect for and protection of minorities, the existence of a functioning market economy as well as the capacity to cope with competitive pressure and market forces within the Union. Membership presupposes the candidate's ability to take on the obligations of membership including adherence to the aims of political, economic and monetary union.[18]

The Commission's 'Opinions' on the three Baltic states' applications were published in July 1997, together with those on the other seven CEE states and Cyprus as part of the *Agenda 2000* package which also contained the Commission's proposals for a strategy for enlargement.[19] Although some reservations were made about the treatment of minorities, especially in Latvia, all three of the Baltic states were judged to meet the political criteria. However, the Commission concluded that whereas Estonia could come close to meeting the economic criteria in the medium term, both Latvia and Lithuania were considerably further behind. It therefore recommended differentiating between them and inviting Estonia to join the other 'first wave' states in opening accession negotiations in March 1998.

The proposal was a vindication of the Estonian government's recent strategy to prioritise EU over NATO accession but was a severe blow to the confidence of the Latvians and Lithuanians, coming just days after the disappointment of the NATO summit in Madrid. They argued strongly that much of the data used by the Commission was out of date or inaccurate[20] and urged that negotiations should be opened with all the applicants in order to avoid undermining the regional co-operation initiatives developed in recent years. Despite strong support from all the Nordic states, however, the European Council at Luxembourg in December 1997 endorsed the Commission's strategy based on differentiation while emphasising that all the applicants were part of the same accession process and 'are destined to join the European Union on the basis of the same criteria', in other words were 'pre-ins' rather than permanently excluded.[21]

Although Latvia and Lithuania were extremely disappointed that they were not yet themselves engaged in accession negotiations, it was recognised that the inclusion of Estonia was of historic significance for the future of the whole Baltic region. Whereas the Madrid decision on NATO enlargement had still left doubts about the future place of the Baltic states in the post-Cold War security order, the invitation to Estonia by the European Union was an unequivocal assurance that they had moved irrevocably out of Russia's sphere of influence into the Western institutional family. If it was indeed a deliberate 'test-case', Russia's acquiescence was equally historic and ensured that the road really was clear for the other two Baltic states to 'catch up' with Estonia and join the EU. They both renewed their efforts to meet the accession criteria and were rewarded in October 1999 by favourable progress reports from the Commission and the recommendation that they should be invited to join the accession negotiations. The Helsinki Council in December 1999 agreed to open negotiations early the following year with all the applicant states except Turkey and so the question of eventual EU membership for the Baltic states appears to have been resolved.

Prospects for EU and NATO membership

For most of the former communist states, membership of NATO has seemed a somewhat easier objective than membership of the EU, with its 80,000 pages of legal documents (the *acquis communautaire*) that need to be adopted and implemented in preparation for accession.[22] It seems likely that the Czech Republic, Hungary and Poland will have been NATO members for at least five years before they finally also become members of the EU.

However, for the Baltic states the position seems to be the opposite and NATO membership is apparently simultaneously more important and yet less attainable. Although membership of NATO was undoubtedly the foreign policy and security priority of all three Baltic states, there is no certainty when they will achieve it and considerable speculation that it might never happen. Indeed, four academic specialists recommend that NATO should outline explicitly the 'limited scope of future enlargement' by naming Romania, Bulgaria, Slovenia and Slovakia as future members and making it clear that the Baltic states will not be included, to 'avoid an irreparable break in relations with Moscow'.[23] By contrast, EU membership now seems reasonably certain and is no more problematic for the Baltic states than for most of the other CEE applicants. It is even possible that if it is decided that it would be easier for the EU to cope with a 'big wave' rather than a series of smaller waves of enlargement, all three Baltic states will become EU members simultaneously after all. The precise date is still impossible to predict with certainty, but is likely to be around 2005.

Although EU membership without that of NATO would not accord with the Baltic states' own security preferences, it is seen by a number of advisers and academics as probably the best outcome to what Asmus and Nurick in a frequently cited RAND report called 'one of the most delicate questions facing the alliance'.[24] They recommended that all three Baltic states should become EU members as soon as possible but not be offered full Western European Union membership until such time as NATO too felt able to extend its security guarantee.[25] Thus the Baltic states would at least initially have the same security status as Finland and Sweden, which would ensure minimal disturbance to the balance of power in the Baltic region and reassure Russia that EU enlargement is compatible with her own security interests. In the light of the Helsinki, Feira and Nice EU Council decisions on the development of the Common European Security and Defence Policy, the WEU issue looks likely to disappear off the agenda[26] and certainly it does not seem to be a major factor in Russia's assessment of the impact of EU enlargement, which remains fairly positive. Russia's attitude in the future will depend on whether the EU's increasingly active role in the Baltic region is seen to enhance collective security in its broadest sense and whether the membership of the Baltic states opens up new opportunities for positive interaction between Russia herself and the Union.

The European Union's contribution to security in the Baltic region

An anchor of peace and stability

The EU itself had its origins as a peace and stability project reconciling historic enemies and creating a security community for the states of Western Europe based on socio-economic interdependence. In the 1980s it extended its zone of democratic stability and economic prosperity to Southern Europe, serving as a valuable anchor for the new democracies in Greece, Spain and Portugal as they 'returned to Europe'. It now hopes to play a similar role in Central and Eastern Europe, and the Baltic region will be one of its main testing grounds, not only in relation to those states aspiring to become EU members but also with respect to Russia, for whom the Baltic retains considerable military and economic importance.

The EU's role in the Baltic region was fairly limited during the Cold War period, but with the accession of Finland and Sweden in 1995 and the expectation that Poland, Latvia, Estonia and Lithuania will become members in the next few years, it has emerged as a major actor. This is a significant change in the balance of power in the region but one that generally seems to have been welcomed by Russia in line with its preference for a multipolar order and its perception of the EU as at least a potential counterbalance to the USA. Although the USSR was rather more sceptical about the EC's role in the Cold War period, the Russian Federation regards European integration positively, particularly recognising its contribution to the overcoming of traditional enmities. It now sees the EU as 'one of the cornerstones of stability in Europe'[27] and the prospect of its enlargement to include the potentially rather volatile countries of Central and Eastern Europe has therefore generally been welcomed as helping to ensure stability on Russia's western borders. This would seem to be particularly true in relation to the accession of the Baltic states, which are seen as 'openly unfriendly' towards Russia.[28] Membership of the EU would impose considerable constraints on both their internal and external policies and almost certainly act as a moderating and restraining factor in their relations with other states in the region. From Russia's perspective, therefore, their accession to the EU would reduce the risk that they could be 'loose canons' on its borders and help to 'normalise' relations with potentially rather difficult neighbours. It would also extend the zone of economic stability and prosperity into North-eastern Europe with potential benefits to Russia's own economic development.

Political leverage in resolving conflicts

The EU (like NATO) has made accession conditional on respect for democracy and human rights, the protection of minorities and the settlement of all outstanding disputes with third parties to avoid the risk of importing instability into the Union. Russia has therefore recognised the important political leverage that the EU can exercise over applicant states in pressurising them to resolve conflicts if they want to meet the accession criteria. Two of the most sensitive and potentially dangerous areas of contention between Russia and the newly independent Baltic states have been their treatment of the large Russian minorities living particularly in Estonia and Latvia and the settlement of the post-independence borders. In both cases,

Russia has seen the prospect of EU enlargement offering opportunities both to exert pressure on the Baltics directly and to use bilateral meetings at political, parliamentary and official level to urge the EU to lean on them to make concessions.

The size of the Russian minorities in Estonia and Latvia inevitably posed a major challenge for newly independent states trying to construct a clear national identity. Ethnic Latvians constituted barely half the total population at the time of independence and in the ten largest cities, including the capital Riga, Russians were the largest ethnic group. It is an undeniably exceptional situation and from the perspective of the Latvians at times makes it 'difficult to maintain their identity in their own country'.[29] In Estonia the position was somewhat less dramatic but in 1989 ethnic Estonians constituted little over 60 per cent of the population of the country. Since independence there has been considerable outmigration of Russian-speakers and by the end of the 1990s the Russian minority in Estonia was 28.7 per cent, in Latvia 30.3 per cent and in Lithuania a relatively small 9.4 per cent of the population.[30]

The most contentious issue was the question of who qualified for citizenship in the newly independent states, and with it the attendant rights of a passport, right to vote and eligibility for many public service appointments. The Lithuanians, significantly with by far the smallest Russian minority, granted almost universal citizenship to all those resident in the country at the time of independence and hence effectively defused the issue as far as relations with Russia are concerned. Estonia and Latvia, however, were reluctant to grant citizenship to those whom they regarded as colonialists and restricted automatic citizenship to residents in 1940 and their descendants. Both states imposed difficult hurdles for other people to gain citizenship, such as long residency requirements, tests on proficiency in the 'native' language and knowledge of the constitution. The consequence of these restrictive citizenship laws was that large numbers of Russian-speaking residents in the Baltic states were consigned to the very difficult status of 'non-citizens' and Russia was able to complain that the discrimination against them constituted a serious violation of human rights.

This apparent mistreatment of their 'compatriots' has been an extremely emotive issue in Russian domestic political debate and the authorities have had little choice but to impose economic sanctions and threaten even more serious 'action'. There has been quite widespread sympathy for the plight of the Russian minorities in the West and of course the EU is extremely anxious to avoid being drawn into conflict with Russia over such an issue after enlargement. Therefore, through the Commission's annual progress reports and numerous bilateral contacts, considerable pressure has been brought to bear on Estonia and Latvia to reform their citizenship laws. In Estonia's case, the desire to get on to the list of 'first wave' states in 1997 was a powerful incentive to introduce revised legislation. Latvia has been slower to respond to international pressure but there is no doubt that the progress that has now been made in adopting citizenship laws that conform to OSCE standards is largely attributable to the leverage exercised by the EU over candidate states. The matter is still not resolved to Russia's satisfaction and President-to-be Vladimir Putin used the occasion of the EU–Russian summit in October 1999 to criticise the EU for failing to improve the position of ethnic Russians in the Baltics.[31] It would appear that Russia believed the Commission was unduly 'soft' on Latvia in its assessment of its record on human rights in the progress report published the previous week. Russia's *Medium-term Strategy for Relations with the European Union* indicates its intention to seek 'consultations' before the next enlargement of the EU in order to secure Russia's interests, including specifically 'to safeguard, in the interests of stability, security and cooperation in Europe, the rights of the Russian-speaking population in the Baltic states'.[32] It therefore clearly expects the EU to continue to exercise leverage over its future members in order to alleviate the problem.

There is less direct evidence of the EU's involvement in the question of the settlement of the borders of the Baltic states but the fact that when they do become members of the EU their borders with Belarus and Russia will be the external borders of the Union itself makes it an important pre-accession issue. Borders became a matter of contention at the time of independence because the Baltic states claimed that the post-war settlement had no legitimacy as they had been under Soviet occupation when it had been imposed. Lithuania was prepared to accept the status quo, although the question of transit rights from the Russian *oblast* of Kaliningrad across her territory involved some sensitive negotiations with Russia. In the case of Latvia and Estonia the border issues were more difficult to resolve because they regarded the 1920 treaties of Riga and Tartu as the only legitimate basis for negotiation, which implied claims to Russian territory. President Yeltsin was under great domestic political pressure to make no concessions and in 1995 declared, 'the border is unchangeable. We don't need foreign land, but we can't give away any single meter of our land either.'[33] The issue was potentially a serious threat to peace in the region and in the mid-1990s there were fears that direct conflicts might flare up along the Estonian–Russian border.[34]

Western governments, in line with the principles of the Helsinki Final Act of 1975, supported the status quo and urged Estonia and Latvia to withdraw their revanchist demands. The knowledge that crucial decisions concerning their applications for membership of the EU and NATO would be taken in the summer of 1997 seems to have been an important factor in Estonia officially withdrawing her demands for reference to the 1920 treaties in November 1996 and Latvia doing likewise in February 1997.[35] Russia, however, seems to have recognised how important it was for them to have concluded the new treaties successfully[36] and continued to use delays in ratification for several years as further leverage for improvements in the treatment of the Russophone minorities.[37] From her perspective, therefore, the EU dimension provided useful political leverage for the furtherance of her policy objectives.

The Northern Dimension

The Nordic states have understandably been particularly committed to the development of a regional security community and Finland made the promotion of the 'Northern Dimension' of the EU's external policy one of the key objectives of its EU presidency from July to December 1999. At a conference attended by the foreign ministers of the EU member states and Estonia, Latvia, Lithuania, Poland, Norway and Iceland in November 1999, it was recognised that EU enlargement made the concept of the Northern Dimension all the more useful 'in enhancing European security, stability, democratic reforms and sustainable development in Northern Europe'.[38] It does not create new institutions, nor indeed have access to any additional funding, but is intended to bring together all the various regional initiatives and co-operative programmes in a co-ordinated strategy to increase their synergy, visibility and effectiveness. An Action Plan[39] for the period 2000 to 2003 identifies a wide range of projects in the fields of economics and trade, energy, nuclear safety, the environment, transport, communications, international crime, asylum and illegal migration, public health and culture. The initiative has been received positively by the Russian government, and the north-western regional authorities, including the Leningrad and Novgorod *oblasts*, are especially interested in greater regional co-operation. In particular, the Northern Dimension offers an EU framework for the establishment of more constructive relations between the Baltic states and Russia and also potentially may hold the key to resolving the Kaliningrad problem. It is probable that sub-national co-operation facilitated through the Northern Dimension initiative may turn out to be its most innovative and important contribution to regional security. The hope is that it will 'encourage Russia to remain outward looking and engaged in Europe'.[40]

Baltic–Russian relations in an enlarged European Union

The accession of the Baltic states to the EU will inevitably have a major impact on its relations with Russia. If the borders between the Baltic states and Russia and Belarus become a barrier shutting them off from their eastern neighbours, their hoped-for security gains may prove illusory. There is increasing recognition of the dangers of EU enlargement creating a new fault-line across Europe, and of course were NATO also to expand to the Baltics the implications would be even more serious. If Russia is not to feel a permanent 'outsider', excluded from the prosperity and stability anticipated in the enlarged EU, then bridges need to be constructed to integrate her into the larger European political, economic and social space. Although the accession of the Baltic states clearly carries risks that the tensions in their relationships with Russia will sour her relations with the EU itself, there is a more optimistic scenario in which, once their security needs have been met, they will act as a bridge to Russia and the other states to the east. Many of the sources of real or potential conflict could also provide opportunities for the development of closer and mutually beneficial relations and thus heal the divisions of recent history. Three case-studies will now be examined in this context: the Russian minorities in the Baltic states, trade and the Russian exclave of Kaliningrad.

The Russian-speaking minorities

After the Baltic states become EU members, there will be one and a half million ethnic Russians living in the Union. So far this fact has been seen as a potential problem, particularly if Russia continues to feel the need to champion their rights in the face of reluctance by the Estonians and Latvians to integrate them fully into their societies. However, if these problems can be resolved, large Russian-speaking communities could come to be an asset in the development of closer social, cultural and economic relations with Russia. For example, during the Soviet period the Baltic coast was a popular holiday destination and with increased prosperity Russian tourism could again flourish, facilitated not just by relatively easy transport links but also the much higher chance of finding people able to speak Russian than elsewhere in Europe. Similarly, the increasingly affluent Russians living in the Baltic states are likely to be attracted to cultural cities like St Petersburg, Novgorod and Moscow, as well as visiting friends and family in Russia. Cultural, educational and business travel is also likely to increase significantly.

However, this rosy scenario of a much increased volume of movement of people between Russia and the Baltic states is obviously dependent on finding ways to overcome the feared tightening of the borders as a result of EU enlargement. The EU is deeply concerned about the 'permeability' of its external borders to illegal immigrants, traffickers in people, drugs and nuclear materials and those engaged in organised international crime generally. Therefore, one of the pre-accession requirements is to tighten border controls and adopt the Schengen *acquis*, including its common visa regime. There is already resentment at the proposed introduction of visas for travel between the Baltic states and Russia and much of the informal cross-border economic activity has been severely curtailed by stricter border formalities. Apart from the practical inconveniences of such restrictions on the free movement of people, they are having a very negative psychological impact on ordinary people, many of whom, of course, remember when they were all part of the same country. If EU enlargement is not to be perceived as creating the kind of new barriers across Europe about which Robert Bideleux warns in Chapter 2 of this volume – a 'paper iron curtain' of visa and custom formalities – ways will need to be found to secure the external borders without unduly obstructing legitimate movement in the region.

The other major contribution the Russian minorities may make to improve relations between Russia and the EU is in the field of business. In both Latvia and Estonia Russophones play a leading role in the private sector, in part because the language requirements for employment in the public sector have forced them to seek opportunities elsewhere.[41] In Latvia most of the banks are controlled by members of the Russian community and they have advertised on Russian television to attract financial deposits from those looking for a safe haven for their money.[42] In many other areas of the Baltic states' economies Russophones play a leading role and not surprisingly they are particularly supportive of EU membership.[43] With the advantage of the language and personal connections, they hope to play a key role in assisting Russian companies to gain a foothold in the Single Market.

Trade

The EU is already Russia's most important trading partner, accounting for about 40 per cent of her trade, and with enlargement the proportion is likely to rise to over 50 per cent. The Baltic states rely heavily on Russian gas and oil for their energy requirements but their markets are too small to be regarded as particularly attractive for other Russian goods. However, their potential role as gateways to the EU market as a whole is viewed with considerable interest among the more outward-looking Russian entrepreneurs. As Russia's historic 'window to the West' they have always been important transit routes to the rest of Europe and the pre-existence of extensive transport links dating from the Soviet era, albeit in urgent need of modernisation, plus the new EU inter-regional projects such as the Via Baltica could transform Russia's interest in the Baltics from geopolitics to geo-economics.[44] This is already the case for the big gas and oil lobbies and Medvedev suggests that they, together with other business elites and the north-west regional leaders, are pressing for a more liberal approach to the Baltics in Russian foreign policy.[45]

The export of Russian gas and oil through the large ice-free ports of the Baltic states is one of the best examples of the kind of economic interdependence that could transform Russian–Baltic relations. The importance of the transit trade to the economies of the Baltic states is considerable, providing the largest single source of hard currency income for Estonia and, particularly, Latvia.[46] They have managed to attract large amounts of Western investment to modernise and generally upgrade major ports such as Ventspils in Latvia, which currently handles 15 per cent of Russia's crude-oil exports, Paldiski in Estonia and Klaipeda in Lithuania. There are a number of ambitious projects for the construction of new oil pipelines from Russia to the Baltic ports which would help to integrate Russia into the European market and bring increased prosperity to the whole region. However, there are counter-pressures in Russia to avoid becoming too dependent on 'foreign' ports and oil terminals and instead develop new Russian ports on the northern shores of the Gulf of Finland. There is expected to be increasingly stiff competition between the Baltic Sea ports and obviously their future will be dependent on a significant growth in the volume of trade in the region. However, if the Russian economy recovers and progress is made towards the creation of a free trade area with the EU, the Baltic ports could come to play similar roles in relation to trade with the East as ports like Rotterdam play in Western Europe.

Direct trade between the Baltics and Russia is also likely to increase, although its value will inevitably be quite modest owing to the small scale of their economies. In the Soviet period the Baltic states' trade was overwhelmingly orientated towards Russia and the rest of the USSR but over the past decade it has shifted significantly towards the EU, especially its northern members. The financial collapse in Russia in 1998 was responsible for a particularly steep decline in Baltic–Russian trade, with the inability of many Russian enterprises to pay for goods delivered. The potential for trade to be increased therefore largely depends on the achievement of both financial stability and economic growth in Russia itself.

From the perspective of the Baltic states, the large Russian market on their borders is very attractive, particularly as it might be easier to penetrate than the more sophisticated EU market and, as discussed above, the Russian-speaking business community has business-development advantages. There used to be a lucrative trade in agricultural goods and processed food and if there is increased prosperity in Russia the market could recover. However, Russia has already flagged up its concern that EU export subsidies, through the Common Agricultural Policy, would give the Baltic farmers an unfair competitive advantage over her own and is hoping to be able to negotiate some compensatory measures prior to enlargement. The EU has made a commitment to hold discussions prior to the next enlargement to try to find ways to alleviate Russia's fears that it might be damaging to her economic interests, and clearly it is important to ensure that new barriers to greater trade between Russia and the EU are avoided. It is Russia's goal to diversify her exports away from the current predominance of raw materials and energy, and she fears that the extension of the Single Market to Central and Eastern Europe may put her manufactured goods at a competitive disadvantage. However, to a large extent the future prospects for increased trade will depend on the willingness and capacity of Russia to adopt EU technical standards, as otherwise the legal barriers may be more significant than either tariffs or other forms of more obvious discrimination.

The Kaliningrad oblast *as a Russian exclave in the EU*

The final case-study is the one that has attracted the greatest amount of concern in both academic and political circles as it involves the prospect of a heavily militarised Russian exclave in the midst of an enlarged European Union. Russian sensitivities about its future regularly give rise in the press, at conferences and other meetings to what is hoped are just 'wild' threats that, if necessary, nuclear missiles will be stationed in Kaliningrad in order to 'defend' Russia's interests. However, the greatest security risks presented by Kaliningrad to the Baltic region are increasingly seen to stem not from its position as a military garrison but as a centre of chronic socio-economic instability, with a high level of organised crime and endemic corruption of the local administrative and business elite.[47] The fear is that with the accession of Poland and Lithuania to the EU, Kaliningrad's economy will lag further and further behind and the gap in living standards in the region will be dangerously widened. The ultimate challenge to the 'bridge or barrier' conundrum is therefore presented by its future prospects and it is generally agreed that 'it will be the touchstone for the new security order in the region'.[48]

The origins of the problem lie in the post-Second World War settlement in which the old East Prussian capital of Königsberg and its surrounding area became part of the USSR, along with the three Baltic states. Almost all the ethnic Germans were forcibly removed and the area was repopulated mainly with Russians.[49] During the Cold War it became one of the most important Soviet military bases due to its geostrategic position and ice-free port and it remains a predominantly militarised zone, frequently referred to as 'an unsinkable aircraft carrier', albeit a rusting one, whose location in the midst of the future enlarged EU arouses strong passions on all sides. Since 1991 it has been completely separated from the rest of Russia and can only be reached by land through Lithuania and Belarus, a state of affairs which has enormous practical as well as political implications. The Lithuanian government has been anxious to avoid undue tension with Russia and negotiated a visa-free regime for Kaliningrad residents for up to thirty days a year and transit agreements for energy and military traffic which seem to work reasonably satisfactorily, but there are concerns as to the impact of Lithuanian accession to the EU. In particular, it is recognised that it would be detrimental to good relations in the region if an unmodified Schengen visa regime were to be imposed on Kaliningrad citizens travelling across Lithuania to the Russian mainland either for business or family reasons. It is proposed, therefore, that a limited number of people will be granted annual multiple-entry visas to minimise the practical and psychological impact of the reinforced EU border and Lithuania will continue to serve as a 'bridge' to the East even after EU accession. However, if Kaliningrad declines further into lawlessness and crime, there will be pressures to tighten the EU borders and impose a state of quarantine to keep out crime and illegal migration. The dangers of it becoming a pariah enclave in an enlarged EU are widely recognised, and therefore there is a shared interest in finding a solution to its endemic socio-economic problems.

In the context of this study, the most significant aspect of the Kaliningrad issue may be quite simply the extent to which it looks set to involve the EU and Russia in intensive interaction. Perhaps surprisingly in view of the fact that it is an *oblast* of the Federation, Russia has been willing to concede that it is a shared problem and indicated its willingness for it to be an agenda item within the framework of the Northern Dimension. In its *Medium-term Strategy* document Russia designated it as 'a pilot region within the framework of the Euro-Russian cooperation in the 21st century'. So far there has been little indication as to what this might mean in terms of substantive policy initiatives but it is assumed that it indicates a willingness to permit Kaliningrad to become increasingly integrated in the Euro-regions in the Baltic Sea area. This would therefore imply a particularly important role for Poland and Lithuania as its immediate neighbours, but also for the other Baltic states in helping to improve the overall security position in the region.

Conclusion: bridge or barrier to the east?

Although the Baltic region has been remarkably peaceful and stable for the first post-Cold War decade, it will inevitably remain sensitive because Russia is not only one of the key actors but also the direct neighbour of present and aspiring EU and NATO members. The Baltic states continue to look to the West for their security and clearly hope that EU and NATO membership will create an invincible barrier against any attempt by Russia to exert direct or indirect pressure on them. There is also a danger that the EU, in its desire to protect its internal security, will insist that its new borders to the east are so impenetrable to the perpetrators of international crime and illegal immigration that in effect a new Iron Curtain will be erected across the region. In the early years after they gained independence, the Baltic states seemed to take the line that the higher and thicker the barriers between themselves and Russia the better. However, there is now increasing recognition throughout the region that permanently excluding and isolating Russia is not conducive to long-term security and stability. Both the EU and NATO have adopted strategies designed to build bridges to Russia and seek to integrate her into the wider European political and socio-economic space on the basis of 'partnership', though not membership. As has been discussed in this chapter, the Baltic states could potentially play an important role in achieving this goal, particularly through increased trade and inter-regional co-operation.

However, there are three crucial conditions that are necessary if the Baltic states are to serve as a bridge linking Russia to the wider Europe.

First, they should become members of the EU as soon as possible but not of NATO, at least for the foreseeable future. This is a very unpopular proposition in the Baltic states themselves but is widely believed elsewhere to be the only scenario from which good Baltic–Russian relations can realistically be developed. Second, it is vital that Russia continues along the path of political and economic reform and evolves into a stable, and increasingly prosperous, liberal democracy interested in participating fully in the economic life of the region. Third, Russia and all three Baltic states need to move on from the post-imperial syndrome of mutual recrimination and distrust and establish the kind of 'normal' relationship in which problems can be resolved quietly and rationally without becoming emotive issues in the domestic press and election campaigns.

It is impossible to predict with any certainty whether these conditions are likely to be met over the next decade, above all because the future of Russia itself remains unclear. However, there are grounds for optimism. Although President Putin remains somewhat of an enigma at the time of writing, initial signs suggested that he intended to encourage an outward-looking, entrepreneurial business culture and was resisting pressures to retreat into isolationism. As has been argued in this chapter, the best prospects for peace and stability in the Baltic region lie in the opportunities for Russia to benefit from what the *Financial Times* described as 'the transformation of the eastern Baltic from stagnant Soviet lake to dynamic trade and investment highway'.[50] The most obvious way in which the Baltic states could provide a bridge to the East is by becoming Russia's gateway to the EU's Single Market, modernising the old Soviet-era transportation infrastructure and expanding links between business communities. Increased social and economic interaction can also be expected to lead to an improvement in the political climate and the recognition of the mutual advantages of moving towards a 'normal' pattern of inter-state relations. In such circumstances, the Baltic states would find it easier to accept the postponement, or even ruling out, of NATO membership. So it is possible, though by no means certain, that the Baltic states could serve as the vital bridge to the East, ensuring that Russia, too, can share in the hoped-for stability and prosperity of the new security order.

Notes and references

1 R. D. Asmus and R. C. Nurick, 'NATO Enlargement and the Baltic States'. *Survival* 38 (2) 1996, p. 137.

2 P. van Ham (ed.), *The Baltic States: Security and Defence after Independence.* (Chaillot Paper 19). (Paris: Institute of Security Studies, Western European Union 1995), pp. 5–6.

3 V. S. Vardys and J. B. Sedaitis, *Lithuania: The Rebel Nation.* (Boulder: Westview 1997), pp. 46–7.

4 This is the well-known article that stipulates that an attack on any one NATO member state shall be considered an attack against them all.

5 L. Jonson, 'Russian Policy in Northern Europe' in V. Baranovsky (ed.), *Russia and Europe: The Emerging Security Agenda.* (Oxford: SIPRI/Oxford University Press 1997), p. 308.

6 E. Bajarunas, 'Lithuania's Security Dilemma' in van Ham *op.cit.*, p. 14.

7 G. Herd, 'The Baltic States and EU Enlargement' in K. Henderson (ed.), *Back to Europe: Central and Eastern Europe and the European Union.* (London: UCL Press 1999), pp. 259–60.

8 Asmus and Nurick *op.cit.*, p. 124.

9 A. Lejinš, 'Joining the EU and NATO' in Lejinš (ed.), *Baltic Security Prospects at the Turn of the 21st Century.* (Helsinki: Aleksanteri Institute/Kikimora Publications 1999), p. 29.

10 Madrid Declaration on Euro-Atlantic Security and Cooperation. NATO website. URL: http://www.nato.int/docu/pr/1997/p97-081e.htm.

11 The Washington summit communiqué and the Membership Action Plan are in *NATO Review* 47 (2) 1999.

12 S. Croft *et al.*, 'NATO's Triple Challenge'. *International Affairs* 76 (3) 2000, p. 502.

13 Lejinš *op.cit.*, p. 39.

14 M. Light *et al.*, 'A Wider Europe: The View from Moscow and Kyiv'. *International Affairs* 76 (1) 2000, pp. 80–1.

15 W. Wallace, 'From the Atlantic to the Bug, from the Arctic to the Tigris? The Transformation of the EU and NATO'. *International Affairs* 76 (3) 2000, p. 482.

16 M. Maresceau and E. Montaguti, 'The Relations between the European Union and Central and Eastern Europe: A Legal Appraisal'. *Common Market Law Review* 32 (6) 1995, pp. 1327–67.

17 *Presidency Conclusions: Copenhagen European Council.* (Brussels: Council of the European Union 1993).

18 *Ibid.*

19 European Commission, 'Agenda 2000 – For a Stronger and Wider Union'. *Bulletin of the European Union* supplement 5/1997 and supplements 10 (Latvia), 11 (Estonia) and 12 (Lithuania) for the Commission's Opinions.

20 Herd *op.cit.*, pp. 264–5.

21 J. Gower, 'EU Policy to Central and Eastern Europe' in Henderson *op.cit.*, p. 14.

22 Lejinš *op.cit.*, pp. 12–13.

23 Croft *et al. op.cit.*, p. 502.

24 Asmus and Nurick *op.cit.*, p. 121.

25 US officials were concerned about the danger of 'underlapping security guarantees' if non-NATO members became full WEU members on the basis of the Amsterdam Treaty, which encouraged EU members to join the WEU. See M. A. Smith, 'The NATO Factor' in Henderson *op.cit.*, p. 57.

26 See the discussions by Wyn Rees in Chapter 6 of this volume.

27 Y. Borko, 'The New Intra-European Relations and Russia' in M. Maresceau (ed.), *Enlarging the European Union: Relations between the EU and Central and Eastern Europe.* (London: Longman 1997).

28 V. Baranovsky, 'Russia: A Part of Europe or Apart from Europe?' *International Affairs* 76 (3) 2000, pp. 443–58.

29 I. Viksne, 'Latvia and Europe's Security Structures' in van Ham *op.cit.*, p. 77.

30 W. Thompson, 'The Baltic States' in P. Heenan and M. Lamontagne (eds), *The Central and East European Handbook.* (London: Fitzroy Dearborn 1999), p. 27.

31 S. Taylor, 'Russia to Raise Fears over EU Enlargement'. *European Voice* 21–8 October 1999, p. 9.

32 *Medium-term Strategy for Development of Relations between the Russian Federation and the European Union (2000–2010).* Available in translation on the Finnish EU presidency website. URL: http://www.presidency.finland.fi.

33 Quoted in *The Baltic Observatory* 14 1995.
34 Jonson *op.cit.*, p. 313.
35 S. Medvedev, 'Geopolitics and beyond: The New Russian Policy towards the Baltic States' in M. Jopp and S. Arnswald (eds), *The European Union and the Baltic States: Visions, Interests and Strategies for the Baltic Sea Region.* (Helsinki: Ulkopoliittinn instituutti and Institut für Europäische Politik 1998), p. 241.
36 Reporting on the conclusion of negotiations with the Estonian government on the border, a leading Russian newspaper observed that 'the Estonians also have an interest in the new agreement: the leadership of the European Union ... would hardly be delighted with a new EU member that has an unresolved border dispute with Russia'. *Sevodnya* 6 March 1999.
37 G. Herd, 'Russia and the Near Abroad' in T. Salmon (ed.), *Issues in International Relations.* (London: Routledge 2000), p. 246.
38 'Conclusions of the Foreign Ministers' Conference on the Northern Dimension'. Available on the Finnish EU presidency website. URL: http://www.presidency.finland.fi.
39 'Action Plan for the Northern Dimension with External Cross-border Policies of the European Union 2000–2003' (press release 9401/00). (Brussels: Council of the European Union 2000).
40 J. Blomberg, 'Challenges in the North of Europe'. *European Foreign Affairs Review* 4 1999, p. 6.
41 N. Melvin, *Russians beyond Russia: The Politics of National Identity.* (London: RIIA 1995).
42 *The Economist* 24 June 2000.
43 Medvedev *op.cit.*, p. 254.
44 Z. Ozolina, 'Latvia' in H. Mouritzen (ed.), *Bordering Russia: Theories and Prospects for Europe's Baltic Rim.* (Aldershot: Ashgate 1998).
45 Medvedev *op.cit.*, p. 263. See also A. Sergounin, 'The Russia Dimension' in Mouritzen *op.cit.*, pp. 50–1.
46 A. A. Pikayev, 'Russia and the Baltic States' in B. Hansen and B. Heurlin (eds), *The Baltic States in World Politics.* (Richmond: Curzon 1998), p. 140.
47 For a detailed analysis of the contemporary situation see P. Joenniemi *et al.*, *The Kaliningrad Puzzle – A Russian Region within the European Union.* (Finland: The Åland Islands Peace Institute 2000).
48 G. Herd, 'Competing for Kaliningrad'. *The World Today* 55 (11) 1999, p. 7.
49 J. M. Godzimirski, 'Soviet Legacy and Baltic Security: The Case of Kaliningrad' in O. Knudsen (ed.), *Stability and Security in the Baltic Sea Region.* (London: Frank Cass 1999), p. 32.
50 A. Robinson, 'Potential Sighted through "Window to the West"'. *Financial Times Survey: The Baltic Sea Region* 11 June 1999, p. iii.

13 Poland

'For Your Security and Ours'

Paul Latawski[1]

Introduction

One of the most famous Polish political rallying cries of the nineteenth century was 'For Your Freedom and Ours' (*Za Wolnosc, Nasze i Wasze*). This slogan characterised the politics of a generation or more of Polish radicals who spilled their blood in numerous revolutionary challenges to the established European order in the hope of regaining an independent Polish state. Today, Poland's effort to contribute to the reshaping of the European order and promote its security following the demise of communism is an altogether more genteel and conventional affair. At the start of a new millennium, the new Polish slogan may be accurately described as 'For Your Security and Ours', reflecting the view that Poland's place in the new European order is bound up with other states in the Euro-Atlantic area and vice versa. At the core of post-communist Polish foreign and security policy is institutionally based integration in the 'Euro-Atlantic community of democratic states'.[2] It reflects the view that Poland's security is thus grounded in an overlapping triad of national interest, international norms and institutional integration into the transatlantic community. In his annual parliamentary address on 5 March 1998, Polish Foreign Minister Bronislaw Geremek summarised the key elements of Polish policy in relation to the new European order:

> We are turning to the West and its institutions, having in mind the attainment of at least four goals: first, strengthening ourselves internally, second, introducing a new sensitivity and different historical experience to the West-European debate and the West-European understanding of Europe, third, strengthening NATO and the European Union not only by adding our potential to their strength, but also by showing new vistas and new challenges and, fourth, strengthening and accelerating the processes of the democratic reconstruction [of] the region and building a new European order. This four-part task is the kernel of the new geopolitics that we initiated nearly nine years ago in this part of Europe.[3]

The explicit element of this policy has been the pursuit of the goal of membership in NATO and the European Union, the principal institutions of European political, economic, social and security integration. Membership in both these institutions, however, means the acceptance of norms. Therefore, implicit in this institutionally based approach is the adoption, preservation and extension of the norms associated with the Western community. What is striking about the Polish position is that integration (and its concomitant adoption of norms) is linked to the internal development of the country. Moreover, Poland is not only seeking to import norms but to export its own regional perspectives in the evolving European security order.

Foreign and security policy: framework and priorities

Polish efforts to shape and find a place in the European security order since the end of the Cold War have been characterised by remarkable consistency. It was under the first post-communist Polish Foreign Minister, Krzysztof Skubiszewski, that the basic elements of Polish foreign and security policy were first assembled. It must be remembered that in 1989–91, the security landscape was still in a state of significant flux and the boundaries of change were not known. For Poland this meant proceeding with some caution as long as the USSR remained in existence and potentially could retreat into security recidivism. In this period, articulating the Polish policy *raison d'état* and buttressing the regained sovereignty were immediate priorities.[4] Nevertheless, Skubiszewski also laid the groundwork for a long-term reorientation of Polish policy to an emphasis on integration into Western institutions. Speaking at a meeting of NATO's North Atlantic Assembly in November 1990, Skubiszewski made as his departure point the idea of 'equal security for all'. He stated that 'all of Europe, including Central and Eastern regions, need to be considered as a single area as far as security is concerned. There is no room for any selective treatment of European security'.[5] He went on to stress that 'the new European order should be built in such a way as to exclude military dominance by any single country or group of countries as well as rule out the capability to mount a surprise attack'.[6] For Poland, this statement led to the conclusion that these conditions could only be met by the redirection of policy towards the goal of integration into Western institutions. By 1991, the Western orientation of Polish policy moved into the public domain.[7] By 1993, the shift was complete towards a policy 'to maintain and intensify the process of Poland's integration into European and Euro-Atlantic institutions'.[8]

In policy terms, institutional integration was inextricably bound to a set of norms. Poland both aspired to be part of them and saw its security enhanced by their underpinning of European security. Speaking at Chatham House in March 1993, Hanna Suchocka, the Prime Minister, made plain this linkage: 'the family of democratic Western European countries, supported by the trans-Atlantic partnership, is what we aim at. Not because we need some umbrella, but because we all share the same values and objectives. Because we want Europe to be secure.'[9] The focus on integration into institutions in Europe coincided with a strong emphasis on the promotion of a broader international normative regime that helped to consolidate security and stability. Skubiszewski in his 1990 address to the Polish Sejm stressed: 'in international relations we will strengthen law-abidingness [*praworzadnosc*], in other words we will boost the functions of international law, with special attention drawn to the protection of human rights and basic liberties'.[10] Dariusz Rosati, one of Skubiszewski's successors from the post-communist part of the Polish political spectrum, echoed this line when he stressed that Poland sought 'a friendly international setting, guided by principles of democracy and international law'. Rosati went on to describe a European order that is characterised by the 'universal acceptance of democracy, pluralism and the free market as the organising elements of . . . European societies and relations between states'.[11]

Although integration into Euro-Atlantic institutions lay at the core of Polish foreign and security policy, it formed part of a more complex web of relationships Polish policy endeavoured to build in a comprehensive and mutually supporting fashion. The five key priorities of this policy were set out by Skubiszewski and thereafter adhered to with relatively little modification by his successors:

1   To make Poland's orientation still firmer by a step-by-step process of getting the country included in the integration structures and in the network of West European and North American interdependencies.
2   To take part in the shaping of a new European order based on the co-operation of states and on the co-ordination of pursuits of international institutions with particular regard for the establishment of an all-European system of security.
3   To strengthen and develop the best possible options with Poland's neighbours.
4   To reinforce and expand the new regional relationships in this part of Europe.
5   To promote bilateral co-operation in all fields with the states of Western Europe and North America – which means, in other words, the Euro-Atlantic dimension of Poland's bilateral relations.[12]

Skubiszewski's successors adhered, as noted, to these basic elements even if these goals underwent some repackaging. The only notable change was the increased prominence of the aim of developing 'intense economic relations with rapidly growing world markets'.[13] The five priorities essentially form an integrated whole. At the core is the integration into institutions such as NATO and the EU. Buttressing this main effort, however, is the development of bilateral relations and multilateral co-operation that transcends several layers of the international system. The promotion and consolidation of norms conducive to Polish security is a leitmotif at all policy levels. This raft of aims outlined in the early 1990s represents the post-communist vision of Poland's place in the European order. These Polish foreign and security policy objectives have enjoyed a remarkable degree of continuity in their pursuit and consensus in their support among the political establishment of Poland.

Return to Europe

Integration into NATO

At the heart of Polish foreign and security policy goals is membership in NATO. From 1990 onwards, it consistently occupied the top position among Poland's external policy goals.[14] Alongside the aim of membership in the Atlantic Alliance, becoming part of the European Union formed the second major pillar of a policy popularly described as the 'Return to Europe'. In combination, these twin goals made institutionally based integration the key theme of Polish external policy. From the start, however, it was recognised that the timeframes for obtaining membership in these two organisations would differ, as would the weight of Polish efforts in seeking NATO and EU membership. NATO was clearly seen as the more quickly realised goal. Indeed, in the November 1992 official paper on 'Security Policy and Defence Strategy of the Republic of Poland', membership in the EU was described as a 'long-term objective' while the effort to join NATO was viewed as an immediate and ongoing process.[15] In short, for practical reasons NATO membership was bound to be initially the central effort of Polish policy.

Polish priorities in seeking NATO membership were undoubtedly conditioned by the country's twentieth-century insecurity. Loss of statehood, domination by foreign powers and genocidal population losses in wartime have left an indelible mark on Polish thinking regarding national security. The legacy of these historical events has been a desire to find security arrangements, or a security order, that would provide predictability, strong external guarantees of military support and that ultimately would provide the best possible environment for the maintenance of a sovereign Polish state. Pooling sovereignty is designed to preserve as much of it as possible. In 'hard' security terms, NATO is seen as the key post-Cold War provider in meeting these criteria. In September 1995, a group of key foreign and security policy figures published what was the most comprehensive study, entitled *Report: Poland–NATO*, of the 'obstacles and difficulties encountered in Poland's drive to membership in the North Atlantic Alliance'.[16] This study reflected the thinking that underpinned Polish motivations for wanting to join a coalition such as NATO:

Poland's independence can be effectively safeguarded only within a coalition framework . . . An effective coalition is, therefore, a system with high 'entry' and 'exit' costs and an advanced degree of integration and specialization of roles. Hence the importance of Poland's full participation in all of NATO's political and military structures after being invited to join the Alliance.[17]

It was recognised in *Report: Poland–NATO* that obtaining membership in the Alliance was dependent not so much on such things as any real or potential threats but rather on the degree to which Poland conformed to the norms embedded in NATO:

> The geostrategic factor (and advantages) should not, however, be overemphasized. Geostrategic arguments no longer play a role *per se*. Poland can count on integration with the West only if it is a democratic state with a market economy and effective civilian control of the military. In the process of European and Transatlantic integration 'values' (i.e. democracy) and 'interests' (i.e. security) form an interlocking whole.[18]

Meeting Poland's post-Cold War hard security requirements has been a process of convincing the country's NATO interlocutors that it fully meets a set of norms. Indeed, the NATO members' 1995 *Study on NATO Enlargement* contained a discussion of the normative component of membership that was tantamount to criteria for entry into the organisation.[19] When Poland realised its goal of entry into NATO in March 1999, the credible adherence to norms was one of the key factors in the Polish acquisition of Alliance membership. Polish integration into NATO was more than simply gaining hard security guarantees, it was very much linked to a Polish view of the kind of European order of which Poland desired to be a part.

This view can be substantiated in opinion poll evidence regarding support in Polish society for this aspect of Polish external policy. An examination of the views of Polish political parties at the time of the autumn 1997 parliamentary elections indicated a virtually unanimous view in favour of joining NATO among all the major parties with only some reservations expressed by minor parties. These reservations, however, concerned the pace of integration into NATO and not its desirability.[20] Elite opinion in favour of NATO membership for Poland has been more than matched by public support. Between 1993 and 1996, public support in Poland had been steadily growing and in January 1996 an opinion poll indicated 72 per cent of respondents favouring NATO membership.[21] Opinion polls taken in June 1997, December 1997 and May 1998 indicated that this support remained at high levels with 80, 76 and 74 per cent, respectively, supporting entry into the Alliance.[22] Polling within the armed forces has also indicated high levels of support among the group most directly affected by NATO membership.[23] On the eve of joining NATO, a very solid 65 per cent of those polled supported Polish membership in NATO and 58 per cent believed that it would enhance Poland's security.[24] NATO's action during the Kosovo conflict did not diminish Polish enthusiasm for it. An opinion poll conducted in February 2000 saw public support at a steady 63 per cent.[25] The commitment of the Polish public is best measured by its willingness to pay for the additional costs associated with membership. Predictably, when Polish public opinion was asked about making greater financial contributions to the public purse, support tended to dip concerning the prospect of meeting the cost of membership. Nevertheless, a majority of the public remained willing to pay more for any additional defence costs that may come with membership of NATO.[26]

Integration into the EU

For Poland, membership of the European Union was always going to be a longer-term process. Since the European Council summit in Copenhagen in June 1993, the EU has devised criteria for membership and a process that has advanced cautiously.[27] Poland's entry into NATO in March 1999 led to a major shift in emphasis towards accelerating preparations for accession into the EU. Geremek in 1999 stressed in a Sejm speech that 'our top priority is to have Poland included in the integration system of the European Union'.[28] Unlike NATO membership, where the adaptation would have the most far-reaching consequences on a segment of Polish society (armed forces), preparations for EU membership are more complex and represent a symbiosis of external and internal policy in their normative impact. Because of its domestic implications, EU membership has been a more controversial feature of Poland's aim of integration into Western institutions. Meeting the post-Cold War political, economic and social criteria of membership in the EU requires more time and more discomfort for a broader spectrum of Polish society. Added to the impact of preparations for EU membership is the perception that the EU is lukewarm about enlargement and that the goalposts of membership keep moving as a result of this reluctance.

Paralleling the heightened official efforts to prepare for EU membership was growing frustration regarding the pace of the EU enlargement process. The Minister of Foreign Affairs spoke of the lack of political will among existing EU members to move forward with the enlargement process in June 2000.[29] In an interview in the Polish newspaper *Rzeczpospolita*, Geremek attributed this lack of will to social attitudes prevalent in the EU. 'Some EU societies are scared', he said, ' "barbarians" have come to their doorsteps. Those "barbarians" will want to take their workplaces, sell their products on EU markets, and demand financial aid from the EU . . . Never before have we seen such big obstacles on our road towards the EU.'[30] According to opinion polling evidence in EU member states, public perceptions are of a Poland steeped in religiosity and conservatism, although Poland is generally viewed favourably concerning its economic reforms.[31]

Growing frustration over the perceived slow pace of its enlargement process has had an impact on the general popularity of the EU in Poland. In June 1998, around 80 per cent of those polled supported Polish membership.[32] Thereafter, there was evidence of a downward trend. Support stood at 64 per cent in September 1998, 55 per cent in December 1998 and 47 per cent by May 1999. It remained at 47 per cent in October 1999.[33] In the course of 2000, Polish support recovered with 65 per cent of those polled in July 2000 indicating that they would vote in favour of membership if a referendum were held.[34] What this evidence demonstrates is that support for integration into the EU has remained substantial but there exists a certain amount of ambivalence about the way in which the enlargement process has been managed by the current member states.

In the broadest sense, Poland sees membership in the EU as enhancing its security. The adherence to a spectrum of political, social and economic norms associated with EU membership provides a normative foundation for Poland's security. However, it is also evident that the Polish official view sees limits to the amount of sovereignty Poland will be willing to pool in the EU. Geremek made this plain in an interview he gave shortly before leaving office.[35] Another example can be seen in Polish preferences that the EU concentrates on 'soft' security issues while the 'hard' security matters are left to NATO. Polish caution towards the development of a European defence identity within the EU reflects this view. Poland is very 'Atlanticist' in its foreign and security policy. It is a long-standing Polish position that 'the presence of the United States in Europe is necessary for the security of the continent'.[36] Polish policy towards EU membership can be summarised as being committed to integration but cautious about 'excessive federalist tendencies'.[37] For the Poles, acceptance of political, economic and social norms is less problematic than the construction of a possible 'European state'.

Security subsidiarity: sub-regional co-operation

Alongside Poland's drive for integration into Western institutions, sub-regional co-operation is seen as another major level of its foreign and security policy for the pragmatic cultivation of norms beneficial to Polish security. The place of sub-regional co-operation in the wider picture of European security was clearly framed by Polish Foreign Minister Geremek in a keynote address to a major international conference in October 1998:

> Sub-regional co-operation makes a tangible contribution to security in the OSCE area. It is the embodiment of the principle of subsidiarity in security terms. It is designed to solve problems at the lowest possible platform of interaction. Sub-regional co-operation underlines

the importance of the 'neighbourhood' as a security factor. Good neighbourliness constitutes the fabric of European security. Without a solid bilateral basis of relations between neighbours, all references to a new security era will ring hollow.[38]

In another speech, Geremek described Poland's policy of sub-regional co-operation as an attempt to 'construct comprehensive microsystems of regional security'. A wide remit of activity falls under the rubric of regional and sub-regional co-operation. This is one of the reasons why it is seen as being so important to Polish foreign and security policy:

> Regional activities are seen as one of the basic tools for strengthening Polish independence and enhancing our position in the region and on the continent as well. Such co-operation also helps to improve our potential in many fields, since the regional co-operation agenda is very broad – from economic projects and infrastructure to cultural and educational questions.[39]

Poland has certainly been very active in regional and sub-regional co-operation. It was one of the founding members of the Visegrad group in February 1991.[40] Other regional groupings that Poland has joined include CEFTA (Central European Free Trade Area), CEI (Central European Initiative) and the Council of Baltic Sea States. In its policy, Poland has stressed the need for these processes to yield concrete results instead of constructing hollow sub-regional institutions. 'We give our support for institutionalisation of this co-operation', stated Geremek, 'only if it is a result of real activities and not a substitute for them'.[41]

The practice of good neighbourliness: cross-border bilateral relations

The normative aspects of Poland's foreign and security policy aims are most vivid in the most basic level of its external policy: bilateral relations with its neighbours. This area may be the most basic building block of policy but it is also one where norms play a fundamental role. One of the most important vehicles in Poland's post-communist bilateral relations has been the 'good neighbourliness' treaty. Between 1991 and 1994, Poland signed such treaties with all six of its neighbours.

These treaties serve a number of important functions in Poland's bilateral relations. With some of the neighbours, the good neighbourliness treaty is an important instrument of reconciliation. The treaties with Germany, Lithuania and Ukraine fall into this category. With other states, such as the Czech Republic and Slovakia, the dominant theme is solidarity in the common aspiration of integration into Western institutions. Whatever the motivation for concluding the treaty, each of them embraces a wide agenda of principles, norms and specific projects to develop positive bilateral relations. Their normative function is neatly illustrated with regard to the issue of protection of national minorities. Each of these bilateral treaties contains strong commitments to protect the identity of any ethnic minorities within the boundaries of the signatory states. The obligations towards national minorities are consistent with the norms for minority protection in Europe set out by the Council of Europe and the OSCE.[42]

Poland's cross-border relations have been generally progressing in a very constructive and positive fashion. Concerning relations with Belarus and Russia, however, progress has not proceeded as smoothly as Poland had hoped. Tensions between Poland and its two eastern neighbours have been evident from time to time. While the significance of the periodic political ruptures between Poland and Russia in particular should not be overdrawn, the lack of a sustained effort to discard the burdens from the past only highlights the need for a reconciliation along the lines of the German–Polish rapprochement.[43] Indeed, the success of post-Cold War German–Polish relations showcases the benefits that have resulted from Poland's policy of good neighbourliness in its bilateral relations. The key to the bilateral successes would, therefore, appear to lie in the degree to which both parties adhere to a common set of norms guiding their vision of European security.

Conclusion: Poland and international norms

In the wider international sphere, Polish foreign and security policy has sought to 'contribute to the building of a permanent, just and peaceful order in Europe and the world based on the values of democracy, human rights, rule of law and solidarity'.[44] This broad view of the norms most desirable for the international system as a whole has been reflected in Polish official attitudes towards the Organisation for Security and Co-operation in Europe and the United Nations. The Polish perspective on the role of both of these organisations has recognised their importance in promoting norms but it has been reluctant to assign them a central place in terms of Polish security. This reluctance stems from an unwillingness to have Poland's security resting on the practice of collective security, which has not met Polish expectations since the formation of the League of Nations in 1919. Taking the OSCE as a prime example, Polish policy has been unwilling to assign it any 'leading or co-ordinating functions', preferring instead to strengthen its 'normative function'.[45] The same approach is evident in Polish policy towards the UN.[46] Clearly, Polish policy has preferred to see the application of norms linked to organisations bound by commitment rather than non-binding co-operation. This is why Poland has pursued a foreign and security policy with integration into NATO and the EU as its cornerstone. The sub-regional and bilateral aspects of Polish policy are designed to complement the main effort of institutional integration.

The consequence of this approach is an attempt to anchor Poland to a European order based on a set of norms sustained and made predictable through institutional integration.

Notes and references

1 The views expressed here are personal and should not be construed as representing the views or policy of the British government, Ministry of Defence or the Royal Military Academy, Sandhurst.
2 Policy Statement by Bronislaw Geremek, the Polish Minister of Foreign Affairs, presented to the Plenary Session of the Sejm, 8 April 1999. URL: http://www.msz.gov.pl/english/polzagr/expose99us.html.
3 *Materials and Documents* 8 1998, p. 1663.
4 Skubiszewski is credited with being one of the principal architects of Poland's post-communist foreign and security policy and the political consensus behind it. See L. Vinton, 'Domestic Politics and Foreign Policy, 1989–1993' in I. Prizel and A. A. Michta (eds), *Polish Foreign Policy Reconsidered: Challenges of Independence*. (London: Macmillan 1995), pp. 23–7. See also K. Skubiszewski, 'Racja stanu z perspektywy polskiej' in B. Wizimirski (ed.), *Rocznik Polskiej Polityki Zagranicznej 1992*. (Warsaw: PISM 1994), pp. 35–44.
5 'Poland and European Security'. Address by the Polish Foreign Minister Krzysztof Skubiszewski to the North Atlantic Assembly. London, 29 November 1990. *Zbiór Dokumentów* XLVII. (Warsaw: PISM 1991), p. 9.
6 *Ibid.*, p. 13.
7 K. Skubiszewski, 'Polka polityka zagraniczna w 1991 rok' in B. Wizimirski (ed.), *Rocznik Polskiej Polityki Zagranicznej 1991*. (Warsaw: PISM 1993), pp. 15–25.
8 'Poland's Foreign Policy in 1993'. Sejm exposé by the Polish Foreign Minister Krzysztof Skubiszewski. *Zbiór Dokumentów* XLIX. (Warsaw: PISM 1993), p. 10.
9 Address by Prime Minister Hanna Suchocka. Chatham House, London, 3 March 1993. *Zbiór Dokumentów* XLIX. (Warsaw: PISM 1993), p. 31.
10 Sejm exposé by the Polish Foreign Minister Krzysztof Skubiszewski, 26 April 1990. *Zbiór Dokumentów* XLVII. (Warsaw: PISM 1991), p. 12.
11 Sejm exposé by the Polish Foreign Minister Dariusz Rosati, 9 May 1996. *Materials and Documents* 5–6 1996, p. 1097.
12 'What is the Polish Reason of State in the Face of Current Political, Economic and Social Challenges?' Sejm address by the Polish Foreign Minister Krzysztof Skubiszewski, 21 January 1993. *Zbiór Dokumentów* XLIX. (Warsaw: PISM 1993), p. 10.
13 This objective gained a higher profile during Olechowski's and Bartoszewski's tenures as Minister of Foreign Affairs in 1994–5. See, for example, Sejm exposé by the Polish Foreign Minister Wladyslaw Bartoszewski, 24 May 1995. *Materials and Documents* 4 1995, p. 808.
14 For a summary of Polish policy statements on NATO membership see *Polska – NATO wprowadzenie i wybór dokumentów 1990–1997*. (Warsaw: ISP–PAN 1997).
15 'Polityka bezpieczenstwa i strategia obronna Rzeczypospolitej Polskiej' in *Wojsko Polskie Informator '95*. (Warsaw: Bellona 1995), pp. 21–2.
16 A. Ananicz *et al.*, *Report: Poland–NATO*. (Warsaw: September 1995).
17 *Ibid.*
18 *Ibid.*
19 *Study on NATO Enlargement.* (Brussels: NATO 1995).
20 'Mala sciagawka dla wyborcy 97'. *Polityka* 20 September 1997 and 'Wybór Polski'. *Wprost* 21 September 1997.

21 'Polish Attitudes toward Poland's Integration with NATO. Findings Based on CBOS Polls, 1993–1996'. (Warsaw: Public Opinion Research Centre 1996).

22 Opinion poll by CBOS, 15–18 June 1997 in report by the Polish News Agency PAP; Opinion poll by Demoskop, 4–9 December 1997. *Rzeczpospolita* 21–2 February 1998; Opinion poll by Centre for Market Research, May 1998. *Rzeczpospolita* 30–1 May 1998.

23 T. Mitek, 'Aprobata warunkowa'. *Polska Zbrojna* 20 February 1998.

24 Opinion poll by OBOP, 20–2 March 1999 in report by the Polish News Agency PAP, 5 April 1999; Opinion poll by SMG/KRC, 3–10 March 1999. *Zycie Warszawy* 27–8 March 1999.

25 Opinion poll by CBOS, 3–8 February 2000 in report by the Polish News Agency PAP, 9 March 2000.

26 See Opinion poll by Demoskop, 4–9 December 1997 and Opinion poll by Pentor Public Opinion Research Centre, September 1997 in report by the Polish News Agency PAP, 15 December 1997.

27 See Martin A. Smith and Graham Timmins, *Building a Bigger Europe: EU and NATO Enlargement in Comparative Perspective*. (Aldershot: Ashgate 2000), ch. 2.

28 Policy statement by Bronislaw Geremek, the Polish Minister of Foreign Affairs, presented to the Plenary Session of the Sejm, 8 April 1999. URL: http://www.msz.gov.pl/english/polzagr/expose99us.html.

29 Report by the Polish News Agency PAP, 22 June 2000.

30 Interview with the Minister of Foreign Affairs, Bronislaw Geremek, 'Barbarzyncy u progu'. *Rzeczpospolita* 26 June 2000.

31 Report by the Polish News Agency PAP, 27 July 2000.

32 Report by the Polish News Agency PAP, 14 July 1998.

33 Report by the Polish News Agency PAP, 2 November 1999.

34 Report by the Polish News Agency PAP, 18 July 2000.

35 'Barbarzyncy u progu'. *Rzeczpospolita* 26 June 2000.

36 Statement to the Sejm by the Minister of Foreign Affairs, Andrzej Olechowski, 21 January 1994. *Materials and Documents* 3 1994, p. 333.

37 'Barbarzyncy u progu'. *Rzeczpospolita* 26 June 2000.

38 Keynote Speech at International Conference on Sub-regional Co-operation by Bronislaw Geremek, 13 October 1998. URL: http://www.msz.gov.pl/english/polzagr/osce/keynotespeech.html.

39 *Ibid.*

40 This sub-regional group counted Czechoslovakia, Hungary and Poland among its initial members. With the break-up of Czechoslovakia in January 1993, the trio expanded into a quartet with the birth of the Czechoslovak successor states: the Czech Republic and Slovakia. See P. Latawski, *The Security Route to Europe: The Visegrad Four*. (London: RUSI 1994), pp. 14–32.

41 Keynote Speech at International Conference on Sub-regional Co-operation by Bronislaw Geremek, 13 October 1998, *op.cit.*

42 'Poland's International Obligations with Regard to National Minorities'. *Polish Quarterly of International Affairs* 1 (1–2) 1992, pp. 189–98.

43 See P. Latawski, 'Germany's Reconciliation with its Eastern Neighbours'. *RUSI Journal* 139 (6) 1994, pp. 65–9 and Latawski, 'Russo–Polish Relations: Elusive Reconciliation'. *RUSI Newsbrief* 20 (4) 2000, pp. 32–4.

44 *Security Strategy of the Republic of Poland*, 4 January 2000. URL: http://www.msz.gov.pl/english/polzagr/security/index.html.

45 Speech by the Minister of Foreign Affairs, Andrzej Olechowski. Vienna, 7 September 1994. *Zbiór Dokumentów* L. (Warsaw: PISM 1993), pp. 93–4.

46 Speech at the United Nations General Assembly by the Minister of Foreign Affairs, Bronislaw Geremek. URL: http://www.msz.gov.pl/english/polzagr/onz54sesjazo.html.

14 South-east Europe

Collision of norms and identity?

Paul Latawski[1]

Introduction

The concept of international order as articulated by Hedley Bull[2] and others provides a very important template for assessing international efforts at peace-building in South-east Europe in the wake of the disintegration of Yugoslavia. The Yugoslav wars of succession have led to international intervention and post-conflict reconstruction that amount to a sustained effort to create a new international order in the Balkans. In principle such efforts, as K. J. Holsti has argued, can 'include the definition of norms regarding the use of force; systems of governance for the society of states; conflict-resolving mechanisms and procedures; the resolution of war-producing issues . . . and some consideration of the types of issues that may generate conflict in the future'.[3] Elements of Holsti's notion can be seen in the European Union's 'Stability Pact for South-eastern Europe' launched in June 1999 in Cologne as the key vehicle for introducing a new order in South-east Europe and one that aims to resolve and prevent conflict in the Balkans. At the heart of the Stability Pact are norms of respect for democracy, human rights and multiculturalism together with a political agenda to impart them in the Balkans. In the eyes of the Pact's promoters, these are viewed as essential building-blocks of a more stable and secure order both within and between states in this sub-region of Europe.

'International orders', as John MacMillan has observed, 'are not value-free or politically neutral, but are constructed and directed to suit certain political purposes and interests.'[4] The Stability Pact's role in building a new and more peaceful international order in the Balkans raises some serious questions concerning the built-in normative assumptions regarding democracy, human rights and multiculturalism that underpin this project. In particular, how do these norms relate to that old enemy of previous attempts to build orders in South-east Europe: ethnic nationalism? The norms of democracy, human rights and multiculturalism embedded in the Stability Pact are seen as being both in opposition to and the cure for the ethnic nationalism in the region. The agenda of ethnic nationalism in the region has been driven by the desire to obtain security for the ethnic identity of the nation (often at the expense of other nations). This potential conflict concerning the application of these norms boils down to how one understands nationalism and how this understanding is applied in building an international order. What if the application of norms such as democracy, human rights and multiculturalism is linked to a specific understanding of nationalism held by the norm-givers? If those endeavouring to build an international order embrace one kind of nationalism and those in the region cling to another variety, then it potentially creates formidable obstacles for introducing generally accepted norms.

Stability pact: aims, process, agenda

Since the early 1990s, the former Yugoslavia has witnessed some of the most brutal conflicts in post-communist Europe. The suffering can be measured in the tens of thousands of deaths, the hundreds of thousands displaced from their homes by ethnic cleansing and physical destruction of property and infrastructure reminiscent of Europe in the Second World War. The conflicts of the former Yugoslavia have not only affected the peoples of that broken country but have had a ripple effect of instability throughout the Balkan region. The spillover of the Yugoslav conflicts was felt in such areas as economic costs associated with loss of trade and social costs of having to host, in some cases, sizeable refugee populations. The response of the international community has brought major military and political engagement by interested governments and a host of international and non-governmental organisations. The Stability Pact stemmed from the recognition that solutions had to be found to the decade-long conflict in the former Yugoslavia and to the persistence of instability in the Balkan sub-region.

The European Union was, as noted, the initiator of the Stability Pact process. The Cologne summit hosted by the EU saw the launch of the Stability Pact process on the eve of the end of the Kosovo conflict. The summit sought to bring into existence an integrated and comprehensive approach to political, social and economic reconstruction in the Balkan region and brought together an impressive assemblage of 'foreign ministers, representatives of international organisations, institutions and regional initiatives' towards this end.[5] According to the Cologne summit's final communiqué, the aim of the Stability Pact was to achieve 'lasting peace, prosperity and stability for South Eastern Europe'.[6] The Stability Pact process is meant to function as a 'framework for co-ordination' for its multifarious participants. Organisationally, the Stability Pact spawned four 'Working Tables' to carry forward its agenda. They were: the South-eastern Europe Regional Table; Working Table on Democratisation and Human Rights; Working Table on Economic Reconstruction, Development and Co-operation;

and Working Table on Security Issues. The Regional Table serves as the co-ordinating body for the other three tables.[7] In July 1999, at a follow-up summit in Sarajevo, the Stability Pact process received the endorsement of its regional participants in the Balkans and the formal organisational machinery for the process was set in motion. Providing overarching direction for the Stability Pact is a Special Co-ordinator appointed by the Council of the European Union but coming under the auspices of the OSCE. Bodo Hombach, a German diplomat, took up the post of Special Co-ordinator at the Sarajevo summit.[8]

The objectives of the Stability Pact are essentially to introduce security, economic prosperity and democracy into the Balkan sub-region. It is the last of these objectives – democracy – which imports into South-east Europe the most challenging set of norms to the Balkan status quo. Indeed, a substantial number of the Stability Pact's 'headline goals' touch upon democracy, human rights, multiculturalism and the treatment of national minorities. In the Cologne summit communiqué, participants pledged to work for the attainment of the following goals:

- Bringing about mature democratic political processes, based on free and fair elections, grounded in rule of law and full respect for human rights and fundamental freedoms, including the rights of persons belonging to national minorities, the right to free and independent media, legislative branches accountable to their constituents, independent judiciaries . . . deepening and strengthening of civil society.
- Preserving the multinational and multi-ethnic diversity of countries in the region, and protecting minorities.
- Ensuring the safe and free return of all refugees and displaced persons to their homes.[9]

The summit document also unambiguously concluded on these matters that 'lasting peace in South Eastern Europe will only become possible when democratic principles and values, which are already actively promoted by many countries in the region, have taken root throughout, including the Federal Republic of Yugoslavia'.[10]

The most important vehicle for the realisation of these aims is Working Table I on Democratisation and Human Rights. In its workplan, Working Table I sets out the following as a primary task:

> The main strategic aim of the Working Table on Democratisation and Human Rights is to anchor democracy and respect for human rights throughout the region, including by institutionalising OSCE commitments and principles in the countries in the region, also through membership of the Council of Europe, including accession to its Convention on Human Rights and implementation in practice of its political and human rights codes, where appropriate.[11]

In order to realise these aims, it has produced a number of 'task forces and initiatives' covering areas such as human rights and national minorities, good governance, gender issues, media, education and youth, refugee returns and parliamentary exchange.[12] Working Table I obtained initial funding of 165 million Euros (£100 million) to finance its projects.[13] It is significant how the democratic and human rights norms are linked into the major international treaties embodied in the OSCE and the Council of Europe. This underscores the importance of grounding the Stability Pact norms in the established overall regimes of the international system.

The objectives of the Stability Pact in building democratic values certainly reflect the views of a number of the major states engaged in the problems of the Balkans. The role of democracy in promoting stability is almost axiomatic in US policy. A December 1999 White House report, *A National Security Strategy for a New Century*, stressed that 'in crafting our strategy, we recognize that the spread of democracy, human rights and respect for the rule of law not only reflects American values, it also advances our security and prosperity'.[14] Deputy Secretary of State Strobe Talbott, in a speech entitled 'Self-determination: From Versailles to Dayton and beyond', spoke of the US view of the benefits of bringing democratic values to the Balkans:

> Democracy, of course, is the political system most explicitly designed to ensure self-determination. That makes democracy the best antidote to secessionism and civil war, since in a truly democratic state, citizens seeking to run their own lives have peaceful alternatives to taking up arms against their government.[15]

US policy has been paralleled by major European states. In the UK, Foreign Secretary Robin Cook stressed, in a major address at the Royal Institute of International Affairs, that 'diplomacy for democracy' was an important feature of British policy designed 'to promote British values of democracy and freedom'.[16] Similarly, German policy advocates the filling of the 'deficit in democratisation' in South-east Europe.[17]

These democratic norms, so central to the Stability Pact process and integral to the policies of the major powers, are being promoted in a part of Europe that has experienced brutal conflict in which ethnic nationalism was a major factor in driving the violence. Nationalism and ethnicity in the Balkans are factors that must be reckoned with in the imparting of democratic norms to build a peaceful and stable order there. Unfortunately, the introduction of these norms brings into sharp focus the extent to which the Stability Pact's success or failure will depend on how nationalism is understood by both the norm-givers and their recipients. Therefore, it is necessary to examine the meaning of the ideas of nationalism and ethnicity and how they impact on the international system.

Which nationalism? Identity and international relations

Since the end of the Cold War, there has been an explosion of interest in the study of nationalism and the related subject of ethnicity across many academic disciplines. Although there has been a proliferation of scholarship, nationalism remains a field of study that is 'vast and ramified'.[18] Despite the varieties of meanings and disciplinary approaches ascribed to the study of nationalism, nations and ethnicity, there is a dominant orthodoxy that sees nationalist phenomena as a product of modernity and grounded in instrumentalism. According to the instrumentalist approach, national or ethnic identities are 'situational' and are the 'property of individuals rather than of collectivities'.[19] In the instrumentalist view, national identity and ethnicity are secondary issues able to be swept aside by more potent universal forces such as social class, economic development, global interdependence or secularisation.[20] Anthony D. Smith has summarised the major strands of this dominant modernist and instrumentalist school in the following manner:

> First, nations and nationalism are regarded as inherently modern – in the sense of recent – phenomena; that is, they emerged in the last two hundred years, in the wake of the French Revolution. Second, nations and nationalisms are treated as the products of the specifically modern conditions of capitalism, industrialism, bureaucracy, mass communications and secularism. Third, nations are essentially recent constructs, and nationalisms are their modern cement, designed to meet the requirements of modernity. Finally, ethnic communities, or ethnies, to use a convenient French word, though much older and more widespread, are neither natural nor given in human history, but are mainly resources and instruments of elites and leaders in their struggles for power.[21]

The result for the instrumentalists is a nation that is seen as the 'imagined community'. Benedict Anderson's highly influential study produced this seductive phrase that encapsulates the artificiality of nations and nationalism in the eyes of the instrumentalists. According to Anderson, 'the convergence of capitalism and print technology on the fatal diversity of human language created the possibility of a new form of imagined community, which in its basic morphology set the stage for the modern nation'.[22]

In contrast to instrumentalist interpretations is the school of thought labelled primordialism. There are a number of hues to primordialism, but they all hold to some degree that nations and consequently nationalism are more deeply rooted in history and can be seen as organic, part of the naturally occurring order or representing unbreakable social bonds. One critic of primordialism has argued that its proponents consider that 'ethnic identities have biological and even genetic foundations, and that the motivation for ethnic and kinship affiliation comes from these socio-psychological forces internal to the individual and related to primordial human needs for security and, more importantly, survival'.[23] The primordialist position has gained some popularity due to the events in the former Yugoslavia but it has also been heavily criticised for its determinism.[24] Primordialist views certainly cover a broad spectrum. They can form the foundation of thought of ethnic nationalist extremists while in gentler academic circles they represent an attempt to identify immutable elements of national identity that condition the problems of the present. What all of these views have in common is that nations and nationalism are seen to have qualities that are deeply rooted and unchanging.

Falling between the instrumentalist and primordialist approaches is the work of Anthony Smith. He defines nationalism 'as an ideological movement, for the attainment and maintenance of self-government and independence on behalf of a group'.[25] His definition is entirely consistent with similar instrumentalist views of nationalism. For Smith, the nation, nationalism and ethnicity are changeable and changing phenomena. Smith departs from the instrumentalist approach in his views concerning the deep-rooted and durable cultural qualities of national identity which, he argues, are firmly rooted in early modern ethnic communities he calls *ethnies*. Although Smith considers many cultural attributes, language is clearly one of the most important elements of national identity:

> Authenticity and dignity are the hallmarks of every aspect of ethnic culture, not just its ethno-history. Of these the best known and most important is language, since it so clearly marks off those who speak it from those who cannot and because it evokes a sense of immediate expressive intimacy among its speakers. The outstanding role played by philologists, grammarians and lexicographers in so many nationalisms indicates the importance so often attached to language as an authentic symbolic code embodying the unique inner experiences of the ethnie. Though language is not the only significant aspect of the nation . . . it remains a vital symbolic realm of authentication and vernacular mobilisation.[26]

Thus Smith, at least tangentially, also has something in common with the primordialists. The implication of Smith's thinking, however, is to underscore the diversity and staying power of nations and nationalism. Unlike the instrumentalists who see nationalism as a transitory phenomenon overtaken by new forces such as globalisation, or the primordialists who see nationalism as part of an enduring natural order, Smith sees it as something that continues to have necessity, function and embeddedness within a 'modern plural world order'.[27]

The implications of these broad strands of thought on nationalism are enormous for those trying to make sense of the phenomenon in the international arena. One of the historical criticisms of the international relations field has been how little attention has been given to the problem of nationalism.[28] The literature on ethnic conflict has recently swelled but it has not particularly considered the basic assumptions of how nationalism is understood in the context of these conflicts.[29] When typologies of nationalism are considered at all in this literature, it is instrumentalist thinking that dominates analysis of the international challenges posed by nationalism. Depending on which theory of nationalism one subscribes to, it can have a major impact on one's perceptions at the level of theory, analysis, policy and action. This has important implications, not the least in attempting to measure the prospects of introducing democratic norms in an area stricken with ethnic conflict. Importing norms based on an understanding of nationalism alien to the region might well produce some significant difficulties for the norm-givers.

The state: crossroads of democracy and national identity?

On the issues of democracy, nationalism and international order, the state stands at a significant crossroads. 'Modern democratic governance is inevitably linked to stateness', wrote Linz and Stepan; 'without a state, there can be no citizenship; without citizenship, there can be no democracy'.[30] The notion of citizenship is also central to the idea of 'civic nationalism'. Where civic nationalism prevails, one's citizenship determines national identity. The focus in the civic model of nationalism is on the individual rather than any collective ethnic identity:

> In a liberal democracy the individual is taken as the cornerstone of the deeply divided society while ethnic affiliations are ignored by the state. All individuals are accorded equal civil and political rights and judged by merit. They compete and are free to mix, integrate, assimilate, or alternatively form separate communities as long as they do not discriminate against others. The privatization of ethnicity in liberal democracy maximizes individual rights but minimizes collective rights.[31]

Countries such as the United Kingdom and the United States clearly possess a civic national identity where democracy, citizenship and national identity are intimately intertwined with the state. The focus on the individual's rights in both democracy and civic nationalism is meant to mitigate potential conflict within the diversity contained in the state. This instrumentalist model has been effectively translated into international norms regarding democracy and the treatment of national minorities. Therefore, the international norms relevant to democracy and national identity largely reflect the experience of states possessing a civic form of nationalism. This situation raises two important questions. First, how effective is civic nationalism in preserving ethnic identity while preventing inter-communal conflict? Second, can democracy exist in circumstances other than alongside civic nationalism?

On this first question, the track record of democratic states possessing a civic nationalism is seen as generally good. There are, however, critics who see the democratic–civic nationalism model as having serious shortcomings regarding treatment of ethnic communities. Hans Köchler has argued that:

> The traditional nation-state is based on an authoritarian ideology in terms of the ethnic, religious and regional status of the individual (the citizen). This ideology corresponds to a centrist power structure and to the regrettable fact that population groups which differ from majority populations (in terms of their ethnic, religious, cultural orientation and so forth) do not enjoy equal rights.[32]

Under the civic nationalism model, the majority group in the democratic society has the ability to impose a collective identity at the expense of other ethnic groups in the state. Anthony Smith has gone further in saying that civic nationalism is no better than its ethnic counterpart in the treatment of minorities:

> The common view fails to grasp the nature of civic nationalism. From the standpoint of affected minorities, this kind of nationalism is neither as tolerant nor as unbiased as its self-image suggests. In fact, it can be every bit as severe and uncompromising as ethnic nationalisms. For civic nationalisms often demand, as the price for receiving citizenship and its benefits, the surrender of ethnic community and individuality, the privatization of ethnic religion and the marginalization of the ethnic culture and heritage of minorities within the borders of the national state.[33]

The consequence of the 'price for receiving citizenship', according to Smith, is that it 'delegitimizes and devalues the ethnic cultures of resident minorities . . . and does so consciously and deliberately'.[34]

On the second question, of whether democracy can exist without civic nationalism, the conventional wisdom suggests that democracy and civic nationalism have a symbiotic relationship. The existence of democracy in conditions of ethnic nationalism is seen as being unworkable. George Schöpflin, in his *Politics in Eastern Europe*, observed that:

> the nation in its ethnic dimension functions in politics as a category that is connected primarily to the state and to definitions of identity. It is not the medium through which the multiplicity of cross-cutting and contradictory interests find articulation and, it is hoped, aggregation.

Rather, the nation is a relatively static entity, as it must be if it is to act as the foundation of the community, and one that transcends everyday politics. The nation is sacralised and cannot be the subject of the bargains and compromises needed for the smooth functioning of democracy.[35]

This view, however, can be empirically challenged by the fact that states exist that are practising 'ethnic democracy', a model that combines 'a real political democracy with explicit ethnic dominance'.[36] The examples of post-Second World War Germany, Israel and the post-communist Czech Republic, Hungary, Poland and Slovenia all bring together strong ethnic national identities and 'real political democracy'. These examples suggest that democratic aggregation of interests can take place in a largely mono-cultural ethnic state.

Despite these critiques of the relative benefits of civic nationalism versus other types and the possibility of having democracy outside a civic national identity, the most commonly held assumptions see civic nationalism as benign and argue that modern democracy cannot exist alongside anything other than it. These assumptions form the foundation of current international norms concerning democracy and ethnicity. Nevertheless, it can be argued that the shortcomings of civic nationalism at the state level described by Köchler and Smith have been translated into the international arena. Ethnic national identity is equally 'delegitimized and devalued' in terms of the application of international norms. As an issue in international relations, civic nationalism is regarded axiomatically as good and ethnic nationalism as bad. In Chapter 2 of this volume, Robert Bideleux reflects this conventional wisdom when he writes about the need to 'liberate Central and East Europeans from the tyranny of ethnic collectivism'. Ethnic nationalism is seen only in the light of being the 'nemesis of democratic alternatives'.[37] While no one can deny the savagery that has attended ethnic nationalism in places such as the former Yugoslavia, to see ethnic nationalism as illegitimate and, in normative terms, as needing to be trans-mogrified into a civic identity assumed compatible with democracy carries its own dangers. Apart from anything else it limits the responses of the international community in dealing with such vexing issues as conflict in the former Yugoslavia. These problems are brought into sharp focus with regard to the question of applying democratic norms and the multi-culturalism of the Stability Pact in the face of ethnic nationalism in Southeast Europe.

Applying stability pact norms: the cases of Bosnia and Kosovo

The Stability Pact's Working Table I on Democratisation and Human Rights produced a draft report on *The Promotion of Multi-ethnic Society and Democratic*

Citizenship in South Eastern Europe in February 2000. Produced by a team of advisers from the Council of Europe, the preparation of the report enjoyed the co-operation of the OSCE High Commissioner on National Minorities and included a consultation process that saw a delegation travel to four Balkan states (Albania, Bosnia and Herzegovina, Croatia and the Former Yugoslav Republic of Macedonia).[38] The report was envisaged as forming the basis of an 'action plan' to be adopted by the Stability Pact project. Under the section headed 'basic concepts and general objectives', the report stated the basic principles to underpin democratisation:

> The concept of 'multi-ethnic and multi-cultural society' is put forward as an important avenue for overcoming the problems which have resulted from – an often ethnocentric – thinking in rigid categories: a heritage of exclusivity, exclusion and compartmentalisation which did not allow for a genuine dialogue between all people, a common forum (both in a political and in a social sense) for the articulation of the different wishes and needs and a common ground for living together.[39]

The paper stressed that this basic principle needed to be moved into the realm of policy:

> it is now urgent to move forward and re-create the pillars of multi-ethnic and multi-cultural society. This should be done not in an ad hoc manner but through a principled approach on the basis of existing common European standards that are directly relevant and should be applied in each country.[40]

Flowing from these basic principles were two objectives to guide Working Table I: 'the promotion and, where necessary, rehabilitation of multi-ethnic and multi-cultural society, and the development of democratic citizenship'. According to the report, both must be developed hand in hand:

> these two objectives have to be seen in conjunction: multi-ethnic and multi-cultural society must be firmly rooted in a common effort to promote democratic values, especially equal citizenship rights and the equal empowerment of all citizens for sharing responsibility for the life of the country as a whole.

Thus the multi-ethnic society and democratic citizenship, in the view of the report's authors, have to be seen as 'mainstreaming concepts' and an 'integral part of decision-making in all policy areas'.[41] How likely is it that these 'mainstreaming concepts' will succeed in building democracy and supplanting ethnic identity in the cases of Bosnia and Kosovo?

By examining the progress registered towards the attainment of these goals, one might gain some insight into their prospects. The dual objectives of democratic citizenship and multi-ethnic society are already principles embodied in the agreements that ended the conflicts in Bosnia and Kosovo. The 1995 Dayton agreement for Bosnia and the 1999 UN Security Council Resolution 1244 for Kosovo both emphasised these principles in the peace processes that they constructed.[42] Therefore, these agreements and the efforts to implement them provide litmus tests to assess the prospects for success. In the case of Bosnia, the repatriation of refugees and internally displaced persons to areas across the inter-entity lines (dividing the Serbian Republic from the Muslim-Croat Federation) has been very limited by all accounts. The statistics collected by the UN High Commissioner for Refugees or the Office of the High Representative of the UN Secretary-General do not always make clear how many people are refugees returning to Bosnia and how many are moving back to areas where their group had been ethnically cleansed. Reading the reports of the High Representative from 1996 to 2000 does not give the impression that efforts to restore something akin to the pre-conflict multi-ethnic settlement pattern had made much progress.[43] Although a report by the International Crisis Group (ICG) argued that there had been some positive movement, press reports indicated that very little had changed.[44] Ironically, a pessimistic *Washington Post* article quoted an ICG official as saying that 'the ethnic cleansers are winning the battle to shape postwar Bosnia'.[45] Only 80,000 people out of the 600,000 that had returned to Bosnia had 'gone to areas where their ethnic groups are in the minority' between 1995 and 1999.[46]

The efforts to restore the multicultural features of Kosovo have seen even less success. A Serbian exodus spurred on by fear and violence and attacks on Serbian cultural and religious sites has replaced the earlier flight of Albanians from Kosovo.[47] By early 2000, some estimates reckoned that around three-quarters of the pre-conflict Serbian population had left the province, with approximately 100,000 Serbs remaining and concentrated in ghetto-like enclaves.[48] The hardening of lines between the two communities was violently symbolised by the tensions in the divided city of Mitrovica.[49] In the face of the *de facto* separation or departure of the Serb population, some members of the international community continued to make vigorous efforts to keep remaining Serbs in Kosovo and entice back those who had departed.[50] Significantly, the United Nations Interim Administration Mission in Kosovo (UNMIK) was cautious about promoting the too-rapid return of Serbian refugees in the absence of a secure environment.[51] Despite these efforts, Kosovo had seen its Albanian majority increase to approximately 95 per cent of its total population. There can be few geographical entities in Europe today that are more ethnically homogeneous.

If efforts to restore multicultural societies in Bosnia and Kosovo have seen little measurable progress, then efforts to cultivate democratic citizenship have fared little better in the face of collectivist ethnic identities and questions of self-determination. In the case of Bosnia, the Dayton settlement at least provided a state that could bestow citizenship on its citizens. Despite this clear advantage, individual identification remains strongly tied to ethnic groups and/or neighbouring states such as Croatia and Serbia rather than the Bosnian state to which only the Muslims have any affinity.[52] In Kosovo, the central obstacle to cultivating democratic citizenship is structural. If citizenship requires a state, then this is a basic condition currently lacking for the inhabitants of Kosovo. The province of Kosovo is in a *de jure* sense still part of a Yugoslav state that has little or no legitimacy in the eyes of Kosovar Albanians. Moreover, UN Resolution 1244 is rather ambiguous about the possibility of Kosovo obtaining statehood (the earlier Rambouillet accords offered a more concrete path of self-determination towards statehood). The issue of statehood for Kosovar Albanians holds out the prospect of secession from Yugoslavia with huge implications not only for Kosovo, but also for the whole Balkan region.[53] According to the conventional wisdom discussed earlier, however, citizenship and the state are inextricably linked, making the prospects for cultivating democratic citizenship seemingly limited.

Conclusion: a need to rebase the norms?

The apparent difficulties in introducing democratic reforms and a multicultural society consistent with the civic national identity embodied in many Western democracies and the Stability Pact can be attributed to the obduracy of ethnic nationalism in the Balkans. Despite the stubborn persistence of this nationalism in the face of international efforts to introduce a new normative base, very often analysts are dismissive of its importance and power. Susan L. Woodward, a highly respected observer of the Yugoslav conflict, wrote that 'the label of nationalism is not sufficient to describe a situation or predict behaviour, however, because of its empty-vessel character – its absence of programme outside the insistence on political power for some imagined community'.[54] The limited inroads of Stability Pact norms in places like Bosnia and Kosovo suggest that ethnic nationalism is far from being an 'empty-vessel' and it is an identity that will not be easily replaced. General Sir Michael Jackson, who commanded the NATO-led international peacekeeping force when it entered Kosovo, offers some sobering thoughts on the task of introducing Stability Pact norms:

> We have soldiers living in Serb apartments where they are isolated. We have permanent guards on all Orthodox churches and monasteries without which they would be burnt and bombed. We even escort little old ladies to the bread shop to buy their bread, but on the way a Kosovar Albanian teenager will give the sign of throat-slitting to her face. In terms of what outside intervention in the sense of soldiers and policemen and civil administrators can achieve, what this tells me is that there is a limit: we're talking about people's attitudes, people's perceptions – and that's what needs to be changed if we are to achieve

the concept which underpins [UN Resolution] 1244 of a new Kosovo: democratic, liberal, reconciled, multi-ethnic. I'm afraid that my deduction is that there's a very long way to go indeed.[55]

One of the serious limitations of efforts to introduce core Stability Pact norms is the adherence to concepts of democracy linked to civic national identity that has little resonance in the Balkans. This linkage presupposes an emphasis on individual over collective rights, a privatisation of ethnicity and, in the cases of those areas that experienced ethnic conflict, a reintegration of ethnic groups displaced by fighting. The assumption that this is a universal model to be applied everywhere shows little regard for cultural diversity and its power in relation to ethnic identity. It is not the core values and attributes of democracy that are flawed, but the promotion of democratic models coupled to a civic national identity that would be more familiar in Pittsburgh than Prizren. The consequence of this kind of approach is to make ethnic national identity something delegitimised and devalued in relation to international norms. Patronising those who have ethnic national identities is not likely to win their hearts and minds to the cause of democracy. If earlier efforts to recast Balkan orders are any indication, such an approach offers little prospect of durable stability replacing real or potential Balkan conflict.

Finding a way of making democratic norms accessible to those possessing an ethnic identity is the key to tackling Balkan problems. Taking a more differentiated approach to norm transmission may yield better long-term prospects for stability. It also entails contemplating approaches at odds with conventional Western notions of multicultural society. In areas that have seen the separation of ethnic groups because of violence, it may be more viable to attempt to build democracy in a mono-ethnic context. This applies to the two 'entities' of Bosnia and the province of Kosovo. Some analysts see such an approach as abhorrent, arguing that it legitimises 'ethnic cleansing' and does not bring lasting stability.[56] Others, however, recognise that such solutions have been adopted in the past and that they may be the only viable option.[57] Such an approach should only be considered in areas where ethnic separation has already occurred as a result of violence and conflict. In parts of South-east Europe where multicultural societies have not been wrenched apart by violence, the Stability Pact efforts to link democratic citizenship and multicultural society may be the best way forward. Accepting ethnic separation as the starting point for introducing democratic norms is driven by the need to bring security not only to regions but also to individuals. The definition of security has undergone a process of 'deepening' and 'widening' since the end of the Cold War.[58] The implications of this process of redefinition on projects such as the Stability Pact must not be underestimated. In particular, the increased emphasis on 'individual security' in academic analysis and the more recent discussion of 'human security' in the international political arena clearly have implications for Stability Pact norms.[59] If the needs of individual or human security and the promotion of democratic norms are best advanced together in a mono-ethnic setting, then the prize of long-term stability may justify the appropriate rebasing of Stability Pact norms. The failure to do so may produce an imagined order that brings neither security nor stability to South-east Europe.

Notes and references

1 The views expressed here are personal and should not be construed as representing the views or policy of the British government, Ministry of Defence or the Royal Military Academy, Sandhurst.
2 H. Bull, *The Anarchical Society: A Study of Order in World Politics.* (Basingstoke: Macmillan 1977).
3 K. J. Holsti, *Peace and War: Armed Conflicts and International Order 1648–1989.* (Cambridge: Cambridge University Press 1991), p. 22.
4 J. MacMillan, *On Liberal Peace: Democracy, War and the International Order.* (London: Tauris 1998), p. 5.
5 The Stability Pact has 29 participants including states in Europe, North America and Asia (Japan) and a host of institutions including the EU, NATO, WEU, OSCE, Council of Europe, UN, UNHCR, OECD, IMF and World Bank. See Stability Pact Information Note. URL: http://www.seerecon.org/News/ETSP/SPC.htm.
6 Stability Pact for South Eastern Europe. Cologne, 10 June 1999. URL: http://www.seerecon.org/KeyDocuments/KD1999062401.htm.
7 *Ibid.*
8 Sarajevo Summit Declaration, 30 July 1999. URL: http://www.stabilitypact.org/SUMMIT.htm.
9 Stability Pact for South Eastern Europe, *op.cit.*
10 *Ibid.*
11 Workplan: Stability Pact for South Eastern Europe. URL: http://www.ceps.be/Research/SEE/workplan.htm.
12 Working Table I: Democratisation and Human Rights, Task Forces/Initiatives. URL: http://www.stabilitypact.org/WT-1/TOC-WT1.htm.
13 Address by Stability Pact Special Co-ordinator Bodo Hombach. Tokyo, 15 May 2000. Text available on the Stability Pact website. URL: http://www.stabilitypact.org.
14 *A National Security Strategy for a New Century.* URL: http://www.usia.gov/regional/ea/easec/natsec2k.htm.
15 Address by Strobe Talbott, Deputy Secretary of State: 'Self-Determination: From Versailles to Dayton and beyond'. Office of Public Affairs, Embassy of the United States, London.
16 Address by Robin Cook, the Secretary of State for Foreign and Commonwealth Affairs: 'Foreign Policy and National Interest'. Royal Institute of International Affairs. London, 28 January 2000. UK Foreign Office website. URL: http://www.fco.gov.uk/text_only/news/speechtext.
17 *Ein Stabilitätspakt für Sudosteuropa.* German Foreign Ministry website paper. URL: http://www.auswaertiges-amt.de/3_auspol/2/3-2-2j.htm.
18 J. Hutchinson and A. D. Smith (eds), *Nationalism.* (Oxford: Oxford University Press 1994), p. 3.
19 A. D. Smith, *Nations and Nationalism in a Global Era.* (London: Polity Press 1995), p. 30.

20 M. Weiner, 'People and States in a New Ethnic Order?' *Third World Quarterly* 13 (2) 1992, pp. 317–18.
21 Smith (1995) *op.cit.*, p. 29.
22 Quoted from B. Anderson, *Imagined Communities.* (London: Verso 1991) in Hutchinson and Smith *op.cit.*, p. 95.
23 F. P. Harvey, 'Primordialism, Evolutionary Theory and Ethnic Violence in the Balkans: Opportunities and Constraints for Theory and Policy'. *Canadian Journal of Political Science* 33 (1) 2000, p. 3.
24 *Ibid.*, pp. 1–24. See also Smith (1995) *op.cit.*, pp. 31–5.
25 A. D. Smith, *Theories of Nationalism.* (London: Duckworth 1971), p. 171.
26 Smith (1995) *op.cit.*, p. 66.
27 *Ibid.*, p. 153.
28 See, *inter alia,* F. H. Hinsley, *Nationalism and the International System.* (London: Hodder and Stoughton 1973) and J. J. Pettman, 'Nationalism and after' in T. Dunne *et al.* (eds), *The Eighty Years' Crisis: International Relations 1919–1999.* (Cambridge: Cambridge University Press 1998), pp. 149–64.
29 For a small sampling see: M. E. Brown (ed.), *Ethnic Conflict and International Security.* (Princeton: Princeton University Press 1993); W. R. Duncan and G. P. Holman Jr, *Ethnic Nationalism and Regional Conflict: The Former Soviet Union and Yugoslavia.* (Boulder: Westview Press 1994); S. I. Griffiths, *Nationalism and Ethnic Conflict: Threats to European Security.* (Oxford: Oxford University Press 1993) and T. R. Gurr and B. Harff, *Ethnic Conflict in World Politics.* (Boulder: Westview Press 1994).
30 J. J. Linz and A. Stepan, *Problems of Democratic Transition and Consolidation.* (Baltimore: Johns Hopkins University Press 1996), p. 28.
31 Quoted from S. Smooha and T. Hanf, 'The Diverse Modes of Conflict Regulation in Deeply Divided Societies' in J. Hutchinson and A. D. Smith (eds), *Ethnicity.* (Oxford: Oxford University Press 1996), p. 332.
32 H. Köchler, 'The Concept of the Nation and the Question of Nationalism: The Traditional "Nation State" versus a Multicultural "Community State"' in M. Dunne and T. Bonazzi (eds), *Citizenship and Rights in Multicultural Societies.* (Keele: Keele University Press 1995), p. 43.
33 Smith (1995) *op.cit.*, p. 101. See also E. Mortimer, 'A Mild Patriotism'. *Financial Times* 7 August 1996.
34 Smith (1995) *op.cit.*, p. 102.
35 G. Schöpflin, *Politics in Eastern Europe.* (Oxford: Blackwell 1993), p. 278. This view is echoed in B. Denitch, *Ethnic Nationalism: The Tragic Death of Yugoslavia.* (Minneapolis: University of Minnesota Press 1994), p. 143.
36 See Smooha and Hanf *op.cit.*, p. 330.
37 Denitch *op.cit.*, pp. 100–26.
38 Report of the Stability Pact for South Eastern Europe: *The Promotion of Multi-Ethnic Society and Democratic Citizenship in South Eastern Europe.* Strasbourg, 1 February 2000. URL: http://greekhelsinki.gr/english/reports/stability-pact-1-2-2000.html.
39 *Ibid.*
40 *Ibid.*
41 *Ibid.*
42 The Dayton peace agreement. Annex 4 Article II. NATO website. URL: http://www.nato.int/ifor/gfa/gfa-an4.htm; Security Council Resolution 1244. UN website. URL: http://www.un.org/Docs/scres/1999/99sc1244.htm.
43 Reports by the High Representative for Implementation of the Peace Agreement to the Secretary-General of the United Nations, March 1996–May 2000. URL: http://www.ohr.int/reports/.

44 'Bosnia's Refugee Logjam Breaks: Is the International Community Ready?' *ICG Balkans Report* 95. URL: http://www.crisisweb.org/projects/bosnia/reports/30may00.pdf. See also I. Guzelova, 'Bosnia Refugees Trickle Back Home'. *Financial Times* 3 July 2000.
45 R. J. Smith, 'Outside Efforts Do Little to Mend Fractured Bosnia'. *Washington Post* 23 January 2000.
46 Statement by Principal Deputy Special Advisor to the President and Secretary of State for Kosovo and Dayton Implementation, Ambassador James W. Pardew Jr, to the House International Relations Committee, 4 August 1999. (Washington DC: United States Information Agency 1999).
47 See K. Done, 'Bombing of Serb Cathedral Condemned'. *Financial Times* 2 August 1999; P. Smucker, 'NATO and UN Clash as KLA Terror Campaign Goes On'. *Daily Telegraph* 24 June 1999 and R. Wright, 'Fear Sparks Move toward Ghettos'. *Financial Times* 24 June 1999.
48 E. Cody, 'Out of Work and Hope, Serbs Evacuate Kosovo'. *Washington Post* 17 February 2000 and R. J. Smith, 'A Year after the War, Kosovo Killing Goes On'. *Washington Post* 12 June 2000.
49 R. J. Smith, 'Diversity Divides a Town in Kosovo'. *Washington Post* 16 February 2000 and S. Wagstyl, 'Razor Wire to Stay in City Filled with Hate'. *Financial Times* 24 March 2000.
50 Report of the Secretary-General on the United Nations Interim Administration Mission in Kosovo. S/2000/538. (New York: UN Department of Public Information 2000). See also P. Finn, 'US Plans to Return 700 Serbs to Kosovo'. *Washington Post* 16 April 2000 and 'New Plan to Help Serbs in Kosovo'. *The Times* 27 June 2000.
51 House of Commons Foreign Affairs Select Committee, *Kosovo, Volume I. Report and Proceedings of the Committee.* (London: Stationery Office Ltd 2000), p. xvii.
52 Smith, 'Outside Efforts Do Little to Mend Fractured Bosnia' *op.cit.*
53 For a range of views on the vexing question of self-determination and secession see: A. Buchanan, 'Self-determination and the Right to Secede'. *Journal of International Affairs* 45 (2) 1992, pp. 347–65; A. Etzioni, 'The Evils of Self-determination'. *Foreign Policy* 89 1992–3, pp. 21–35; J. Mayall, 'Sovereignty, Nationalism and Self-determination'. *Political Studies* 47 (3) 1999, pp. 474–502 and K. S. Shedadi, *Ethnic Self-determination and the Break-up of States.* (Adelphi Paper 283). (London: IISS 1993).
54 S. L. Woodward, 'War: Building States from Nations' in T. Ali (ed.), *Masters of the Universe? NATO's Balkan Crusade.* (London: Verso 2000), p. 204.
55 M. Jackson, 'KFOR: The Inside Story'. *RUSI Journal* 145 (1) 2000, pp. 17–18.
56 The arguments for this view are fully explored in M. Kramer and A. Siljak, 'Separate Doesn't Equal Ethnic Peace'. *Washington Post* 21 February 1999 and R. Kumar, *Divide and Fall? Bosnia in the Annals of Partition.* (London: Verso 1997).
57 See two articles by C. D. Kaufman: 'Possible and Impossible Solutions to Ethnic Civil Wars'. *International Security* 20 (4) 1996, pp. 136–75 and 'When All Else Fails'. *International Security* 23 (2) 1998, pp. 120–56. See also the 'Introduction' in J. McGarry and B. O'Leary (eds), *The Politics of Ethnic Conflict Regulation.* (London: Routledge 1993), pp. 1–40.
58 S. Terry, ' "Deepening" and "Widening": An Analysis of Security Definitions in the 1990s'. *Journal of Military and Strategic Studies* Fall 1999, pp. 1–13. URL: http://www.stratnet.ucalgary.ca/journal/.
59 A. Suhrke, 'Human Security and the Interests of States'. *Security Dialogue* 30 1999, pp. 265–76 and B. Buzan, *People, States and Fear: An Agenda for International Security Studies in the Post-Cold War Era.* (London: Harvester-Wheatsheaf 1991), ch. 1.

Part IV

Uncertain Europe?

15 Whose Europe? Whose security?

Martin A. Smith[1] and Graham Timmins

In this volume, our team of contributors has set out to examine the changing nature and evolution of the key concepts of 'order' and 'security' through a variety of institutional, regional and national perspectives. We did not begin with a set of preconceptions as to whether a 'new security order' has or has not developed since the end of the Cold War. Rather, we asked our contributors to consider the core concepts from their own given perspectives. Is it, therefore, possible to draw general conclusions from what has been written here hitherto? While a measure of caution is undoubtedly in order, it is both possible and desirable, in the interests of not leaving readers 'hanging', to offer some general, if tentative, conclusions here. The discussions in this final chapter will, therefore, be focused first on the general question of whether a solid and recognisable security order now exists throughout Europe. Attention will then turn to the pivotal issue of the role of international institutions in extending order and security from the part of geographical Europe where they are well established and strong to those where they are weaker or barely existent at all. This process is fraught with institutional, political and cultural difficulties from the perspective of both the 'givers' and the 'receivers', as has been made clear by several of our contributors here.

What kind of 'Europe'?

A major conceptual issue that confronts analysts in this area is concerned with the task of defining what we understand by the term 'Europe'. No consensus exists among commentators and observers on this matter and a number of different conceptions of Europe have been explored and discussed by academic writers.[2] In Chapter 2 of this volume, Robert Bideleux opts firmly for a definition based upon the notion of Europe not as a fixed geographical entity, but rather as 'an idea, a states system, a civilisation and a set of values and norms'. Bideleux's definition also stresses the extent to which this *normative* Europe has been shaped by many different peoples over the centuries. He thus pinpoints a key issue; that of *inclusivity*. Viewed in terms of its objective historical development, normative Europe is an inclusive Europe of many differing nations and peoples.

There exists another conception of Europe. This may be termed *political* or *institutional* Europe. Journalists and commentators often use the generic label 'Europe' when dealing specifically with the European Union. As a result, the political and popular debates about Europe can be focused almost exclusively on matters relating to one particular international institution. This has often been the case in the UK. Perhaps more seriously, the notion of a more limited and exclusive Europe is present, at least implicitly, in many of the debates that surround the future evolution of both the EU and NATO. The starting point for both institutions is that to be fully 'European' a country must be a member. These institutional viewpoints thus do share one important characteristic with those of the proponents of normative Europe. This is that definitions cannot and should not be strictly limited by geography. A fundamental part of the official ideological basis of NATO is that the United States is, if not a European country in the geographical sense, a 'European power' none the less. This view has been articulated at a high level. In congressional testimony in March 1995, for example, Richard Holbrooke, the Assistant Secretary of State for European and Canadian Affairs and soon to achieve fame as the main broker of the Bosnian peace agreement, declared that:

> The United States has become a European power in a sense that goes beyond traditional assertions of America's 'commitment' to Europe. In the 21st century, Europe will still need the active American involvement that has been a necessary component of the continental balance for half a century. Conversely, an unstable Europe would still threaten essential national security interests of the United States.
> This is as true after as it was during the Cold War.[3]

In one important sense, therefore, the conceptual foundations of NATO are inclusive, resting as they do on the notion that the security of the member states, at least in the sense of responding to a direct attack on the territorial integrity of any one of them, is indivisible. The key article five of the NATO Treaty states, as is well known, that the members shall consider an attack on any one of their number as being an attack against them all.

Yet it is precisely the perceived solidity of this 'security guarantee' that has led NATO members to be very cautious in practice about allowing other countries to join their institution. They have also refused outright to countenance any kind of associate membership arrangement. As the officially endorsed *Study on NATO Enlargement* put it in September 1995: 'there must be no "second tier" security guarantees or members within the Alliance and no modifications of the Washington Treaty for those who join'.[4] The principle of one-tier membership has been firmly adhered to, despite academic interest in a variety of possible associate membership options. Suggestions put forward include Jeffrey Simon's proposal to create *de facto* associate membership by permitting Central and Eastern European countries to sign up to all but the core articles five and six of the NATO Treaty (the latter defines the geographical area within which the article five guarantee is operative). Douglas Stuart, meanwhile, has come up with a proposal to create a three-tier NATO membership; with a 'European core' (*sic*) of EU states; a middle tier embracing the rest of the NATO membership; and, finally, an outer ring of new 'affiliates' from Central and Eastern Europe.[5] All such schemes have been, in institutional terms, non-starters, however. As William Johnsen and Thomas Durell-Young have argued, 'none of these pundits . . . have adequately delineated exactly what constitutes less than full membership in a collective defence treaty organisation: either a state has reciprocal [military] security obligations or it does not'.[6]

The European Union, in its various guises, has always been rhetorically open to the acceptance of new members. The Treaty of Rome, which established the original European Economic Community in 1957, began, as is well known, with the declaration that its framers were 'determined to lay the foundations of an ever closer union amongst the peoples of Europe'. They also rhetorically called 'upon the other peoples of Europe who share their ideal to join in their efforts'.[7] It is fair to say that there have been periods when member states did appear outward looking and inclusive. In the late 1970s and early 1980s, negotiations were initiated and followed through for the accession of Greece, Portugal and Spain, following the termination of military rule in those three countries. These rounds of institutional enlargement were explicitly premised on encouraging democratic consolidation in these states by inculcating the EC's institutional *acquis* and norms into their leaders and populations. In the mid-1990s it was the turn of a group of Cold War European neutral states (Austria, Finland and Sweden) to join.

Since that 1995 round of EU enlargement the picture has changed substantially. During the late 1990s, attention, both official and academic, had begun to focus much more on the problems and prospects of applicant countries being *excluded* rather than included, or at least having their membership delayed for protracted periods of time.[8] Applications from CEE states began to come in from 1994, at a time when the EU was preoccupied with internal matters – principally Economic and Monetary Union and, to a lesser extent, developing common foreign and defence policies. Enlargement was not seen by EU members during the 1990s in the same positive way in which most of them had viewed it during previous decades.

As the new millennium began, therefore, from the standpoint of those who saw things in terms of institutional Europe, non-EU and non-NATO countries seemed caught in a double bind. In order to be considered fully European they would have to join at least one, and preferably both, of these institutions. Yet their prospects of doing so, at least within the short to medium term, appeared if anything to be decreasing. In addition to the problems they were finding in interesting EU members in further enlargement, once the Czech Republic, Hungary and Poland had joined in March 1999, momentum towards further enlargement of NATO's membership appeared to decline.[9]

Pal Dunay usefully divides post-Cold War Europe into three distinct areas. With regard to Western Europe Dunay argues, in common with most others, that an established 'security community' exists.[10] In Central Europe, which Dunay defines as the non-Soviet former Warsaw Pact countries or their successor states together with the three Baltic republics and Slovenia, there have, he believes, been some clear indications of an emerging security community, although it is not yet firmly established. The positive indications are evident in, for example, the extent to which countries in this region have sought to tackle problems and disputes by non-military means. Dunay also emphasises the fact that every one of the states within his definition of Central Europe has indicated a desire to join the EU and NATO. The third and final area in Dunay's typology is Eastern Europe: that is, Russia, the former Soviet republics and the successor states of the former Yugoslavia with the exception of Slovenia. All of these states are fighting each other, enmeshed in other kinds of military activity or in situations of high tension with one or more of their neighbours which might potentially erupt into war.[11] Against this background, Dunay argues that:

> What we should aim at in Europe is not the unification of the old continent but a redrawing of the dividing lines. The reason for not unifying Europe is not that there are forces, which oppose unification, it is rather that the developments of recent years have proved that *unification is impossible* [emphasis in the original].[12]

If the construction of a genuinely pan-European security order is impossible, as this view suggests, we are left with an effective two-option choice. The West could put up the shutters and concentrate on preserving and, where possible, deepening its own established security community. Alternatively it could proceed with selective enlargement of the membership of the two premier institutions underpinning this security community. Dunay argues that this process will, by definition, involve the drawing of new dividing lines between the 'ins' and the 'outs'.

The core roles of international institutions

International institutions are fundamental to discussions about European security, as the prominence given to them by many of the contributors to this volume attests. Their importance does not derive from their physical characteristics, such as a headquarters and international staffs. These are but the outward reflections of something more profound. Robert Keohane's much-cited definition suggests that international institutions 'involve persistent and connected sets of rules (formal or informal) that prescribe behavioral roles, constrain activity and shape expectations'.[13] International regimes in large part supply the 'rules' which are central to Keohane's core definition of an institution. They in turn both reflect and are brought into being by the development and general acceptance among the member states of a set of basic beliefs and principles. Regime theorists have managed to agree on a basic definition of what they believe a regime to be: 'a set of principles, norms, rules, and procedures around which actors' expectations converge'.[14] Institutions and regimes are thus, at bottom, *social* constructs; that is, they shape and regulate human behaviour. In the international arena this means the behaviour of those who make and influence the policies and attitudes of the states which are the members of the institutions. Thus, the regimes that underpin institutions provide, as Clive Archer puts it in Chapter 1 of this volume, 'the sinews for the international society'.

Broadly speaking, institutions and their regimes play four important roles in European security affairs. First, they are important in defining the core values and principles that their member states adhere to. Following on from this, the mechanisms which are established and maintained within institutions serve to ensure compliance with the rules and procedures which member states adopt in order to operationalise these core values and principles. This type of 'enforcement' does not necessarily depend upon the international institution possessing formal supranational competencies, although this has been the case with the European Community/ Union from the start. NATO and the CSCE/OSCE, on the other hand, have not been endowed with any supranational components.

NATO has evolved a number of informal mechanisms that have enabled it to influence significantly the defence planning and policies of its member states. In addition to providing for a more efficient and effective joint defence effort, these spring from the widespread belief that NATO embodies a 'community of values' among its members. Common values are written into the preamble of its founding treaty. This speaks of the signatories being 'determined to safeguard the freedom, common heritage and civilisation of their peoples, founded on the principles of democracy, individual liberty and the rule of law'.[15] This preamble has been dismissed by some. They point out that the declaratory commitment to 'democracy' did not extend to debarring the military regimes that formerly existed among the member states. One should not underestimate the importance of perceptions of shared values, however. Thomas Risse-Kappen has shown convincingly that these have been instrumental throughout NATO's history in persuading member states to adapt or modify their policies, attitudes and behaviour in the military arena in order to conform with, and thus help strengthen, the common values and maintain the institution's health and vitality. This can be seen in the case of the United States, which has, Risse-Kappen contends, as a result been susceptible to influence from its

European NATO allies to a significantly greater extent than a simple consideration of relative power politics would suggest.[16]

The OSCE has, by contrast, failed to develop thus far into an institution of comparable robustness and importance. As Andrew Cottey notes in Chapter 3 of this volume, 'the European Union and the North Atlantic Treaty Organisation, rather than the OSCE, have become the institutional core of the new Europe'. Cottey notes the conventional explanations for the OSCE's relative institutional weakness (a large, disparate membership, consensus-based decision-making and lack of supranational competencies) but adds an additional, explicitly norm-based, factor to his assessment. He argues that a large part of the problem confronting the OSCE springs from its attempt to establish and uphold diverse and sometimes contradictory norms relating to both its member states' international behaviour and their internal affairs. The most obvious tensions are 'between the principles of respect for state sovereignty and non-intervention in internal affairs on the one hand and those of respect for human rights and democracy on the other'.

A third important role of international institutions is, as noted earlier, to contribute to the definition of European identity. This lies at the heart of the whole 'institutional Europe' view. For people who subscribe to this line of thinking, institutions embody what it is to be 'European'; hence, in order to be European a country has to be a full member of the core institutions. This has become a prevailing belief and it is evident among members, prospective members and 'outsiders' alike. EU officials and leaders in particular are very prone to equate membership of their institution with 'Europe' *per se* and to take it upon themselves to define the parameters of the wider Europe. In an address by EU Commission President Romano Prodi to the European Parliament in Brussels in October 1999 he said, speaking of the Balkan region, that:

> We should devise new and innovative forms of co-operation with these countries . . . *In this way, we should make it clear to Albania and the countries of the former Yugoslavia that we see them as members of the European family of nations,* and that once they have met the criteria for membership we shall welcome them into the EU, provided certain important steps are taken beforehand [emphasis added].[17]

Prodi evidently believed that the European Union has the right to bestow the status of being or becoming European on to non-member states. This would seem conceited were it not for the fact that the leaders of many non-member states have, *de facto*, conceded the point. They have spoken repeatedly since the collapse of the Warsaw Pact and the USSR in 1989–91 of a desire to 'Return to Europe' by joining the EU and NATO. This conveys a sense of being cut off from and denied the right to be 'European' during the period of Soviet control from the 1940s to the late 1980s.[18] The phrase 'Return to Europe' is often attributed to Czech President Vaclav Havel, but was first used as the theme for a meeting of the leaders of Czechoslovakia, Hungary and Poland in April 1990. Havel did deliver a speech at this meeting which left little doubt as to the institutional context of the hoped-for 'Return':

> The successful Western European integration mechanisms are predominantly referred to as European and not Western European, which implies that the Western countries ought to be prepared to accept, gradually, in varying degrees and in various ways, the countries that were cut off from them decades ago.[19]

Hard-headed concerns related to the military dimension of defence and security have also played a role in encouraging leaders in, for example, the Baltic states to seek NATO membership, as Jackie Gower notes in Chapter 12 of this volume. Nevertheless, the underlying desire to 'Return to Europe' in a more profound cultural and ideological sense has been widespread in the Central and Eastern regions. In 1994, for example, the Estonian Foreign Minister said, on the occasion of the signing of his country's free trade agreement with the European Union, that:

> Association with the European Union is extremely important for Estonia. It is a means to achieve one of my country's primary foreign policy goals, which is to become fully integrated into the New Europe. The logical conclusion of this process would be eventual full membership in the European Union . . . integration into Europe is also an integral part of our security policy.[20]

Six years later the Lithuanian Foreign Minister greeted the opening of accession talks with the EU in expansive terms:

> The negotiations which are starting today are an extraordinary event in the relations between Lithuania and the European Union. For the EU member states and Lithuania the development of European integration is a matter of mutual interest. Lithuania and Europe are bound together by common values, common history, common aspirations for the well being, stability and security of their peoples. Lithuania's accession to the Union is the only logical outcome of our common destiny.[21]

The final, and some would argue most important, role of the two core international institutions in Europe is to provide security for their members. In the post-Cold War strategic environment this is not concerned principally, or even mainly, with defence against external aggression. Rather, it lies in the maintenance of a security community among the members themselves.

For a fully developed security community to come into being, war must become both structurally and conceptually impossible among the states involved. In other words the states concerned should, first, be incapable of mounting military operations against one another – the so-called 'structural incapacity to attack'. Second, their leaders should share an unwritten but general understanding that war would never be considered against other states within the security community however serious and protracted disputes with them may become.

These are stiff tests and, contrary to the impression sometimes conveyed, it should not simply be assumed that Western Europe, as is often cited, has become a fully fledged security community. A structural incapacity to attack does not exist among all members of the supposed security community in Western Europe. In terms of the size and capabilities of their armed forces, both France and the UK can certainly mount significant offensive operations if they want to. Some would argue that Germany could too, though here the picture is somewhat more complicated. Because of special historical and, until recently, constitutional constraints, the German armed forces do not have the same structural capacity, experience or indeed willingness to project military power outside their own country as do the French and British.

Granting, therefore, that in structural terms the existence of a West European security community does not look quite as assured as is often assumed, what can be said about the state of affairs in the conceptual arena? In other words is it credible to believe that West European leaders would ever seriously consider going to war against a fellow EU or NATO member or, conversely, feel threatened by the prospect of military attack by their allies? Here the case for stating that a developed West European security community does exist seems stronger. After all, the bottom line is that no NATO or EU member has gone to war with another member since 1949 and 1957, respectively, nor, discounting the Greco-Turkish fringe in NATO, ever seriously threatened to do so.

A popular explanation among academic analysts for the absence of war between the states of Western Europe is one that emphasises the role played by increasing interdependence among them. According to this view in its simplest form, the greater the network of ties and contacts among states, especially in the economic and commercial arenas, the lower the risk of war. This is because these states will have come to depend increasingly on one another for supplies of vital materials and for export markets and will not wish to see their access to these disrupted.

Although the connection between interdependence and peace might appear to be self-evident, it should not be accepted at face value. As John Lewis Gaddis has reminded us, there is very little historical support for the assertion that relations of apparent interdependence *automatically* promote international peace. Gaddis makes his point by citing the specific examples of economic interdependence which existed among the major powers in

Europe on the eve of the First World War, and also notes that the USA was Japan's largest trading partner in 1941.[22]

In a pioneering study, Robert Keohane and Joseph Nye developed the concept of complex interdependence. They argued that in a few regions of the world (Western Europe and North America) relations of interdependence were marked by a web of connections, links and relations which provided contact and communication not only between governments but also between a range of other interest groups within wider societies. The role of international institutions was, they argued, important. These provided further forums for communication and co-operation. Keohane and Nye also argued that as the web joining states and societies together had become so dense, distinctions between military, economic and political issues became increasingly blurred. As a consequence, the importance and use of military power has come decreasingly to be seen as the final arbiter of disputes and disagreements in regions where complex interdependence exists.[23]

Jaap de Wilde has argued that the existence of interdependence neither presumes nor leads to equality between states and, as a result, the potential for conflict remains and may even increase as two or more unequal states are drawn ever closer together. What really matter, in de Wilde's view, are perceptions. As he puts it, 'the existence of economic and ideological interdependence by itself [is] not enough; it [has] to be recognized'. Citing other writers, he elaborates on this point:

> Since 1945 the Western democracies seemed to have learned the lesson. Marshall aid was offered and within a few years the enemy states were accepted as equal partners in all kinds of international organizations. Mutual interests outweighed national sentiments. Russett and Starr affirm that this had more to do with the perception of interdependence (the psychological dimension, as they call it) than with the mere facts of interdependence. Much of what is being seen as interdependence is not new, but is just being recognized for the first time. The 'material' facts of interdependence do not necessarily make for peace by themselves; the 'immaterial' facts must be present as well.[24]

Following on from this, it can be seen that the essential foundations of the West European security community are the perceptions of interdependence that have developed among those states which make it up; that is, members of the EU and NATO. This has enabled discrepancies in size and relative power to be overlooked, especially within the EU where, for example, the Benelux states appear to have no problem integrating themselves further alongside a united Germany which, by most objective measurements, is the single most powerful state within the Union.

What exists today in relations among all the states of the EU and almost all the states of NATO (i.e., with the exception of Greco-Turkish relations) is the closest that any group of states has yet come to a security community, with the possible exception of relations between the United States and Canada. War is still theoretically possible in Western Europe because France, the UK and Germany all possess substantial and sophisticated military forces, and the first two at least have not as yet reconfigured these to create a defence posture based on structural incapacity to attack. Yet it does seem inconceivable that, again with the possible exception of Greece and Turkey, two or more members of either the EU or NATO will ever consider using armed force against each other. While the wide-ranging and deep perceptions of interdependence developed within the European Union are often given the major share of the credit for having brought this state of affairs into being, the importance of NATO should not be underestimated. It is the latter that has been, after all, centrally concerned with 'hard' security and questions of defence policy, posture and the application of force. Then there is its transatlantic dimension. As Mathias Jopp notes, NATO has grown into 'more than purely an alliance' and has 'developed an important culture of multilateral consultation and cooperation'. Overall, it is 'still the only institution linking the US and Western Europe in a security community'.[25] Both the EU and NATO thus have vital roles to play in maintaining and extending the security community that exists in Western Europe. Tom Dodd, in a report prepared for British Members of Parliament, summed this up as follows: 'although in the post-war period, membership of the EC might have made conflict in Western Europe unthinkable, it was perhaps membership of NATO which made it impossible'.[26]

The discussions above point towards two conclusions that, although controversial, are ultimately difficult to avoid. First, 'normative' and 'institutional' Europe converge in the institutional processes and regimes which are embodied in the EU and NATO. Therefore, in so far as it exists, the contemporary European security order is tangibly embodied principally in the European Union and NATO. Second, for all the doubts, hesitations and, occasionally, outright opposition which they have provoked, the EU and NATO enlargement processes offer the most viable means by which institutional security and order can ultimately be extended from 'haves' to 'have-nots' in Europe.

The importance of enlargement

The end of the Cold War produced a backlash against what many saw as the traditional concept of 'security', which stressed its military dimension above all else. That this backlash developed can be seen by the extent to which Western leaders have felt the need at least to acknowledge and pay their respects rhetorically to broader definitions of security, although often these have been placed uneasily alongside military-based arguments and considerations. At their Rome summit in November 1991, for example, NATO's heads of state and government adopted a new Strategic Concept which stated that 'it is now possible to draw all the consequences from the fact that security and stability have political, economic, social, and environmental elements as well as the indispensable defence dimension. Managing the diversity of challenges facing the Alliance requires a broad approach to security.' Yet the Strategic Concept made no attempt to detail how NATO and its member states proposed to do so and 90 per cent of the document was in fact concerned with military restructuring issues and the preparation of new defence guidelines.[27]

The subsequent evolution of NATO strongly suggests that its member states have never really intended to allow it to take on a broad security agenda in any practical way. In the immediate aftermath of the fall of the Berlin Wall, in 1989, various ideas were bandied about for NATO, for example, to organise environmental task forces or provide expertise and practical help in interdicting the trade in illegal drugs.[28] But such ideas enjoyed only a short shelf life and all of NATO's meaningful activities since 1989, whether in Bosnia, Kosovo or in developing co-operation with the CEE states and others, have been firmly military-based in nature. Moreover, NATO has been seen as a military-centred institution by those CEE states which have signalled an interest in co-operating with and eventually joining it.

NATO leaders have effectively taken a gamble that the military dimension of security will remain sufficiently important and relevant in post-Cold War Europe to justify keeping their institution in business. Is their calculation justified? Among academic analysts and commentators, some still do take the view that military power and the pursuit of national interests remain of central importance to the future of European security. The best-known proponent of this position has undoubtedly been John Mearsheimer. His gloomy 1990 prognosis for Europe following the collapse of Cold War bipolarity was based on the view that military issues have been and will remain the most important determinant of international power and hence the key factor in conditioning relations between states in Europe. Mearsheimer's analysis was particularly relevant for NATO because in large part his pessimism was based on the supposition that the demise of the Warsaw Pact would lead to the inevitable weakening, if not dissolution, of the institution, which in turn would increase instability and the risk of war in Europe.[29]

While one or two voices have been raised in support of Mearsheimer, or at least the basic views which he articulated in 1990,[30] many fellow-analysts have tended to be dismissive of them. On the other hand, considering the changes that have taken place since the late 1980s, remarkably few have argued that NATO can be disbanded with no serious risk to overall security in Europe.[31] Most have taken what seems to be the safe middle course and, while criticising Mearsheimer for being excessively pessimistic, have refrained from calling for NATO's dissolution. The consensus belief can thus be boiled down to two points. First, the military dimension, while undoubtedly less central than in the Cold War period, remains at least a significant background component in European security. Second, NATO, by virtue of its long experience of military co-operation coupled with its integrated military structures, remains the best-placed institution to safeguard and oversee European military affairs. NATO has, in any event, evolved into 'more than a military alliance'. It has become, along with the European Union, one of the main institutional embodiments of the normative basis of the post-Cold War security order in Europe.

Having said that, NATO *by itself* is unable to satisfy the desires of the CEE states. Two main reasons for this are apparent. First, the very existence of the EU as one of the two most important institutions in Europe ensures that accession to NATO by itself would not be sufficient to provide CEE leaders with the assurance that they would, from henceforth, be fully regarded as having 'Returned to Europe'. Thus the desire for these states to complete their 'Return' would remain significantly unfulfilled. The second key factor is the drawing power of the EU-wide Single Market. Since the mid-1980s, membership of the EU has given states in theory, and increasingly in practice, barrier-free access to what has become in effect the largest internal market in the world, comprising some 370 million people at the turn of the millennium.

In light of the decisions taken at the Cologne and Helsinki European Council summits in 1999, assessed by Wyn Rees in Chapter 6 of this volume, the EU may at last be on the way to developing an operational military capability. NATO, it seems certain, will never be able to offer its member states anything which compares to the EU's Single Market. Although article two of the NATO Treaty commits the signatories to 'seek to eliminate conflict in their international economic policies and . . . encourage economic collaboration between any or all of them', it is well known among students of NATO affairs that this article has always been a dead letter in the eyes of virtually all NATO member states.[32] Today only very occasional suggestions are made for changing this state of affairs and the authors of such suggestions have little prospect of seeing their recommendations being adopted.[33]

As is well known, political differences among the member states over the development of a common defence policy were for a long time instrumental in preventing the EU from developing military characteristics. There are, as Martin A. Smith and Graham Timmins note in Chapter 5 of this volume, those in the academic community who go beyond this and argue that the EU should not develop such characteristics even if the political barriers were to be removed. This perspective has a reasonably long pedigree and can be traced back at least to the early 1970s and the work of Johan Galtung and, especially, François Duchene. Galtung in his 1973 book *The European Community: A Superpower in the Making?* deplored what he saw as the EC beginning to assume the characteristics of a conventional military superpower.[34] Duchene, meanwhile, in a series of articles and book chapters, was developing the idea that the EC was, in fact, evolving into a new and distinctive type of international power. He adopted the term 'civilian power' to describe this, arguing that the EC's strength and profile in the world was coming to rest mainly on its integrated economic and commercial strength and also on its ability to provide a prominent example of successful international integration and co-operation. Underlining this second element for Duchene and other civilian power theorists was the idea that EC member states had good working examples of successful economic and democratic political systems to offer the world.[35] Although the whole concept of civilian power was subsequently challenged and, to an extent at least, discredited in the eyes of analysts and practitioners,[36] its appeal has never completely disappeared. It is useful to refer to it in the present context because it aids exploration of the question as to what, in concrete terms, the EU can offer to the consolidation and enhancement of security, broadly defined, in Europe.

To begin with, by placing the emphasis on non-military factors of power, the civilian power concept provides a potential framework within which supporters of the EU and European integration can define a role for their institution within the context of a broad understanding of what security is. Anybody who accepts that the military dimension of security is either all-embracing or at least its single most important element also, almost by definition, believes that NATO is, if not 'the only game in town', then at least clearly the most important of the European security institutions. Conversely, for those who argue for a broader understanding of security, a more significant 'security' role for the EU becomes at least a possibility.

By serving to enhance the economic, and especially the commercial, strength and hence prosperity of its member states the EU arguably helps to promote pacific relations among them. This proposition is based on liberal thinking about the links that exist between prosperity and peace.[37] It is closely related to the so-called 'democratic peace' school of thought, too. Democratic peace theory in particular draws heavily upon the West European experience, and especially relations among member states of the EU, for empirical support of its basic propositions about mature democracies never going to war with each other.[38]

Notwithstanding the common view that the EC began life in the 1950s and 1960s as a simple economic and commercial arrangement, the requirement to have democratic political systems in place has always been a key criterion for those aspiring to membership. The Copenhagen meeting of the European Council in June 1993 placed democracy at the head of the list of requirements for membership.[39]

The EU undoubtedly possesses better all-round credentials as a force for encouraging the consolidation of democracy in Central, Eastern and South-eastern Europe than does NATO. This is not to belittle the contribution that the latter can make, and has been making in specific areas, such as promoting democratic control of the military, through its Partnership for Peace programmes. But NATO has comparatively little to offer by way of influence and example in other areas. Barry Buzan *et al.* are correct in describing the Western-based security community, despite its having 'grown up within the common military structure of NATO' as being, today, 'politically and societally distinct from it'.[40]

NATO's primary attraction to CEE leaders is that it ties US military strength into a joint defence arrangement for its member states and, it is hoped by many, also – at least indirectly – for those with whom NATO has good co-operative relations. Even in the absence of a clear military threat, there is a strong sense that NATO is still needed to provide background reassurance. Sir Michael Howard defined this concept in the Cold War context in 1983 and the essence of his definition is, if anything, even more valid today. Howard argued that NATO, and through NATO the US military presence in Europe, fulfilled two roles during the Cold War. The first, and easily the most discussed, was the deterrence of possible Soviet aggression. The second was reassurance. This means, as described by Howard in 1983, 'the kind of reassurance a child needs from its parents or an invalid from his doctors against dangers which, however remote, cannot be entirely discounted'.[41] It is precisely this kind of vague but still vital military-based reassurance that many CEE states are seeking from the West, and specifically from the United States through NATO, as part of an overall 'security order package'. Paul Latawski has argued elsewhere that CEE leaders have perceived a choice between two basic models of military alignment. One is the 'commitment security' offered by NATO membership and based on 'mandatory commitment rather than voluntary cooperation' with the strength and permanence of this commitment symbolised by NATO's integrated military structures. The second is based on the well-known concept of collective security. This, Latawski argues, is much less popular among CEE leaders both because of its looser and less binding nature and because this kind of security operated through the OSCE has, since 1994, been promoted from time to time by the Russian Foreign Ministry as its preferred alternative to NATO enlargement.[42]

The conclusion that emerges from the discussions in this section is that neither the EU nor NATO is able to construct a new European security order on its own. The EU has not been able to deal with crises and contingencies requiring a military response in an effective manner. Hence it will be unable to displace NATO in this arena until such time as it can either respond effectively or else the military dimension of security ceases to have any real salience in Europe. Notwithstanding the outline decisions taken during 1999 on potential militarisation, substantial obstacles remain to this actually happening, as Smith and Timmins, and Rees make clear in their chapters on the EU and WEU in this volume.

Dealing with the 'outsiders'

This is not the end of the story, however, for it leaves one vital issue unaddressed: what to do with the 'outsiders'. This is a label that can be applied to two groups of countries. First, there are those that seek to join the EU and/or NATO but are unlikely to be invited to do so, at least in the short to medium term. Second, there are those which have not yet indicated a firm desire to join either institution and, additionally, are unlikely to be invited to join even if their leaders did. The single most important country to fall within the latter category is Russia.

The member states of both the EU and NATO have, of course, established engagement programmes with non-member states. In the EU's case the PHARE[43] and TACIS[44] aid and assistance programmes have been augmented by the so-called 'Europe Agreements', the first of which were signed in December 1991. In addition to the strengthening of economic and commercial links leading to the establishment of a free trade area, the Europe Agreements cover cultural co-operation and a 'political dialogue'. The latter was to be conducted via a multilateral 'structured' dialogue, which would concern most areas of EU activity, including the Common Foreign and Security Policy and justice and home affairs issues. Furthermore, the aspiration of participating CEE states to become members of the EU was recognised and the agreements were officially designed to assist them in achieving this objective.[45] By 1996 all ten of the CEE states which had indicated a wish to join the EU had signed one of these agreements. Cyprus, Malta and Turkey, the other would-be applicants, already had similar agreements dating from the 1960s and 1970s. However, in the 1990s EU members refrained from agreeing membership enlargement as a joint objective with their new interlocutors and also from providing an unambiguous statement supporting accession as part of the Europe Agreements initiative. This encouraged CEE governments to question the real intentions of Western leaders and the long-term value of the Europe Agreements.[46] The agreements have been officially linked by the EU to a CEE enlargement process. However, the nature and robustness of this linkage has been left deliberately vague and unquantified, leading to doubts among CEE leaders as to whether the Europe Agreements are really designed as an alternative to, rather than a path towards, eventual EU membership.

The growing disenchantment in some quarters[47] fuelled basic dilemmas, which have been faced by both the EU and NATO. To begin with, the member states of both institutions have perceived a need to be seen to be offering *something* to non-members for political and diplomatic reasons. They have not wanted to be accused of perpetuating 'dividing lines' in post-Cold War Europe, though many believe these to be inevitable anyway. Yet, are the initiatives on offer intended as an apprenticeship or substitute for eventual membership in the institution proper? Also, if the underlying political goal is the avoidance of new dividing lines, can this be achieved unless eventual membership is seen to be on offer to *all* European countries?

NATO has faced similar questions with regard to its Partnership for Peace programmes. At the same time as launching the PfP initiative at their 1994 Brussels summit, NATO members also officially opened up a debate on enlargement. They did this by stating that 'we expect and would welcome NATO expansion that would reach to democratic states to our East, as part of an evolutionary process, taking into account political and security developments in the whole of Europe'. From the very beginning of the PfP's life, therefore, it was inextricably linked in many people's minds with the issue of NATO enlargement. As with the EU's Europe Agreements, however, the nature of the linkage was only vaguely and generally set out. The 1994 summit documents stated that 'active participation in the Partnership for Peace will play an important role in the evolutionary process of the expansion of NATO' without being specific about what this meant.[48] Subsequent analysis has suggested that, despite what was said in the summit communiqué about the 'important role' of PfP in preparing the way for future NATO enlargement, most member states in 1994 hoped that it might act as a substitute for membership for participating CEE states. At the same time they hoped that it might serve as a useful framework for promoting military co-operation.[49] The idea of the PfP constituting a possible path to NATO membership was only accepted subsequently under pressure from Central European states, especially the Czech Republic, Hungary and Poland.[50]

During the late 1990s the perceived dangers of new dividing lines appearing between members and frustrated aspirants became a major issue for both the European Union and NATO. The problem for the EU arose because of the way in which it had decided to proceed with an enlargement process in 1997. This approach, recommended by the European Commission, was based on the division of aspiring members into two groups called, in EU-speak, the 'ins' and 'pre-ins'. The former group consisted of countries judged fit by the Commission to enter into accession negotiations, which were duly opened in March 1998. Six states fell into this category: the Czech Republic, Hungary, Poland, Estonia, Slovenia and Cyprus. The remaining five applicant states – Bulgaria, Romania, Slovakia, Latvia and Lithuania – were judged to have not made sufficient progress in developing either their economies or democratic political systems. Turkey was, alone, effectively cast into the outer darkness. Its application for EU membership was not even formally accepted.

This attempt to separate the applicants into three categories lasted a little over two years. It was abandoned by EU leaders at their Helsinki summit meeting in December 1999. There they adopted a revised approach and stressed 'the inclusive nature of the accession process, which now comprises 13[51] candidate States within a single framework' adding that 'the candidate States are participating in the accession process on an equal footing'.[52] Actually things were not completely equal. The EU summiteers made it clear that they did not envisage admitting new members all at once, nor was every aspirant offered the prospect of membership within a medium-term timeframe. More specifically, while Turkey was, finally, accepted as a candidate for membership, no dates were set for the opening of actual accession negotiations with its leaders. Nevertheless, the EU and its member states had shifted considerably from their previous approach to managing their enlargement process. This supports the view that they had been sensitive to 'dividing lines' arguments as well as aware of the extent to which some of the original 'pre-ins' group were moving ahead of some of the 'ins' with regard to their economic and political preparations for eventual membership.

NATO had faced its own 'dividing line' challenge in the spring of 1999, albeit one which originated in a wholly different set of circumstances. At the 1999 Washington summit nine countries were identified by name in a manner which suggested that they either were or would be under consideration for future NATO membership. NATO leaders noted that 'at the summit in Madrid [in July 1997] we recognised the progress made by a number of countries aspiring to join the Alliance in meeting the responsibilities and obligations for possible membership'. Their statement went on to say that:

> Today we recognise and welcome the continuing efforts and progress in both Romania and Slovenia. We also recognise and welcome continuing efforts and progress in Estonia, Latvia and Lithuania. Since the Madrid Summit we note and welcome positive developments in Bulgaria. We also note and welcome recent positive developments in Slovakia. We are grateful for the co-operation of the former Yugoslav Republic of Macedonia with NATO in the present crisis and welcome its progress on reforms. We welcome Albania's co-operation with the Alliance in the present crisis and encourage its reform efforts.[53]

It is especially ironic that Macedonia and Albania were listed among those whose aspirations to join NATO were now officially recognised. Prior to the spring of 1999 there was unanimity among analysts to the effect that these two states had no chance of getting into NATO and nor should they do so. Their aspirations had been either overlooked entirely,[54] or else brusquely dismissed.[55]

One did not have to look far to see the reason why the official tune had changed, or at least been modified. The Kosovo crisis was then at its height and both these countries had played vital roles in supporting the NATO air operations against Serbia since they were launched the previous month. As well as coping with an influx of over 300,000 Kosovar refugees, Macedonia was host to the build-up of ground forces from NATO countries that would eventually form the initial elements of the Kosovo Force (KFOR) which deployed after the Serbian government sued for peace six weeks later. Albania, meanwhile, was hosting a half-million-plus refugees who had left Kosovo since the start of Operation Allied Force. Under the pressure of immediate operational and political requirements, the leaders of NATO member states felt that they had little choice but to give the two South-east

European states at least a rhetorical perspective on future NATO membership. The same basic considerations applied, though to a lesser extent, with the other seven aspirants named.

Nevertheless, the pressures of the moment were not sufficient to induce the members to agree to a further round of enlargement (following the March 1999 accession of the Czech Republic, Hungary and Poland) there and then. Instead, a 'Membership Action Plan' was proposed in an attempt to demonstrate that more was on offer than mere words. The MAP, as outlined in the summit communiqué, included an invitation to aspirant members to submit 'annual national programmes', detailing their preparations for membership, to NATO, where officials and national representatives would offer 'focused and candid' feedback. A special defence planning process 'which includes elaboration and review of agreed planning targets' was also promised.[56]

On paper, this looked like a serious scheme of preparation for NATO membership. Yet there were grounds for questioning whether the MAP would prove to be a significant initiative. One could argue, for instance, that the MAP contained little more than proposals which were already being developed under the existing PfP and which had been lifted out of that process and given a new name. It can also be argued that the name of this initiative is deceptive, implying as it does that determined activity on the part of aspirant members will lead to NATO membership. The leaders of the existing member states had not abandoned a traditional aversion to setting concrete targets which aspirants might demonstrably meet and then demand entry. This was made quite clear in the summer of 1999 by Klaus-Peter Klaiber who, as NATO's Assistant Secretary-General for Political Affairs, had day-to-day responsibility for overseeing the MAP. Klaiber wrote about the MAP that:

> It does not . . . provide a checklist for aspiring countries to fulfil, nor would their participation in the programme prejudice any decision by the Alliance on issuing an invitation to begin accession talks. Decisions on invitations for membership will continue to be made on a case-by-case basis by all Allies and by consensus, taking into account political, security and military considerations.[57]

This was an interesting statement for the head of the MAP to make. It could be read as a tacit admission that, no matter how hard a government strives to meet the various standards and targets suggested under the plan, NATO members will make their decisions based on other, broader considerations.

A generally cynical assessment published by the Parliamentary Assembly of the Western European Union later in 1999 arrived at a similar conclusion. The WEU report noted that 'even if a candidate country fully meets the requirements for assuming the responsibilities and obligations of membership, it has no chance of being accepted if the Alliance comes to the conclusion that its interests are not served by that country becoming a member'. Referring to the detail of the MAP, the report further concluded that

> the Atlantic Alliance has thus established a whole set of procedures which, while they may be considered by the candidates as marking their entry into a pre-accession phase, expose them to the risk of becoming so bogged down in the numerous details that this can only delay the final decision [on membership]. Indeed, perhaps it is precisely the Alliance's intention to prolong the procedures.[58]

The discussions in this section suggest that neither the EU nor NATO has developed a settled approach to the question of how to deal with non-members. Both responded during the 1990s with a mixture of limited membership enlargement coupled with the development of wider programmes of engagement and co-operation. Yet the basic question of whether and in what ways participation in the wider programmes might provide a clear and orderly path to eventual membership had not been properly addressed by the members of either institution. Moreover, these discrepancies appear quite deliberate. They exist because the current members have been averse to creating mechanisms under which aspirants might demonstrably 'prove themselves' and consequently demand admission to membership as of right.

It is worth spending a little time on two particular countries: Turkey and Russia. Both are currently 'outsiders' in important respects. As such, their treatment by and relations with the two core institutions offer particularly instructive insights into the main problems which confront those who wish to see the extension of institutional order in Europe via the parallel enlargement of the EU and NATO.

Turkey

Turkey's continuing exclusion not only from EU membership but even, currently, from accession negotiations (alone among applicant states) has been used as evidence of an innate desire on the part of existing members to build a socially and culturally exclusive Europe. Officially, the EU and its member states deny being culturally exclusive. Following Turkey's formal application for membership, which was submitted in 1987, an advisory opinion from the European Commission in 1989 rejected the application. This was done on the grounds that it would be 'inappropriate' to consider applications during a period of rapid political change but Turkey's political and economic situation was also cited. There is also, of course, the added factor of the fraught relations between Greece and Turkey in general and in the context of Cyprus in particular, given that the latter is now negotiating for accession itself.[59]

Despite this, suspicion remains that there are additional factors in play over and above legitimate concerns about Turkey's commitment to the norms and institutions of democratic government and the ability of the wider EU to absorb the Turkish economy. Two rounds of enlargement of the European Community took place during the 1980s. These saw Greece being admitted in 1981 and Spain and Portugal joining in 1986. As was noted earlier, in part these countries were included as a means of under-writing and solidifying their relatively recent transitions to democracy fol-lowing periods of military rule. No convincing arguments have been offered as to why a similar approach should not apply in the case of Turkey. Neither should the state of the Turkish economy be an insuperable obs-tacle in itself. Certainly major adjustments and transition arrangements will be needed but they will in the cases of most of the CEE applicants, too, and this has not dissuaded the EU from at least opening accession negoti-ations with all of them.[60]

Nor can it be said with confidence that the positive moves made at the Helsinki summit in 1999, towards at least recognising Turkey as a legit-imate candidate for eventual membership, necessarily reflect a profound change of heart on the part of the EU and its member states. It is more likely that they resulted, at least in part, from tactical political considera-tions and a desire not to antagonise the United States unduly. During the course of 1996 and early 1997, official hints of various kinds began to emanate from the Turkish government to the effect that it might be pre-pared to block NATO enlargement unless satisfactory progress was made in the direction of opening accession negotiations with the European Union. In January 1997, for example, a senior Turkish official was quoted in the Western press as reminding both NATO and EU leaders that the position of Turkey in NATO ensured that the two enlargement processes were 'inextricably linked'.[61] The implied threat being made carried weight because under article ten of the NATO Treaty unanimous agreement is required on the part of existing member states before anybody new can be invited to join.

The Turkish government did not, in fact, exercise its right to veto, or even to attempt to slow down, the NATO enlargement process. Neither in Brussels in December 1996, when NATO Foreign Ministers announced their intention to name candidates for accession in 1997, nor at the Madrid summit in July 1997, when formal invitations were issued, was there any real indication that the Turks would try to derail these decisions. This raises the question of what behind-the-scenes diplomatic bargaining had taken place to head off this danger to NATO enlargement.

There is evidence for the development of an understanding between Turkey and the USA. The United States, for its part, seems to have under-taken to do what it could to press the EU to look sympathetically at eventual Turkish membership in exchange for the Turks agreeing not to veto NATO enlargement. US statements on European affairs during the course of 1997 often included references to its support for the position that Turkey should eventually become a member of the EU. At the beginning of the year, shortly after the Turkish threats noted above, Secretary of State Madeleine Albright met with Sir Leon Brittan, the EU Commissioner then in charge of External Relations, and the Dutch Foreign Minister (representing the EU presidency) in Brussels. When questioned about the content of their discussions, a State Department spokesman said that 'she [Albright] gave them a strong sense of the American view towards Turkey, and that is that Turkey is a European country . . . that we need all of us to make sure that Turkey is embedded in the major Western institutions – not only in NATO but in a stronger affiliation with the European Union'.[62] The impression gained from this and similar comments made at the time was that a deal of sorts had been struck between the USA and Turkey whereby the former would attempt to influence proceedings in Brussels in return for the latter's compliance on NATO enlargement. In addition, the USA attempted to smooth relations between Greece and Turkey towards this end, in brokering a meeting between the Greek Prime Minister and the Turkish President on the margins of the NATO Madrid summit. After this meeting, a short communiqué was issued containing six points. These included respecting each other's sovereignty and 'vital interests and concerns in the Aegean' and also a 'commitment to settle disputes by peaceful means based on mutual consent and without use of force or threat of force'.[63]

At their December 1997 Luxembourg summit, EU leaders managed to achieve consensus on a number of conciliatory measures. In view of the pro-Turkish line being pushed by the USA, it seems likely that at least part of the reason why these moves were made was to try to head off the threat of Turkey disrupting the NATO enlargement process in the future. The official statement issued at the conclusion of the Luxembourg meeting contained three important elements. First, it included the politically and psychologically significant declaration that the EU was committed to helping create conditions which would make eventual Turkish membership possible. These were elaborated in the second conciliatory element of the Luxembourg statement. It contained a section setting out a 'European strategy for Turkey' which, it was stated, was designed to 'prepare Turkey for accession by bringing it closer to the European Union in every field', including in discussions on the EU's Common Foreign and Security Policy. Finally, while confirming that accession negotiations would open with Cyprus during 1998, the EU leaders 'requested that the willingness of the Government of Cyprus to include representatives of the Turkish Cypriot community in the accession negotiating delegation be acted upon'.[64]

The Turkish government caused a diplomatic flurry by refusing an invitation to attend the Luxembourg summit, along with the other applicant countries. Yet it is noteworthy that the official statement which it put out at the end of the meeting neither specifically refused any of the EU's proffered olive branches nor made any reference to reconsidering Turkish support for NATO enlargement. Moreover, threats to break off diplomatic relations with the EU and to withdraw the application for membership were not carried through. Scope for future tension and discord does remain, however. Notwithstanding the conciliatory gestures made by EU members in Luxembourg in 1997 and Helsinki in 1999, the long-standing impasse with Turkey over membership remains essentially unresolved. Cyprus could easily become a particular source of dispute, too.

This story of EU–Turkish relations is included here not only because Turkey is an intrinsically important country in a geostrategic sense, but also because it illustrates important debates and limitations on the potential extension of a European security community. Notwithstanding official denials, and the existence of legitimate grounds for international concern over the treatment of Kurdish and Islamic groups within Turkey, it is difficult to avoid the conclusion that the underlying reason why Turkey has been denied EU membership is the innate perception that it is not a 'European' country in some profound cultural, social or historical sense. Thus, despite its long-standing membership in NATO, Turkey, in terms of its relations with Greece, has continued to form one part of the exception to the prevailing belief that war has become a conceptual impossibility among members of NATO and the European Union.

Russia

In Turkey, there has been both majority popular support and a basic consensus among the political and military elite over the desirability of full participation in both the EU and NATO.[65] In Russia, however, there has long existed the well-known division between the 'Westerners' and the 'Slavophiles'. Some would also add a third distinct group – the 'Eurasionists'. They believe that Russia has a distinct vocation as a great power that reaches deep into both Europe and Asia.[66]

This basic division of opinion within Russian society underlines the key importance of the question of identity. As Laura Richards Cleary argues in Chapter 11 of this volume, identity is a fundamental security issue for Russians.[67] Furthermore, the lack of a settled identity capable of inspiring loyalty and support from across the many disparate groups that comprise the patchwork quilt of the Russian Federation has two important consequences for security in Europe more generally. To begin with, Russia's unsettled identity has helped to reinforce a widespread sense of vulnerability among its rulers and its people, especially vis-à-vis 'the West', which many Russians continue to regard as the principal 'other' – an alien, unwelcoming, or even potentially threatening entity. Elsewhere we have conceptualised this by looking at the influence of Russia's 'geopolitics of vulnerability'.[68]

This geopolitics of vulnerability has two dimensions. Most fundamentally it exists at a spatial and territorial level. Most commentaries on the 'Russian condition' refer to an ingrained fear of territorial assault and invasion, in particular from the West. Williamson Murray provides a typical example:

> The waves of invasions, beginning with the damage inflicted by Mongol hordes in the thirteenth century, that have washed over Russia have influenced Russian society and culture in a fashion that is difficult for outsiders to understand. Charles XII and Napoleon only added to a paranoia that the Germans reinforced twice more in the twentieth century. Open in both directions, with great rivers that provide rather than deny access, Russia has only time, distance, and weather to block the depredations of its invaders.[69]

This is not the whole of the story, however. Concerns motivated by the geopolitics of vulnerability have also manifested themselves in a distinct political and diplomatic sense. Here, the fear has been over the possibility of Russia being effectively isolated and shut out of European affairs and denied its 'proper place' in deliberations about the future European military, political and economic security architecture. President Boris Yeltsin repeatedly returned to this theme in his statements on foreign and security policy during the 1990s, one example of which will suffice to convey the substance of Russian concerns in this area. In a report to the Duma early in 1995, the Russian President stated that 'decisions on European security that are made without Russia's participation and, even worse, against Russia would be counterproductive. A new split on the European continent would not be in the interests of Russia or in the interests of Europe as a whole.'[70] Mainstream Russian leaders have expected international institutions of all types, but especially the European Union and NATO, to develop a 'special relationship' with their country: that is, one that goes beyond the co-operative links available to other former Warsaw Pact and former Soviet states.

Yet, the deep-seated sense of 'otherness' which many Russians feel has imposed significant constraints on the approach of their government to its relations with the two core institutions. Whereas, as noted, most Turks wish to see their country being integrated into institutional Europe to the maximum possible extent, many Russians are instinctively more dubious about this. Official attitudes towards NATO enlargement illustrate the dichotomies in the Russian outlook. On the one hand, a frequently cited reason for opposing it has been because the process is not open, *de facto*, to Russia. Certainly, it is generally accepted within NATO member states that Russian membership is so improbable that the possibility is scarcely discussed among political leaders or academic analysts.[71] Yet the attitude of Russian leaders towards membership has been ambiguous. A case can be made for saying that, in diplomatic terms, Russia could have profited from submitting and doggedly pursuing an application for NATO membership. This would have faced NATO leaders with the prospect of either admitting Russia, which would fundamentally alter the whole character of NATO in both political and military terms, or else rejecting it or stalling for time. If NATO leaders had opted to pursue either of these latter courses they would have run grave risks of severe political embarrassment and of under-mining much of the official rationale for NATO enlargement, which has been touted, especially by US leaders, as overcoming dividing lines and, of course, extending the parameters of the European security community. Rejecting or stalling Russia might well have provoked splits between the USA and European NATO leaders to the extent that no consensus could have been found on proceeding with any NATO enlargement at all.

Despite the advantages of this approach, there is no evidence to suggest that any mainstream Russian leaders have ever seriously considered it. It is true that Russia's two post-Soviet Presidents to date have both publicly mused upon the long-term possibility of Russia joining NATO. Yeltsin did this in December 1991[72] and Vladimir Putin in March 2000.[73] But neither of these statements was followed up. The fact that both were made at the start of presidential terms of office suggests that they are best seen as political signals that the leader wished to indicate to NATO members a desire for improved relations between Russia and themselves.

The Russian body politic has been unable and unwilling to decide upon the fundamental question of whether, to borrow the title of a recent article on Russian foreign policy, it wishes the country to be 'a part of Europe or apart from Europe'.[74] This only heightens perceptions of vulnerability, most especially with regard to NATO and its enlargement process. There remains a feeling among many military and some political leaders in Russia that the country is physically threatened by NATO enlargement. The most serious threat, however remote, is seen as the possibility of territorial inva-sion; hence the demands by Russian leaders across the spectrum that no significant NATO military infrastructure be deployed on the territory of its new eastern members. But there is also a perception, little noticed out-side Russia, that the wider NATO eastern engagement programmes are designed, at least in part, deliberately to disrupt Russia's core geopolitical 'space'. The Russian foreign policy and military establishments have de-fined this since 1991 as embracing the so-called 'near abroad' states: that is, the other former Soviet republics.[75]

Russians have accused the NATO Partnership for Peace programme on both counts. It is hardly surprising to hear a Russian general state that 'Partnership for Peace is a program for establishing strategic influence in Eastern Europe and moving NATO's forward lines right up to Russia's western borders'. But no less a 'dove' than Mikhail Gorbachev has written in very similar vein: 'let's call a spade a spade. Partnership for Peace means that the NATO infrastructure would gradually draw closer to Russia's bor-ders . . . with all the ensuing consequences; joint military maneuvers and movements of NATO armed forces in direct proximity to Russia's bor-ders.'[76] It is also charged that PfP critically undermines attempts to breathe life into the moribund Commonwealth of Independent States, which groups Russia with most of the other former Soviet states and which Russian leaders have sought to turn into a more significant international institution from time to time.[77] In consequence, it is argued, PfP debilitates attempts to create a Russian-led collective security system for the near abroad space. This line has been adopted by, among others, Vladimir Lukin, the Chairman of the Russian Duma's International Relations Committee, and the Foreign Intelligence Service, led at the time by Yevgeny Primakov, who subsequently went on to become Foreign Minister and Prime Minister under Boris Yeltsin.[78]

In summary: many of its leaders see Russia as being an innately vulnerable country, and the Russian people have not adopted a settled European identity. Thus, their country is likely to continue to behave in a way that will appear to many European leaders to be unpredictable, erratic and sometimes hostile.

Conclusion: uncertain Europe

The future role and place of Russia is one of the major uncertainties which complicate attempts to predict the prospects for and potential nature of a wider European security order. A discernible order already exists among a group of countries in Western and Central Europe. It is evidenced in the security community that has developed among them, ensuring that war as a means of settling differences and advancing political goals has become effectively impossible. This community is not a creation of the post-Cold War world. Indeed, and perhaps ironically, it developed during the Cold War years. Yet its continued existence has defied those pessimists, most famously Mearsheimer, who seemed certain in the early 1990s that, absent the Soviet threat, the 'glue' binding the members of NATO together (and perhaps the EC/EU too) would be bound to degrade.

This Western-based security order is essentially normative in nature. But it is both solidified and given tangible expression by the two core institutions – the European Union and NATO. If the question put is whether and how the Western-based security order can be extended to include other Europeans, then the only real prospect of doing this lies in enlarging the memberships of these two institutions. This is not a simple mechanical process. The member states of both institutions have, quite rightly, decided that before new members can be admitted, they must prove themselves able and willing to absorb the core norms that underpin the institutions. In the case of the EU this process is both more formalised and more demanding than it is for NATO. The EU has even developed a term for the process – its officials and members' leaders frequently speak of the necessity of new members absorbing the '*acquis communautaire*'. Yet NATO too has created an 'institutional apprenticeship' mechanism – the Partnership for Peace. As noted by Martin A. Smith in Chapter 4 of this volume, an essential element of this process has been to inculcate 'Western' norms with regard to the proper place of the armed forces in a democratic society into the would-be members' political establishments.

Two principal uncertainties remain. The first concerns to what extent the members of the EU and NATO will be prepared to enlarge their institutions further. The second revolves around the question of what to do with long-term or permanent outsiders. These outsiders cannot be treated as a bloc given their disparate nature and varied reasons for being unwilling or unsuited to membership of the EU and/or NATO. There is a difficult balancing act to be achieved by the current members of the two institutions. If they prove to be overly reluctant to engage in further enlargement they run the risk of maintaining and entrenching 'two Europes', divided into a 'core' of stable and relatively prosperous countries in a security community, and a 'periphery' consisting of the rest. The key distinction between the two groups would lie in the answer to the question of whether armed conflict among their constituent parts remained possible.[79] On the other hand, a rush to enlargement runs the risk of debilitating the institutions in terms of decision-making efficiency and also of diluting the norms that they embody if poorly qualified or underprepared countries are brought in precipitously. In addition, as Paul Latawski has argued vigorously in Chapter 14 of this volume, attempts to try to *impose* Western norms and values on countries and peoples elsewhere in Europe, such as in the Balkans, are not only morally questionable, but are also likely to be counterproductive. There are no easy answers to the enlargement conundrums that confront the EU and NATO. Perhaps more disturbingly, the 1990s did not yield much evidence that their member states had been seriously engaged in a search for potential answers and solutions.

Notes and references

1 The views expressed here are personal and should not be construed as representing the views or policy of the British government, Ministry of Defence or the Royal Military Academy, Sandhurst.
2 For a useful historical and general overview see M. Emerson, *Redrawing the Map of Europe*. (London: Macmillan 1998). See also B. Buzan *et al.*, *The European Security Order Recast*. (London: Pinter 1990), ch. 4.
3 'Overview of European Security Architecture'. (London: US Embassy 1995), p. 2.
4 *Study on NATO Enlargement*. (Brussels: NATO 1995), p. 23.
5 J. Simon, 'Does Eastern Europe Belong in NATO?' *Orbis* 37 (1) 1993, pp. 32–4; D. Stuart, 'NATO's Future as a Pan-European Security Institution'. *NATO Review* 41 (4) 1993, pp. 18–19.
6 W. Johnsen and T. Durell-Young, 'NATO Expansion and Partnership for Peace: Assessing the Facts'. *RUSI Journal* 139 (6) 1994, p. 49.
7 Consolidated version of the treaty establishing the European Community. EU website. URL: http://europa.eu.int/eur-lex/en/treaties/dat/ec_cons_treaty_en.pdf.
8 See D. Phinnemore, 'The Challenge of EU Enlargement: EU and CEE Perspectives' in K. Henderson (ed.), *Back to Europe: Central and Eastern Europe and the*

European Union. (London: UCL Press 1999), ch. 5; P. O'Neil, 'Politics, Finance and European Union Enlargement Eastward' in J. Sperling (ed.), *Two Tiers or Two Speeds? The European Security Order and the Enlargement of the European Union and NATO.* (Manchester: Manchester University Press 1999), ch. 5; 'Who Will Join Europe's Club – and When?' *The Economist* 8 April 2000, pp. 45–6; 'Knocking on the Union's Door'. *The Economist* 13 May 2000, pp. 45–6; 'Make it Ten, Set a Date'. *The Economist* 10 June 2000, pp. 16–17.

9 The reasons why are explored and discussed in M. A. Smith and K. Aldred, *NATO in South East Europe: Enlargement by Stealth?* (London: Centre for Defence Studies 2000), ch. 1.

10 Clive Archer in Chapter 1 of this volume (p. 16) defines the security community concept.

11 These categories are not unchangeable. Countries can move from one to another. For example, following the effective end of the Tudjman era and the installation of a reformist democratic government late in 1999, Croatia began moving from being an 'Eastern European' country to a 'Central European' one. In March 2000 tangible evidence was forthcoming when the country was invited to join the NATO PfP.

12 P. Dunay, 'Whence the Threat to Peace in Europe?' in I. Gambles (ed.), *A Lasting Peace in Central Europe?* (Chaillot Paper 20). WEU website. URL: http://www.weu.int/institute/chaillot/chai20e.htm.

13 R. Keohane, *International Institutions and State Power.* (Boulder: Westview 1989), p. 163.

14 D. Puchala and R. Hopkins, 'International Regimes: Lessons from Inductive Analysis'. *International Organization* 36 (2) 1982, pp. 245–6.

15 Quoted from the text of the NATO Treaty in *The North Atlantic Treaty Organisation: Facts and Figures.* (Brussels: NATO 1989), p. 376.

16 T. Risse-Kappen, *Cooperation among Democracies: The European Influence on US Foreign Policy.* (Princeton: Princeton University Press 1995).

17 Romano Prodi, *Speech/99/130.* (Brussels: European Commission 1999).

18 Paul Latawski discusses this, in the case of Poland, in Chapter 13 of this volume.

19 'A Meeting of Leaders from Three Neighbouring Countries'. Czech President's website. URL: http://www.hrad.cz/president/Havel/speeches/index_uk.html.

20 Estonian Foreign Ministry website. URL: http://www.vm.ee/eng/index.html.

21 Lithuanian Foreign Ministry website. URL: http://www.urm.lt/eu/open.htm.

22 J. L. Gaddis, 'The Long Peace: Elements of Stability in the Postwar International System'. *International Security* 10 (4) 1986, pp. 111–12.

23 R. Keohane and J. Nye, *Power and Interdependence* (second edn). (Boston: Scott, Foresman 1989).

24 J. de Wilde, 'Promises of Interdependence: Risks and Opportunities'. *Bulletin of Peace Proposals* 19 (2) 1988, p. 163.

25 M. Jopp, *The Strategic Implications of European Integration.* (Adelphi Paper 290). (London: IISS 1994), p. 39.

26 T. Dodd, 'NATO's New Directions'. UK House of Commons website. URL: http://www.parliament.uk/commons/lib/research/rp98/052.html.

27 *The Alliance's Strategic Concept.* (Brussels: NATO 1991), p. 7.

28 See P. Corterier, 'Quo Vadis NATO?' *Survival* 32 (2) 1990, pp. 141–56.

29 J. Mearsheimer, 'Back to the Future: Instability in Europe after the Cold War'. *International Security* 15 (1) 1990, pp. 5–56.

30 See, *inter alia,* J. Wyllie, *European Security in the New Political Environment.* (London: Longman 1997).

31 For examples of the comparatively rare academic arguments in favour of NATO's dissolution see R. Steel, 'NATO's Last Mission'. *Foreign Policy* 76 1989, pp. 83–95 and J. Clarke, 'Replacing NATO'. *Foreign Policy* 93 1993/94, pp. 22–40.

32 Article two was originally included at the suggestion of the Canadians, who were the only real enthusiasts for economic collaboration within a NATO framework. After one or two tentative attempts to activate article two during the early 1950s were met by hostility or indifference by their fellow-members, the Canadians gave up and today the article has no practical meaning for NATO.

33 For a recent argument in favour of developing NATO as an economic forum see J. Tedstrom, 'NATO's Economic Challenges: Development and Reform in East-Central Europe'. *Washington Quarterly* 20 (2) 1997, pp. 3–19.

34 J. Galtung, *The European Community: A Superpower in the Making?* (London: Allen and Unwin 1973).

35 See, *inter alia*, F. Duchene, 'Europe's Role in World Peace' in R. Mayne (ed.), *Europe Tomorrow*. (London: Fontana 1972), ch. 2 and Duchene, 'The European Community and the Uncertainties of Interdependence' in M. Kohnstamm and W. Hager (eds), *A Nation Writ Large? Foreign Policy Problems before the European Communities*. (London: Macmillan 1973), ch. 1.

36 H. Bull, 'Civilian Power Europe: A Contradiction in Terms?' *Journal of Common Market Studies* 21 (1/2) 1982, pp. 149–64.

37 On the links between liberalism and peace see, *inter alia*, M. Doyle, 'Liberalism and World Politics'. *American Political Science Review* 80 (4) 1986, pp. 1151–69 and B. Buzan, 'Economic Structure and International Security: The Limits of the Liberal Case'. *International Organization* 38 (4) 1984, pp. 597–624.

38 On democratic peace thinking see, *inter alia*, C. Layne, 'Kant or Cant: The Myth of the Democratic Peace'. *International Security* 19 (2) 1994, pp. 5–49 and J. Owen, 'How Liberalism Produces Democratic Peace'. *International Security* 19 (2) 1994, pp. 87–125.

39 'Membership requires that the candidate country has achieved stability of institutions guaranteeing democracy, the rule of law, human rights and respect for and protection of minorities, the existence of a functioning market economy as well as the capacity to cope with competitive pressure and market forces within the Union'. See the text of the European Council communiqué, reprinted in *Bulletin of the European Communities* 6 1993, p. 13.

40 Buzan *et al. op.cit.*, p. 40.

41 M. Howard, 'Reassurance and Deterrence: Western Defense in the 1980s'. *Foreign Affairs* 61 (2) 1982–83, p. 310.

42 P. Latawski, 'Central Europe and European Security' in W. Park and G. W. Rees (eds), *Rethinking Security in Post-Cold War Europe*. (London: Longman 1998), pp. 92–4.

43 For more on PHARE see Smith and Timmins, Chapter 5 in this volume.

44 Technical Assistance for the Commonwealth of Independent States. The equivalent of the EU's PHARE programmes for the former Soviet republics.

45 *The Europe Agreements with Poland, Hungary, Romania, Bulgaria and the Czech and Slovak Republics*. (Brussels: European Commission 1995).

46 A. Mayhew, *Recreating Europe: The European Union's Policy towards Central and Eastern Europe*. (Cambridge: Cambridge University Press 1998), pp. 22–3.

47 In a March 1999 address to the French Senate, for example, Vaclav Havel told his audience that: 'the opportunity that is now opening before Europe will be fulfilled only when everyone is allowed to participate. Each new candidate for membership obviously must meet a number of common requirements, but once a nation has met them no other considerations should delay its acceptance. If it were to become evident that there is a policy of double standards; if there is distrust towards the new democracies; if there is fear that they might consume too large a piece of the cake; or, if there is an overall fear of them, as of something new and difficult to fathom, Europe will once again begin to divide and this new division will soon become a much more serious reason for

alarm than the novelty, or the unrefined state, of today's post-Communist democracies'. Address by Vaclav Havel, President of the Czech Republic to the French Senate. Czech President's website. URL: http://www.hrad.cz/president/Havel/speeches/1999/0303_uk.html.
48 Press Communiqué M-1(94)2: Invitation. (Brussels: NATO 1994).
49 B. Boczek, 'NATO and the Former Warsaw Pact States' in V. Papacosma and M. A. Heiss (eds), *NATO in the Post-Cold War Era: Does it Have a Future?* (Basingstoke: Macmillan 1995), pp. 214–15; G. Auton, 'The United States and an Expanded NATO' in P. Dutkiewicz and R. Jackson (eds), *NATO Looks East.* (Westport: Praeger 1998), p. 181.
50 J. Borawski, 'Partnership for Peace and beyond'. *International Affairs* 71 (2) 1995, pp. 234–5; J. Eyal, 'NATO's Enlargement: Anatomy of a Decision'. *International Affairs* 73 (4) 1997, pp. 702–3.
51 Malta and Turkey joined the eleven countries that had been divided into 'ins' and 'pre-ins' in 1997.
52 'Presidency Conclusions Helsinki European Council 10 and 11 December 1999'. EU website. URL: http://ue.eu.int/en/info/eurocouncil/index.htm.
53 Washington summit communiqué. NATO website. URL: http://www.nato.int/docu/pr/1999/p99-064e.htm.
54 See, *inter alia*, S. Larrabee, 'NATO Enlargement after the First Round'. *International Spectator* XXXIV (2) 1999, pp. 73–86.
55 See, *inter alia*, H. Binnendijk and R. Kugler, 'Open NATO's Door Carefully'. *Washington Quarterly* 22 (2) 1999, p. 134.
56 *Membership Action Plan.* NATO website. URL: http://www.nato.int/docu/pr/1999/p99-066e.htm.
57 K. P. Klaiber, 'The Membership Action Plan: Keeping NATO's door open'. *NATO Review* 47 (2) 1999, p. 25.
58 'Security of the associate partners after the NATO summit'. WEU Assembly website. URL: http://www.weu.int/assembly/eng/reports/1649e.html.
59 To be more specific, accession negotiations are taking place with the Greek Cypriots who form the internationally recognised government. It is not clear at the time of writing what will happen if these negotiations are concluded successfully and yet the division between the Greek and Turkish Cypriot parts of the island is not overcome.
60 Adam Bronstone illustrates and explores this point with a comparison of the EU approach to Turkey and Poland. See A. Bronstone, *European Security into the Twenty-first Century.* (Aldershot: Ashgate 2000), pp. 200–7.
61 *Financial Times* 20 January 1997. See also *Independent* 15 October 1996.
62 'Daily press briefing, Wednesday January 30 1997'. (Washington, DC: US State Department 1997).
63 'Simitis–Demirel meeting leads to joint communiqué on Greek–Turkish relations'. (Washington, DC: Greek Embassy 1997).
64 Luxembourg European Council 12/13 December 1997, Presidency Conclusions. EU website. URL: http://ue.eu.int/newsroom/main.cfm?LANG=1.
65 'Ataturk's Long Shadow: A Survey of Turkey'. *The Economist* 10 June 2000, p. 6.
66 On this see K. Aldred and M. A. Smith, *Superpowers in the Post-Cold War Era.* (Basingstoke: Macmillan 1999), pp. 99–100.
67 For more on identity issues in Russia see, in addition to Laura Richards Cleary, S. Shenfield, 'Post-Soviet Russia in Search of Identity' in D. Blum (ed.), *Russia's Future: Consolidation or Disintegration?* (Boulder: Westview 1994), ch. 1 and G. Dijkink, *National Identity and Geopolitical Visions.* (London: Routledge 1996), ch. 8.
68 See M. A. Smith and G. Timmins, 'Russia, NATO and the EU in an Era of Enlargement: Vulnerability or Opportunity?' *Geopolitics* 5 (2) forthcoming.

69 W. Murray, 'Some Thoughts on War and Geography'. *Journal of Strategic Studies* 22 (2/3) 1999, p. 214.
70 *Rossiiskiye Vesti* 17 February 1995. Translated and reprinted in *Current Digest of the Post-Soviet Press* (*CDPSP*) 47 (8) 1995, p. 14.
71 For a rare exception see D. Yost, 'The New NATO and Collective Security'. *Survival* 40 (2) 1998, pp. 139–40.
72 See 'Yeltsin Says Russia Wants to Join NATO'. *Evening Standard* 20 December 1991 and 'History "Turns Inside Out" as Russia Asks to Join NATO'. *Daily Telegraph* 21 December 1991.
73 *Izvestia* 7 March 2000. *CDPSP* 52 (10) 2000, pp. 5–7.
74 V. Baranovsky, 'Russia: A part of Europe or apart from Europe?' *International Affairs* 76 (3) 2000, pp. 443–58.
75 On Russian attitudes and policy towards the 'near abroad' see Aldred and Smith *op.cit.* (1999), pp. 107–18.
76 Lt-Gen. Leonid Ivashov in *Rossiiskaya Gazeta* 25 March 1994. *CDPSP* 46 (12) 1994, p. 25. Gorbachev in *Nezavisimaya Gazeta* 13 January 1994. *CDPSP* 46 (2) 1994, p. 32.
77 On the CIS see M. Webber, *The International Politics of Russia and the Successor States.* (Manchester: Manchester University Press 1996).
78 Lukin in *Nezavisimaya Gazeta* 18 March 1994. *CDPSP* 46 (11) 1994, pp. 7–8. FIS in *Nezavisimaya Gazeta* 26 November 1993. *CDPSP* 45 (47) 1993, p. 12.
79 This concept is adapted from J. Goldgeier and M. McFaul, 'A Tale of Two Worlds: Core and Periphery in the Post-Cold War Era'. *International Organization* 46 (2) 1992, pp. 467–91.

Index